Real Estate Securities

Syndicating Real Estate

by

Mark Lee Levine, Esq.
Professor

and

Philip A. Feigin, Esq.
Professor in Practice

Professional Publications

and Education, Inc.

Real Estate Securities
Syndicating Real Estate

Mark Lee Levine, Esq.
Professor

and

Philip A. Feigin, Esq.
Professor in Practice

ISBN-13: 978-1975887957
ISBN-10: 1975887956

"Real Estate Securities"

Preface

It is apparent to most business people that securities issues are generating even more interest today than when compared with only a few years ago. Investing in businesses, via securities, is becoming a more common phenomenon.

This material emphasizes cases, statutes and other authorities that impact the area of securities and in particular, the area of real estate securities. The intent is to provide a framework to determine when there might be a security involved, when that security offering must be registered or be exempt, and when the person selling the security must be licensed as a broker-dealer or agent or otherwise be exempt. Of course, there are many other connected issues that must be addressed, following the three areas noted of determining if there is a security, the registration/exemption of the same and the registration/exemption of the vendor of the security. These additional areas are examined later in this Work.

The cases have been abridged to allow the reader to focus, for the most part, on only the relevant parts of the cases as to the securities issues.

It is our hope that the review of this material may enlighten those readers who are concerned with the real estate securities area. A review of the cases and other authorities herein will allow the reader to take advantage of more safe harbors in which there is less exposure in working in this field of real estate securities.

The cases are reported decisions. They are not fictitious suppositions as to what might happen in a given circumstance. It is obvious that decisions can vary from state to state, that any decision can be reversed, and that one court, even the highest court of a given state, may change its philosophy and, therefore, its position as to a given issue in future decisions. All readers must be cognizant of the changing nature of the law and the potential that a decision one day may not be supported on another day. This is true with the changing state of the law on a state and/or federal basis; this point is further exacerbated as new statutes are passed and other regulations and positions are issued by regulatory bodies such as the Securities and Exchange Commission, "blue sky" agencies, and other regulatory bodies that impact real estate securities.

The text would not be complete without attempting to make suggestions to avoid litigation and pitfalls in the area of securities. Certainly, we also attempt to include discussion of the most up-to-date issues in the area of real estate securities. As such, in this edition, there are more references to Crowdfunding and Reg. A+ developments involving the SEC and state securities offices and tax issues impacting real estate securities.

PREFACE

It is hoped that the reader, previous to reading the case, will attempt to project and predict the potential outcome of the case by reviewing the short fact situations that often preview a case. Obviously, the key facts of the case can make the difference in the decision, but this type of approach allows one to concentrate on the issue of the case by attempting to predict the outcome prior to reaching the decision. One might also consider the detailed steps or policies that might be implemented within a given office to attempt to avoid the problem of the case in the future.

There are many real estate law texts and securities materials on the market that attempt to treat numerous areas in the form of a treatise. Such is not the intent of this material. The materials are a sprinkling of various areas in an attempt to analyze the areas of concern and planning when working in this field of real estate securities. (Keep in mind that most of the principles examined in this Work apply to securities in general, even if the security does not involve a real estate matter.)

There are, of course, many other areas of concern with real estate securities that are not covered in this material. However, it is hoped that the material herein will generate an overview of this particular field. There are connected areas, which might overlap with the area that is the focus of this text. For example, there is the area of real estate licensees' liability on the brokerage side, when the item being sold as a security involves real estate.

***

The Authors

MARK LEE LEVINE

Dr. Mark Lee Levine is a full Professor, Chair Holder, and Past Director of the **Franklin L. Burns School of Real Estate and Construction Management, and Past Chairman of the Legal Studies Department,** *Daniels College of Business,* **UNIVERSITY OF DENVER,** specializing in real estate, real estate securities, international real estate, tax aspects of real estate transactions and real estate liability issues. He is a sought-after consultant in these areas as well. Dr. Levine is a principal in **LEVINE SEGEV LLC,** Attorneys, and Chairman of the Board of Directors of **LEVINE, LTD., REALTORS®,** a full-service real estate firm in Colorado.

Dr. Levine is a partner in numerous real estate investments and serves on various publishing and advisory boards. He holds a collection of academic degrees, including a Bachelor of Science in business and economics from Colorado State University; a Doctorate of Jurisprudence from the University of Denver School of Law (JD); a post-law degree (LLM) in tax law from New York University; he is a graduate from the Professional Accounting Program (PAP) at Northwestern University Graduate School of Management; and Dr. Levine also holds a Ph.D. in Business.

Levine is an active member of various tax, legal and real estate committees. He is a member of the Denver, Colorado, and American Bar Associations as well as several other professional groups. He is admitted to the Federal district, circuit, tax, and U.S. Supreme Court. A popular lecturer, he is also author of 22+ books (and over 30 revisions of books) in addition to hundreds of articles in many publications.

Dr. Levine holds (or has held) numerous professional designations in real estate, securities, valuation, law, tax and related fields, including, for example, CCIM, MAI, CIPS, Certified FIABCI, Diploma., FRICS, GAA, GRI, SREA, CA-C, SRS, CRS, CRB, CPM, ALC, CLU, ChFC, DREI, RECS, TRC, etc.

Levine is a three time Fulbright Grant Recipient and he holds numerous other academic, teaching, and professional awards and honors.

PHILIP A. FEIGIN

Phil Feigin is a senior partner at Lewis Roca Rothgerber Christie LLP, working out of the firm's Denver and Tucson offices, where his practice centers on securities law and regulation. Before entering private practice in 2000, he served as a state securities regulator for more than 20 years, starting in Wisconsin as the Chief Enforcement Attorney for the Wisconsin Securities Commissioner (1979-82), then as

Assistant Colorado Securities Commissioner (1982-87) then as Colorado Commissioner (1987-98). He finished his regulatory career as Executive Director of the North American Securities Administrators Association in Washington, D.C. (1998-99) before returning to Denver to begin private practice at (then) Rothgerber Johnson & Lyons LLP.

Phil was involved in the drafting and enactment of each of the five statutes under which the Colorado investment industry is regulated. He has also been involved in the development of various federal laws, as well as the Model State Commodity Code and the Uniform Securities Act of 2002. A good portion of his practice involves serving as an expert witness in criminal, civil injunctive, administrative, arbitration, and private civil litigation involving securities and commodities law and regulation, and investment fraud in general. He has also served as an adjunct professor at the Daniels School of Business, Denver University, and as a professor in practice at the James E. Rogers College of Law at the University of Arizona. When his nose is not buried in a securities book, you may find Phil birding, watching his beloved Denver Broncos and Wisconsin Badgers, playing golf, woodworking, writing and singing parodies accompanying himself (badly) on his guitar, or petting, feeding or cleaning up after his and Barbara's adored cats.

***

Caveat

This publication was created to provide information regarding the subject matter covered. It is sold with the understanding that the authors and/or publisher are not engaged in rendering legal, accounting, or other professional service and/or advice. If legal advice or other expert assistance is required, the services of a competent professional person should be sought. (From a Declaration of Principles jointly adopted by a Committee of the American Bar Association and a Committee of Publishers and Associations.)

Inasmuch as there are differing opinions on a number of legal, tax and related matters that obviously affect many activities, certainly not limited to those involving real estate securities issues, it is important for us to emphasize a general Caveat and Disclaimer. We have no intent to give legal, tax and/or other advice by means of this text.

The intent is to state general propositions, specific points, development of case law and other authorities relevant to the field of real estate securities. Any opinions or positions expressed herein are limited in this respect, and further are qualified in that they are not necessarily the opinions of any or all parties that might be involved in producing this text or any portion thereof.

All parties are advised that careful planning necessitates consulting with their own legal, tax and other counsel. This text should not be a substitute for that advice, but rather, it should be used as a tool to help inform the user and work with your advisors.

This publication is designed to provide accurate and authoritative information about this subject. The reader is advised that the material contained herein may be inappropriate in a given situation. The book is sold with the understanding that the publisher and authors are not engaged in rendering legal, securities, tax, accounting or other professional services through this publication. Further, due to the nature of this publication, the information contained herein is subject to change without notice. The matters contained herein may be utilized only as consistent with all applicable laws, regulations and restrictions. If legal advice or other expert assistance is required, the services of a competent professional should be sought.
***

Acknowledgments
by Mark Lee Levine

I acknowledge the many people who have given strong support and encouragement to the development of this work. There is nothing more bothersome to me as an Author than to exclude a reference to someone who has been very important in the contribution to any work that I have published. However, it is apparent that it is difficult, and in fact many times impossible, to properly acknowledge the many people who are involved in the production of any work. However, knowing this to be a pitfall that one cannot avoid I, nevertheless, specifically acknowledge the strong support of my prior law firm, LEVINE AND PITLER, P.C., especially via my past partner and true friend for over 40 years, Robert L Pitler. There has also been a great deal of research effort provided at the University of Denver, Burns School of Real Estate and Construction Management, where I am proud to be a member of the faculty, Chair Holder, and Past Director and Chairman.

I also acknowledge my colleagues at the University of Denver, several members of the National Association of Realtors, including various Institutes and Councils thereunder, and attorneys Libbi Levine Segev and Aviv Segev, partners in our firm of Levine Segev LLC (and, respectively, our daughter and son-in-law). Libbi and Aviv have contributed support for much of my research in this Work.

In preparing this Work, there is a good deal of activity behind the scenes. This material must be postured in the correct formatting to allow for the hard copy printing as well as the electronic format. For much of this work, and with sincere thanks, I acknowledge Michael Golden (a prior student, friend, and talented professional) and our daughter, Dr. Abbi Levine Rosenthal. I hastily add that much of the layout and the cover of this Work were generated in large part by Abbi's creative abilities and special talents, honed after many years of work in this area.

I thank my unique, gracious, loving and supporting Partner in Life, my wife, Ellie May (Ellen). She is not just "another pretty face." She is a competent Realtor, CCIM, and holder of a Masters in Real Estate; she also has a great deal of experience in the real property area. Her devoted efforts to proofing much of this material, analyzing the same and lending support on the home front as well as technical support is greatly appreciated.

Thank you to Thomson/West Publishing Co.; the Company has been very kind to allow me to reprint a few items from some of my prior works with them.

To those parties not named specifically, I again plead the impossibility of properly acknowledging everyone that helped with this Work, as noted earlier, and I acknowledge and gratefully thank them for their support. There have been many secretaries and clerks in our offices who have supported this

ACKNOWLEDGMENTS

additional administrative load generated by this Work. To those secretaries and clerks, I extend my thanks.

And, to my Co-Author, Phil: Thank you! Thanks for agreeing to write this Work together. Thanks for your sense of humor. Thanks for your work ethic. Thanks for your expertise in this field of securities. And, thanks for being a good friend!

Mark Lee Levine

Acknowledgments

by Philip A. Feigin

Although I have written a great deal over my years in securities law and regulation, this is my first book, so I must begin by thanking my co-author for inviting me to join him in writing it. Mark has been a friend, colleague, counselor, shoulder-to-cry-on and nudge to get me into teaching for more years than I can remember. I am in his debt (though we're still splitting the dinner bill!)

What I know of securities law is the result of more than 35 years of interaction with terrific and skilled regulators at (what was then) the Office of the Wisconsin Commissioner of Securities, the Colorado Securities Division, and the North American Securities Administrators Association, the SEC, the CFTC and FINRA, the dedicated investigators and prosecutors in various District Attorneys, Attorneys General and U.S. Attorneys across the country with and for whom I have had the privilege to serve, and the equally gifted and talented private practitioners of the Denver area securities bar as well as the Federal and State Regulation of Securities Committees of the Business Law Section of the American Bar Association. I express particular thanks to fellow Badgers Jeff Bartell and Conrad Goodkind (for taking a flyer on me and giving me the chance), and Ron Burtch, Bill Lloyd, and Steve Morgan, to the late, great Royce Griffin, Fred Joseph, Jamie Sharp and Sheryl Lemon and my other fellow staffers at the Colorado Division, and to my dear friends and colleagues Denny Crawford, Barry Guthary, Craig Goettsch, Deb Bollinger, Deb Bortner, Dee Harris, Hugh Makens and Joe Borg.

I thank as well my partners and colleagues at Lewis Roca Rothgerber LLP for your support and encouragement in allowing me the time to pursue writing and teaching in my "seniordom," with a special nod to Fred Baumann, Ken van Winkle, Lew and Andy Schorr, Tenn Grebenar, Steve Johnson, Sam Arthur, Kristin Bronson and Greg Kanan. I also thank University of Rochester President Joel Seligman for his friendship and for encouraging me to pursue law school teaching, and to Dean Marc L. Miller and Professor Billy Sjostrom for giving me the opportunity at the University of Arizona James E. Rogers College of Law in my second adopted home of Tucson.

Finally, my eternal love and appreciation to Barbara, for keeping me sane, centered, (too) well fed, stops me from buying purple ties I think are blue, for telling me what color the bird is, and for smiling when I buy yet another book on the Civil War. We are Boze.

Phil Feigin

Dedications

by Mark Lee Levine

I dedicate my part of this Work to the members of my immediate Family, Ellen (Ellie May Lulabell Jones), Libbi (Libbi the Rosebud), Aviv (Mr Aviver), Liat (Liatie), Maytal (Maytalie), Eyal (Eyalie—The Man), Abbi (The Doo), Alon (The Scientist), and Lev (the Little Big Man; and, of Joyce (Our recently lost Big Red Glasses). These and other close Family members and friends continue, daily, to remind me why it is good to get out of bed and enjoy the lives that we have been blessed to lead.

With love and appreciation,
Mark/Daddy'o/Popsie

by Philip A. Feigin

I dedicate my efforts in writing the book to investors wherever they are, without whom none of this would be possible. It is my fervent hope that those who read our book will be better prepared to structure and market excellent investment opportunities, and, heeding our alerts and cautions, offer solid investment projects that will benefit their investors, developers, themselves and the community in general. Let fair, just and equitable be your guide.

With respect,
Phil

Table of Contents

TABLE OF CONTENTS

PART THREE
TAX 91

CHAPTER 1

Tax Considerations in Syndications........................ 93

CHAPTER 2

Tax Classifications for Types of Property 95

PART FOUR
A POTPOURRI OF PRACTICAL ISSUES IN SYNDICATION OF REAL ESTATE 145

PART ONE

SECURITIES REGULATION

CHAPTER 1

Introduction

It is the rare real estate investment seminar indeed where, upon hearing of the potential securities implications of real estate investing, at least one surprised and concerned audience member does not leave the room in the middle of a presentation and place a frantic call to a partner. The call goes something like *"I'm at a seminar, and based on what one of the speakers just said—we might be selling securities, not real estate, and we could be in a lot of trouble!"* In these chapters, we will describe the intersection of real estate investing and securities law, and provide a guide through the pertinent laws, rules and regulations.

Securities regulation in the United States is shared among the federal Securities and Exchange Commission ("SEC"), administering, for our purposes, the Securities Act of 1933 ("33 Act") and the Securities Exchange Act of 1934 ("34 Act"), and state securities authorities, administering various state securities statutes, often described as "blue sky" laws.[*]

While many commentators tend to focus on these federal laws and the rules adopted under them, with only passing reference to state laws and regulations, we view the field as one integrated securities system, and will approach it that way. Being sued by state securities authorities is no more pleasant than being pursued by the SEC. Being sued by investors under state securities law can pose much more serious concerns than being sued under federal law. The goal here is to steer readers clear of both contingencies.

Our securities analysis is divided into four discrete sections or what we refer to as "silos:" Jurisdiction, Registration, Licensing, and Disclosure. Once a determination is made that securities laws apply (the Jurisdiction silo), each remaining "silo" is relatively independent of the other. In other words, a promoter can be in compliance with securities registration requirements but still violate professional licensing and disclosure provisions. Likewise, he can avoid any licensing requirements, but still violate the securities registration and disclosure provisions, or have no registration or licensing concerns but still run into disclosure problems. Compliance with one silo does not provide, let alone guarantee, compliance with another.

---

[*] It would be entirely too unwieldy to attempt to discuss each state's securities law and rules individually. However, we will refer to particular state law provisions as examples when appropriate. Most state securities laws are based on model acts prepared and adopted over the years by what is now called the Uniform Laws Commission. Three versions of the Uniform Securities Act, of 1956, 1985 and 2002, form the basis of most state laws. The most populous states, such as California, New York, Texas, Ohio and Florida, have drafted their own unique statutes. Even then, there are many similarities in many areas, making some generalities possible.

After dealing with the Jurisdiction silo, in dealing with the remaining three, consideration must be given under both federal and state law to the three different levels of response to securities law violations. In other words, what does an errant promoter face if he violates the securities laws? The worst securities violations can be pursued as crimes by federal and state prosecutors. The regulators can bring administrative or civil injunctive enforcement actions (before administrative law judges or in court). Far more commonly, and regardless of the first two, private civil suits by investors can undermine, if not ruin, any venture involving volatile securities conduct.

As foreboding as this all might seem, most find the securities laws relatively easy to navigate, once you learn how to steer clear of the "rocks." It is time now to chart the rocks in the stream and the ways to deal with them.

***

CHAPTER 2

Jurisdiction

The First "Silo"

A. OVERVIEW

There is no question that complying with regulations costs money. Dealing in an environment where there are no regulations is easier than dealing in one where there are. It is completely understandable that people dealing in real estate investing would prefer to avoid securities regulation if at all possible. It should also be understood that securities regulation has been around for a long time, and has evolved to encompass a vast array of arrangements that might not seem to involve securities at first blush. Like tax law, securities law is not always intuitive, and whether you think it should apply in a given situation is not determinative, or even important.

Under the heading **Jurisdiction**, we will analyze two thresholds with fundamental questions:

- *Does my project involve a "security?"* and
- *If so, which securities laws apply?*

Real estate investing comes in all sorts of shapes and sizes. Before addressing these two jurisdictional questions directly, it is useful to spend a moment with a simple model in progression of facts.

Joe Jones buys a house to live in using his own savings. He might refer to his house as an "investment" as well as his residence. He hopes the home will increase in value so that, one day, he can sell it for more and use the increased equity to upgrade and buy a nicer place. While Joe might consider the house an "investment" as well as a place to live, the Realtor who sold the house to him did not sell a security to Joe, he sold him a house.

Encouraged by the market for rental homes, Joe decides to purchase a second house, again using his own savings, to fix up and then rent out as a source of income. Joe might refer to this second rental house as an "investment" too. However, an "investment" though it may be in Joe's view, the realtor who sold Joe this "investment" still did not sell Joe a security.

Taking the example a bit further, let us say that Joe is now so successful with that first rental home he wants to buy another one. However, his own savings are now fully committed. A traditional approach might be for Joe to seek a loan from a bank. Neither the bank nor the realtor who sells the house to Joe has sold him a security here either.

But what if Joe instead turns to a neighbor or friend or business associate and asks to borrow the funds he needs to buy this third house in exchange for his promise to repay the loan with interest? Or, what if Joe decides to form a simple limited liability company ("LLC") and recruit a few family members and friends to invest the cash needed to buy the house in exchange for a share of profits earned on resale with Joe doing all the work to earn them? In these latter cases, Joe has likely ventured into the realm of securities. Although the realtor does not sell a security to Joe in selling the home to the LLC, in raising funds from his investors, Joe has sold securities to them.

If we were to try to describe a litmus test, to draw a bright red line that cannot be crossed if you are to avoid securities law altogether, it is perhaps best stated as "using other people's money," "OPM." As soon as Joe turns from using his own savings to the funds of persons other than himself (who are not professional lenders like banks, savings banks and other professional lenders), the "securities" warning light should start pulsing. As we will see, if those other people are *passive investors*, if they are not going to be pitching in right beside Joe in running the business, in picking and fixing up the house and managing it as a rental, that pulsing light has turned to a steady, bright red and sirens should be going off. Joe is selling securities. Now, we turn to the specifics.

B. The Definition of "Security"

Both the 33 Act and the 34 Act contain definitions of the term "security," as does every state securities statute (known as "blue sky" laws). Not one of these statutory definitions involves a verbal description or explanation of what the term means. Instead, the "security" definition is merely a list of other terms that are themselves, for the most part, undefined. This collection is often described as a "laundry list" of terms. The relevant portions of the 33 Act definition of "security" (section 2(a)(1)) are as follows:

> The term "security" means any note, stock, treasury stock, security future, security-based swap, bond, debenture, evidence of indebtedness, certificate of interest or participation in any profit-sharing agreement, collateral-trust certificate, preorganization certificate or subscription, transferable share, investment contract, voting-trust certificate, certificate of deposit for a security, fractional undivided interest in oil, gas, or other mineral rights, any put, call, straddle, option, or privilege on any security, certificate of deposit, or group or index of securities (including any interest therein or based on the value thereof), or any put, call, straddle, option, or privilege entered into on a national securities exchange relating to foreign currency, or, in general, any interest or instrument commonly known as a "security", or any certificate of interest or participation in, temporary or interim certificate for, receipt for, guarantee of, or warrant or right to subscribe to or purchase, any of the foregoing.

The definition in the Uniform Securities Act (2002) at section 102(28) reads as follows:

> "Security" means a note; stock; treasury stock; security future; bond; debenture; evidence of indebtedness; certificate of interest or participation in a profit-sharing agreement; collateral trust certificate; preorganization certificate or subscription; transferable share; investment contract; voting trust certificate; certificate of deposit for a security; fractional undivided interest in oil, gas, or other mineral rights; put, call, straddle, option, or privilege on a security, certificate of deposit, or group or index of securities, including an interest therein or based on the value thereof; put, call, straddle, option, or privilege entered into on a national securities exchange relating to foreign currency; or, in general, an interest or instrument commonly known as a "security"; or a certificate of interest or participation in, temporary or interim certificate for, receipt for, guarantee of, or warrant or right to subscribe to or purchase, any of the foregoing.

They are functionally identical. The definitions in the prior versions of the Uniform Act were very similar, lacking only the newer references to puts, calls and the like. Individual states have added a number of terms, like "limited partnership interest" and "viatical settlement." When real estate investments are concerned, by far and away, two of the terms in the laundry list come into play much more than any others: "investment contract" and "note."

C. "INVESTMENT CONTRACTS"

Congress and state legislatures left it to the regulators and the courts to construe what was meant by the various terms on the "laundry list." What is meant by the term "investment contract" has been considered by courts perhaps more than any other on the list.

Any discussion today of the term "investment contract" will start with *SEC v. W.J. Howey Company.*[†] The fledgling SEC asked the federal court to enjoin the defendant from selling what the Commission argued were unregistered investment contract securities. The W.J. Howey Company had sold portions of its orange groves to people who visited Florida on vacation. Under the agreements, the owners were required to manage, harvest and market their chunk of orange grove, with Howey taking a percentage. That raised the immediate question as to how vacationers from New York were to fulfill their obligations. They knew nothing of harvesting and marketing oranges. Recognizing the dilemma that might pose, along with the sale agreement, the W.J. Howey Company enclosed a proposed leaseback agreement with a Howey affiliate, the Howey-in-the-Hills Service, Inc. Under this lease, Howey-in-the-Hills Service, Inc. would happily handle everything for the new owner. In sum, the owner who signed the accompanying agreement would not have to do anything but wait for the checks to arrive.

The SEC lost at both the trial level and on Circuit Court appeal. The Supreme Court reversed, siding with the SEC, holding that the combination of the sale agreement from W.J. Howey Company and servicing agreement from the Howey-in-the-Hills Service, Inc. was in combination an "investment contract" security. In doing so, the Court drew from state court interpretations of the term contained in state "blue sky" laws, where the term originated. The Court set forth the elements of an investment contract as:

> a contract, transaction or scheme whereby a person invests his money in a common enterprise and is led to expect profits solely from the efforts of the promoter or a third party.[‡]

The Court went on to note that their definition of the term:

> embodies a flexible rather than a static principle, one that is capable of adaptation to meet the countless and variable schemes devised by those who seek the use of the money of others on the promise of profits.[§]

This so-called *Howey* test has been adopted by virtually every court and regulator construing the term, though some have gone beyond it. It is usually expressed as either a three- or four-part test. We prefer the four-part version, especially given subsequent challenges and court decisions:

1. an investment of money
2. in a common enterprise
3. with the expectation of a profit
4. based solely on the efforts of the promoter or a third party.

[†] *SEC v. W.J. Howey Company*, 328 U.S. 293 (1946).

[‡] *Id.* at 298

[§] *Id.* at 300.

(When expressed as a three-part test, the latter two elements are combined as "with the expectation of a profit based solely on the efforts of the promoter or a third party.")

It is important to remember that the test was provided in a Court decision, not a statute. Even so, virtually each phrase and word of the test has been probed and dissected more than frogs in a biology class by those hoping to reap the rewards of raising money from others without complying with the securities laws that govern the practice (can't you just smell the formaldehyde?)

Rather than turn this work into a securities treatise, we will abbreviate the most common issues and how they are handled:

1. **"Money."** The investment does not have to be in "money." Anything of value contributed to the venture will suffice, including the land or property involved.

2. **"Common Enterprise."** As for the "common enterprise" element, courts are split on whether there must be a pooling of investments, known as "horizontal commonality," or whether there must only be a connection between the success of the investor and that of the promoter (are their fortunes "inextricably interwoven"), known as vertical commonality.

3. **"Profit."** As for what is meant by "profit," a couple of issues have arisen. It is pretty clear that the term is not limited to "profit" in an accounting sense. Interest paid will be construed as a "profit" under the test.[¶] In a few jurisdictions, some benefit other than a monetary profit will suffice, for instance, a lifetime membership in a golf club qualifies as a "benefit" under California law, provided the investor contributed his capital to a start-up venture, the so-called "risk capital" test.[**]

4. **"Solely."** What is meant by "based solely on the efforts of the promoter or a third party" has probably drawn the most attention and controversy. It is rather generally accepted that "solely" has morphed into "essential managerial efforts."[††] When money is solicited by a promoter from investors to become "members" of a limited liability company, "general partners" of what is represented to be a general partnership, or "participants" in what is described as a "joint venture" in which these investors are granted some rights or powers to manage operations, the question becomes rather murky. Has the promoter granted the investors sufficient rights and powers to manage the company to negate a finding they are no longer dependent on the promoter to provide the "essential managerial efforts" of the enterprise? The conclusion is entirely uncertain, and requires careful case-by-case analysis.

Real estate deals involving investors are almost always organized as either limited partnerships ("LPs") or limited liability companies ("LLCs"). Given standard provisions of state LP law, interests in an LP are universally construed to be "investment contract" securities. By statute, limited partners are not permitted to have any managerial participation in the conduct of partnership business; that is reserved exclusively to the general partner. LPs are governed both by mandatory statutory provisions and the limited partnership agreement ("LPA") signed by the partners. Like an LP, an LLC is also formed through a formal filing with a state's secretary of state or similar official, but most LLC statutes do not contain a mandate that members cannot have managerial responsibilities. That is left up to the members and how the LLC Operating Agreement ("Operating Agreement") is drafted.

[¶] See *SEC v. Edwards*, 540 U.S. 389 (2004)

[**] See *Silver Hills Country Club v. Sobieski*, 361 P.2d 903 (Ca. 1961)

[††] See *SEC v. Glenn Turner Enterprises*, 474 F.2d 476 (9th Cir. 1973), *cert.* denied 414 U.S. 821

D. "Notes"

"Note" is the first form of security in the "laundry list" definition. Notes, also known as promissory notes, are everywhere in our business and personal lives. We sign a note to the bank when we buy a house or a car. How can that kind of note be a security subject to all this regulation? Is every "note" a security?

The answer is, "it isn't." This is one of those "I know it when I see it" sort of things. In *Reves v. Ernst & Young*,[††] the Supreme Court rendered a decision on the subject of *"when is a note a security?"* after federal trial and appellate courts struggled with term. Unlike the *Howey* test, the *Reves* test is a bit harder to summarize in a few short lines. Generally speaking—and we do mean *generally*—a simply test to apply to help make the determination is as follows: If the person writing the check is a company, a business engaged in the business of lending money to borrowers, the note the borrower signs is likely *not* a security.

On the other hand, if the person writing the check is not engaged in the business of lending money to borrowers, the note is likely going to be considered a security. That likelihood will move toward certainty if any of the following is true:

- the person writing the check is an individual, a consumer;
- if the person receiving the funds is a business;
- if the funds will be used to for ongoing operations of that business or to finance some new venture; or
- if that business has "borrowed" funds from more than one non-money lending business "lender," particularly if the "lender" is an individual/consumer.

In fact, per the *Reves* decision, *Reves v. Ernst & Young*, 494 U.S. 56 (1990), "notes" are *presumed to be securities* unless one of the excluding factors apply. While to some it may seem like an innocent loan arrangement—you are borrowing money from a few people to carry on your business—under securities law, the arrangement is viewed as an issuer of securities raising funds from one or more investors through the sale of notes. The issuer is selling notes to investors to raise capital for its business or venture.

Understanding this framework is important to any securities analysis, and sheds light on the "laundry list" definition approach. It really does not matter much which of the laundry list items you insert in the blank in the sentence "The issuer is selling _____ to investors to raise capital for its business or venture." The blank could be filled in with "notes," "stock," "bonds," "investment contracts," or most other of the items on the list. The principle is that the blank is a security. The exception to the rule is that the "blank" is not a security in particular circumstances.

For instance, a certificate of deposit issued by a bank has most of the hallmarks of a note security. Even so, a statutory decision has been made that bank CDs will not be considered securities, based on the fact banks and their issuance of CDs is regulated by other authorities, *i.e.*, bank regulators. Another example is fixed and variable insurance products. Insurance products would be construed as securities were it not for the fact that, under most state laws, they are excluded from the "securities" definition. (Note: Variable insurance products, while excluded from the "securities" definitions of most state securities laws, are *not* excluded from the federal "securities" definition—thus the anomaly that insurance agencies and salespeople selling variable annuities must be registered with the SEC and FINRA as broker-dealers and agents but not under the laws of most states.)

[††] *Reves v. Ernst & Young*, 494 U.S. 56 (1990)

E. Notes Secured by Mortgages or Deeds of Trust

Given this discussion of "notes" as securities, it should be clear that, when a consumer buys a house with funds borrowed from a commercial lender, the note signed by the consumer to the lender is not a "security" under the *Reves* test. In a simple world, that would be an unalterable truism, but this is not a simple world.

The allure of a real estate-secured note to individual investors has at times been all but irresistible. Some less than scrupulous promoters have attempted to use that intoxication to their advantage. There have been times, particularly when interest rates are high, when more senior aged sellers of homes are forced to entertain a private transaction in which they take back a note from the buyers secured by a second lien on the home to make the primary sale transaction work. This arrangement is also accompanied by the pledge of the realtor patching the whole transaction together that he will be able to find a buyer to take that second note off the hands of the sellers in short order. A sort of secondary market in secured notes has developed from time to time as a result. This is but one example of real estate-secured notes being marketed as investments.

In another permutation, we have seen cases involving promoters who purportedly acquired a large parcel of real estate, and purportedly subdivided the land into much smaller parcels, all of which they purportedly now owned in fee simple. [Note: in this context, "purportedly" and "purports" is legalese for "conned people into believing they...."] After obtaining what purports to be an independent appraisal for each lot, they offer to sell investors individual notes each secured by a first on each lot at a significant discount to the appraised value, the investor funds to be used to build homes in a new, idyllic community. These were "notes" secured by real estate, but, remembering *Reves*, in this case, the person writing the check is a consumer not engaged in the business of lending funds for the acquisition of real property, and the person getting the funds was the business.

In a twist on this arrangement, there was at least one scam where the perpetrator had in fact acquired a very large estate in fee simple (with investor funds). To monetize the estate for "running around money," the conman started selling smaller notes, each purportedly secured by an interest in the equity. For example, say the equity in the estate is $5 million and he owns it in fee. He sells Investor #1 a note for $100,000 secured by the home, Investor #2, another $100,000 secured note, and so on. In the case we have in mind, none of the security interests was recorded until regulators started investigating. All of the secured interest documents were filed at the same time. The recorder's office required that they be filed in sequence. The result was that, randomly, Investor #6 was granted first position, and they all followed, up to Investor #19, who in fact owned a 19th deed of trust!

Aside from the anecdotal diversion, these arrangements pose regulatory challenges to define. We will discuss securities registration and exemptions from the requirement in Chapter 3. Suffice to say at this point that there is an exemption from registration for any sale of a bond or other evidence of indebtedness (a fancy term for a note) secured by an interest in real property, provided the mortgage, together with all notes secured thereby, are offered and sold as a unit. Generally, the rule is that the exemption only applies to that value of the evidence of indebtedness that is actually secured for true equity in the property. So, if you sold a $1 million note secured by a $100,000 piece of land, 10% of the note is exempt from registration and 90% is not. In the face of the argument that the notes secured by up to that 19th deed of trust were exempt from securities registration requirements, the regulators' response was that they were not in fact exempt because all notes and deeds of trust were not offered and sold as a unit. The position was never contested as fraud subsumed the entire operation and led to the collapse of the operation before any decision was rendered.

These examples are by no means suggested as a means of syndication. However, they point out circumstances when the certainty that real estate-secured notes are not securities may not be so certain after all.

F. "Pushing the Envelope"

Recall the reference in the *Howey* case to "the countless and variable schemes devised by those who seek the use of the money of others on the promise of profits." It should come as no surprise that, in crafting real estate investment deals, if securities law can be avoided lawfully, overall expenses will be that much less, inuring to the bottom line benefit of both the promoter and likely the investors. New and cutting edge developments arise all the time, involving arrangements and instruments that have never before been subject to regulatory or court determination as to whether they involve securities.

So, how should a promoter proceed in such a case? Of course, the promoter should always consult with competent counsel. The ramifications are too great not to do so. If the promoter cannot afford to pay the lawyer's fees, perhaps the promoter is not ready to undertake a project using other people's money. However, it is not uncommon that the newfangled arrangement is something the lawyer brought to the promoter's attention in the first place. So, now what?

The prudent answer in dealing with any real estate (or other investment-oriented arrangement) when you are not sure as to whether the investment will or will not be construed as a security going forward is to *presume it is a security* and act accordingly, even if you disclose your position and belief that the interests being sold are not securities. To ignore securities law requirements and restrictions is a dangerous course of action. The ramifications if you are wrong are dramatic and potentially life changing.

We will delve into the securities law requirements and restrictions on real estate securities offerings in the next few chapters, but suffice to say that any such offering must clear the hurdles posed by securities registration or exemption, broker-dealer and agent licensing, and disclosure requirements and limitations. We will learn that, under the most commonly employed securities registration exemption, Rule 506(b), an issuer can raise an unlimited amount of money from "accredited" investors (and a maximum of 35 investors who are "sophisticated" even if not accredited), provided the issuer has a pre-existing business or personal relationship with them, meaning the issuer does not use general advertising or solicitation to find them. Further, the officers and directors of an issuer are generally permitted to offer and sell their offering securities, provided they receive no commissions or other compensation for doing so, but paid salesmen have to be licensed as securities agents. Finally, securities issuers are generally required to make full and fair disclosure of all material, important facts about any securities being offered or sold.

If we look at these factors in the real estate context, it is the unusual project that will not require significant sums to move forward. Given that a promoter wants to spend his time developing his project rather than finding investors, he will likely not want to raise $5,000 at a crack. That will take forever and be an administrative nightmare even without considering securities law. The promoter will look to raise a lot of money per unit from very high net worth people. He is far more likely to succeed contacting those people he knows rather than total strangers. He is not likely to find such investors by advertising in the Penny Saver or cold calling. In sum, the promoter is likely to stay within the bounds set in Rule 506 even if he has never heard of Rule 506.

Using paid agents might be desirable because, again, most promoters want to develop, not raise money. That poses a dilemma for a deal that may or may not involve securities. If the promoter errs on the side of caution, he will steer clear of using unlicensed sales agents. Perhaps the promoter decides to risk it. The latter option is what we refer to as a *Dirty Harry* situation: "The question you have to ask yourself is, *'Do you feel lucky?'*" Some people may feel the risk is worth it. Others, staring down the barrel of a .38 Magnum regulatory revolver, will decide that it is not.

Finally, as to disclosure, securities-style disclosure is just good business. Not only are investors (securities or not) better informed as to the project and the risks, but full and fair disclosure also serves to deter and defend against later claims that disclosures were not made.

The upshot is, with perhaps the expenditure of a little more time, care and money up front, a real estate promoter can comply with securities requirements without too much trouble, and take a good deal of follow-on risk off the table. Taking the more "devil may care" approach and crossing the securities lines might provide even unjustifiably disgruntled investors an easy means of recovering their money. The daring promoter might pay a steep price if a court were to say his position that the investments were not securities is entertaining but wrong, allowing investors to take full advantage of the powerful securities law private rights of action. Even more grief can be brought to bear at the hands of securities regulators who view the "it's not a security" position as a challenge to their very existence and will pursue the matter until the end of time proving you are wrong and making sure no one else tries the same idea.

G. "Tics"—A Case in Point

Tenant-in-common interests ("TICs") are an excellent example of a few concepts, not the least of which is how tax advantages can drive securities offerings in other than rational directions. Add to that the phenomenon that taxpayers will twirl themselves into arcane financial contortions for the sole purpose of avoiding taxes, well beyond the limits of simple common sense.

In the case of TICs, it all starts with a simple and rational premise. In the years leading up to the housing bubble bursting, in or around 2008, people who invested in real estate saw it repeatedly inflate in price, so that if they sold an investment property at a profit, rather than realize the capital gains and pay tax, they sought ever larger properties to acquire with the proceeds to shield them. An industry evolved to fill the need.

In a "TIC program," a sponsor/promoter sought to sell a maximum of 35 tenants-in-common undivided ownership interests in a large property to people seeking real property to buy with the proceeds of the sale of real estate they already own, thus shielding the proceeds from tax by using Section 1031 of the Internal Revenue Code ("IRC" or "Code"). The property could be residential or commercial, with the majority interest held by the sponsor/promoter. These programs were usually offered and sold as private placement offerings of investment contract securities, with a private placement memorandum, by licensed securities broker-dealers and their agents.

As we discussed earlier in describing investment contracts, there is nothing about a real estate transaction that precludes the application to it of statutes and regulatory schemes beyond real estate law. Generally, federal and state securities laws come into play when what is sold is an *interest in an entity* that owns real estate, like a LP or LLC interest. Sometimes, an interest in a general partnership, or what will be construed under the law as a general partnership, can be a security, and that is where the TIC programs crossed paths with securities laws.

Generally speaking, when property is purchased and then later sold for more than was paid for it, capital gains taxes are due on the difference. In enacting Section 1031, Congress allowed a taxpayer who sells property for more than he paid for it to defer paying capital gains tax on the gain, if there is a valid exchange, meeting all requirements under Code Section 1031. (A discussion of the details for these requirements is outside the intent of this work; however, some of these points will be addressed later in this Work under Part III as to tax issues related to securities.)

In its Rev. Proc. 2002-22 ("2002-22"), regarding the issue to determine if the given TIC group is an entity, *e.g.*, a partnership, for tax purposes, the IRS staff listed 15 conditions. If all these conditions were present, the Taxpayer could apply for a Private Letter Ruling to see if the Treasury would conclude that the TIC group would in fact be treated as a TIC group and not as a legal entity, such as a LLC or partnership. This conclusion is very important, since the interests held by a TIC owner could be exchanged for other qualified property, normally meaning real estate for real estate that is used in the trade or business or held for investment. On the other hand, if the Treasury concluded that the TIC does not exist, but the group investing is a Partnership or LLC, such interests are NOT allowed to be exchanged, tax deferred, under Code Section 1031. Like the "Pirates' Code" in *Pirates of the Caribbean*, the 15 conditions of 2002-22 were more "guidelines" than Code. However, if the Taxpayer desires to seek a favorable Private Letter Ruling, the conditions must be met. As mentioned, this area is discussed in more detail in the Tax Section of this Work, under Part Three.

TIC programs were just the latest in a long line of real estate ownership programs that have emerged over the years, including campgrounds, vacation property, time shares and the like. In each instance, real estate brokers have sought a share of the commissions paid, claiming it was due them for the sale of the *real estate* aspect of the deal. Securities regulators said "no way." Though an effort at an accommodation was floated in 2008, the economic swoon of that autumn doomed the proposed exemption to a place among many others on the regulatory cutting room floor. In the wake of the Lehmann Brothers debacle, TIC programs started failing with regularity. One such colossal failure, of a program widely distributed by smaller and regional brokerage firms and leading to their failure as well, probably tainted and buried TIC private placements for the foreseeable future.

Any investment offering involving the sale of fractional interests in the ownership of real property to investors always presents the red flag of securities. Clearly, there are likely securities law implications. If the group is being formed for the purpose of acquiring the real property, the red flag must be raised higher. If there is a dominant promoter and the investors have only limited authority in the management of the property, the flag is nearing the top of the flagpole. At some point, real estate companies and agents must decide when to salute. To deny those realities takes us back to Dirty Harry—"*do you feel lucky?*" For the prudent and wary, the answer is and should be a resounding "no." (For additional discussion on TIC issues, especially as to the Tax Rules and 1031 Exchanges, see *infra*, Part Three.)

H. Sale of a Business

We mention this subject because so much of our audience will be people from the real estate industry. Some Realtors commonly engage in the selling clients' businesses because the sale will include that sale of real estate. As part of the sale, 100% of the equity of the company will be sold, be it shares of a corporation or interests in a LP or LLC. In such a transaction, interestingly, title to the real estate will often remain in the name of the entity; the only thing that will change is the name of the owners of the equity.

For many years, the SEC and state securities regulators adhered to their "sale of a business" doctrine. A transaction in which 100% of the equity interests of company were sold did not constitute a securities transaction, even though shares of stock or other equities within the statutory definition of "securities" were conveyed.

The U.S. Supreme Court changed all that in the *Landreth Timber* case.[§§] The case involved the sale of 100% of the shares in a corporation. The Court essentially said that shares of common stock were shares in any context, be it 100% of them, or 90% or 1%. That decision turned a lot of business traditions and practices on their collective ear, including the real estate "selling a business" practice. What kind of license did you need to sell 100% of the shares of a company that owned land? Under *Landreth*, the answer was a securities license. That was the federal answer. The answer at the state level was a matter of state-by-state concern. Even at the federal level, the area was not a high priority for regulators.

We raise this point in this work on real estate syndication because of the next case we will discuss.

[§§] *Landreth Timber Co. v. Landreth*, 471 U.S. 681 (1985)

I. "Economic Realities"

Just when you thought you might have a grasp of the concepts we have discussed, another one comes along to throw us back in the soup. In *United Housing v. Forman*,[11] the U.S. Supreme Court tackled a difficult question. New York City apartment buildings were being converted into cooperatives, and tenant/now owner ownership of the coop was represented by a "share of stock" in the cooperative association. A dissatisfied coop owner sought relief under federal securities law.

The Court ruled that the "economic reality" was that the so-called shares of stock were not "stock" in the securities context. Calling ownership of what was in fact a real estate interest could not be turned into a "security" simply by calling it by a word contained in the "security" definition.

The point here is that, regardless of how an interest is denominated, just as with the "investment contract" flexibility described earlier, courts are instructed to determine the economic reality of the transaction. If there is an investor/promoter sense to the relationship, courts are likely to take the position securities laws apply as a matter of "economic reality."

More on this blurring in Part One, Chapter 4.

J. What Laws Apply?

We shift now from what might be called substantive jurisdictional questions to the more mundane questions of geographic jurisdiction, *i.e.*, "which laws do I have to worry about?" The internet and other electronic advances in commerce have posed significant challenges to jurisdiction based on geography. For instance, suppose a Norwegian company raising capital through the sale of securities posts the offering on the internet directed at investors in Sweden, but the offering is accessed by an investor in Boston. Has the Norwegian company made an offer in the United States? Is this any different than an agent of the Norwegian company calling that same Boston investor and describing the offering to her? Certainly, if that same Boston investor happened to pick up a Swedish newspaper and saw an ad regarding the offering, would that created U.S. jurisdiction? Modern media and travel give geographic jurisdiction a major headache.

At the federal level, the answer is relatively clear and easy. If you are selling securities from anywhere into the United States, federal securities law applies. If you are selling securities from the United States to anywhere, federal securities laws apply.

State securities jurisdiction is a little different than one might imagine. At the risk of oversimplifying, it depends on in which state the seller and buyer are located—and we mean *physically located*, feet on the ground—at the time of the sale and purchase of the security. The principle is easiest stated in terms of individuals. In the most extreme example, Tom, 56, has never before traveled outside Colorado. Joe is the president of Xtech, a software company in New Jersey and has been lawfully raising money exclusively in New Jersey. Tom has decided to visit his aunt in Detroit, and is killing time in the United Club at O'Hare waiting for his connecting flight. Joe is also waiting in the O'Hare United Club for a connecting flight. Joe notices Tom reading a software magazine and strikes up a conversation with him. One thing leads to another, and Joe offers to sell Joe some of the Xtech's securities, Tom decides to do so and writes Joe a check on his Colorado bank account. They go their merry ways. Six months later, Joe is back in Colorado and has become dissatisfied with his Xtech investment. He wants to sue to get his money back. Tom sees a lawyer in Denver. Tom expects to be able to apply Colorado securities law because, after all, he is a lifelong resident, the check was written on a Colorado bank, Joe received mailings from Xtech at his home, and Joe knew he was from Colorado when he sold him the securities. At the same time, Joe thinks that anyone who sues Xtech will have to do so under New

---

[11] *United Housing v. Forman*, 421 U.S. 837 (1975)

Jersey law. The office is in New Jersey, the factory is in New Jersey, Xtech's bank is in New Jersey, all its investors save Tom are New Jersey residents, and Xtech pays New Jersey state tax.

Imagine the surprise to both Tom and Joe when their respective counsel explain to them that the only state's law implicated in the transaction is that of Illinois! The significant contacts that might compel jurisdiction for other purposes and in other circumstances is not what governs when state securities laws are concerned. It is where the purchaser and seller are physically located at the time of the transaction that governs. In the Xtech case, both seller and purchaser were located in Illinois at the time of the transaction. Illinois securities law, and only Illinois' law, applies to any securities dispute.

We understand that a seller and buyer might be things, *i.e.*, companies or partnerships, when a security is purchased and sold. These are more difficult situations to define with certainty, but the location of the heartbeat actors at the time of the sale and purchase will have a major role in determining which state securities laws apply.

One can conjure up an array of circumstances that pose fascinating questions. What if a Nevada issuer made an initial pitch to a snowbird investor in Arizona where the offering is lawful to sell, but the sale is not consummated until after the snowbird returns in the summer to Pennsylvania, where the offering is not lawful to sell? The answer is that Nevada, Arizona and Pennsylvania law would apply to the transaction. Suffice to say that real estate investment promoters would do well to consult with counsel *beforehand* to identify the requirements posed by each potential jurisdiction, and decide whether complying with upfront regulations or risking after-the-fact liability is worth offering and selling in particular states.

***

CHAPTER 3

Securities Registration and Exemptions

The Second "Silo"

A. WHAT IS SECURITIES REGISTRATION?

The focus of this book is private placement real estate syndications and not those few, enormous offerings that are registered with the SEC. Therefore, we will direct our attention to the exemptions from registration available to, and most frequently relied upon by, real estate syndicators. Even so, some background on securities registration is useful for context.

One of the foundational premises of American securities regulation is that, before securities can be offered or sold, they must be registered, *i.e.*, submitted to, reviewed by and cleared for sale by, securities regulators, unless the security itself or the transaction in which it is offered and sold qualifies for some exemption from the requirement.

In 1911, at the urging of J. N. Dolley, the Kansas Banking Commissioner, what is generally agreed to be the first modern securities law was adopted in Kansas. As a threshold matter, the age-honored commercial principle of *caveat emptor*, "buyer beware," was turned upside down. Issuers/sellers were required to make full and fair disclosure of all material facts regardless of what information any potential buyer might request, in other words, *caveat venditor*, "seller beware."

Under the new law, all issuers wishing to offer their securities in Kansas had to first submit the terms under which they would be sold to the Kansas Commissioner. He was empowered to prohibit any such offering in Kansas if he determined it contained any provision that, in his judgment, was "unfair, unjust, inequitable or oppressive to" investors or if he believed the issuer did "not intend to do a fair and honest business" or "promise a fair return" to Kansas investors.[***]

It is hard to imagine any such broad and arbitrary legislation passing today. However, as extreme and expansive as these standards might be, they were a natural, equal and opposite reaction to the offering practices of the time. This point is underscored by the fact that, whereas there was virtually no state or federal securities regulation in place to speak of before 1911, in the two years following enactment of the Kansas legislation, 17 states had adopted virtually identical laws, and six others had formulated and enacted their own versions.[†††]

[***] Kan. L. 1911, c. 133, §5

[†††] Loss and Cowett, *Blue Sky Law*, at p. 10, Little, Brown and Company, 1958

State securities laws came to be known as "blue sky" laws, though people differ on the origins of phrase. It probably arose in reference to the term "blue sky merchant" of the era, salesmen who sold goods made of nothing more than the big blue sky. The substantive, judgmental authority to deny securities registration contained in the new statutes came to be known as "merit review." State securities laws and merit regulation evolved over the years, with the Uniform Securities Act (1956) having perhaps the greatest single influence on blue sky laws since 1911.

Between 1911 and 1956, a comprehensive scheme of federal securities regulation was implemented, beginning with the 33 Act dealing with registration of securities. Congress made a conscious decision to adopt a full disclosure standard for federal review as opposed to the substantive "merit" standards adopted by most states. In essence, as horrible as the terms of an offering might be for investors, the SEC's job was done once the staff determined the issuer had fully and fairly set forth all material facts.

And so, the two modes of registration policy came to be known as "full disclosure" (adequate and accurate) and "merit review" (fair, just and equitable). As merit review developed, it became less an effort to predict the success or failure of the enterprise or whether the investors would reap profits, and more an effort to equate the risks of the venture between promoters and investors. Further, as staunchly as advocates of full disclosure registration regulation in the 33 Act at the federal level may decry state merit review, the Investment Company Act of 1940 is replete with features clearly consistent with merit review. But we digress.

The federal and state statutory provisions dealing with securities registration are very similar and highly coordinated and integrated (even though it must be noted the reach of state securities registration authority has been cut to the quick and made largely irrelevant due to federal preemption, discussed later). Under both federal[†††] and state[§§§] law (except New York), it is unlawful to offer or sell securities unless first registered or exempt from the requirement. Under the 33 Act, basic requirements are set forth for what information registrants are required to provide, but the real meat of the registration requirements is provided in the SEC's rules and regulations, most notably Regulation S-K dealing with fact disclosure and Regulation S-X dealing with financial disclosure, and the forms for particular types of registration. For instance, initial offerings of securities, IPOs, are filed on Form S-1. Among the provisions of Regulation S-K, the SEC has promulgated guides to assist issuers and their counsel making offerings in specialized areas as to the particular information required and the format in which it is to be disclosed. Most pertinent to real estate syndication is Guide 5 for real estate limited partnership offerings.

The standard model for "blue sky" law registration law for our purposes involves at least two different forms of securities registration: registration by qualification and registration by coordination. Registration by qualification is the full bore version where an issuer is required to register at the state level without regard to what is happening in any other federal or state jurisdiction. Qualification filings are subject to full merit review, with requirements set forth both in statute and in rules (as well, some would argue, as the caprice of the examiner). Registration by coordination is designed to correlate with federal registration of the same deal. Merit states applied their merit standards to such offerings as well (causing no small amount of rancor among the issuer and issuer counsel communities).

If an offering clears muster, an order of registration is issued. If perceived problems in an offering cannot be resolved with regulators, they are most often withdrawn. However, in rare instances, the regulators elect or are put in a position they believe necessitates commencing a hearing to deny registration to an offering. This is done by means of what is called a stop order. A process ensues including a hearing on the merits under federal or state administrative procedures if things get that far.

[†††] 33 Act Section 5

[§§§] See, for example, Colo. Rev. Stat. § 11-51-301

Although public offerings of direct equity investments in real estate are, obviously, provided for under federal registration law and rules, they are not very common. For the most part, IPOs and the securities exchanges are the realm of corporate shares and bonds. Real estate limited partnership interests are particularly difficult to value on a marked-to-market basis. Investors acquire such interests with a long term view; they are notoriously illiquid. Further, real estate partnerships offer certain tax incentives that are unavailable in a corporate form. It is far more common that a real estate offering will have liquidation, rather than merger, sale or public offering, as an exit strategy for owners.

In sum, securities registration can be a costly and time consuming process. More often than not, real estate deals organized as LPs or LLCs elect to rely on exemptions from the registration requirements, and that is where we now turn.

B. Securities Registration Exemptions in General

There are two kinds of securities registration exemptions: (i) securities exemptions; and (ii) transactional exemptions. Exempt securities are things like U.S. Treasury Notes, Bills and Bonds, municipal securities, other securities regulated by other regulators, like bank, insurance company and railroad stock, securities issued pursuant to court orders, and the like. Exempt securities are always exempt from securities registration requirements, regardless of how many times they are offered or sold. The exempt securities list is of no particular relevance to real estate syndicators, except to know how they fit in the scheme of things.

If you are not dealing with a registered offering or an exempt security, to offer or sell any security, the offer or sale must qualify for a transactional exemption, and must do so all over again *every time* the security changes hands. Until 2012, the exempt transactions section of the 33 Act, Section 4, remained relatively unchanged from its 1933 form. Three of the subsections, (1), (3) and (4), dealt with secondary market transactions, *i.e.*, resales. Under the second subsection, 4(a)(2), transactions "by an issuer not involving any public offering" were exempt from federal securities registration requirements. Short, simple, and open to interpretations that could fill the Grand Canyon.

The landmark case interpreting what at the time was 33 Act Section 4(2) is *SEC v. Ralston Purina Co.*[111] The Court held that, to qualify as a "not part of any public offering," the investors in the offering must be "sophisticated," *i.e.*, not in need of the protections provided by securities registration under the 33 Act.

Both before and since *Ralston Purina*, the SEC promulgated various rules and issued interpretations they hoped would provide guidance as to the scope of what is, since enactment of the JOBS Act in 2012 (see below), Section 4(a)(2). Rules promulgated under broad statutory exemptions are generally referred to as "safe harbors." Though safe harbors do not define the ultimate bounds of the statutory exemption, if you comply with the bounds of the rule, you are assured of compliance with the slightly broader but less certain statutory provision. Safe harbors are very popular with issuers and their counsel because, with rare exception, most federal and state securities registration exemptions are "self-executing" (not a reference to *hari-kari*). In other words, there is no provision for an issuer or other applicable person to file an application with the regulator and then receive some sort of certification or permission to proceed in reliance on the statutory or safe harbor exemption. Generally, there are no pre-filings, and there is certainly no assurance forthcoming from regulators that, "Yes, you have qualified for the exemption." Instead, you must proceed in reliance on the statute or rule at your own risk, and subject to later scrutiny and second guessing.

---

[111] *SEC v. Ralston Purina Co.*, 346 U.S. 119 (1953)

C. Regulation D (before the jobs act)

The predominant safe harbor of our era is Regulation D ("Reg. D"), adopted by the SEC in 1982. This regulation in turn is composed of a number of rules. With relatively minor adjustments, the six rules in the 1982 version of Reg. D remained constant until the JOBS Act in 2012. After 2012, per Congressional mandate, the SEC revised and amended Reg. D dramatically, as we shall see.

1. Rule 501

Reg. D begins with three rules of general applicability to the Regulation. In Rule 501, the SEC defines terms.

a. Rule 501(a) "accredited investor"

The "accredited investor" definition has broad impact across securities law, regulation and the markets. For our purposes, an "accredited investor" is an investor with $1 million in net worth (limited now to *exclude* the equity value of the investor's principal residence), or an investor who has earnings of $200,000 or more in the last two years and expected that to continue, or $300,000 when combined with a spouse. The definition applies to other categories of investors as well, but these two qualifications are the ones that apply predominantly to "heartbeats."

A number of different entities can also qualify as accredited investors. As a general premise throughout the securities law when dealing with numeric limits, you cannot avoid exceeding such a limitation by forming some sort of entity and counting it as one rather than counting its constituent parts. Without going overboard on minutiae here, suffice to say that a promoter cannot evade the individual accredited investor limitations by forming groups to form one corporate entity. There is a general "look through" principle, so that the entity status will be ignored to look through to the individual members. So, while investors may have perfectly valid reasons for forming an entity to invest in a particular deal, it will not serve to avoid any numeric limitation.

Entities already in existence when considering a Reg. D offering may be treated as one investor in certain circumstances, but either the asset tests for such entities are much higher than those for individuals, or you must look through to the individuals for accredited investor status.

It should be noted that these standards, adopted in 1982, have not been changed in any material way since then. In Dodd-Frank, Congress mandated that the SEC review the "accredited investor" standards every four years, beginning in 2014. That review remains underway as of September, 2016. There is no way to know what the SEC will do, but no matter what they conclude, it will be controversial.

b. Rule 501(e)—Calculation of Number of Purchasers

As we will see in a moment, both Rules 505 and 506 contain limits on numbers of investors. Under Rule 501(e)(1), certain purchasers are excluded from being counted among this limited number of purchasers: (i) family members residing under one roof count as one, and not as each individual; and (ii) various business entities, like trusts, corporations and benefit plans as well.

One other exclusion seems rather innocuous but packs a heavy punch; "(iv) any accredited investor." We will see in the text of Rule 506 that sales may only be made to a maximum of 35 "sophisticated investors." Tracking things through, however, per the Rule 501(e)(iv) exclusion of "accredited investors" from that count, the result is that there is *no limit* on the number of accredited investors to whom securities offered in reliance on Rule 506 may be sold.

c. Rule 501(i)— "Purchaser Representative"

Jumping ahead just a bit, we will see in the discussion of Rule 506 below that sales may only be made to a maximum of 35 "sophisticated investors." Essentially, "sophisticated investors" are those who have such knowledge and experience in dealing with securities that they do not need the protections of the securities law. Such persons may have those attributes on their own, or may rely on the services and skills of a "purchaser representative" who possesses them. This can be a family member, an attorney, an accountant, an investment adviser or some other knowledgeable professional person. They lend their expertise to the investor for purposes of making the investment decision. Purchaser representatives may be subject to securities licensing requirements unless they are exempt or excluded from them, and it should be obvious they take on some potential liability for providing their guidance.

2. Rule 502

In Rule 502, the SEC describes some conditions generally applicable to one or more of the rules that follow.

a. Rule 502(a)—Integration

Although set forth in specific terms here for Reg. D purposes, the concept of integration applies throughout the securities law when dealing with numeric limitations. Say an issuer developing 100 acres of land is limited to selling only ten LP interests a year under Exemption X. Can the issuer simply divide the parcel into two 50 acre plots and make two identical offerings selling 10 interests in Lot A and eight more in Lot B that year? The answer is "probably not," because the sales in Lots A and B will be "integrated" as simply one offering artificially divided in an attempt to evade the limit.

Of course, it is rarely that obvious or easy a calculation. In the Rule, five factors are set forth to consider in attempting to determine if offerings will be integrated:

1. Are the securities sales part of a single plan of financing?
2. Are the securities to be sold of the same class of interests?
3. Are they being sold at or about the same time?
4. Is the same or similar consideration being received for both?
5. Are the sales being made for the same or a similar purpose?

There is no surefire way to know if what you think are two distinct offerings will be integrated if put to the test. For practical purposes, concerns about integration waned a bit in recent years because experienced issuers relying on Rule 506 elected to limit sales to accredited investors only. That meant they did not have to worry about selling to a 36th non-accredited investor. However, the advent of the JOBS Act has given rise to new integration concerns. We will discuss them below in the discussion of Rule 506(c).

b. Rule 502(b)—Information Requirements

Another reason to decide not to sell to any non-accredited investors is found here, in Rule 502(b). Basically, if sales are made to even one sophisticated but not accredited investor, the issuer is first required to provide such investors with disclosure about the offering and specific levels of financial information (based on the size of the offering), provide the opportunity to ask questions and provide answers, and inform the investor that the securities are subject to resale restrictions. The SEC cautions that, if such disclosure is given to non-accredited investors, the issuer would be well-served to give to all investors.

In the real world as discussed throughout this Work, it has become common practice to prepare and distribute a full PPM package to all investors regardless of their category and sophistication.

c. Rule 502(c)—Manner of Offering

Per Rule 502(c), prior to the changes noted below for Rule 506, issuers were generally not permitted to use public solicitation of advertising in offering securities in reliance on Rule 506. This rule, or predecessors like it, precluded public solicitation and advertising of exempt offerings until the JOBS Act gave rise to a new paradigm, discussed below.

d. Rule 502(d)—No resale

One of the most vexing problems regarding exempt offerings is that the securities the investors receive must be restricted as to their resale. The restrictions and the means to lift them are set forth in 33 Act Rule 144. In Reg. D offerings (with the one exception being public Rule 504 offerings), the issuer must disclose the resale restrictions and place a restrictive legend on the securities issued either in print or electronically.

3. Rule 503—Form D

Within 15 days after the first sale is made, the issuer or someone acting on his behalf must file with the SEC a completed Form D. These forms must now be filed using the SEC's online EDGAR System. Under the laws of virtually every state (save New York), Form D must be filed with the securities authority of each state within 15 days of the first sale in that state. These filings carry with them a widely-varied filing fee. The states are in the process of implementing their own electronic Form D filing regime. The filing of the Form D is expressly *not* a condition of the exemption, meaning if an issuer botches the filing or fails to file at all, the offering does not lose the exemption. Although the SEC holds true to this premise, it is not unusual for state securities authorities to react very aggressively to any such failure.

It is on Form D where issuers run into trouble if they employed or associated with agents to sell the offering interests and paid them commissions if they were not licensed or registered in some fashion. Misrepresenting facts in an official filing is theoretically a felony. Declaring the information accurately is to confess to violating the law. Many states will follow up on such information following their review. If the issuer toed the line, there will be no problem. If the issuer stepped over it, bad things are likely to happen. (An important new rule was added after the JOBS Act. See Section G below for a discussion of Rule 507.)

Through April 20, 2107, there were three principal safe harbors in Reg. D: Rule 504, Rule 505 and Rule 506. The statutory authority under which Rules 504 and, in part, Rule 505, are adopted is 33 Act §3(b), under which the SEC is authorized to adopt exemptions from registration for offerings of up to $5 million. The original statutory authority from Rule 506 was Section 4(2), now 4(a)(2).

4. Rule 507

Prior to the November 21, 2016, there wasere no express repercussions for failure to file Form D with the SEC. Even so, many states issued cease and desist orders and imposed fines for late filings.

At least some federal consequences for failing to file took effect in November, 2016 in new Rule 507. Pursuant to this new rule, persons who are the subjects of orders, judgments or decree of a court of competent jurisdiction for failure to comply with Rule 503, the Form D filing requirement, are disqualified from relying on Rules 504, 505 (now extinct) and 506, unless the disqualification is waived by the SEC. State cease and desist orders are not enough to invoke the Rule 507 disqualification.

5. Rule 504

Rule 504 has two parts. Pursuant to the **private offering part of Rule 504**, an issuer is allowed to make a private offering of securities to raise up to $1 million (see Section F. below, which changed the $1 million rule to a $5 million limit, effective April 20, 2017) in any 12-month period. There is no (federal) restriction as to whom the securities may be sold. Public solicitation and general advertising are not allowed. The securities sold in a private Rule 504 offering are restricted securities, meaning they may not be traded by purchasers, publicly, absent registration with the SEC or the applicability of some other exemption. As we will see, as is required of any Reg. D offering, the issuer is required to file Form D with the SEC within 15 days of the first sale, although the filing is not a condition of the exemption. To illustrate, it is clear that raising more than $1 million will preclude reliance on Rule 504. By contrast, failing to file Form D will not preclude relying on Rule 504. The issuer simply failed to comply with the form filing requirement.

Pursuant to the **public offering part of Rule 504**, an offering of up to $5 million (before April 20, 2017, only $1 million) is exempt from federal securities registration, provided that the offering is registered with each state in which the offering will be made. The state registration requirements must include a review for full and fair disclosure of all material facts and the distribution of a disclosure document (since New York's securities law contains no such requirements, a public Rule 504 offering to be made in New York must be registered in at least one other state that does require this disclosure, and that disclosure document must then be distributed to prospective New York investors.) Once registered, the securities may be offered and sold publicly in those states. Form D must be filed with the SEC no later than 15 days after the first sale.

None of the Uniform Securities Acts includes a statutory exemption to complement Rule 504. Most state laws do not. As a result, the standard (if there is such a thing) private placement exemption found in state securities laws imposes added burdens and limitations on private issuers. In Section 402(b)(9) of the Uniform Securities Act (1956), the maximum number of investors was set at 10, the issuer had to have a reasonable basis to believe the investors were acquiring the securities for investment purposes, and payment of commissions to agents was not permitted. We will discuss this state model in a few moments. Suffice to say, for now, that it did not jive well with the private Rule 504 model, and that made private Rule 504 a rather meaningless abdication of authority by the SEC regarding private $1 million offerings ($5 million after April 20, 2017). Even though the SEC washes its hands of such deals, they are much more restrictively regulated under most state laws.

On the other hand, in adopting the public Rule 504, the SEC expressly invoked and relied upon state securities agency securities registration for offerings up to $1 million (now $5 million). These offerings would be registrations by qualification at the state level absent some other individualized state treatment. The states and the American Bar Association joined forces to create the Small Corporate Offering Review or ("SCOR") form, a "fill-in-the-blanks" registration format that theoretically would ease the burden of registration for such $1 million (now $5 million) offering issuers. Many states eased, but did not eliminate altogether, the merit review burdens imposed on other full registrations by qualification. Though well-intentioned, SCOR has met with only very limited success. In our experience, it is not that the application or even merit review jurisdictions prohibit the offerings. Once registered and cleared for sale, the issuers have found it all but impossible to sell their securities. Indeed, private offerings of every shape and size have a very steep hill to climb in finding investors.

There was one other important change to the Rule 504. The change is brought about in the overarching impact of disqualification under Rules 506(d) and (e). We discuss these Rule amendments in more detail in Section I, below.

In summary, until new SEC rule making, under, private Rule 504 offers and sales could be made to anyone without qualification with sales limited to $5 million, but per most state laws, that latitude was reeled back dramatically. Public Rule 504 offerings were also limited to $1 million (now $5 million) and had to be registered in the states where sales will be made. In our experience, the $1 million limit served to cross Rule 504 in either form off the practical list of potential exemptions by comparison. Now that the rules have changed, it will be interesting to see if Rule 504 proves more useful.

6. Rule 505 (repealed effective April 20, 2017—see Section F., below)

We will not spend much time on Rule 505 because it has gone the way of the phonograph and eight-track tapes. Rule 505 was promulgated under 33 Act Section 3(b) and what was then Section 4(2). Per the Rule, an issuer was permitted to raise a maximum of $5 million in any 12 months, sales could be made to a maximum of 35 non-accredited purchasers, and issuers were subject to disqualification if they had been in any legal or regulatory trouble in the past. Issuers had to file Form D.

From 1982 to 1996, Rule 505 was the exemption of choice because the states undertook to conform their statutes and rules to it. The effort was to devise and adopt the Uniform Limited Offering Exemption ("ULOE"). Although a model was produced by the joint efforts of the North American Securities Administrators Association ("NASAA")[****] and the ABA, when it got to the individual states, it was not uniformly adopted. Virtually every state tweaked it here or there, making the coordination problem even worse than before. That regulatory Tower of Babel contributed to the need for a decisive federal solution in 1996. (See below as to National Securities Markets Improvement Act ("NSMIA") in 1996.)

7. Rule 506 (through September 23, 2013) (Legacy)

Pursuant to Rule 506 as originally drafted, an issuer was permitted to raise an unlimited amount of money from an unlimited number of investors. Given that the Rule was adopted under original Section 4(2), the issuer was not permitted to use general solicitation or advertising in finding investors. In fact, the issuer was supposed to have a pre-existing business or personal relationship with them. A new term came into play: "accredited investor." A Rule 506 issuer could sell to an unlimited number of "accredited investors," but was only permitted to sell to a maximum of 35 non-accredited—but still "sophisticated" investors (see the discussion of *Ralston Purina*, above).

Given that, in 1982, there was no state law complement to Rule 506, its application was limited. That all changed in 1996.

As part of the National Securities Markets Improvement Act ("NSMIA") in 1996, Congress preempted the states from regulating any offering *that is exempt* from SEC registration pursuant to any rule adopted by the SEC under what was then Section 4(2) of the 33 Act. If you have been keeping track, this means Rule 506. Virtually overnight in 1996, Rule 505, ULOE, and almost every state private placement exemption provision became all but obsolete. Rule 506 became the universal exemption of choice for any private issuer.

There was, however, a bit of a problem with the preemptive language. We harken back to the discussion of safe harbors and self-executing exemptions. For NSMIA's preemption to apply to a Rule 506 offering, it had to *be* exempt under the Rule. However, there is no way to know if an offering is or is not exempt, at least, that is, until a judge declares it is or is not exempt.

That led to a fascinating anomaly that state regulators and private plaintiffs pursuing rights under private state remedies, as opposed to the SEC, federal courts and federal law, began bringing actions in state courts to show that an issuer of one offering or another had somehow acted in a way contrary to the requirements of Rule 506, and thus, did not qualify for the safe harbor exemption. If the claim had substance, the issuer was then challenged to scramble around looking for some other exemption,

---

[****] NASAA is an organization whose members are the securities regulators of the 50 states, the Canadian provinces and territories, Mexico, Puerto Rico, and the U.S. Virgin Islands.

both federal and state, to cover his errant offering. To the SEC, it must have been a scary prospect that state courts would begin construing terms like "public solicitation" and "advertising" when the SEC had avoided doing so for years.

Today, nothing has changed with that dynamic. State regulators and private investors pursuing state remedies in state and federal courts continue to try to take advantage of issuers they believe have crossed the Rule 506 lines. Sales to more than 35 non-accredited investors, failure to provide requisite "registration-like" disclosure and financial information if even one non-accredited investor is involved; and, public solicitation or advertising are among the "low-hanging fruit" that can form the basis of such enforcement and court actions. Any issuer that fails to adhere to the bounds of Rule 506 does so at its peril.

8. Rule 508

Under Rule 508, even though an offering may involve what the SEC labels "insignificant deviations" from a term, condition or requirement of Regulation D, the offering could still qualify for the safe harbor of Regulation D, notwithstanding the insignificant deviation.

D. REGULATION D (AFTER THE JOBS ACT)

1. New Rule 506(b) (after September 23, 2013)—Old Rule 506

Per the JOBS Act of 2012, sea changes were brought about in 33 Act Section 4, Regulation D, and in particular, Rule 506. We will start with "new" Rule 506(b). New Rule 506(b) is nothing more than old Rule 506. It was left intact and remains a perfectly viable, popular and state law-preempting exemption.

Just as before, there is no limit on the amount raised. There is no limit on the number of accredited investors to whom sales are made, but sales to "sophisticated" investors are limited to 35. Public solicitation and advertising are prohibited. If a Rule 506(b) offering is made exclusively to accredited investors, there is no particular disclosure requirement, although issuers are advised that they are still subject to the general anti-fraud, full and fair disclosure provisions and requirements. However, if even a single sale is made to a non-accredited—yet a "sophisticated"—investor, disclosure providing the same factual information that would be required if the offering was registered must be made to *all* non-accredited investors, along with financial disclosure that becomes more complex as the size of the offering increases. At that point, there is absolutely no reason not to provide it to the accredited investors as well, and not doing so might even prove to be problematic under the anti-fraud provisions. Further, the issuer is required to have a good faith belief the accredited investors are in fact accredited, and that any others meet the qualifications of being "sophisticated" investors.

There was one important post-JOBS Act change to the previous iteration of Rule 506(b). The change is brought about in the overarching impact of two other new rules adopted by the SEC, Rules 506(d) and (e). We discuss Rules 506(d), (e) and 507 in more detail in Section I below.

2. New Rule 506(c)—public solicitation and advertising allowed

In the JOBS Act, Congress amended 33 Act Section 4 by creating subsections. Former Section 4 became Section 4(a). A new subsection 4(b) was added. Under new subsection 4(b), Congress directed the SEC to create a new exemption from securities registration by rule under which public solicitation and advertising are permitted. In other words, Congress mandated that the SEC create an exemption for "public" private offerings. The SEC did so, at new Rule 506(c). The Rule was effective on September 23, 2013.

The Rule is not particularly complicated. An issuer is able to raise an unlimited amount of money from an unlimited number of accredited investors, just as in legacy Rule 506. The big change is that, under new Rule 506(c), an issuer is not prohibited from publicly soliciting or advertising for investors. There is, however, a *quid pro quo* to this new latitude. Sales are restricted to *accredited investors only and exclusively*. Further, the issuer is required to *verify* that each of the investors in fact meets the qualifications of an accredited investor.

As guidance from the SEC as to the term "verify," the SEC staff provided three examples in the final rule release of what would constitute satisfactory verification. In addition to the investor's own written attestation in each instance, an investor's tax returns and forms could be used to verify income status. Bank or brokerage statements could be used to show assets in excess of $1 million. Finally, written confirmation from an investor's attorneys, brokers, bankers and advisors would also suffice. Again, the SEC stressed these were only examples of satisfactory verification methods. Other means and methodologies can and will be developed. There is also a bit of a fudge factor. The issuer must have a good faith belief that each investor's income and or $1 million + assets have been verified.

The problem with Rule 506(c), if there is any, is that an issuer has nowhere else to turn if it violates some term in attempting to comply. 33 Act Section 4(b) and Rule 506(c) are generally the only provisions under which public solicitation and advertising is permitted. Once an issuer crosses that line and goes out to the public, it is committed. One misstep, such as selling securities to an investor who is not accredited, could lead to the necessity of abandoning the offering and waiting out a six-month "dark period" to purge the violation and reoffer.

The new pairing of Rule 506(b) and (c) gives new life to the integration problem. Suppose a syndicator sells Offering A in reliance on Rule 506(c), using public solicitation, thus selling solely to accredited investors the syndicator verifies to be properly accredited. The syndicator then sells Offering B, this time a private offering, made in reliance on Rule 506(b). Offering B can include sales to sophisticated, but not accredited, investors. As long as the Offering A and Offering B are deemed to be separate transactions, everything should be fine. However, if it was later determined that the two deals were simply one larger offering artificially distinguished as two, without any substantive difference, the two offerings could be "integrated" under Reg. D.

In such instance, there is a big problem. It would mean the syndicator made an invalid Rule 506(c) offering because sales were made to non-accredited investors; and the offering does not qualify as exempt under Rule 506(b) either, because the syndicator employed public solicitation, and that is not permitted under Rule 506(b). That leaves the syndicator in a bit of a fix. The alternatives for proceeding are few and potentially painful. The syndicator can:

- Abandon the offering and return any funds already invested. Not fun, and sometimes not possible; or
- Disclose to investors the potential exemption misstep and offer to rescind the investments. If this is done soon after the investments have been made, there is a good chance no one will accept. [Note that: (i) many states require that rescission letters be filed with the agency before being sent out; (ii) a rescission letter is an "offer to purchase" under both federal and state laws; and anti-fraud provisions apply to both the representations made and any facts omitted; and (iii) most regulators take the position that the person offering rescission must have the means to honor all accepted offers at the time the offers are made, and the offers must be made to all affected investors at the same time. This last part is usually the deal breaker, due to lack of funds.] If no one or only a few investors accept, the original offering can proceed, and the investors who rejected the offer are precluded from later filing a claim on the basis disclosed, assuming the rescission process was followed correctly. However, Rule 506 may still be unavailable to the "same offering" unless the issuer waits to re-offer for six months or so. (We never said this would be easy!); or

- Decide to take his chances and rely on 33 Act Section 4(a)(2) and not the Reg. D safe harbors. Should that be the course, because securities sold without registration in reliance of Section 4(a)(2) are not covered securities like those sold in reliance on either Rule 506, the issuer must find state law exemptions on which to rely; and they are generally far more restrictive and limited than either Rule 506.

It is far better not to have the problem, using careful planning and execution, than to try to solve it once you have it.

There is no question that, prior to the JOBS Act, private issuers had for years implored the SEC and Congress to permit public solicitation and advertising of private offerings in one form or another. Just as regularly, their urgings were ignored. With passage of the JOBS Act and the promulgation of Rule 506(c), their pleas were fulfilled. Even so, it is no panacea for small business.

Entrepreneurs of start-up businesses, by definition, ooze eternal optimism. It is their hope and dream that get them up every morning. After they have tapped every source they can think of for funding, it is natural for them to believe that generally soliciting and advertising their deals will help them find equally optimistic and hopeful investors who can understand a gem when they see and get in on the ground floor of the next Apple or Microsoft, except it usually does not work that way; and that may me particularly true when it comes to real estate.

Under the old regulatory regime, issuers in Rule 506 private placements were limited to approaching people with whom they had a pre-existing business or personal relationship. It was natural for prospective issuers to want to expand beyond that circle and publicly seek investors. However, it well may be that the only people who might be interested in investing in such an offering are those in that circle.

In making investment decisions, investors seek a safe place to invest, want to make a profit and liquidity so they can sell out when they desire. It is most likely that only those in your inner circle will have a strong basis to judge and rely on you to be honest should they entrust their funds to you. With little track record, investing in any small business is very risky, with profitability perhaps years away, if ever. Further, it is hard enough to find someone to invest once, let alone someone who will take an investor's place. In sum, investing in small business is usually going to require some intangible reason above and beyond the merits that can be portrayed in written documents. With hundreds of thousands of investment opportunities, large and small, abounding on the Internet, how is any one offering going to stand out? Without some other factor attracting investors to one over another, the viability of public solicitation and advertising may prove to be far less of an ultimate answer to small business capital formation than its proponents projected. Prospective issuers that do not have a reliable and strong source of capital among a circle of personal contacts may need to think twice about relying on public solicitation and advertising for that next raise.

3. New 33 Act Section 4(b)(1)—Internet intermediaries OK without a broker or dealer license

Congress did not stop there. In a move the SEC could and should have made years before, Congress added a new subsection 4(b)(1) to 33 Act Section 4 regarding *internet intermediaries*. Such intermediaries are not to be considered as brokers or dealers under federal law provided they operate within prescribed limits. It was a natural outgrowth of the advent of the Internet. For years, universities and others sought to allow embryonic businesses to post business plans on independent websites that anonymous angels could peruse and even engage in online conversations with the principals without being identified. If the angels grew interested enough in a project, they could identify themselves to the sponsor and engage in negotiations directly.

There were two problems. First, prospective issuers were engaged in what amounted to public solicitation and advertising, so that there was no available securities registration exemption. Second, even if the first problem was overcome, the webhost, which almost always had to agree to be compensated with securities in the new venture, because the start-ups were already cash-starved, were construed by the SEC to be "brokers" requiring broker registration. New subsection 4(b) and Rule 506(c) addressed the first problem, and new subsection 4(b)(1) addressed the second.

An Internet intermediary connecting hopeful net posters and intrigued angels will not be construed as a federal broker or dealer even if they invest in the deals as long as they provide only "ancillary services." Such intermediaries:

- may not be paid any form of commission on a sale the originates from a web "match;"
- may not take possession of customer funds or securities; and
- are precluded from serving in this capacity if they are subject to any statutory disqualification from broker or dealer registration.

The term "ancillary services" is defined to include:

- performing due diligence and helping negotiate, provided no special compensation is paid for providing investment advice or recommendations; and
- providing standardized documents that could, but need not, be used in handling the deal, but not being involved in developing deal terms on behalf of the issuer.

Rather than seeking the proverbial needle in a haystack, it is not hard to imagine internet intermediaries evolving over time, and gathering significant followings for specific sectors. This one will gain a reputation as the site of choice for biomed deals; that one for hi-tech; another for great real estate deals. Investors and promoters both will gravitate to the sites containing the best offerings and providing the most promising prospects in particular genres. As exciting and inexpensive as the prospects of such Internet involvement may be, whereas perhaps one in 10 people with whom you have a pre-existing business or personal relationship may be capable and/or interested in investing in your private offering (or 20, or 30 or whatever …. Pick a number.) There will be a shifting from that circle to strangers, potential investors who access a website and your prospective offering changes that equation exponentially, to one in 1,000 or to one in 10,000. (Again, pick a number—it will be much higher for sure). At least the cost will be relatively less expensive than mailings or cold calling.

A reader asked a few questions about offerings that are best addressed here. First, he noted that Rule 506 deals with sales and not offers. Therefore, he asked if an issuer discusses a deal with a prospective investor before the issuer has determined the prospect is accredited, has the issuer run afoul of the Rule? The answer is "it depends." It is true that Rule 506 applies only to sales and purchasers. So, making an offer to a non-accredited investor does not implicate the Rule's restrictions. However, public solicitation and advertising are restricted under Rule 506(b), so more information is needed for a complete answer.

The question gives rise to another subject, "what constitutes an 'offer'?" The best answer is "almost any discussion of the subject once the idea of an offering has crystallized in the minds of the issuer" can be construed as part of the offer. An offer can be a process as well as a finite moment in time. Lawyers seek to control the offering process to make sure that anything said about an offering is well thought out and accurate through written statements contained in a private placement memorandum. Many promoters find that approach restricting and unrealistic. The best practice is in there somewhere. It should suffice that anything said should be kept general and to a minimum.

The reader next asked "can an issuer form a new entity, Entity II, and try to get it right after doing something to cause the first offering through Entity I to be ineligible to rely on Rule 506?" That question gives rise to another important topic, who is the 'issuer'? The entity limited partnership, LLC or the like is clearly the issuer, but it does not end there. The general partner or manager is going to be considered the "issuer" as well. Generally speaking, one should proceed on the premise that any individual or entity that can be construed as a controlling person of the deal can be described as the "issuer." With that in mind, the answer to the initial question is "no." Forming a new entity will not change the identity of the heartbeats involved. It will likely not alter the goals of the project either. Thus, the second Entity II will be "integrated" with Entity I. The general rule is that an issuer that missteps on a Rule 506 offering must sit on the sidelines for at least six months before giving the project another try; or they can register the deal. Neither is a particularly attractive option, making attention to detail in the first instance all the more important.

The reader's next question addresses the issue as to whether new Rule 506(c) changes some understandings held about "old Rule 506." He stated that, under old Rule 506, an issuer first had to determine whether a prospective investor is accredited (usually by a questionnaire); the issuer should not have a particular offering in mind when the investor is approached; and then the issuer must wait 30 days before approaching that prospect with a real offering proposal. This proposed three step process confuses, conflates and misstates a few important premises. First, Offerees need not be accredited. Purchasers must be accredited. There is a big difference. A Rule 506(c) issuer can make an offer to anyone on earth. However, it makes little sense to do so because an offer to a non-accredited investor is a waste of time and effort relying on Rule 506(c); only accredited investors can purchase, so why bother with non-qualified Offerees? In the second and third points, the reader is really asking about Rule 506(b). Under Rule 506(b), to steer clear of any suggestion the issuer engaged in public or general solicitation and advertising, the maxim is that the issuer should have a pre-existing business or personal relationship with any person to whom the issuer makes an offer. The reader was suggesting a means of fabricating such a relationship by using the old two-step process from cold calling: "I don't have anything to offer you now, but I'll call you if and when something comes along." I would not want to go into court and argue that "relationships" originated in that manner did not involve "public solicitation" within the meaning of Rule 506(b)!

The next reader question was whether proposing a joint venture to a prospective partner wherein the prospect would be a full participant in management in a real estate venture could be turned into a security were the prospect to later change his mind and desire a passive, non-management role. The answer lies in the timing, and involves basic investment contract law. We presume that the first "joint venture" proposal would involve the prospect relying on his own efforts to manage the project and generate profits. Assuming that is the case, there is no investment contract. The fact pattern fails the "efforts of others" component of the *Howey* test. If a participant in a joint venture decides on his own after entering the deal that he would rather take a back seat and let others assume the laboring oars, he will have a hard time convincing a judge that he invested on the premise that he would earn a profit based on the efforts of others. He will likely fail in his attempt to turn a non-security into a security after the "sale" is made by reneging on and abdicating responsibilities. This will be a fact-intensive inquiry as to what he really believed when he committed; but on the facts presented, it is doubtful he will succeed.

The reader's last question is a familiar one: "What about all those real estate and inventor clubs out there where all sorts of people attend a monthly meeting and listen to perfect strangers make proposals about investment ideas?" The reader surmised that the presenters at these meetings violated the law pre-JOBS Act but they are legal post-JOBS Act, again presumably based on the availability of Rule 506(c). The question raises another reality of securities regulation. It is true that there are such gatherings and such presentations in most cities. It may be a dirty little regulatory secret, but our sense is that, absent some express harm emerging from them, they were simply tolerated. Technically, yes, they violated the law. They made illegal offers; but illegal offers do not create private, civil damages. That claim is left to illegal sales. The question both before and after the JOBS Act is: To whom are the sales made? So, the answer to this final question is "yes," they were likely illegal under prior law, but are permissible under Rule 506(c) as long as any resulting sales are restricted to accredited investors.

The unfortunate bottom line for prospective small offering issuers is that no statute or rule change is going to alter the fundamental dynamic that small offerings are risky and illiquid, and those are not characteristics of much interest to mainstream investors. That said, Congress went one step further in the interests of reaching potential investors that might be out of the mainstream, and that is where we turn next.

This discussion of using the internet to raise capital is tied to the concept of Crowdfunding, discussed next.

E. New Section 4(6) and Section 4A—Crowdfunding

The most controversial feature of the JOBS Act was the introduction of "crowdfunding" for equity or debt. The concept was to allow small issuers to raise up to $1 million in a 12-month period[††††] through registered "funding portals" (a lot like the internet intermediaries discussed in the previous section, but regulated) from anyone. The prospect of such a "democratization" of investing (as crowdfunding supporters saw it) brought chills to the spines of consumer advocates and investor protection interests who saw nothing but fraud in the idea. As a result, so many "bells and whistles" were imposed in the law, they strangled most of the potential out of the proposal to the extent it had any in the first place.

Although the statute contained express directions for much of the new mode of capital formation, enabling SEC rule making was still needed to complete the picture. The final rules were not effective until May 2016.

Given the amount of capital usually called for in real estate offerings, the $1.07 million total capital restriction, and the per investor maximum annual crowdfunding investment cap, SEC Rule crowdfunding may be more trouble than it is worth for real estate deals.

Even before the SEC's crowdfunding rules became effective, when interested parties put pencil to paper, it was hard to figure out how anyone was going to make any money as a service provider. There was simply not enough "food on the table" to go around. The maximum amount that can be raised is $1.07 million. Issuers are likely to need legal assistance to help chart a course around the many legal "landmines" that will pose challenges to even experienced securities counsel. The issuers are likely to be rather unsophisticated in securities disclosure regimes; thus, this type of offering will require a lot of hand holding and guidance. There are also the accounting disclosure requirements to consider. Further, the funding portal will have to be compensated, as will the escrow agent. It is not outlandish to suggest that, of a maximum of $1 million that might be raised, 10 to 15% could be eaten up by offering expenses before the venture sees its first dollar of new capital. That also means the venture must make up that same 10 to 15% just to return to zero.

Those people who believed in crowdfunding as a mechanism for raising capital, but saw Sections 4(6) and 4A crowdfunding as unlikely to present great opportunities, simply changed the paradigm. They realized the same marketing principles based on social networking could be employed using a combination of the new Rule 506(c) and existing broker-dealers willing to adopt a new business strategy.

Registered broker-dealers advertise and solicit for new clients every day. Issuers previously restricted to soliciting potential investors they knew were liberated by the new Rule to publicly solicit. Without waiting for or relying on the registered funding portals of the future, the broker-dealers could perform the portal functions—and more—seeking potential investors through public solicitation and advertising of Rule 506(c) offerings. Using social media to solicit investors poses some challenges under existing brokerage rules dealing with recordkeeping, but not enough to deter a fledgling means of investor and client marketing.

[††††] The amount has since been adjusted for inflation to $1,070,000.

It was not long after September 23, 2013 that we started to hear of experiences involving "crowdfunding" and "crowdfunded offerings." It took a while to figure out whether these were gun-jumping Sections 4(6) and 4A crowdfunding efforts, going forward with neither final rules nor registered portals to guide them, in another word, "illegal," or they were offerings being made under new Rule 506(c) that were simply utilizing social media to spread the word, with or without a broker-dealer's involvement, which was and is perfectly lawful. With no limit on the amount that can be raised, the number of investors, a cap on how much an individual investor may invest in a 12-month period, or a host of other restrictions and limitations, if generic crowdfunding has a future in private placement capital formation, it seems much more likely to happen at the Rule 506(c) level than under whatever rules are finally adopted under 33 Act, Sections 4(6) and 4A.

While waiting for the SEC to act, another complementary phenomenon arose, worthy of noting. Many states adopted their own crowdfunding statutes or rules. Under these provisions, issuers are permitted to proceed with crowdfunded offerings relying on the state mandate under state securities law and the intrastate offering exemption in federal law (discussed more fully in Sections E and F below). Whether such an offering is permitted in any particular state is a question of local law. The SEC has, in a phrase, washed its hands of such deals, provided they do not cross state lines, physically or electronically.

There are also a number of interesting tax issues when employing the label of "Crowdfunding." Many of these issues are discussed in the Tax Section of this Work.

F. "REGULATION A+"

The JOBS Act contained another mandate to the SEC to change a regulatory exemption, this time Regulation A ("Reg. A"). Reg. A is transactional securities registration exemption promulgated under 33 Act, Section 3(b) in 1936. While refinements have certainly been made to the Rule over time, it has remained relatively unchanged in principle for 79 years! Under old Reg. A, an issuer was permitted to raise up to $5 million through the sale of securities in a 12-month period. There is no limit on the number of investors. There are no investor qualifications. In addition, prospective issuers are permitted to "test the waters" using a very brief and restricted description of a prospective offering to determine if there is enough investor interest to justify moving forward with a full-fledged filing with the SEC. Under Rule 262, "bad actors" are disqualified from relying on Regulation A (this disqualification is broader than the Regulation D Rule 506(d) and (e) disqualification discussed in Section I below).

Unlike any of the other exemptions we have discussed to date, Reg. A is known in the patois of the industry as a "mini-registration." A proposed "offering circular" (as opposed to "prospectus" with registered offerings) is filed with the SEC and is reviewed by the staff of the Division of Corporation Finance. Comments and responses are exchanged between staff and issuer as with the full registration process. *Once allowed for use by the staff*, the issuer is permitted to begin the selling process as far as the SEC is concerned. There are a few other features, but of no particular impact here. So, this is the one federal exemption that an issuer knows "*is exempt*" for preemption and "covered security" purposes, except Congress chose not to preempt state authority over such offerings. Go figure!

There is another catch to old Reg. A. As stated, Congress did not include Reg. A offering securities among the list of covered securities in NSMIA. As a result, state securities registration jurisdiction over old Reg. A offerings was *not* preempted. Hence, to sell a Reg. A offering at the state level, the documents filed with the SEC had to filed with the states as an application for registration by qualification, meaning a separate disclosure review in most every jurisdiction and application of full merit standards in merit states. Review in multiple states drove up the expense of even a well drafted offering. The SEC review process, the state review burden in general, the merit burden in particular, the $5 million limit on the amount that could be raised, and the resulting disinterest of broker-dealers in marketing such deals made old Reg. A pretty much a dead letter as an exemption. Reg. A offerings had fallen to a mere trickle at the SEC and the states in the last decade or two. Then came the JOBS Act.

In the JOBS Act, 33 Act Section 3(b) was amended to authorize the SEC to adopt a new form of Regulation A by rule to allow for capital raised of up to $50 million. Among other features, the SEC staff will review the offering materials as they would any registration filing, and shares sold in such offerings would be freely tradable (not restricted as with Rule 506 offering securities). Congress did the SEC no political favor when it left it up to the Commission to determine by rule if state securities registration authority would be preempted. The SEC released its proposals, immediately nicknamed on the street as "Reg. A+," on December 18, 2013. The new rule was announced in May 2015 and became effective on June 19, 2015.

Predictably, state preemption was a key area of controversy when the proposed rule was released; and it remains so, at least to the state securities administrators. In its Release, the SEC proposed creating two tiers of Reg. A offerings. The Rule in place today (for offerings up to $20 million) would became "Tier 1" offerings , and the states continue to have the authority to review them. However, the SEC preempted the states from regulating new "Tier 2" offerings of up to $50 million.

The SEC gave state securities regulators a chance to follow through on plans developed through the auspices of NASAA to create a streamlined, "one stop" filing and review regime for such offerings. Key to that proposal would be whether NASAA's merit state members would agree to relent on application of some of the most common and, for members of the issuer community, most problematic merit review requirements. On March 11, 2014, NASAA announced publicly that its members had voted to adopt a coordinated and expedited review procedure for Reg. A+ offerings. In fact, under the state regime, the applicability of the "promoter's equity," the "promotional shares," and "loans to officers" merit rules were limited for such offerings.

Notwithstanding all this regulatory and political "excitement," it is an open question as to whether the advent of new Reg. A+ will have an impact on real estate syndications. In the past, Reg. A deals have principally involved offerings of corporate shares with a view toward a traded secondary market, and thus, not of particular interest to most real estate syndicators. Real estate deals tend not to lend themselves well to stock offerings, given that the corporate form obviates some of the benefits offered investors in a limited partnership or limited liability company, such as passing the benefits through to investors, etc. Even so, the cachet of having the offering reviewed and allowed for use by the SEC (and the states) may ease the resistance some investors may have to other private offerings. [Chart follows]

COMPARISON OF REGULATION A

TIER 1 AND TIER 2

Both Tiers
Freely tradable securities
No blank checks or "extractive industries" (oil & gas, mining)
"Test the Waters"
'33 Act, Sec. 12(a)(2) private liability

Tier 1 (reviewed by SEC *and* States)	Tier 2 (reviewed by SEC alone)
$20 million cap Audited financial statements *not* required by the SEC	$50 million cap Audited financials required

Audited financial statements not required by the SEC No more than $6 million or 30% in selling shareholder shares	Audited financials required No more than $15 million or 30% in selling shareholder shares
No more than $6 million or 30% in selling shareholder shares	No more than $15 million or 30% in selling shareholder shares
No reporting requirements	Quarterly, Annual and Material Event reporting required
No investor qualifications	Sales limited to accredited investors, or non-accredited investors who invest $\leq$10% annual income or net worth
States *not* preempted	States *are* preempted
No express Sec. 12(g) exemption (but Sec. 12(g) unlikely to apply anyway)	Exempt from Sec. 12(g) registration if: • uses registered transfer agent • files required reports and is current • public float is $\leq$ $75 million or $\leq$ $50 million annual revenue

Some old Reg. A features take on new significance in Reg. A+. For one, good old Form 1-A, known better as the Small Corporate Offering Registration ("SCOR") form, states have accepted for use for years to register offerings exempt under Rule 504, can be used to file information under Reg. A+. If nothing else, the questions posed on the Form are invaluable in helping prospective issuers to organize their materials and get an understanding of what is required of them in virtually any competent offering. Gathering and organizing all the information required and at least considering the answers to the questions posed will help save time and money, once the issuer visits the securities lawyer.

The other feature from old Reg. A that went relatively unused was the "test the waters" process. I (Feigin) was a member of the SEC-organized task force whose work led to the addition of "test the waters" to the regulation and to encourage states to do the same. Under the "test the waters" process, prospective issuers are permitted to circulate a simple and abbreviated solicitation of interest to the public about their proposed offering. It does not take much work or legal advice to get the thing put together; and it can save the issuer a lot of money and time if the responses are weak. It may be "back to the drawing board" time, but at least the issuer did not go to the expense of assembling a full offering circular, filing package before any real evaluation as to whether it would be well received among investors. There are restrictions on retreating to a Reg. D offering, if the "test the waters" process is employed; thus, careful consideration should be given to taking one path or another before the first step.

Note the manner in which the SEC chose to preempt the states. It was an indirect approach. Back in 1996, in the National Securities Markets Improvement Act of 1996 (NSMIA), Congress provided that the states would be preempted from creating and applying securities registration regulation on "covered securities." Covered securities included exchanged-offered and traded securities, mutual fund shares and a few other forms of security that made sense to those with a national market perspective. But Congress also created another form of "covered security;" securities sold to "qualified purchasers" would also be covered securities, although defining the term would be the SEC's burden. So, the states would be preempted from regulating securities sold to qualified purchasers.

It is fair to presume that what Congress had in mind was the creation of a class of investors who did not need the registration protections of federal (and state) securities law given some characteristics, such as sophistication, experience, professional guidance, wealth, and the like. The lines were to be drawn by the SEC, if they ever chose to draw them.

Although there was one attempt early on to define "qualified purchasers" as "accredited investors," that was quickly abandoned. The only power to preempt available to the SEC in the JOBS Act was the "qualified purchaser" definition under the 33 Act (as distinguished from the term "qualified purchaser" under the Investment Company Act of 1940). No other "covered securities" were created in the Act. Therefore, if the states were to be preempted from review of Reg. A+ offerings, it was using the "qualified purchaser" definition or nothing. The SEC elected to define "qualified purchaser" as anyone, *anyone*, to whom a Tier II Regulation A offering was made. No other qualifications were required! No other standards applied!

As one might imagine, the states were displeased. They abhor preemption in the first place. For the SEC finally to define "qualified purchaser" to mean any carbon-based, life form was considered a virtual slap in the face. The SEC really had nowhere else to turn.

Securities regulators in Montana and Massachusetts filed appeals with the SEC and the DC Circuit Court arguing that the SEC's action is improper under and contrary to Congressional intent of NSMIA. The SEC rejected the appeal as did the DC Circuit Court. It was rejected by the Circuit Court for the District of Columbia as well, and is thus a dead letter.

In a blog in March 2015, I (Feigin) described some "reality checkpoints" as to whether anyone is likely to file under Tier I as opposed to Tier II. Those points follow.

Before the small company issuer community uncorks the champagne, it is important to recognize some practical realities and limitations about the new Regulation A regime.

SEC Review. Both Tier 1 and Tier 2 offering statements will be reviewed by the SEC's Division of Corporation Finance examiners, and Corp. Fin. is on record as stating that Reg. A offering statements are subjected to the same regulatory scrutiny as any S-1 registration filing, applying Regulations SK disclosure and SX accounting standards. Preparation of a Reg. A offering statement is going to require significant legal and accounting expense. It follows that the Staff will rely on Guide 5 for guidance on how real estate-related offerings should be presented.

Registrations by Qualification. At the state level, Regulation A offerings are **registrations by qualification**, *i.e.*, full registrations, akin to S-1 filings with the SEC. There is no Reg. A exemption complement at the state level, nor did the SEC impose Reg. A on the states. At the state level, registration by qualification filers are usually required (either by state statute or rule or both) to provide audited financials. So, under Tier 1, although the SEC will not require audited financials, the states might, and might have to *require* them (absent waiver authority), making the Tier 1 waiver rather meaningless.

Merit Review. Generally, merit states have the power to limit sales by insiders and affiliates more strictly than the SEC's Tier 1 limits. Even with waiver of loan repayment and cheap stock guidelines, merit states might pose problems here. Merit review can be avoided by selling shares exclusively in those states that do not apply merit standards, *i.e.*, the "disclosure" states.

Broker-Dealers/Underwriters

Financials. At least in Middle America, offerings of more than $10 million by early stage or other lesser known private companies are likely going to have to be made by one or more broker-dealers to succeed. Will these broker-dealers be willing to take on an offering by such a company that does not have audited financials, regardless of what the regulators require?

Reporting. It is one thing to say that shares will be freely tradable, and another to say there is an actual market for them. Will broker-dealers be able to market the shares to investors on the basis they are freely tradable if the company does not commit to making periodic, public reporting? Will the Tier 1 reporting waiver even be relevant?

Suitability. While there may be no minimum investor qualifications in Tier 1, and only limited qualifications in Tier 2, the SEC did not exempt broker-dealers that sell the securities from their *suitability obligations.* Will such offerings be "suitable" investments for non-accredited investors, even if the investors are investing less than 10% of income or net worth?

FINRA. How will FINRA's Corporation Finance section handle these new Reg. A offerings made by their member firms on behalf of client issuers? Will FINRA apply full registration review to the offerings, or will the deals be treated as some sort of exempt offering with lesser or no standards imposed? It is highly unlikely FINRA will ease its suitability requirements on broker-dealers. Nor are the states likely to do so.

The biggest disconnect between new Reg. A+ and real estate offerings is the fact that one of the biggest benefits of a Reg. A+ offering is that it results in freely tradable stock, and for all practical matters, C corporation shares of stock are not a particularly advantageous way to syndicate a real estate offering. There is double taxation of any dividends, and significant corporate action usually requires a cumbersome vote of the shareholders, as contrasted with the pass-through benefits of the limited partnership or limited liability companies, and their relative ease of operation. That said, this "ill-fitting suit" has been what has been. Innovations and the relative ease of getting to the marketplace may give rise to promoter and investor interest we have not see 7.

G. SECTION 3(A)(11), RULE 147 AND 147A

There is at least one other weird duck of an exemption to consider in the real estate securities area. Among the various exempt securities, there is 33 Act Section 3(a)(11), known as the "intrastate offering exemption." Unlike their Section 3(a) brethren, securities sold in reliance on Section 3(a)(11) are not exempt from securities registration for secondary trading, *i.e.*, a resale of the interests acquired in the first sale. These securities are exempt from SEC securities registration requirements because they lack one characteristic essential to federal jurisdiction, *i.e.*, they are not offered or sold by interstate means. If they are offered and sold solely within one state, the SEC has no jurisdiction.

To address these questions (though not necessarily answer them), the SEC developed Rule 147, effective in 1974. This is the safe harbor for Section 3(a)(11). Although the 33 Act contains this exemption on the federal level for an offering that is solely in one state, as noted, it is unclear what is "intrastate." After many requests, the SEC finally issued guidance and the Rule 147 safe harbor. Mistakes in attempting to comply with the Rule were commonplace, and led to loss of the exemption. See Appendix.

In the age of the Internet and social media, it is not easy to establish that any commercial transaction took place solely within one state, without using some form or interstate means. Using the mail across states lines is certainly out of the question. What about using a bank? It is federally insured even if a state chartered bank. Can you use the phone? What if you drive to meet an investor and you take an interstate highway? Keep in mind that, under securities law, the burden of proving the applicability of any securities registration exemption is on the person claiming it.

Old Rule 147 was relatively complex and detailed; many counsel shied away from attempting to rely on it, because there were so many ways to slip up. The restrictions imposed in the Rule were neither natural nor intuitive, but the SEC took the position they were necessitated by the limits of Section 3(a)(11), the statute under which it was promulgated. Some problems were beyond an issuer's control. The issuer could do everything perfectly well, and then have an investor move unexpectedly to another state and put the whole transaction in jeopardy.

Section 3(a)(11) and old Rule 147 are exemptions from SEC registration requirements only; "Nothing in this rule obviates the need for compliance with any state law relating to the offer and sale of the securities." That left the issuer to register at the state level or find a state exemption.

Any issuer desiring to rely on old Rule 147 also had to keep in mind the discussion earlier in the text as to "integration." Suppose an issuer sells Offering X in reliance on Rule 147 in State A in January, and then, in May, sells Offering Y in State B, the possibility looms that the two offerings will be integrated. Why? Because if the two offerings were to be combined (integrated), they were offered and sold in two different states, precluding reliance on the intrastate exemption. The integration concepts mentioned in Regulation D, discussed earlier in the text, also apply to Rule 147. There are five factors to consider in Rule 147, just as with Reg. D:

1.   Are the securities sales part of a *single plan of financing?*
2.   Are the securities to be sold of the *same class of interests?*
3.   Are they being sold at or about the *same time?*
4.   Is the *same or similar consideration* being received for both?
5.   Are the sales being made for the *same or a similar purpose?*

Of course, as mentioned, with regard to any safe harbor, failing to comply with the terms of the rule does not necessarily mean you have exceeded the bounds of the statute under which it is promulgated, but can and will lead to sleepless nights. In general practice, while Section 3(a)(11) and old Rule 147 are viable exemptions, prospective issuers generally steer clear of them, unless there is no other alternative than preparing and filing a registration statement.

The advent of intrastate crowdfunding provisions placed new emphasis on Section 3(a)(11) and Rule 147 and led the SEC to address some of the more vexing questions and stumbling blocks of the provisions. Significant changes to both Rule 504 and the intrastate offering exemption resulted, effective April 20, 2017.

H. Summary Changes to Rules 504, 505 and 147 and the Addition of New Rules 147 A and 506(d) and (e)

1. Changes to Rule 504

As mentioned, two important changes were made regarding Rule 504 effective on April 20, 2017. First, the amount of money that can be raised was increased from $1 million to $5 million, the statutory limit for such exemptions under Section 3(b)(1). Second, as of April 20, 2017, per Sections 506(d) and (e), the bad actor disqualification provision applies to Rule 504 issuers as well. The remaining provisions of and applicable to Rule 504 continue as before.

Although the increase to $5 million may make the exemption more attractive to some issuers, this remains a federal and not a state exemption. Securities sold in reliance on Rule 504 are not "covered securities," and thus state securities law requirements are not preempted. To rely on Rule 504 for a private offering, although federal law poses no problem, state laws do. For any such offering to be offered or sold in a state, it must be registered in that state or exempt from the state registration requirements. Although Rule 504 (old or revised) contains no minimum investor qualifications and no limit on the number of investors, state law exemptions are usually much more restrictive: public solicitation and advertising usually are prohibited, and there is usually a rather small number of investors allowed.

Rule 504 also contains a provision under which a public offering for up to $5 million can be conducted without SEC registration, provided the offering is registered in each state in which the offering will be made. (If a state law does not provide for securities registration, like New York's Martin Act, the

504 public offering must be registered in another state that does require registration and that offering document must be used in the state with no requirement.) A benefit of going through this state registration process is that the resulting securities are usually freely tradable.

In summary, all the provisions of old Rule 504 are retained in the new version effective April 20, 2017--with two important changes. The former cap of $1 million is raised to $5 million, and the "bad boy" disqualifiers apply.

What will the changes mean? No one knows. Few issuers relied on Rule 504 in its original form. The latitude provided in the private version of Rule 504 was a mirage; state law restrictions still applied. The $1 million limit for registered deals was not enough money to attract any but the most embryonic issuers; and notwithstanding the SCOR program and state efforts to assist them, the now state-registered offerings usually failed even though the issuers could publicly solicit and advertise where registered. The increase to $5 million may attract more seasoned issuers and breathe life into the SCOR program. Even so, even simplified and expedited state securities registration processes are not particularly well suited for real estate offerings.

2. Rule 505 repealed

Increasing the amount that can be raised under Rule 504 to $5 million made the already moribund Rule 505 even more superfluous. It has now officially been laid to rest and repealed.

3. Changes to Rule 147 and New Rule 147A

The most complicated of the new wave of rule changes came in the intrastate offering realm of Section 3(a)(11), Rule 147 and the creation of new Rule 147A. The changes were motivated, at least in part, to accommodate the wave of intrastate crowdfunding state laws and rules.

At the outset in understanding the changes, remember that Rule 147 is promulgated under Section 3(a)(11) and cannot exceed its statutory limits. It is for this reason that, although new Rule 147 and Rule 147A look very similar, the SEC adopted new Rule 147A under its general exemption authority in the 33 Act, Section 28, and *not* Section 3(a)(11).

Rule 147 is left largely intact. The SEC left it alone given that many state crowdfunding provisions are keyed to the existing rule. Changing current Rule 147 would necessitate multiple amendments at the state level. While this may be accurate, it is likely that new Rule 147A will give rise to new legislation, state rulemaking or both; but, who knows? It is the thought that counts.

New Rule 147 is changed in three principal ways. The staff of the SEC issued Compliance and Disclosure Interpretations ("CD&Is"), effective May 16, 2016, to accompany the effective date for the SEC's crowdfunding rules. In the crowdfunding CD&Is, the staff provided that they would not consider Internet postings of issuers relying on state crowdfunding provisions to be interstate offers as long as the issuer included a disclaimer to the effect that only in-state investors could purchase the securities. That was one of the biggest concerns facing intrastate crowdfunders. While worthwhile, a staff position does not an SEC rule make, and private civil liability still haunted any such conduct. That staff position is incorporated in new Rule 147. That makes a difference for private civil liability.

Second, while the issuer must still be incorporated in the state of the offering, have its principal place of business in that state, and must be "doing business" in that state, under the new rule, "principal place of business" is amended to mean where their principal business is conducted as opposed to where they have their principal office. Third, old Rule 147 was also modified as to the issue of the residency of investors. Under the revised rule, the issuer need only have a reasonable belief that each investor is a resident of the state. Notwithstanding a reasonable belief, the fact of non-residency was enough to lose the safe harbor under the prior rule.

Although these changes to old Rule 147 are of some help, and while Rule 147 may remain the cornerstone of existing state crowdfunding provisions, the greater latitude of new Rule 147A makes it a more attractive option. Under new Rule 147A, old Rule 147's state of incorporation requirement is replaced with the simpler and more realistic "principal place of business" and "doing business" tests. While sales of securities remain restricted to in-state residents, offers can be made anywhere. Purchasers can resell their securities to non-residents after six months as opposed to the nine months required under Rule 147.

These new Rule 147 and Rule 147A provisions do not change the fact that, as with Rule 504, the SEC merely steps out of the way and defers to state law. The focus then shifts to what is permissible or required under state law. The states have been very willing to attempt to accommodate start-up businesses using this federal latitude, but those efforts generally have not applied to real estate syndications, even though they can often be rather local in nature. While there is no federal limit on the number of investors or amount raised in an intrastate offering, they have tended to be rather small at the state level. The overwhelming opportunities and simplicity afforded by Rules 506(b) and (c) are likely to cause offerings relying on these provisions to overshadow and eclipse reliance on even revised Rules 504, 147 and 147A in the foreseeable future, but the latter should not be ignored altogether as one or another may serve in niche situations. We shall see.

All the changes in federal exemptions brought about in the wake of the JOBS Act were implemented by an SEC under a Democratic administration with a Republican Congress looking over its shoulder. It is anyone's guess what will occur with an SEC under a Republican administration with a Republican Congress. Suffice to say that the subject of securities regulation and exemptions is likely to remain volatile and necessitate close attention to the latest developments.

Summary by SEC Staff as to Comparison of Rules 147 and 147A

"On October 26, 2016, the Commission adopted final rules that modernize how issuers can raise money to fund their businesses through intrastate offerings while maintaining investor protections. The final rules amended Securities Act Rule 147 to modernize the safe harbor under Section 3(a)(11)[2] so issuers may continue to use state law exemptions that are conditioned upon compliance with both Section 3(a)(11) and Rule 147. The final rules also established a new intrastate offering exemption, Securities Act Rule 147A, that further facilitates intrastate offerings by allowing offers to be accessible to out-of-state residents and making the exemption available to issuers that are incorporated or organized out-of-state.[3]

Requirements of Rules 147 and 147A

In order to conduct offerings pursuant to Rule 147 or Rule 147A, issuers[4] must meet certain requirements. The table below broadly summarizes the Commission requirements for each rule. We refer to "in-state" as the state or territory in which the issuer is resident and doing business at the time of the sale of the security.

	Requirements of Rule 147 (safe harbor under Section 3(a)(11))	Requirements of Rule 147A
The issuer is organized in-state.	✓	
The officers, partners, or managers of the issuer primarily direct, control and coordinate the issuer's activities ("principal place of business") in-state.	✓	✓

	Requirements of Rule 147 (safe harbor under Section 3(a)(11))	Requirements of Rule 147A
The issuer satisfies at least one of the "doing business" requirements described below.	✓	✓
Offers are limited to in-state residents[5] or persons who the issuer reasonably believes are in-state residents.	✓	
Sales are limited to in-state residents or persons who the issuer reasonably believes are in-state residents.	✓	✓
The issuer obtains a written representation from each purchaser as to residency.	✓	✓

"Doing Business" In-State

Issuers conducting an offering pursuant to Rule 147 or Rule 147A must satisfy *at least one* of the following requirements in order to be considered "doing business" in-state:

- the issuer derived at least 80% of its consolidated gross revenues from the operation of a business or of real property located in-state or from the rendering of services in-state;
- the issuer had at least 80% of its consolidated assets located in-state;[6]
- the issuer intends to use and uses at least 80% of the net proceeds from the offering towards the operation of a business or of real property in-state, the purchase of real property located in-state, or the rendering of services in-state; **or**
- a majority of the issuer's employees are based in-state.

Restrictions on Resale

Securities purchased in an offering pursuant to Rule 147 or Rule 147A can only be resold to persons residing in-state for a period of six months from the date of the sale by the issuer to the purchaser. Issuers must disclose these limitations on resale to offerees and purchasers and include appropriate legends on the certificate or document evidencing the security. Although securities purchased in an offering pursuant to Rule 147 or Rule 147A are not considered "restricted securities," persons reselling the securities will nonetheless need to register the transaction with the Commission or have an exemption from registration under federal law.[7]

Filing Requirements and Relationship with State Securities Laws

Issuers conducting an offering pursuant to Rule 147 or Rule 147A are not required to file any information with or pay any fees to the Commission. Issuers, however, must comply with state securities laws and regulations in the state in which securities are offered or sold. Each state's securities laws have their own registration requirements and exemptions to registration requirements. Issuers wishing to obtain information should contact the state securities regulator in the state in which they intend to offer or sell securities for further guidance on compliance with state law requirements. Issuers may also obtain useful information on state securities law registration requirements and exemptions to registration requirements by visiting the website of the North American Securities Administrators Association (NASAA) at www.nasaa.org.

Integration

The integration doctrine provides an analytical framework for determining whether multiple securities transactions should be considered part of the same offering. This analysis helps to determine whether registration under Section 5 of the Securities Act is required or an exemption is available for the entire offering. Rules 147 and 147A provide issuers with a safe harbor that offers or sales conducted pursuant to Rule 147 or Rule 147A will not be integrated with:

- prior offers or sales of securities; or
- subsequent offers or sales of securities that are:
    - registered under the Securities Act, except as provided in Rule 147(h) or Rule 147A(h);
    - exempt from registration under Regulation A;
    - exempt from registration under Rule 701;
    - made pursuant to an employee benefit plan;
    - exempt from registration under Regulation S;
    - exempt from registration under Regulation Crowdfunding; or
    - made more than six months after completion of the Rule 147 or Rule 147A offering."

I.   DISQUALIFICATIONS

Historically, both Reg. A and Rule 505 contained a bad actor disqualification, known colloquially as "bad boy" provisions. If any officer, director or principal of an issuer or any affiliate has been the subject of an adverse enforcement order imposed after September 23, 2013, the issuer is disqualified from relying on any Rule 506 exemption, barring a waiver of the ban from the Commission. If the action occurred prior to September 23, 2013, the issuer is not prohibited from relying on Rule 506(b) or (c), but must disclose the facts regarding the adverse action. After the JOBS Act, these disqualifying events were made applicable to Rule 506 offerings as well. In addition, effective April 20, 2017, the disqualification was made applicable to issuers intending to rely on Rule 504. As discussed above, Rule 507 disqualified issuers that had been the subject of enforcement action for failure to file Form D. Rule 507 and the Reg. A disqualifier section are provided in full in the Appendix. While the SEC reserved the power to waive the disqualifiers, they are not likely to do so, having imposed strict guidelines.

J. THE REGISTRATION CONTINUUM

From the standpoint of setting regulatory policy for capital formation under federal and state law, one can perceive a sort of cascading in the rules and regulations. An issuer just starting out might raise some seed money using Rule 504 (the least burdensome of the safe harbors). The company can move up to an offering under Rule 506(b) to raise second tier funds both from wealthy supporters and close-in friends and colleagues. Perhaps the issuer can then utilize Rule 506(c) to more generally seek capital through use of the internet or other networking opportunities. Then, the growing company can make a Reg. A+ offering as a precursor to a full-blown registered IPO. It is not hard to see how things might flow. For real estate issuers, the process may be modified somewhat, given the large amounts of funding required and the fact that they do not often lend themselves to traded stock deals, but the opportunities are there to consider.

***

CHAPTER 4

Licensing of People Deemed "Engaged In The Business" of Selling Securities

The Third "Silo"

A. ORIENTATION

Once upon a time, there was a difference between a system requiring *registration* of businesses and people and one imposing *licensing* requirements on businesses and people. Presumably, in a registration system, there was no qualification testing, no prior experience required. As long as you were not statutorily disqualified from being registered, for instance, a criminal record, filed the requisite form and paid the fee, you could obtain registered status and your name was listed on the registry for all to see.

In a licensing structure, you had to establish your qualifications, by training or by passing an examination, or both. Doctors, lawyers and certified public accountants are traditional examples of licensed professions. Their license theoretically indicates not only registration but also a minimum level of competency.

The distinctions between registration and licensing in modern practice have all but disappeared and can lead to some confusion. Under securities law, an issuer "registers" securities, but a broker-dealer, an investment adviser and both their agents also "register" with securities authorities even though, being subject to minimum qualifications and examinations, are likely obtaining "licenses" within the traditional meaning. For the sake of clarity here, we will refer to what broker-dealers and agents obtain to engage in business as licenses, as opposed to registering.

A national regulatory structure has evolved in dealing with securities broker-dealers and their agents. Licensing responsibilities are shared among the SEC, FINRA and state securities regulators. The SEC licenses (registers) broker-dealers and has authorized FINRA to license broker-dealer agents and oversee the conduct of broker-dealers and their agents. The SEC does not directly license broker-dealer agents. Under state laws, state authorities require the licensing of both brokerage firms and their agents "doing business" in their state, a term very broadly interpreted. Although this shared responsibility might seem to create a lot of overlapping effort, it has developed into a cooperative system modernized by electronic application and monitoring systems.

For the most part, this national regulatory system is irrelevant to real estate promoters. Though some real estate syndications are sold through broker-dealers, more are not. They are sold directly by the sponsors. The questions that must be addressed and frequently arise in the real estate syndication area are: "How am I going to sell these interests?", "Do I need a license?" and "Does he need a license?" We will address them shortly.

B. What is a "Broker-Dealer" and who is an "Agent?"

Very generally speaking, a broker-dealer is a person that engages in the business of effecting transactions in securities for its own account or for the account of others. Although there is nothing in the definition that precludes an individual from being a broker-dealer, the term is better construed to be a company of some sort. An agent is an individual, other than a broker-dealer, who represents a broker-dealer or issuer in effecting or attempting to effect transactions in securities on their behalf.

Given these definitions, it is important to note that, in the securities realm, there is no such thing as an "independent" agent. Under securities law, an agent must be associated with a broker-dealer or an issuer, or the agent is a broker-dealer himself. Generally speaking, under securities law, everyone reports to someone. Said another way, it is almost always the case that someone is charged with the responsibility to oversee and supervise the (mis)conduct of another. That is certainly the case when it comes to broker-dealers and their agents.

Traditionally, under the 33 and 34 Acts, the terms "broker" and "dealer" were treated separately. A "broker" was a go-between, a pure agent who had no principal role or stake in the transaction. The broker was paid a commission for facilitating the transfer of shares to a buyer and cash to a seller. On the other hand, a "dealer" was a principal in the transaction, selling shares from or buying shares for its own account or inventory. They bought or sold their own property. Those distinctions blurred over time, so that the terms have become joined as "broker-dealer."

In Part One, Chapter 2, we mentioned the sale of business doctrine, and the not uncommon circumstance where a licensed real estate broker is retained to sell a business because the business owns real property. In a broader context, there is any number of developments in which land and securities seem to coexist, for instance, campgrounds, fishing camps, condo developments with rental pool agreements, and more. Does the individual retained to sell these interests need both a securities license and a real estate license?

The answer is, unfortunately, "maybe." Obviously, the SEC could care less about state real estate licensing. So, if a security is involved, SEC registration will be required. At the state level, the answer is a mixed bag. In some states, where the transaction could be construed as a real estate deal if the buyer is buying to use or live in the unit himself, it will be viewed as a real estate transaction and not a securities transaction. If the buyer is buying as an investment and not for personal use, it will be a securities transaction. If both, securities licensing is required. The securities conclusion will be enhanced if there is a voluntary rental pool, and enhanced further if pooling is mandatory. Purchase of multiple units will also send the dial over to the securities part of the gauge. It is best to consult with local counsel to determine local law and practice.

C. The Licensing Process

There are dozens of terms used to describe the people who act on behalf broker-dealers. They are "agents" under the Uniform Securities Act 1956, "sales representatives" under the Uniform Securities Act 1985 and back to "agents" under the Uniform Securities Act 2002. Under federal law, they can be referred to as "persons affiliated" with a broker-dealer and elsewhere as "associated persons."

FINRA uses "associated person" in places, but more often, "registered representative." In common slang, agents are often referred to as "reps." Suffice to say they are all the same individuals working for or on behalf of broker-dealers or issuers.

Broker-dealers "register" with the SEC and FINRA (FINRA actually handles the process) completing Form BD and submitting it through an electronic licensing system known as the Central Registration Depository ("CRD"), which is administered by FINRA with the database jointly owned by FINRA and the states via NASAA. Broker-dealer registration is no simple task. That fact is underscored by the internal FINRA requirement that the application process for membership as a broker-dealer must be completed within *six months*. For agent licensing, a Form U4 application is completed and filed through the CRD by a broker-dealer acting on behalf of a sponsored agent. The applications are distributed electronically to all designated jurisdictions by the CRD. Each state has direct access to the CRD.

All applications are reviewed to determine if there is any basis for disqualification. Typical among the bases for disqualification are past criminal convictions, past enforcement actions by regulators, filing misleading information and failing to meet minimum standards like designated principals failing exams, missing filing deadlines or failure to pay fees.

As with any disciplinary issues involving licenses, applicants and licensees, regulators do not have the authority to make final denial determinations on their own. Applicants and licensees are entitled to notice of grounds for denial of an application or intended discipline of a licensee and an opportunity for hearing on the merits before a designated authority, under what are generally known as administrative procedures acts ("APAs"). The particulars of the system of each jurisdiction vary, but the principles are generally the same. Regulators are often empowered by statute to take emergency action in appropriate circumstances, but it is always followed by opportunity to contest the action at a hearing. Most matters involving applications that run into problems are resolved by voluntary withdrawal of the application as opposed to a formal proceeding wherein the facts become matters of public record and formal findings are rendered.

Applicants to be the principals and agents of a broker-dealer are required to take and pass various national examinations administered by FINRA. Most of the exams are FINRA-related, the most common being Series 24 for principals and Series 6 for agents to sell mutual funds and Series 7 for agents to handle general securities products like stocks and bonds. Principals and agents are also generally required to take and pass Series 63, an exam owned by NASAA and administered by FINRA that deals with state securities law and compliance. Each applicant for agent licensing is issued a CRD number that will track his actions for the remainder of his career.

It is a commonly held misconception that, once an agent has taken and passed Series 7 and 63, he holds a "Series 7 and 63 license." There is no such thing. Any time an agent leaves a firm, his authority to conduct business—and what is truly his license—terminates; it ceases to exist at the same instant. He is no longer entitled to act as an agent. If and when he is hired by or associates with a new broker-dealer, the new firm will submit a new application for agent licensing with the firm, and the CRD will connect the exam passage record with him by means of his CRD number.

The agent need not retake and pass any of the exams to become licensed at the new firm, *provided* the period between his last association and the new application is less than two years. If more than two years have passed since he was last associated with a firm, he must start over and take the exams again. Given this circumstance, in some instances, agents who have been out of the industry for a while seek to find some brokerage firm willing to list the agent as an active broker even though he does nothing for the firm, simply to prolong the two year period. It is a practice known as "parking," and, needless to say, it is seriously frowned upon by regulators and bad news for both firm and agent if discovered.

D. COMPLIANCE

In the grand scheme of things, broker-dealer and agent oversight is both comprehensive and intensive. Firms are examined on a regular basis by FINRA examiners, the SEC conducts oversight exams to make sure FINRA is doing its job, and state regulators conduct exams of both headquarter offices and branch locations that the other two might not review. All of the regulators conduct "for cause" exams as they see fit.

All three regulators have adopted extensive books and records requirements, financial requirements and rules of conduct. Unlike regulators that oversee financial institutions and insurance companies, securities regulators, particularly state regulators, are much less concerned with the financial stability or "safety and soundness" of their licensees, and tend to focus more on consumer protection. Broker-dealer regulatory compliance is no simple matter, and requires a significant annual expenditure of resources.

One of the hallmarks of securities regulation is the rather paternalistic requirement imposed on licensees that before recommending an investment to a customer, the brokerage firm and agent must "know their customer" and determine that, before recommending an investment to a customer, must determine that it is "suitable" for them given the customer's financial situation, risk tolerance and degree of sophistication. Notwithstanding that the "know your customer" and "suitability" requirements are exclusively regulatory requirements enforceable solely by regulators by means of administrative processes, it is quite common for private litigants to allege that violations of these rules constitute grounds for recovery of lost investment funds in private litigation.

Among the records that firms are required to maintain are complaint files. Not only is a firm required to maintain and act upon written complaints received, but they are also required to report such complaints on the CRD records of the agent involved. Frankly, this drives firms and agents nuts. What information appears on an agent's CRD record can become a significant battle given a widely held belief that adverse information appearing on an agent's Form U4 can have disastrous ramifications to subsequent agent licensing and the ability to compete successfully for new clients.

If a regulator can establish there are grounds for sanctions against a licensee, such as rule violations or that some other statutory disqualification has arisen, the regulator can initiate an administrative action. More often than not, such matters are dealt with by means negotiations resulting in a stipulated consent order. These become matters of public record, including on CRD records. Such adverse actions can have serious repercussions for the licensee in following years as well.

When an agent gets in trouble, the first place regulators will look is to his supervisor. As we said previously, everybody is supervised by somebody in the securities world. That is especially true for broker-dealers and agents. Failure to supervise is one of the most commonly asserted regulatory concerns. Given that firms generally do not want to get into regulatory trouble, they are hard on their supervisors to make sure it does not happen. In turn, supervisors can be hard on their reps for the same reason. The degree to which firms and supervisors oversee firm operations varies greatly from firm to firm.

E. BROKER-DEALERS AS PRIVATE OFFERING "PLACEMENT AGENTS"

Broker-dealers engage in a wide variety of business, from helping retail clients in developing and implementing financial plans and buying and selling stocks in personal accounts, to acting as underwriters of initial public offerings on the New York Stock Exchange. When a broker-dealer is retained to help sell private offering securities, the firm is generally referred to as a "placement agent."

When it comes to private offerings, including real estate syndications, while many deal sponsors make the decision to retain broker-dealers to help sell their interests, the fact is that broker-dealers are expensive, sometimes prohibitively so in the private offering arena. In fact, many sponsors find that broker-dealers are unwilling to market their interests to their customers. For many promoters, the thought of hiring a broker-dealer to market their securities is a luxury they cannot afford.

The harsh reality is that private offering interests have always been hard securities to sell. They are inherently very risky investments, and by definition illiquid to boot. These natural concerns were exacerbated in recent years by the collapse of some very widely marketed private placements (involving medical receivables, tenant-in-common real estate interests, and oil and gas) sold by many perhaps too trusting, careless mid-range brokerage firms. When the offerings proved to be fraudulent, many of the broker-dealers that marketed them simply collapsed in the face of regulatory and private civil litigation.

In the wake of the frauds, FINRA imposed heightened restrictions on their member broker-dealers electing to sell private placements. The SEC, FINRA and the states placed greater emphasis on private placements in their examination efforts. With heightened supervision, awareness and scrutiny, fewer firms to begin with (given the demise of many that were willing to deal in private placements in the first place), and a healthy traditional stock market, it is not hard to understand that attracting brokerage firms to the private placement market is no small feat.

F. Issuers

As you might imagine from reviewing this comprehensive regulatory system for those "engaged in the business of selling securities," you probably do not want to be a licensed broker-dealer or agent if you do not have to be and still be able to achieve your goals. This all leads to the inevitable question: *Does an issuer selling its own securities need a broker-dealer or agent license?* The answer ranges from an equivocal "probably not" to a more worrisome, "in some cases."

The analysis starts with the principle that "issuers" are excluded from the definition of "broker-dealer" in the statutes. Even so, that is not the end, only the beginning. Why? Because that begs that question, "Who is the issuer?" A corporation issues stock, so the corporation is the issuer. That corporate issuer is just a legal fiction; we know it can only act through the efforts of people. The catch is that, while the statutes contain an exclusion from the "broker-dealer" definition for "issuers," it does not contain an exclusion for the people who run them. For how they are treated, we must look further.

For better or worse, there is generally no express statutory exclusion or exemption from licensing for the people who run or are employed by issuer businesses. That said, we know that the officers, directors, general partners, managers and other principals of small companies across the country offer and sell their companies' securities every day. So, we are either in the midst of an unprecedented licensing crime wave, or there is some other answer.

It comes in the form of regulatory and court guidance as to the meaning of the term "engaged in the business" contained in most every "broker-dealer" definition. The latitude with which the term is viewed varies wildly from jurisdiction to jurisdiction, so it is important for any prospective syndicator to consult with competent securities counsel to ascertain the answer for any particular state. With this "ask your lawyer" caveat firmly in place, there are some general tendencies worth noting. We will commence with federal law.

1. Federal Law

Unlike under state securities law, "issuers" are not excluded from the definitions of "broker" or "dealer" in the 34 Act. So, one must look elsewhere to find relief from the federal licensing requirement. Generally speaking, per a safe harbor set forth in SEC 34 Act, Rule 3a4-1, an individual associated with an issuer will not be construed as a "broker" and may thus sell the securities of that issuer without being registered with the SEC as a "broker" so long as he:

- is not subject to statutory disqualification from serving as a rep;
- receives no special compensation or commission for selling;
- will perform significant duties for the issuer after completion of the offering;
- has not been associated with a broker-dealer for at least the past year; and
- has not offered or sold the securities of any other issuer within the last 12 months.

In Rule 3a4-1(b), the Commission states affirmatively that failure to meet any of these factors does not necessarily mean that a particular individual violated the 34 Act bar on unregistered conduct. This constitutes specific notice that the statute is broader than the safe harbor. So, there is built-in, express latitude. It is also important to note that, unlike under state securities laws, there is no express private civil liability under the 34 Act for engaging in business as a broker or dealer without being so registered.

It is important to stress one overarching reality looking at the area in general and the five factors noted under Rule 3a4-1 specifically. Regulators are likely to pounce all over any unlicensed individual who is paid to sell securities, period. Regardless of any other characteristic or fact, in their view, if you get paid for selling, you need a license. So, keep in mind that paying some unlicensed person to sell your securities for you is like waving a red flag at a bull in your bathroom.

What about the "dealer" definition? This is one place where the federal law distinction between "broker" and "dealer" comes into play. Under federal law, a "dealer" is a person engaged in the business of buying *and* selling securities for its own account, whereas a "broker" is an intermediary between "seller" (issuer) and "buyer" (investor) in an issuer setting. Since an issuer only sells securities (and does not buy them too) for its own account in making an offering, the practical effect is that issuers are generally not dealers under the 34 Act. If the issuer is not a dealer, the people selling on behalf of the issuer can, at best, be brokers, and that falls back to the Rule 3a4-1 safe harbor.

Above and beyond the relative safety of Rule 3a4-1 is the question of the limits of "engaged in the business." We know that under Rule 3a4-1, selling an issuer's securities once in a 12-month period is within the express limits of the safe harbor, but what about twice, or four times in a year? This is a question not beyond the pale of reality, where a real estate promoter may be developing and managing a few different projects at the same time. How many times in a 12-month period may the principals of the developer sell the issuer's securities before they are considered "engaged in the business" of acting as an intermediary, a broker, between the issuer entity and its investors? There is simply no clear answer.

Finding an answer will certainly entail a case-by-case, intensive factual analysis. It may very well come down to whether the principals are doing any real developing or simply spending all their time raising money. If their capital raising efforts are merely incidental to where they are truly spending their time, on developing the project, they are not likely to be called brokers. If the opposite is true, they are treading on thin ice. The relationship between the various deals will also come into play. Are these truly separate deals, or is this merely one larger raise split up for some perhaps nefarious purpose? Again, consultation with counsel on such close and potential volatile questions is strongly recommended.

2. State Law

It is fair to say that *most* state securities laws and regulators provide for an outcome at least similar to that of federal law. One slightly narrower feature of state law and interpretation is that the exception to the licensing requirement is limited to principals of the issuer, and not just anyone who works for the issuer. As under federal law, receiving compensation for selling will all but certainly void any application exemption or exclusion from licensing. That said, the state laws and policies of the jurisdictions in which you will sell must each be reviewed with counsel to ascertain the local answer. Given that selling without a license can not only provide a regulatory basis for injunctive relief and restitution, it can serve as a basis for private civil liability (and it is a strict liability violation) for damages, and criminal culpability in the worst cases, for both the unlicensed individual *and* the company that hired him, the licensing question is nothing to fool around with.

G. SUMMARY

Now armed with some basic information, we will address those three questions that challenge any prospective real estate syndicator.

1. "How am I going to sell these interests?"

This is both a legal and a practical question. From a legal standpoint, issuers and their principals are generally permitted to sell the issuer's securities without first obtaining a securities broker-dealer or agent license, provided they are not affiliated with a broker-dealer and do not receive any transactional compensation. From a practical perspective, if a promoter does not have a pool of ready investors already lined up waiting to invest, the offering is not likely to succeed. The promoter may be able to retain the services of a licensed broker-dealer to market the investments for him, but that is not likely.

2. "Do I need a license?"

Probably not, provided you are a principal of the issuer, *and* you will not be paid any commission or similar selling compensation, *and* you will have significant duties for the issuer after the selling is completed. However, it is critical that the laws of the states in which sales will take place are reviewed to determine the correct local answer.

3. "Does he need a license?"

If "he" is a reference to some third party you as an issuer or principal of an issuer would hire to assist you in selling the securities of an offering, the answer is likely "yes, he will need a license." Further, given that there is no such thing as an independent agent in securities law, it is difficult to simply hire a salesman. An issuer must retain a licensed brokerage firm to serve as placement agent of its offering. While some states allow people to become licensed as "agents for issuers," there is no universal system, and inquiry should be made on a state-by-state basis with competent counsel.

***

CHAPTER 5

Disclosure

The Fourth "Silo"

A. OVERVIEW

Securities disclosure is an art. The mantra is that, in offering and selling a security, "an issuer must make *full and fair disclosure of all material facts.*" Earlier, we discussed how modern securities regulation goes well beyond the general commercial principle of *caveat emptor.* For example, under general real estate law, a real estate agent is not required to disclose to her young couple clients looking at house for sale that the charming, vacant, wooded open space down the block they are so impressed with will be turned into a major construction zone in six months for a new housing and retail development unless they ask her about it. *Buyer* beware. Under securities law, the agent would be required to disclose that fact to them even if they never asked about it. If she did not disclose it and the couple bought the house, the agent could be sued for failing to disclose a material fact. *Seller* beware.

B. THE LAW

The root source of this disclosure mandate is the anti-fraud provision found in one form or another in virtually every securities law:

It is unlawful for any person, in connection with the offer, sale, or purchase of any security, directly or indirectly:

(1) to employ a device, scheme, or artifice to defraud;

(2) to make any untrue statement of a material fact or to omit to state a material fact necessary in order to make the statements made, in the light of the circumstances under which they are made, not misleading; or

(3) to engage in any act, practice, or course of business which operates or would operate as a fraud or deceit upon any person.[††††]

Note that this was the very first section of the foundational Uniform Securities Act drafted in 1956, widely adopted by the states. It sets the tone for the entire act. While anti-fraud provisions appearing in various places in federal securities law contain important variations to the preamble, the three

---

[††††] § 101, Uniform Securities Act (1956)

subsections are rather uniform and universal. Rule 10b-5 under the 34 Act is probably the best known anti-fraud provision of federal law.

The first subsection is generally regarded as a restatement of good old, common law, Garden-variety fraud. The actor knowingly misrepresented or omitted facts to the victim with the intent of defrauding him, and the victim in fact relied on the misrepresented or omitted facts to his detriment. In modern parlance, he ripped him off.

The third subsection is the vaguest of the three. It is intended to apply to those circumstances that are wrongful but may not be covered directly by the first two subsections for one reason or another.

The second subsection is the one that draws the most attention and most clearly embodies the securities law disclosure theme. Rather than prohibit the making of a "false" statement, care is taken to preclude any hint that intent to deceive is required; thus, the choice of "untrue" over "false." Omitting to state facts that make what is said misleading is given equal weight. Continuing our home-buyers' analogy, if the agent represented to the couple that the open space was owned by the Nature Conservancy when she knew that was not the case would be making an untrue statement. If she made no mention of the open space at all, but described how quiet and peaceful the neighborhood was, knowing about the plans for construction and development, she would be omitting to state facts that made what she said misleading. Same effect.

C. "MATERIALITY"

That leads us to what is meant by the word "material?" The generally accepted, court-devised definition is paraphrased as follows:

> A misrepresented or omitted fact is "material" if there is a *substantial likelihood* a *reasonable investor* would consider the matter *important* at arriving at his investment decision. Whether a fact is "important" turns on whether knowing of the misrepresented or omitted fact would *significantly alter* the *total mix* of the information presented.[§§§§] (Emphasis added).

The first thing to notice is that this is an *objective* test, considering what a *reasonable* investor would think important at the time of the investment. This makes great sense. Disclosure must be full and fair *before* it is presented to investors. The standard is equally important in the context of litigation. While the accuracy of disclosures made at the time of an investment is not likely to be contested if the investment is profitable, investors who have lost money will aver after-the-fact that, had they known of virtually any fact the issuer failed to disclose during the investment pitch, they would never have invested. It is simply human nature. Therefore, disclosure must be judged as of the moment before the first dollar is raised, as if the whole package was presented to a regulator for review *before* the offering commenced.

The second facet of note in the definition is that the untrue or omitted fact need not be **THE** crucial factor in making the investment decision. It must just be important to the decision. Further, there must be more than a mere likelihood; there must be a *substantial* likelihood, and knowing the true fact must do more than merely alter the total mix of information; it must *significantly* alter it. All that said, it should be abundantly clear that the materiality of facts in any offering is a judgment call, one that requires experience and understanding of the manner in which the standard is applied.

[§§§§] See *TSC Industries, Inc. v. Northway*, 426 U.S. 438 at 449 (1976)

D. In Practice

As we stated in Part One, Chapter 3 on **Securities Registration**, there are no express disclosure requirements for making an offering under 33 Act Section 4(a)(2), or in offerings made in reliance on Reg. D Rule 506(b) or (c) provided sales are made exclusively to accredited investors. If any sale made in reliance on Rule 506(b) is made to an unaccredited but sophisticated investor, the issuer is required to provide to that unaccredited investor the same kind of factual disclosure that would be required were the offering to be registered, and gradually complex financial information depending on the size of the deal. In Reg. D Rule 502(b)(2), the SEC reminds issuers that, although not expressly required under the Rule, general anti-fraud provisions always apply to sales of securities, and they should consider whether they should provide such disclosure to accredited investors as well.

In theory, the stated purpose of the disclosure requirements is to give a prospective investor all the information he needs to make an informed investment decision. In practice, full disclosure up front, at the time of investment, serves as a sort of issuer insurance policy against later assertions of fraud. Setting aside for a moment the ability to publicly solicit investors under Rule 506(c), Rule 506(b) deal investors will be persons with whom the promoter has a pre-existing business or personal relationship. It is more likely those prospective investors are considering the investment based on that relationship than on any written disclosures. People invest with people more than on the basis of the documents they are given.

Issuers should disclose everything under the sun. If investors are interested in investing in a deal, it is far more likely they are interested because of the trust and expectations developed in their personal and professional relationship with the promoter than anything presented to them in writing. Skillful and experienced counsel will work with the promoter to identify all material information that must be disclosed and craft a way to disclose it in a manner most favorable to the promoter yet still fairly and fully presents it.

It is months or even years later when disclosures are truly put to the test. If things are not going well, or they are going well but some investor does not think they are and sees a lawyer, the first thing any investor lawyer should ask is "did they give you a disclosure document?" In some cases, investors might not even remember they did. In many other cases, the investor will say "yes, I got one, but I really didn't read it because it was just typical legal mumbo jumbo." When the lawyer inquires further, when he finds a comprehensive, signed subscription agreement in which the investor warranted that all disclosures were made and any questions answered, and a private placement memorandum that contains full disclosure of exactly what the investor is complaining about, it is then that the "insurance policy" feature of the disclosure documents have done its job. That is one case that will likely not be filed at all, and if one is filed, it will be far more susceptible to a motion to dismiss.

E. Past Versus Future

Material information should be considered in two groupings: *historical information* and *forward-looking information*. Historical information consists of things that have already happened, whereas forward-looking information involves what might, or is hoped will, happen in the future. Obviously, in dealing with historical information, there is much less "wiggle room" than there might be with forward-looking information. The managing partner either went to Harvard or he did not. The partnership either bought the land last March or it did not. Whether a manager's projection that lease revenue will increase 5% per year over the next five years is something an investor can count on is far more speculative, dependent on an array of factors. As long as projections as to what might or is hoped will happen are arrived at in good faith, they are viable provided the bases for them, the presumptions used in arriving at them, are disclosed as well for evaluation by prospective investors.

With initial public offerings of registered securities, the goal is to make sure the disclosures are accurate for that one brief, shining moment when all the initial sales are executed. Private placements only rarely afford that opportunity. It is far more likely sales of such offerings will occur over an extended period of time. That makes disclosure more challenging. It is presumably accurate at the point in time when counsel provides final copies of the private placement memorandum, subscription agreement and operating agreement to the issuer. But does it remain accurate and up-to-date three months later, when the issuer is still selling? Updates to and refreshing of disclosure are subjects that must be discussed beforehand between issuer and counsel, but generally speaking, the answer is "yes," the disclosure must be accurate at the time of every sale. Counsel should take into consideration the offering period intended, draft language accordingly, and have an understanding with the issuer as to periodic updating.

Updates are necessary to describe changed circumstances, if any, and particularly, how sales are going. It may be a lot easier to sell the 25th and last interest in a deal than to sell the first two. It is important to understand that each investor must be offered the same deal. For instance, if in selling to the first five investors, some issuer fee was set at 2% up front, but later investors conditioned their investments on that fee being 1% and in arrears, the initial five investors must be advised of the change and must accept it for the issuer to retain their investments.

F. REAL ESTATE SPECIFIC

So, what must a real estate syndicator disclose in a private placement offering? The simple answer is "all the material facts." Full disclosure will only come after full discussion between issuer and counsel. That said, there are some bases for review. Guide 5 to SEC Regulation S-K is a set of guidelines for how a real estate limited partnership would prepare its registration statement to register the partnership interests with the SEC on Form S-1. Obviously, an issuer doing a private placement is not registering, but it is useful to review Guide 5 to get a general idea as to the disclosure that would be required in a registered offering.

It will also be useful to review NASAA's merit guidelines for real estate offerings. Again, merit regulations are targeted at offerings that are registered at the state level, and not at private placements. Even so, it is useful to review the standards set forth in the merit guidelines in fashioning your private placement terms.

A typical private offering package is composed of private placement memorandum, subscription agreement and operating agreement. In addition to describing the project, the principals, risk factors, conflicts, use of proceeds, means of distribution and tax ramifications, the PPM usually contains a synopsis of the important features of the operating agreement.

It is in the operating agreement that the Constitution and statutes of the business are set forth. As syndicator, crucial decisions will have to be made as to how the business will be run, how people will be compensated and the like.

Describing a deal that will involve one discreet project from beginning and middle to end is a commonplace task. But what about "blind pools?" To begin, what are they? They have been around for many decades. They are to be distinguished from "blank check" offerings involving penny stocks that were at one time mistakenly referred to as "blind pools." In a blind pool offering, the promoter raises funds to invest in property, and more often, properties, not yet identified specifically. In the offering document, the promoter describes the parameters for properties to be chosen, but for one reason or another, does not identify them presently. Typical parameters might be descriptions like: "high rise apartments with at least 75% occupancy in metropolitan areas in the southern U.S. with populations of at least 750,000." The prospective investor then knows that the LLC will not be investing in raw land, warehouses or golf courses. Investors may ask for even finer restrictions to fit their investment model.

Blind pools provide a good deal of flexibility to the promoter, and also allow for acquisitions subsequent to the offering period of the deal. Given the latitude afforded the promoter in blind pools, start-up developers with no investment track record are likely to have more difficulty raising funds for them than would a promoter with a proven track record of offering, selling and operating a blind pool venture.

　　***

CHAPTER 6

Violations

Violations of federal and state securities laws can have administrative, civil injunctive, criminal and private civil repercussions. Regulators can take licensing actions against broker-dealers and agents, issue cease and desist orders to any violator, file complaints in federal or state courts, respectively, seeking injunctive relief like receiverships, restitution and disgorgement, and they can refer matters they believe to involve criminal violations to federal and state prosecutorial authorities. Private parties have private civil remedies available to them, although their options are fewer and in some cases, subject to higher proof standards.

It is unlawful to offer or sell a security unless it is registered or exempt from the requirement. It is unlawful to act as a broker-dealer or agent unless the entity or individual is licensed or exempt from the requirement. It is unlawful to violate the anti-fraud provisions. The three are unrelated as a general matter, meaning that someone can violate the first but not the second or third, or the third but not the first two, and so on. All three have administrative, civil, criminal, and private civil ramifications.

The question frequently arises, "How likely are we to get caught if we do something that's a bit over the line?" Statistics are hard, if not impossible, to gather. An issuer who violates the securities law is far more likely to be sued by a disgruntled investor than to be investigated or pursued by a regulatory agency. The likelihood of suit is directly proportional to the amount of the investment and the assets available on recovery.

It is a matter of coincidence as to whether a particular problem will come to the attention of a regulator. The higher the profile of the offering, the greater the likelihood a regulator will see it. Regulators come across many, many more potentially problematic matters than they can reasonably pursue, so they perform a sort of triage or prioritization based on an array of factors. They consider the number of investors involved, the amount being raised, and per investment, the nature of the offerees and investors (elderly more vulnerable than younger sophisticated investors), the subject matter (oil and gas, gold mines vs. mutual funds), the manner of offering (friends of friends or newspaper ads and cold calls), whether the actors have been in trouble before, whether it is currently underway or happened six years ago, whether it is a plausible or ridiculous offering (a new medical building vs. a formula to turn lead into gold), to name just a few. It does not take the presence of many of these factors to lead to an investigation.

Even before matters proceed to court, regulators have broad administrative subpoena power and do not hesitate to use it. Responding to an administrative subpoena can be a significant burden on a young business. Dealing with an investigation in general can take a small business to the brink. Securities regulators are zealous about protecting investors and care far less about the solvency of the businesses they investigate if they suspect securities violations have occurred.

In summary, when a developer crosses the line from using his own money to relying on the investment dollars of other people, a spectrum of protections come into play that can be brutal to a violator. Securities laws are nothing to fool around with. While we will discuss in some depth how to structure deals and raise funds from investors in the following pages, the prudent real estate syndicator and developer will make sure to retain and heed the advice of competent, experienced, real estate securities counsel at every step in the process.

***

PART TWO

BASIC REAL PROPERTY PRINCIPLES

CHAPTER 1

Types of Real Property Interests

A. Introduction

Because the material in the Work discusses "real estate" securities, it appeared reasonable to include a brief discussion on real estate interests and related matters, allowing the reader a "refresher" on this area. The experienced reader can simply choose to quickly move past this area, if the refresher is not needed.

Property law is *generally* the same from state to state. However, because specific review of each state's variances cannot practically be developed herein, the following discussion in part utilizes Colorado law as a *prototype* to illustrate basic principles of real estate law.

B. Definition of Property

Property signifies dominion or right of use, control, and disposition that one may lawfully exercise over things or objects.

1. Relationships

Property involves relationships, *e.g.,* one distinction of relationships included in the Restatement of Property is:

- **Right**—a legally enforceable claim of one person against another, that the other shall do a given act or shall not do a given act.
- **Privilege**—a legal freedom on the part of one person as against another to do a given act or a legal freedom not to do a given act.
- **Power**—an ability on the part of a person to produce a change in a given legal relation by doing or not doing a given act.
- **Immunity**—a freedom on the part of one person against having a given legal relation altered by a given act or omission to act on the part of another person.

2. Situs

Property usually has a locus or place of rest. This resting place is important in the procedural area of the law in order to gain jurisdiction, etc. For example, the courts refer to jurisdiction over the property by looking to its *situs* or location (*in rem*).

***

CHAPTER 2

Grouping of Property Types—
In General

Property can be grouped in many ways. The following are only a few.

A. REAL VERSUS PERSONAL

One of the most basic classifications is real property as opposed to personal property. The extremes on the continuum, as is true with most demarcations, are easy to define; thus, a piece of raw land is easily placed in the real property area. Likewise, a pencil is easily placed in the personal property classification. A significant problem arises when there is an attempt to distinguish property that has the characteristics of both groups, for example, leases or fixtures. These will be referred to subsequently.

B. TANGIBLE VERSUS INTANGIBLE PROPERTY

Another basic property classification involves those types of property interests that have physical substance, referred to as tangible property. There is an overlap of property noted in the first classification; both real and personal property may be in either the tangible group or the intangible group. Thus, an easement is included in the intangible group (intangibles in the real estate area are often referred to as incorporeal interests). Tangible property includes interests in property (rights, etc.) that are capable of physical possession. Thus, ownership of a pencil or fee simple is a tangible interest. (The physical assets that are capable of actual physical or symbolic livery of seisin are often referred to as corporeal interests.)

C. FUTURE VERSUS PRESENT INTERESTS

These groups are discussed subsequently in the area of Future Interests.

D. REAL PROPERTY; FREEHOLD VERSUS NON-FREEHOLD INTERESTS

In addition to the classifications noted above, there are further sub-classifications within many of the earlier noted groups. For example, there is the sub-classification of freehold versus non-freehold interests. This distinction is of extreme importance in many states. See below.
    * * *

CHAPTER 3

Grouping of Property Types
Freehold Interests

There are often four classes of freehold interests in many states.

A. FEE SIMPLE OR FEE SIMPLE ABSOLUTE

This interest is the largest and greatest estate in land. Technically where land is free from all other ownership rights, it should be referred to as a fee simple absolute (F.S.A.), not fee simple.

The fee simple or fee simple absolute may be inherited. Further, if the fee is not otherwise limited, it is deemed by some states to be a fee simple absolute. However, the fee can, of course, be limited. Thus, the fee could be followed by some limitation, a few examples of which are noted and discussed subsequently. Thus, one may own a fee subject to a special limitation.

B. LIFE ESTATE

In addition to the fee simple discussed above, there can also be a grant, and thus an ownership in real property that is referred to as a life estate. Thus, to A for his life and then to B, A would own a (real property) life estate interest; that interest would exist for the remainder of A's life. Further, if X conveys Blackacre to Y for life, Y will own a life estate that will cease upon Y's death. X has a retained vested fee simple (not absolute) that is referred to as a reversion. Upon Y's death, the reversion vests in *possession*. (We say "vests in possession" since the estate of X is already vested, as to other rights. See the discussion of "vesting" noted in the Future Interests area). The life estate and reversion are transferable.

As was earlier stated, when A conveys an interest of a life estate to B, A would retain the reversion. However, it is possible for A to convey immediately what would otherwise be a reversion. Thus, if A conveyed a life estate to B and the remainder of the estate to C, A would, of course, have no reversion, because he transferred his remaining interest to C at the same time he created a life estate in B. C's interest is vested, as that term is technically meant in the subsequent discussion.

The remainder must be created simultaneously to the preceding life estate. The interest in C, in the above example, is vested.

It is also possible for the grantor owning the fee simple absolute to convey not only one life estate but successive life estates. For example, X may convey a life estate to Y, and on the death of Y a life estate to Z. This would result in life estates in two parties, with the reversion in the grantor. There is no limit to the number of successive life estates that may be granted by the holder of the fee simple absolute.

As indicated above, there may be successive life estates with a reversion in the grantor or there may be a simultaneously created remainder in a third party. In all cases, both the life estates and the reversion or remainder are presently vested. As such, they are fully alienable.

The interests are vested, notwithstanding an earlier death of a life tenant where said tenant never received the benefit of the life estate. For example, if A conveys a life estate to B and then a life estate to C and then the remainder in D, if C predeceases B, C's interest was still vested; however, C never received the benefit of the enjoyment and use of the property since his interest terminated before the termination of the prior estate, in this case B.

1. Life Estate, *Per Autre Vie*

In addition to the above example, there may be a life estate created for the duration of the life of another. D could convey a life estate to E, but the life estate for the benefit of E could end on the life of D or the life of someone else in addition to the life of E. Thus, if the life estate would end with the death of D, the party making the conveyance, then even though E died, E's interest would pass to his heirs since the life estate would remain until the death of D.

2. Curtsy and Dower Abolished

Under some state statutes the concepts of curtsy and dower, *i.e.*, rights in property to a spouse, on the death of a spouse, have been abolished. Therefore, the concept of a life estate in certain property to the spouse as existed under common law no longer exists.

C. FEE TAIL

The concept of fee tail is only briefly covered here because it has been abolished in many states. This concept is where the grant is "to X and then to the issue of X, in perpetuity." Some states' abolition of this estate, however, is not a complete denial of its existence but rather somewhat of a slight modification. For example some states provide that a person who is seised in fee tail of any land, that is, receives a grant of a fee tail interest, is deemed to be seised of the land only for a life estate with a remainder in fee simple absolute to the person or persons to whom the estate would pass on the death of such first grantee, according to the course of the Common Law. Thus, in effect under the statute, one who receives an interest by means of a grant as a fee tail will be deemed to hold only a life estate, and a person who would take from him, under Common Law, will take a fee simple absolute.

Under Common Law, the person who would take from the grantee would be the oldest son because the rule of primogeniture applies (at least if the language of the statute is taken literally primogeniture would apply). This interpretation is open to question. However, some authorities argue that rather than applying the rule of primogeniture, *i.e.*, the position that the oldest son takes all property, as opposed to dividing the property among all children, the courts would probably attempt to apply the Statute of Descent and Distribution. However, again the literal reading of the statute requires the primogeniture application.

D. DEFEASIBLE FEE, SPECIAL LIMITATIONS, AND CONDITION SUBSEQUENT

There are also types of fee simple estates that are limited, due to events that may occur that should reduce or increase estates. As discussed subsequently, there were grants of a fee simple subject to a special limitation. Thus, where A receives a grant of land, with a restriction that said land can never be used for purposes of serving alcoholic beverages, and if in the event the same is served, the interest to A will immediately terminate and revest in the grantor, A's interest is a fee simple subject to a special limitation. Likewise, there may be other limitations on the grant, such as a fee simple subject to a condition subsequent.

One important definition that has not been mentioned and that should be kept in mind when discussing freehold estates in Part Two, Chapter 5, Future Interests, is the concept of *seisin. Seisin* is the possession of land under a claim of title of freehold. Thus, *seisin* is not the equivalent of a freehold estate because a freehold estate may exist without the current possession, *e.g.*, a non-possessory life estate.

Some authorities do not include the defeasible fee, special limitation, condition subsequent and other limitations in the freehold category; rather, they are discussed separately as Future Interests.

To fully comprehend the demarcations between interests, whether they be freehold or otherwise, the following examples should be studied and the terminology noted:

- If A conveys to B for life, B has a life estate and A has the reversion;
- If A conveys to B for life, with remainder to C, B has a life estate and C has a vested remainder in fee simple;
- If A conveys to B for life, then to C for life, and then to D for life, B will have a life estate, C will have a life estate, and D will have a life estate. A will have a reversion in fee simple;
- If A conveys to B for life, then to C for life, and then to D, A will have no remaining interest, B will have a life estate, C will have a life estate, and D will have a vested remainder in fee simple;
- If A conveys to B for life and then to the heirs of B's body, B has a fee tail interest. As noted, this interest would be limited under Colorado law and under similar statutes;
- If A conveys to B, so long as the property is used for a school, and at such time as it terminates its use for a school the property will revert to the grantor, A has a possibility of reverter, to be discussed under the Future Interests area, and B has a fee simple subject to a special limitation; and
- If A conveys to "B and his heirs," it is generally held that B has a fee simple absolute because "and his heirs" are words of limitation of the interest granted to B, not words of conveyance to the class known as "B's heirs."

***

CHAPTER 4

Grouping of Property Types
Types of Non-Freehold Estates

A. IN GENERAL

In addition to the conveyance of the freehold estates earlier mentioned, there may be conveyance of property that is not of sufficient importance to be classified as a freehold estate. These non-freehold interests might include any of the following, as listed below.

Under Common Law the non-freehold interests were often referred to as chattels real. Chattels real, as that term was used under the Common Law, are treated as real property under some state statutes. Therefore, under that type of statute they may be inherited and are also devisable by will. As such, they are also freely transferrable during life, except as otherwise limited by statute or contract among the parties.

Generally, non-freehold interests are leases. In most states, there are four general groups of leases. Before proceeding to the types of leasehold estates, it is worthwhile to note some basic points. First, where land is leased, there is no limit as to the period of time it may be leased, and it still constitutes a lease so long as the interest is less than a life estate. Even though the conveyance is for 100 years (unless the courts would construe this as an actual grant of the fee, which is usually not the case), it is a non-freehold estate, even though it might last longer than most life estates.

Where a lease involves a period in excess of one year, most states require a writing to be able to enforce the lease.

B. TYPES

The four types of tenancies or non-freehold interests regarding leases include:

I. Tenancy for a period

A tenancy for a set period of time expires under the given period, without a requirement of notice under most state laws.

If the tenant remains in possession past the stated period of time, the tenant is deemed a tenant at sufferance, and therefore may be ejected through proper statutory means unless the landlord recognizes the tenant as a tenant from period to period, or a continuing tenant. The tenancy that may be created by the recognition by the landlord of the hold-over tenant at sufferance may be for a period equal to the original term of the prior lease or it may be a tenancy at will, or the period to period tenancy. The decision would depend upon the circumstances and of course upon statute. Most courts favor a period to period tenancy. What period this will be, when the period to period tenancy is employed, would depend on the facts but is often a period equal to the prior period.

2. Tenancy at sufferance

A tenancy at sufferance is not truly a tenancy, but is a situation where there is a limbo state. The tenant who does not pay his or her rent is treated as a tenant at sufferance. For example, as noted above, where a tenant for a fixed period holds over improperly, he is a tenant at sufferance until the landlord elects to eject the tenant or create a new period to period tenancy.

3. Tenancy from period to period

This tenancy, which is usually employed with the rental of apartments or many other short rental periods, involves a rental from year to year, month to month, or so forth. This type of tenancy results in an *automatic* renewal for the given period, such as year to year, unless otherwise terminated as may be provided in the contract or as provided in statute.

Where this type of tenancy exists, the landlord or the tenant must terminate the tenancy in the manner provided by statute, unless otherwise agreed. Under many statutes notice must be given to terminate the tenancy. Such notice requirements are often similar to the following:

Period of Tenancy	Amount of Notice
For less than one week	One day
For one week or longer, but less than one month, or a tenancy at will	Three days
For one month or longer, but less than six months	Ten days
For six months or longer, but less than one year	One month
For a year or longer	Three months

4. Tenancy at will

Where the landlord and tenant agree that there is a tenancy, as opposed to a tenancy at sufferance, but the period of time is indefinite, it is a tenancy at will. In this case, either the landlord or tenant may terminate the agreement at any time providing the statutory notice is given.

Note: Most states provide that no notice is required for termination of a tenancy for a set period or for a tenancy at sufferance.

C. FORCIBLE ENTRY AND DETAINER ACTION (F.E.D.)

Where a tenant fails to surrender the premises as required under statute, a hold-over tenant or a tenant at sufferance may usually be evicted, as may be a tenant who is otherwise in default. Where a tenant without permission of the landlord defaults on rent or otherwise breaches the lease agreement, he may be given notice, in writing, properly served, to, in the alternative, pay the rent or vacate. The notice under an F.E.D. action under many statutes is not identical to and does not constitute notice of termination of the periodic tenancy or tenancy at sufferance. The reason for this limitation is that the notice that is served under the F.E.D. action gives the tenant the alternative of *either* paying the rent *or* leaving the premises.

   ***

CHAPTER 5

Ownership by Multiple Parties

A. In General

In addition to the simple ownership of land by one individual, there are many types of ownership of land that involve multiple parties. The following discussion illustrates the more typical methods of common ownership of land.

B. Tenants in Common

A tenancy in common ("TIC") involves an undivided interest in the ownership in property by multiple parties. It exists, generally, whenever two or more parties own, simultaneously, concurrent interests in the identical property, and the property is not otherwise classified as provided hereunder.

Unities of interest, time, and title are not required for a tenancy in common. These concepts are discussed subsequently under the joint tenancy discussion.

Although the interests of the tenants must be undivided, even though partitioning may occur later, the interests do not have to be equal. However, if the tenants do not designate otherwise and their interests are derived from a common instrument, the interests will be assumed to be equal.

Partitioning may occur where the tenants do not agree. Thus, if the tenants in common cannot agree or they otherwise wish to have the land divided, the tenant or tenants may petition the court to seek a partition of the land. If such a division is not practical, the property will be sold and the proceeds divided according to the respective interests of the tenants in common.

Notwithstanding the different proportional interests in the tenancy in common that may exist, all tenants have equal rights to concurrent possession in the property. One tenant may not prevent another tenant from enjoying equal use of the property.

However, some courts have held that although all tenants have equal rights to use the property, one tenant may use the property if the other tenants do not choose to use it; he is not required to account to the other co-tenants if they fail to likewise utilize the property. There are limitations on this concept with regard to mines where it has been held that a co-tenant is required to account to and divide the profits with the other co-tenants. Although it might seem unjust, a co-tenant is not entitled to seek contribution or payment from the other co-tenants if the mine suffers a loss if the other parties do not choose to join him.

Even though the co-tenant may generally use property and not account to his other co-tenants, there are limited fiduciary relationships between the co-tenants so that one co-tenant may not attempt to assert a title that is paramount to the others. There is the fiduciary relationship that no co-tenant is allowed to occupy or otherwise use the property if such use causes destruction or waste of the property.

Each tenant owning interest in the tenancy at common can otherwise transfer or deal with his interest separately and apart from the other tenants, so long as it does not breach the fiduciary duties or other requirements earlier mentioned. The interests of tenancy in common, as contrasted with a joint tenancy interest, may be transferred by the Statute of Descent and Distribution.

There is more discussed later in this Work as to tax and securities issues for TIC.

C. Joint Tenancy

Another type of common ownership, which is often used by husbands and wives to own real property together is joint tenancy. Joint tenancy has the unusual characteristic, as contrasted with tenancy in common, of *right of survivorship.* Thus, on the death of one joint tenant, the other joint tenant(s) survive to the interest of the decedent. Therefore, there is nothing to convey by will or by descent and distribution when the property is jointly owned. Because it was feared that many people would not be aware of the fact of this right of survivorship many states provide specifically for limitations on the joint tenancy agreement, *e.g.,* that no estate in joint tenancy in real property can be created, except as between executors, trustees, and fiduciaries unless the instrument creating this interest in joint tenancy *specifically* states that the property is to be conveyed in joint tenancy. Under certain statutes the words "and not as tenants in common" are not necessary to create a joint tenancy relationship even though they are often used to stress the fact to the parties involved that a joint tenancy relationship exists. If there is an error in the statement of the deed, where language of joint tenancy is used, but tenancy in common was intended, the deed may be corrected in some instances.

D. Unities Under Joint Tenancy

Joint tenancy historically requires four unities: interest, possession, time, and title. This is contrasted with the earlier discussion of the tenancy in common, which requires only the unity of possession.

1. Unity of title

This requires the interests of the joint tenants to be created at the same time and from the same source. However, this particular requirement of unity of interest is modified under many statutes to provide that one or more of the grantees involved in a joint tenancy relationship can create the joint tenancy relationship; that is, one of the grantees may also be the grantor. Thus, X holding the entire interest may convey to X and Y as joint tenants.

2. Unity of time

This requires each joint tenant's interest to vest at the same point in time. Again, this has been modified by the earlier cited statute.

3. Unity of possession

This requires that each joint tenant have an undivided interest in the *entire* property.

4. Unity of interest

Estates of the same type and duration must be held by the tenants.

The distinctions noted above as to joint tenants and tenants in common as to the unities are not as important today. Again, the key distinction or key importance of joint tenancy, as compared with a tenancy in common, is the right of survivorship.

Joint tenants, like tenants in common, have an equal right of possession and use. A joint tenancy may also be terminated by partitioning or, in some states, by a conveyance by one of the joint tenants; this terminates the joint tenancy and creates a tenancy in common. Note also, however, that even though a tenancy in common may be created by a transfer of a joint tenancy interest, this must be done during the life of the joint tenant, not by an attempted testamentary transfer. The testamentary transfer would, of course, be ineffective since the interests of the joint decedent tenant would be terminated on his death and the interest would pass to the surviving joint tenant.

The creation of joint tenancy interests is not limited to real estate; they may be used with personal property, bank accounts, and other interests. Many statutes specifically provide there may be a creation of joint tenancy for bank accounts, union accounts, and securities.

E. OTHER TYPES OF CO-TENANCY INTERESTS

In addition to the tenancy in common and joint tenancy, there is the tenancy by the entirety. This is a joint tenancy relationship between husband and wife. The only distinction of a tenancy by the entirety as opposed to a joint tenancy is that a *husband and wife* are involved in a joint tenancy. This type of interest is not recognized as separate from joint tenancy under some state laws; if created, it will often be treated as a joint tenancy.

There are also other types of co-ownerships, such as a tenancy in partnership, real estate trusts, cooperative arrangements and mining partnerships.

***

CHAPTER 6

Rights and Liabilities from Owning Land

A. IN GENERAL

In the tort area there are certain rights given to the landowner that may be employed to seek compensation where the property or the use of the property has been damaged. For example, trespass to property may be abated by an action in tort. A loss of land as a result of an improper taking of possession or a holding over may be remedied by a forcible entry and detainer action (F.E.D.).

Actions in ejectment, actions involving condemnation, actions involving damage to property and encroachments, may also be maintained.

B. STATE CONDOMINIUM OR HORIZONTAL PROPERTY ACTS

In many states, condominium ownership is becoming increasingly popular. Many state statutes provide for fee simple absolute ownership in the individual air space, such as the apartment unit, and an undivided tenancy in common interest with the other tenants with regard to the common space.

The common elements would include such areas as the common parking spaces, common grass and recreational areas, hallways and corridors. The individual air space is defined under the statute as the enclosed room or rooms of the given contemplated building.

In this area, there are additional problems, *e.g.*, what if the building burns? A tenant occupying an apartment on the third floor would, of course, be left with an empty air pocket space as his separate interest. Therefore, it is generally provided in the condominium agreement that re-building may occur upon a vote of a fixed percentage of the tenants. The re-building would presumably use the insurance proceeds. However, it is important to have this possibility spelled out on the agreement, which will be perpetual in nature to assure the tenants not occupying the ground area that they will in fact have some feasible space to occupy. Such an agreement could violate the Rule Against Perpetuities, discussed subsequently. There is a special exception in most condominium acts that states that the Rule Against Perpetuities (discussed below) is not applicable.

C. OTHER INTERESTS IN LAND ANCILLARY TO NORMAL USE

I. General

Questions have arisen as to the rights to occupy subsurface, surface, and above surface. Questions arise as to whether one can prevent an airplane from flying over "their" property.

Before the advent of the airplane, it was common to assume that there was no limitation on the use of property, whether down to the center of the earth or up to any point in the sky. Separate estates in real estate were allowed as in the case where there is a conveyance of the mineral interests with retention of the surface interest.

2. Above the land

Since the advent of the airplane, some rules were needed that would limit the interest of a surface owner. There have been multiple theories employed by the courts.

    a.   some courts held there could only be a limited zone of use. This theory placed a limitation upon the upper limit or boundary upon which ownership extends, such as a thousand feet.

    b.   other statutes were more nebulous, they provided the estate in land only allowed the use to the landowner of whatever was *necessary* to protect any *actual* use of his land.

    c.   other statutes simply provided an easement for the right-of-way for planes and construed that this was implied in every grant of land.

3. Beneath the surface

There are also subsurface interests in real estate. As such, there may not be trespass under the surface of land, nor may an outsider remove the substance of the land, such as the minerals, without approval from the surface owner, assuming that he owns both the surface and mineral interests.

There is the right of lateral support, *i.e.*, the digging by a contiguous landowner cannot destroy the interest owned on adjacent land. No person may excavate on his land if it causes injury to adjacent land, where, in its natural condition, the adjacent land would not otherwise be damaged. The concept of lateral and subjacent support is not premised upon negligence principles.

The excavation must cause damage to the adjacent land *as a result of the lack of lateral support where the land is in its natural condition.* Where damage would not have been caused, except for the building of a heavy building on the adjacent land, it is the duty of the owner of the adjacent land to support his existing building. The lateral support concept only applies to the duty of support of land adjacent to the property where that land is in its natural state. Obviously this is a difficult factual problem

If the lateral support is destroyed by the building on land and such damage would have occurred even if the land had only been in its natural state without the improvements on the property, the consequential damages to the buildings and improvements on the land, as well as to the adjacent land itself, are actionable.

In this context, many statutes allow the surface owner to require a bond from a miner who is attempting to remove minerals from the land where such removal might cause lack of lateral support.

    ***

CHAPTER 7

Easements

A. GENERAL

An easement is a real property interest. It is the right to use the property of another. Easements are commonly created for rights-of-way in order to have access to other property; they are also commonly used with regard to utilities.

The party having the use of the easement is referred to as the *dominant* owner or tenement. The property subject to the easement or use by another is referred to as the *servient* owner.

B. EASEMENT APPURTENANT

An *easement appurtenant* is an easement that is annexed to and used for the benefit of another piece of land, such as access. An *appurtenant easement* will pass with the title to the land, which is the dominant tenement or dominant estate. It need not be specifically set forth in the deed conveying the dominant land itself. Such type of easement cannot normally be separated from the dominant estate and transferred separately.

C. EASEMENT IN GROSS

In contrast with an appurtenant easement, an *easement in gross* is for the benefit of an individual, not a given piece of land. As such, in contrast with the appurtenant easement, it may be exercised only by the party to whom the easement is granted. It is not normally assignable or otherwise transferrable, whether by grant or devise. An easement in gross is not the equivalent of a license; a license is generally revocable; an easement is a property interest and therefore not revocable.

D. CREATING AND ENFORCING

Easements may be created in various ways, such as by grant, prescription, or implication. An easement created by grant is derived from the servient estate. However, as is many times the case, an easement may be created by consistent use. This is sometimes referred to as a *prescription*. A prescriptive use is analogous to the acquiring of title in real property by adverse possession. The elements for acquiring an easement by prescription are also like adverse possession, and therefore the discussion of those elements is deferred until the latter subject is reviewed. The period for creation of the prescriptive easement is usually in the range of 18 to 21 years.

An *implied easement* may be created where there is a conveyance of property by the grantor that gives the grantee no access, absent a right-of-way over other land retained by the grantor. The law may imply that this is an *easement of necessity;* the same will be favored because it is against public policy to provide a conveyance of land without allowing access to the same. The law does not favor land that is locked in and therefore unproductive.

Since an easement is a real property interest, if that easement is interfered with, the dominant tenement, *i.e.,* the holder of the easement, may take steps to secure his interest.

Easements in some cases may be terminated, as noted earlier, by a conveyance (easement in gross). The death of the owner of an easement in gross will terminate the easement. There may also be a voluntary agreement by the parties, a release, or waiver of an easement. There can also be an abandonment of the easement, even though most interests in real property may not be abandoned.

An easement is a lesser interest than the entire ownership of the land; therefore, a purchase by the dominant tenement of the servient estate will result in the merger and destruction of the easement. There may also be a termination of the easement by adverse possession of the servient estate. The owner of the servient estate could block and prevent the tenant of the dominant estate from using the easement. Such interference must be *active,* because generally it is held that the owner of the easement has the privilege to use or not to use the easement, at his election.

***

CHAPTER 8

Licenses

A license is not an interest in land and therefore is distinguished from the easement concept noted. A license involving real estate involves the consent by the owner of the land to allow someone to occupy the land or otherwise use the land in a manner that, absent the license, would constitute trespass. An ineffective easement is often construed to be a license.

As indicated, licenses are generally revocable at the election of the party giving the license. They are generally non-assignable, personal in nature, and destructible by death of the licensee. One exception to this is a license coupled with an interest. If one has a license coupled with an interest to enter upon land and remove a given substance, such as minerals or crops, the license is often treated by the courts as irrevocable by the grantor of the license.

***

CHAPTER 9

Protective or Restrictive Covenants

A. IN GENERAL

It is often advantageous for landowners to make a conveyance of land subject to certain restrictions. Euphemistically, "restrictive" covenants are referred to as "protective" covenants, especially in the more modern subdivisions. The concept is that the covenants *protect and aid* the individuals rather than *restrict* them. Common questions in the restrictive covenant area are whether the restrictions are valid, and, if so, how long will they continue. Restrictions on the transferability of land are invalid if they are against public policy. They are often deemed against public policy if they restrict the transfer of land without any reason or purpose.

B. COVENANTS RUNNING WITH THE LAND AT LAW

In many states, for covenants to "run with the land" at law they must:

1. **display intent**—display an intent to run with the land. This would depend upon the surrounding circumstances.
2. **"touch and concern the land"**—it is thought a covenant touches and concerns the land if it can be performed and is for the sole benefit of the owner of the land. It must be beneficial rather than adverse to the owner of the land.
3. **privity in title**—be created between persons who are privity in title, such as, between the grantor and the grantee. The covenants in such a case would exist and extend only to the land granted to the grantee and that amount of land retained and held by the grantor.
4. **be negative**—under the strict interpretation of covenants running with the land, only negative burdens or covenants could run with the land as opposed to positive positions.

C. COVENANTS RUNNING WITH THE LAND IN EQUITY

In contrast with the rules of covenants running with the land in law, equity allowed covenants to run with the land with fewer restrictions. The privity requirement was not required as between the original grantor and grantee. Separate owners of land could agree as to covenants that would bind one another, for example, an agreement that the minimum square footage or floor space of a house would be 1,200 feet.

The intention element continues as a requirement, even in equity. This could be construed by reasonable implication. Likewise, the "touch and concern" requirement under law is also required in equity. The requirement that the burden be negative in nature as opposed to positive was usually also required in equity. In some cases equity would allow an affirmative burden to run with the land where the affirmative burden was a benefit to the landowner as opposed to a restriction.

In addition to the privity, intention, touching and concerning, and negative burden questions, equity imposed an additional requirement that the landowner have *notice* of the existence of the burdens. The Courts also weighed the amount of *benefit* involved from the restrictions. Some cases hold that such notice, and the extent of it, must be included within the chain of title.

Sometimes the requirement of privity may be implied. For example, where B conveys Lot One to purchaser Y and then conveys Lot Two to purchaser X, the question arises whether Y can enforce the restrictive covenants against X, since X did not own the land at the time Y purchased his interest. (It is clear that X may impose the restrictions on Y.) Whether Y may impose the restrictions on X is unclear but it seems plausible that he could do so by implication, since many times the situation is such that the intention of reciprocal enforcement of the restrictions may be implied.

***

CHAPTER 10

Title to Real Property

A. ACQUISITION IN GENERAL

1. Patent

Most ownership in real property is evidenced by a grant from the federal government via a patent. The patent may be granted as a result of compliance with homestead rules or under other special statutes.

Most property that is owned by individuals was initially derived from a grant from the United States, since title to the public property was vested in the United States (except as otherwise conveyed to the states).

As far as state land is concerned, enabling acts that allowed the state admission to the United States also allowed the state land that was granted by Congress to the particular state. Obviously, although each state has boundaries, the state does not own all of the real estate. Sections 16 and 36 in each township were granted by the United States to the state to be used for schools and other governmental purposes. There is also "in lieu of land," *i.e.*, additional land conveyed to the state by the United States where, before the state became a state, part of sections 16 and 36 of a given township had been previously conveyed by the United States to a private party. Where this occurred, the additional land conveyed to the state to compensate for the lost land is referred to as in lieu of land.

Land may (generally) not be acquired, as against a sovereign, such as the United States or a state, by means of adverse possession. As far as states are concerned, part of the sovereign immunity doctrine has been eliminated.

2. Titles

In addition to grants from the United States, grants were made by foreign governments in territories that were previously under their control and jurisdiction.

Certain types of grants or patents are not a grant of all the land; a reservation may be maintained. Many patents contain reservations whereby the United States reserves the right for miners to seek a proprietary interest in a vein or lode. There may be a reservation by the United States of rights-of-way for canals and future ditches.

3. Adverse possession

In addition to acquisition of land by a normal grant or patent, real property may also be acquired by adverse possession. Adverse possession is the concept whereby one takes property and uses it as against the true owner; after the requirements of the statute are met, that party acquires the ownership.

The requirements of adverse possession are sometimes referred to as the *Cohen Rule*. This rule is derived from the statute requiring the land to be held continuously, openly, *hostilely*, exclusively, and notoriously for the period of time required by law. These requirements are:

a. Continuous

The requirement of continuous occupancy does not mean the land cannot be left for a given period of time if there is an intention to retain the control and use of the land. The continuous requirement is terminated when an outside person takes possession of the property without permission.

b. Open and notoriously

The requirement that the property be held openly and notoriously is such that the immediate community would know that the adverse possessor is attempting to claim title. The fact that the actual owner did not receive actual knowledge of the same is not required. If there is an attempt to *conceal* the adverse nature of ownership, the requirement is not met.

c. Exclusive

The use must be exclusive in nature. What exclusive means depends on the nature or general use of the land. It could be "exclusive" in nature where the land is used only for part of the year, *e.g.*, where the land is pasture land and that is the "normal" use.

d. Hostile

The use must be hostile in nature as against the true owner. Use of land under lease or under a contract allowing permission for use, or as a co-tenant, or otherwise deriving the land under the express or implied consent of the true owner is not hostile. This does not mean that one cannot claim adverse possession where he is a lessee, co-tenant, or otherwise uses the land with permission. (He specifically gives notice of his position and disclaims the relationship to claim adverse possession.)

e. Title

A further requirement is possession under claim of title. The possessor of the land must claim it under claim of title and not merely for temporary use. There is a distinction between a claim of title and a claim of right. The latter is not required. The party taking possession may claim there is a better title, so long as he does not claim that his title derives from such better title (and thus is subordinate to said title), and so long as he asserts his title as against all other claims.

There is a special advantage under some state laws where claim of title is made and *color of title* exists. Under one such statute (Colorado), where there is a claim of title and it is made under color of title, that is, a claim that the possessor has title to the property, made in good faith, with the paying of taxes for a seven-year consecutive period, the seven years will apply for adverse possession (as opposed to the normal period that is often much longer, as noted subsequently).

f. Time period

The required number of years of occupancy to meet the time period requirement for adverse possession differs from state to state. In Colorado, the required period is 18 years.

4. Constructive adverse possession

Where there is actual possession of *part* of the land, constructive adverse possession may be maintained for *additional* adjacent land. However, the constructive adverse possession portion of the land may not be of a substantially disproportionate nature to the area actually occupied. For example, occupancy of a farm area may allow constructive adverse possession to adjacent pasture lands, even though they were not actually used; however, the amount of the pasture may not be substantially more than the farm. Some state statutes provide that a person not in possession of real estate may sell it even though another is in adverse possession; see Colorado Law.

5. Limitation on adverse possession

Adverse possession only applies against persons who would have a cause of action against the adverse possessor because of his action to attempt to control the land. The adverse possession doctrine does not apply against holders of future interests where the future interests are not yet possessory.

6. Tacking

Where one is an adverse possessor, meeting all the requirements previously discussed, and that adverse possessor has held the land, at least in some states, for 15 years, his period of holding may be tacked to a subsequent purchaser from the adverse possessor.

B. Taxes

In addition to the methods earlier discussed, title to property may be acquired by a tax deed. Thus, where an owner of real property fails to pay his taxes, the property may be levied on and sold. A treasurer's deed will eventually be issued to the purchaser, absent redemption. It is established that tax title is deemed original title. Therefore, a tax title can be an advantage; it may clear up previous ambiguities or uncertainties in the title.

Title under a Treasurer's deed is usually to the property where it is assessed and sold. There are, however, positions to the contrary. In one case from Colorado, the assessment, levy, tax sale, tax certificate and subsequent Treasurer's deed described the land in general terms and did not reduce or eliminate any mineral interests. The description was broad enough to encompass the entire interest, including the mineral interest. It was held that the sale did not transfer the oil and gas mineral interests to the land, which had been previously severed by a reservation of that interest, even though no separate assessment had been made by the tax division for such separate mineral interests.

Care must be exercised to see that there is complete ownership, including the mineral interests, since under some state laws, the tax deed would not be sufficient, based upon the general description of the land, to convey the mineral interests where there had been a previous reservation of the same.

C. OTHER GENERAL METHODS FOR ACQUIRING OWNERSHIP IN LAND

The other methods of acquiring ownership in land are more the exceptions rather than the general rule. The methods discussed subsequently herein are those that are sometimes referred to as derivative titles. That is, the title is derived from a former owner. The transfer may include the normal grant or conveyance by sale, a transfer by death, whether testamentary or intestate, foreclosures, levy and execution, dedication to the public, abandonment, acquisition from insolvency proceedings or court decree, gifts, or in other manners.

D. NORMAL CONVEYANCE

I. General

The most typical example of a transfer of land is by deed from the record owner. Usually, any person, association, body politic or corporate, can convey real property by deed.

Some state statutes, *e.g.*, Colorado, provide that except in cases where water rights are represented in the form of stock, they are conveyed as real estate; thus, title may pass under an appurtenant clause in a deed if the circumstances establish the intent. Livery of seisin is often not necessary.

2. Consideration

Under general principles, consideration is not necessary. Under some statutory deed forms there is a *statement* of consideration. Therefore, it is often uncertain whether a deed is valid without the statement of consideration. It is the author's opinion that such deed would be valid, notwithstanding the lack of the recitation of consideration. Apparently, the statute, as earlier cited, is only a permissible means of making the conveyance, not a required form for making the conveyance; however, most deeds include a statement of consideration. Most conveyances carry the right of possession. It is an immediate right of possession unless a future day of possession is specified. Even though the executory contract postpones possession, the contract might merge into the deed.

3. Required Elements of a Deed

Aside from the *consideration* element, there are other items that must be included in a deed to make it valid. There must be a designation of the *grantor*, a *description* that is sufficiently clear to identify the property, *signature* of grantor (to avoid the problem of the Statute of Frauds), *delivery* of the deed, and in some states certain other requirements, *e.g.*, Words of Conveyance.

a. Grantor identified

The grantor must be specifically designated in the body of the deed. Capacity is presumed in Colorado where it is a natural person, unless the contrary appears; the same is not true with a corporation. Capacity is not, of itself, required. Therefore, in the case of a corporation, the certificate of incorporation should be shown of record.

b. Description

Land must be conveyed by sufficient description so it may be identified. A deed without any description, or a deed that does not sufficiently identify the property is not sufficient to convey property. To be marketable, as opposed to being a good conveyance, the land must be sufficiently described from the deed itself.

c. Signature of grantor

The grantor must sign the conveyance. To avoid technical defects, the grantor should sign the deed in the *same name* he received it when he was the grantee. This is discussed subsequently under the concept of marketable title.

Where a corporation is involved, the corporate officer should sign. The proper officer to sign depends on state statute. In many states, *e.g.,* Colorado, the statute requires a single signature of the executive officer, even though the general form used will provide for signature places for the president and the secretary. If there is an attorney in fact involved acting for the record owner, the attorney should sign the name of the owner for him as attorney in fact. The power of attorney should, of course, be recorded for reference.

Some states, *e.g.,* Colorado, provide that powers of attorney must be recorded. If an instrument is executed under a power of attorney, the power of attorney must be properly acknowledged and recorded in the county in which conveyance is required to be recorded.

4. Delivery

A deed to be effective must be delivered. Delivery requires the overt *act* and manifestation of the *present intention* to make the conveyance. The transfer of the deed must be meant to transfer the property as opposed to temporary possession of the deed or review of the same. Delivery is also effective where the deed is put in escrow, providing it is beyond the control of the grantor for recall of the deed. That is, the escrow agent cannot be an agent who is subject to complete control of the grantor. For the escrow to be effective, the deed should be required to be transferred to the grantee upon the happening of the condition upon which the deed was placed in escrow.

Properly prepared, an escrow creation can often be effective even though the conditions occur subsequent to the death of the grantor, or even where the death of the grantor is a condition precedent to physical possession of property.

e. Other elements usually in the deed

Another requirement in the deed is that the grantee be clearly identified. If a deed is delivered in blank because the grantor is uncertain as to the grantee or for other reasons, the deed is ineffective at that point in time.

i. Seals

In most state seals are not required for the valid execution of a deed. Seals are utilized by corporations; this often has the effect of creating a *prima facie* case for the position that the same was executed properly by the corporate officer under the theory that the seal would not be on the deed unless it was proper.

ii. Acknowledgment

Acknowledgments in a deed are not normally required to create a valid deed. The appearance before a notary is not usually a necessary element to a valid deed. The acknowledgment usually creates a *prima facie* case for the authenticity of the deed and often makes it admissible in Courts of record without further evidence of the proper execution by the grantor. If the deed is properly acknowledged and properly recorded, it usually creates a *prima facie* case that in fact it was delivered.

As stated, acknowledgments are not usually necessary for a *valid* deed; however, it is often a necessary element to have a *marketable* deed.

E. RECORDING

Generally, under most state laws, deeds, mortgages, and other encumbrances on property along with other instruments *may* be recorded. It is not normally a requirement to have the deed recorded to make it valid. Where the statute allows the recording, it is generally provided that such instrument is valid as against any person who is charged with constructive notice; that is, notice that appears of record. Placing an instrument of record will not accomplish the purpose of constructive notice unless the statute authorizes the recording of the instrument and gives it the effect of constructive notice. Many states provide for the recording of tax levies, sheriff's certificates of purchase, *lis pendens*, and other types of instruments.

In most states recording is of extreme importance. It is of particular importance if the state is a "modified race" statute state. That is, the first grantee to record his instrument, assuming he is without notice of any prior unrecorded interest, will prevail, as opposed to another person, even though the other person took title prior in time.

Many state statutes protect not only a *purchaser,* that is, one paying value, but also any good faith class of persons with *any kind* of interest. One receiving a gift or devise can prevail, as opposed to an earlier unrecorded purchaser's interest.

Recording is generally only valid as against other interests that could have been recorded. The interests of an adverse possessor in property cannot be recorded; therefore, those interests will not be terminated or cut short by a sale by the actual owner (record owner) to a bona fide purchaser for value. (Most title policies exclude coverage as to parties in possession.)

F. OTHER RESTRICTIONS OF RECORD

Where an instrument is of record and it refers to another instrument and the subsequent instrument is not of record, it is usually not sufficient to result in constructive notice.

Often statements contained in the deed or other instrument that affect title to real property, where that instrument has been of record in the Clerk and Recorder's Office of a given county for a set period of time, *e.g.,* 20 years or more, constitutes *prima facie* evidence of the facts recited. Anyone attempting to oppose those facts has the burden of rebutting the *prima facie* case.

Many statutes provide that any instrument that refers to the grantee in a fiduciary capacity will not be notice of the fiduciary capacity unless the instrument shows the name of the beneficiary represented and defines the trust or other document involved. Reference to the trust or other document is usually sufficient if the deed refers to another document and incorporates it by reference or otherwise identifies it where that instrument is of record.

G TITLE INSURANCE

In addition to reviewing the record for instruments recorded that affect title, title protection may also be assured by means of title insurance, which is of course an insurance policy issued by an insurance company that attempts, except for exclusions and other limitations, to insure either the mortgagee or the owner-mortgagor, or both, that the title is as stated in the commitment and insurance policy. The insurance policy, if it covers the given insured, only protects up to the purchase price, as a general rule. Such insurance generally does not cover the profit element where a purchaser acquires property at a reduced price and could sell it for a substantial gain, but there is a title defect.

H. THE TORRENS SYSTEM

In addition to the recording system mentioned earlier and title insurance, title might be held in a different manner and the ownership and marketability delivered in another manner. This is under the Torrens system, which applies in some states, *e.g.*, Colorado.

This registration system developed from an individual who worked with the registration of ships. The thought was, rather than having all the complicated title questions that exist under the normal recording system, possibly one could register land similar to registering ships and keep a better, more accurate, record.

A parcel of land may be registered, except for a tax title, which has certain limitations under the statute, by applying certain steps. The applicant applies to the court for registration. The court will decree title to be registered, assuming basic registration requirements are met and proof of title is shown. The registrar then registers the title according to the court decree and holds the original certificate in the registrar's office.

A duplicate of the registration certificate is issued to the landowner and also to the holder of the lien, if one is involved.

Once registration is accomplished, the registered title cannot be conveyed or otherwise transferred or encumbered except by noting the encumbrance upon the registration certificate of title.

Where registered land is to be conveyed, the duplicate certificate is surrendered to the registrar who issues a new certificate to the new grantee. If the certificate is lost or otherwise destroyed, the duplicate certificate must be obtained by order of the court.

The value of the registration method is that the subsequent recipient of the certificate of title will take title, assuming he is a good faith purchaser for value, with no notice, free and clear from all encumbrances except those noted on the certificate of title, except for certain rights of appeal under the Registration Act, certain rights or claims existing under the Constitution or statutes that do not appear of record, certain public highways and other easements, ditches, special tax or other assessments for which a sale of land has not yet occurred prior to the time of the registration, existing leases not exceeding three years, and certain other limitations.

One important advantage of the registration system, as opposed to the normal recording system, is that the registered property cannot be lost by adverse possession. Registered titles are not normally subject to a general judgment lien as is the case with recorded titles.

Recording of most documents will not affect registered title. Exceptions to this are the recording of a Treasurer's deed that can initiate a new title that will be paramount to the registered title. A federal tax lien can be valid against a registered title.

I. ENCUMBRANCES UPON REAL ESTATE

1. Mortgages and deeds of trust

One of the most common methods of creating an encumbrance upon real property is by a deed of trust or mortgage.

A mortgage may be released only by the mortgagee. Deeds of trust utilize either a public or private trustee. If a private trustee is used, it is treated like a mortgage. If it is a public trustee, a release is by the public trustee but certain documents, such as a cancelled note and request for release, must be executed by the creditor-beneficiary under the deed of trust.

A mortgage or deed of trust lien often expires 15 years after the last due date of the final principal payment. The 15-year period may often be extended for an additional 15-year period by an instrument in writing signed by the beneficiary or creditor-owner of the indebtedness.

2. Judgments

A judgment usually becomes a general lien upon all the real property of the judgment debtor within the county where the creditor records the transcript of judgment. Judgment liens of a general nature and liens of levy and execution expire six years after entry of the judgment.

The judgment lien can usually be released by recording with the Clerk and Recorder of the county in which the judgment is located a statement to the effect that the judgment has been satisfied or by recording of the instrument that releases the property. The latter instrument is executed by the judgment creditor or the assignee from the judgment creditor.

The general judgment lien can usually be destroyed by the execution upon such judgment and levy against the property. The levy will be destroyed by release, by order of court, or by satisfaction of the judgment by the debtor. The levy is often valid for six years or more after its recording.

3. Mechanics liens

Most states allow a lien for mechanics where they supply services or materials in the construction or improvement of property.

Under many state laws a mechanic's lien may be created by a material-man, contractor, subcontractor, builder, a mechanic, and all other persons of every class who perform labor upon or furnish materials to be used in the construction or improvements or for value of services rendered or labor done or materials furnished, etc.

The lien is not usually automatic. The mechanic claiming the lien must file a statement, signed and sworn to by the claimant or his agent, which sets forth the material required by statute.

Liens for labor must often be filed within a given period, *e.g.,* two months, after the completion of the building, structure, or other improvement.

J. FORECLOSURE

Where foreclosure is required involving a trust deed, the public trustee may generally foreclose the deed of trust. The foreclosure by public trustee is initiated by the creditor completing a notice of election and demand for sale and presenting the same to the public trustee. The public trustee then causes the property to be advertised and sold in compliance with the statute.

K. REDEMPTION

Redemption periods vary from state to state. The following is an illustration from Colorado law. Where deeds of trust and mortgages were executed prior to July 1, 1965, the owner of the property, the mortgagor-debtor, has six months after sale in which to redeem his property by paying to the public trustee the amount bid at the sale plus interest and costs. If such redemption takes place, a certificate of redemption is issued that in effect discharges the lien of the prior deed of trust.

During the redemption period any person holding a junior encumbrance who would have his interest cut off by the foreclosure, as provided under Colorado statute, may file a notice of intention to redeem the property. If the owner does not redeem the property, each holder of a junior encumbrance has successive 10-day periods in which to redeem the property after the expiration of the initial redemption period.

If the deed of trust has been executed subsequent to June 30, 1965, in Colorado, the owner of the property has only 75 days after the foreclosure sale, as opposed to the six month period earlier referred to, in which to redeem, unless the sale involves agricultural (non-platted) real estate, in which case the old six month period applies in Colorado.

With regard to the foreclosure, the public trustee may usually sell the property after a given number of days after the filing of the notice of election and demand for sale. (A court order authorizing the sale is also usually necessary.) If the only default by the owner-mortgagor-grantor under the deed of trust is a failure to make timely payments, he may often cure that defect by giving written notice of his intent to pay, within a given number of days prior to the date of the foreclosure sale; payment must often be made by the day prior to the date of sale. Such payment includes principal, interest, and costs.

If there is a redemption by the holder of the junior encumbrance from one having a prior lien, the holder of the junior encumbrance must pay, in addition to the amount bid at the sale, plus interest and costs, the amount due to any prior redeeming party.

If the owner chooses not to redeem his property within the time stated above, the public trustee issues a public trustee's deed to the holder of the certificate of purchase at the foreclosure sale or to any redeeming party if one is present.

Where a public trustee is not involved, the mortgage or deed of trust (private) must be foreclosed by a full action in court. If this is done, upon obtaining judgment, a writ of special execution may be issued to the sheriff who then advertises the property, as opposed to a public trustee. Redemption periods here are the same as those involving a deed of trust with a public trustee.

The earlier referred to mechanics' liens, contracts for sale, general judgment liens, and others not covered by a public trustee must be foreclosed in the same manner as a mortgage or a private deed of trust. **Caution:** The above discussion is intended as a general overview of the area, with Colorado as an example. State laws vary. Each state law must be reviewed separately.

L. MARKETABLE TITLE

In most standard real estate forms used by real estate brokers and salesmen, there is reference to having a good and marketable title. It is generally thought that a title is marketable if it can be derived of record from the United States or the State and the same is free from any liens or other defects or encumbrances that would lead a reasonable person, who desires to buy the property, to refuse to purchase the land without a reduction in price due to some defect or restriction on title.

Marketability concepts were earlier discussed, although not specifically labeled as such. Thus, the previous discussion on mortgages and other encumbrances are restrictions on marketability as noted in the above definition. Additional concepts and restrictions on marketability are noted hereafter, the same being modeled after Colorado law.

Generally, each successive record holder within a given chain of title, that is, a given ownership from the grantor to the grantee to grantor to grantee, and so forth, is presumed to be a bona fide purchaser for value without notice of outstanding claims.

A conveyance or encumbrance from a person who is not, at that point in time in the chain of title, that is, he is not a record holder, may be ignored unless such person subsequently acquires title to the questioned property.

Sheriff's deeds, public trustee's deeds, court decrees, and certain other types of deeds concerning title and other official acts that have been of record for nine years in the county where the land is located, and where no action has been commenced to avoid such title, are very difficult to oppose.

Where land is under option, such option ceases to be notice of the potential purchaser's right to an interest under said option one year after the date for which the conveyance was noted in the option where no conveyance took place and no action was brought to enforce or procure the conveyance.

No action can be brought to enforce the conveyance of any real estate under a bond for deed or agreement for the sale and purchase of real estate unless the action is brought within a given statutory period from the day upon which the conveyance was due, unless the purchaser was in possession of the property.

An unbroken chain of title must be maintained. Thus, from the inception, such as the patentee to every subsequent owner of record, there must be sufficient identification tracing ownership from one to the next.

Names that are pronounced somewhat alike or substantially alike are referred to as *idem sonans*. They are often presumed to be the same person, notwithstanding the difference in spelling. However, surnames, although pronounced alike, which are spelled sufficiently different so they will not be indexed in the same section of the Recorder's indices will often produce a break in the chain of title. The surname Cohen and Kohen illustrates this type of situation.

Where identical names are used, such as the grantee then becomes the grantor, they are often presumed to be the same person unless contrary evidence is illustrated.

Likewise, use of nicknames or abbreviations of the common name will not destroy the presumption of identity. The same is true with titles, prefixes, suffixes, and the like. The use of Mr. or Miss illustrates this issue. These are not part of a name and their use or omission from the record will not normally affect the presumption of identity unless of course they are inconsistent with the *subsequent use*, such as the use of Miss Smith and the subsequent use of Mr. Smith.

Notwithstanding the above, it has been held that the middle initial or middle name is a material part of the name. Under some state statutes, after a given period, variances between names of the grantee and subsequent grantor, involving any one of the following three variations, will not destroy the presumption of identity that would otherwise exist:

- if one instrument contains a middle initial and the other instrument contains no middle initial;
- where one instrument contains a name with the full Christian name and another instrument contains a name with only the initial of such Christian name; or
- if one instrument contains the full middle name and the other instrument contains only the initial of the middle name.

M. CONSTRUCTIVE NOTICE

All parties acquiring interest in property are on notice of all instruments that are necessary to their own chain of title whether they are of record. They are also of notice of any rights of any person in possession of or making actual use of the property they are acquiring, even if the instrument is not of record. They are also on notice as to all matters that they have actual knowledge of or matters that may require them to make inquiry, which could derive the notice in question.

N. HOMESTEAD

Some states (and federal law) allow a homestead interest not to exceed a specified amount. This homestead interest is exempt from certain executions and attachments arising from any debt, contract, or other obligation.

The creation of a homestead can often occur in one of three ways:

- the owner who has title to the home may record an instrument in writing that describes the property, sets forth the nature and source of the owner's interest in the property, and states that the owner is claiming a homestead in the property;
- the clerk may, assuming it is feasible, permit the owner or spouse, in lieu of recording the above statement, to make what is referred to as a "marginal homestead entry" upon the deed itself, which is presently of record; or
- it may be created automatically, by Statute.

Homestead refers to occupancy of the home for use as the residence. Therefore, it often only applies so long as the home is occupied in that manner. It will, however, normally extend to the widow, widower, or minor children.

The homestead allowance is in addition to the allowances allowed to a widow and orphans under many of the probate statutes.

To convey or otherwise encumber or destroy the homestead interest, the husband and wife, jointly, assuming marriage exists, must normally execute the conveyance or conveyances. A separate instrument may be executed that releases the interest in the homestead rights and signed by the husband and wife or other parties who are involved in the homestead interest. A conveyance of the property in question from one spouse to the other spouse usually does not destroy the homestead.

A creditor is normally entitled to levy upon homestead property, but only the excess of the sales price over the homestead allowance, plus costs and expenses, is available to the creditor. If there is no surplus, often statutes provide that the property cannot be sold.

The parties entitled to the homestead may sell the property and segregate the proceeds from the sale. If the same is invested, in some states, within one year of the date of the sale, and if within a given number of days from the date of the purchase of a new home, there is recorded an instrument reflecting the homestead, the new property will carry the benefit of the old homestead exemption.

O. FUTURE INTERESTS

1. Definition

A future interest is commonly defined as an interest that will or may become a possessory estate at some future time.

2. Classification

There are different classifications for future interests. The Simes & Smith Treatise on the Law of Future Interests discusses the "usual" classification based upon certain historical distinctions, and on that basis the classes of future interests are as follows: reversions, remainders, executory interests, possibilities of reverter, and rights of entry for breach of condition.

Another often used and proper classification of future interests has to do with the determination of whether the correlative interest is in the grantor or a third party. The following text section illustrates that type of classification. [Chart follows]

P. Correlative Interest in Grantor or Third Party

		Correlative Interest in <u>Grantor or Third Party</u>	Correlative Interest <u>that Passes</u>
	a.	Reversion	Granting of life estate or fee tail
Reversionary Interests	b.	Possibility of reverter	Defeasible fee, fee simple subject to special limitation or fee simple determinable
	c.	Right of entry for condition broken (power of termination)	Fee simple subject to a condition subsequent
Remainder Interests	d.	Remainders in third party	Vested remainders (indefeasibly vested, vested subject to open, and vested subject to complete defeasance)
	e.	Remainders in third party	Not vested remainders; that is, contingent remainders
Executory	f.	Executory interest or limitation	Springing executory interest
Limitations	g.	Executory interest or limitation	Shifting executory interest

In the above chart, we illustrate the correlative interest held by one party as opposed to the other. For example, where A grants a life estate to B, A has a reversion in fee simple and B has a life estate. The first three items in column one are referred to as reversionary interests; items four and five in column one are referred to as remainders; and items six and seven are referred to as executory interests.

It is sometimes stated that a vested remainder or reversion subject to a present life estate or an estate for years is not a future interest because the estate presently exists and only the actual physical possession is postponed. Again, there seem to be conflicting definitions in this regard. Usually these interests are discussed in the future interest area.

Q. Reversions and Remainders that are Vested

When there is a conveyance from a fee simple absolute to an estate less than the entire fee simple absolute, there must be either a retention of an interest (reversion) or a "conveyance of the other part(s)" to a third party. For example, if A conveys a life estate to B, the reversion remains in A. A might convey a life estate to B, with remainder to C, in which case C has a remainder interest and A has no interest. All reversions are vested as that term is defined subsequently.

R. DEFINITION OF VESTING

An interest is vested in B when throughout its continuance, B or his successors in interest will be immediately entitled to seisin whenever and however the preceding freehold may determine. If A conveys to B for life and then to C and his heirs, A has no interest, he has conveyed all his interest; B has a life estate; C has a vested remainder. It is vested in C because whenever and however the preceding freehold (life estate) terminates, C will be immediately entitled to seisin; that is, possession under a claim of title of freehold.

S. CONTINGENT REMAINDERS

A contingent remainder is a remainder that is not vested. A contingent remainder can be created only at the *same time* as the prior interests are created *and* by the *same act* or instrument. If this simultaneous creation does not exist, the interest would be an executory interest, as discussed subsequently. If the definition of a vested interest cannot be met, the interest must be contingent.

T. REMAINDER INTERESTS

There are four types of remainder interests:

1. "Indefeasibly vested"

A conveys Blackacre to B for life, then to C and his heirs. (To C and his heirs are words of limitation and not words of grant).

2. "Vested, subject to open"

A conveys to B for life, and then to the children of B. The first child would receive a vested remainder that would be subject to open for other children who are subsequently born.

3. "Vested subject to complete defeasance"

A conveys to B for life, then to C and his heirs, unless C dies without children, and then to D and his heirs. C may be defeased by the executory limitation over, if he dies without children. (Stillborn children do not constitute children for purposes of this rule.)

4. Contingent remainder

If A conveys to B for life and then to the sons of C, if they are admitted to the State Bar, this is a contingent remainder to C's sons, assuming they are not admitted to the Bar at the time of the conveyance.

U. REVERSION

A reversion is defined as the residue of an estate left in the grantor or in the heirs of the grantor commencing in possession at the determination or ceasing of one or more particular estates granted or devised previously.

A reversion will never exist following a grant of the fee simple because all the interest is granted; there is no residue. Usually reversionary interests are transferrable. A reversion is a vested estate; therefore, a reversion is not subject to the Rule Against Perpetuities (see the definition of the Rule Against Perpetuities). A reversion arises automatically by operation of law, not by words of retention by the grantor.

V. POSSIBILITY OF REVERTER

A possibility of reverter (sometimes referred to in the correlative as a fee simple subject to a special limitation or a determinable fee) is the interest remaining in the grantor or the heirs of the devisor when the owner of the land in fee simple absolute has conveyed or devised the land subject to a special limitation. The important characteristic of a possibility of reverter is that it occurs automatically when the event or special limitation occurs. It usually uses the words "until," so long as," "while" or "during" to create the interest.

W. RIGHT OF ENTRY FOR CONDITION BROKEN

This is a type of reversionary interest. It is a *power* to terminate an estate upon a breach of the condition subsequent to which such estate is subject. It is an interest remaining in the grantor, his heirs, or the heirs of the devisor when land has been granted or devised subject to the condition subsequent. It does *not operate automatically,* as contrasted with the fee simple subject to a special limitation; therefore, it requires the exercise of the power to re-enter.

Words used to indicate the condition subsequent are usually "upon condition," "providing that" or "but if" Obviously, such words are not controlling; it is a question of intent as to what was created. A condition subsequent cannot be created in a stranger, but must be created in the grantor or his devisors. The re-entry on a condition subsequent need not be in a physical form but may be symbolic or through use of letters, etc. Commencing an action is usually sufficient to constitute the re-entry.

Although a condition subsequent cannot generally be transferred, the interest owned may be transferrable *subsequent* to the exercise of the right of re-entry.

X. EXECUTORY LIMITATIONS

I. Overview

This interest involves a conveyance by virtue of which the interest subject thereto, upon the occurrence of the stated event, is to be divested before the normal expiration thereof (cut short) in favor of another interest in a person other than the conveyor or his successors in interest.

An executory limitation may have the usual characteristics that it: (i) cuts short an existing interest; (ii) involves a freehold to begin in the future; and (iii) involves a gap in the seisin. These characteristics, all of which might exist at one time, were *not allowed at common law.* This is the key distinction between this interest and a contingent interest. The contingent interest exists at the common law, executory limitations did not.

An executory limitation is like a fee simple subject to a special limitation, since the occurrence of the event, that is, the condition precedent, automatically affects the interest subject to the limitation. It is also like a condition subsequent in that it can divest the property. It differs, however, from the condition subsequent and special limitation in that an executory interest cannot operate in favor of the grantor.

Executory interests are executory, not in the sense that it does not presently exist, but rather in the sense that possession has not occurred.

2. Types

a. Shifting executory interests

A shifting executory interest cuts short a prior use (estate) in a person other than the grantor. If A conveys land to C and his heirs, but if C does not marry, then to B and his heirs, B will have a shifting executory interest.

b. Springing executory interests

A springing executory interest cuts short an estate in the grantor. If A conveys to B for life, then to C one year after B's death, there is a reversion in A and a springing executory interest in C that will occur one year after the reversion to A. Without the one year gap, C would own a vested remainder.

Y. Additional Concepts

Other concepts in future interests that might be important, for a quick over-review, are:

1. Doctrine of Worthier Title

This is sometimes referred to as the *Rule of Pivis v. Mitford* (which is the better description). This, in effect, is a rule against making a conveyance to one's own heirs simply because one does not have, by definition, *heirs* while alive. In effect the rule creates a presumption that a grant by A to B for life, and then to the heirs of A, is in effect a reversion, not a remainder to the heirs of A, unless the presumption is adequately rebutted. The rule will not apply where the grantor expressly states to the contrary or where he uses such terms as "children," "issue" or reference is made to "heirs" as if they were determined at a particular time; for example, as if the grantor had died at the time of conveyance, or use of a named person, or use of kin or next of kin.

2. Rule in Shelley's Case

A similar rule is the Rule in Shelley's Case. The Rule, in effect, states that where a conveyance is made by A to B and then to his heirs, the conveyance is a fee simple absolute in B; there is no conveyance to the heirs of B because the words are used as words of limitation rather than words of conveyance.

Shelley's Rule and the Pivis Rule have something in common in that they reflect upon the use of the word "heirs." Shelley's Rule refers to the heirs of the third party, and the Pivis Rule refers to the heirs of the grantor.

3. Right of entry for condition broken

The right of entry for a condition broken:

- apparently descends to the heirs as is true with the possibility of reverter. Apparently neither can be transferred by deed or will;

- is not alienable by deed or by will in any manner—the attempt to transfer it will destroy it and convert the fee simple subject to a condition subsequent into a fee simple absolute;
- is not subject to the Rule Against Perpetuities—the theory is that this interest became recognized and established before the development of the restrictions on contingent remainders; and
- is often referred to as a power to terminate; therefore, it is subject to forfeiture or destruction through waiver and laches.

4. Springing and Shifting Interests

Under common law, as indicated earlier, there were restrictions as to what could be created; the springing and shifting interests described did not exist at common law.

For example, an attempted conveyance in January by A to B for life, beginning after June 1, was ineffective at common law.

A conveyance by A to "B and his heirs, so long as liquor is never used on the premises, and if so, then to C" was disallowed because it was an attempt to make what would otherwise be a special limitation effective for a third-party *stranger*.

If A conveyed to B and his heirs, so long as B and his heirs operate a printing shop on the property, then to C, this was not allowed at common law because, once again, it was an attempt to create a shifting ownership interest in a third party, not the grantor.

If A conveyed to B for life, and the year after B's death then to C, this was not allowed under common law because it would create a *gap* in the seisin.

If A conveyed to B and his heirs, and then to C and his heirs, this would not be allowed at Common Law because no grant could follow the granting of what appeared to be the fee simple absolute in B.

Executory interests dealing with uses involving springing and shifting executory interests could begin in the future by springing from the grantor or shifting between grantees. A use such as this could be raised by bargain and sale, covenant to stand ceased, or resulting use. To illustrate: (i) bargain and sale, A conveys to B and his heirs; (ii) covenant to stand seisin, A conveys or gives a covenant to stand ceased to the use of B and his heirs; and (iii) resulting use, X enfeoffed or conveyed to A and his heirs to hold for the use of C for life, and one year after C's death to the use of Z and his heirs.

5. Statute of Uses

The Statute of Uses was created in 1536. It if if any person was enfeoffed or stood seised for the use of land for another person, such person would have the use and benefit of such land. The effect of the Statute of Uses was to change the relationships so that one who had the *use* would have the *legal* estate. The statute executed the "use."

Z. RULE AGAINST PERPETUITIES

No interest is good, unless it must vest, if at all, not later than 21 years after a life in being, plus a period of gestation if necessary.

The *period* of the Rule Against Perpetuities is measured from the time when the instrument making the gift *becomes effective*. If the gift is by testamentary transfer, it is measured from *the date of death of the decedent*. If the conveyance is by deed, it is measured from the date of delivery of the deed.

The Rule Against Perpetuities applies notwithstanding the facts are clear that in fact the event will occur before the expiration of the required period under the Rule. This is the distinguishing point between the Rule Against Perpetuities and the Rule of Destructibility of Contingent Remainders, discussed in a moment.

Many times it is difficult to determine who the measuring life is to apply the Rule Against Perpetuities. For example, if a gift is made to the children of A if they reach 21 years of age, and A is living, the gift to the children of A will be vested at age 21. The gift must be valid because the children of A, if A is the measuring life, must be determined upon the death of A. And in fact, the interests will vest in said children, "if at all" by age 21.

Although the rule against perpetuities, as stated above, applies under the common-law position in many states, numerous other states have abrogated the common-law rule in favor of a statutory rule that, effectively, in many instances, eliminates the rule against perpetuities on non-donative transfers. This concept is based on the uniform statutory change as to the rule against perpetuities, the same crafted by the Uniform Law Commissioners.

AA. THE RULE OF DESTRUCTIBILITY OF CONTINGENT REMAINDERS

This rule provides that contingent remainders are destroyed unless they vest at or before the termination of the preceding freehold estate. This rule is usually open to interpretation, based on what might happen; compare the Rule Against Perpetuities.

***

PART THREE

TAX

CHAPTER 1

Tax Considerations in Syndications¶¶¶¶

Tax Principles

A. INTRODUCTION

Tax matters in real estate transactions have long been crucial in the real estate field. The decision whether to invest in a given piece of property, to make improvements, to sell or rent property, or to raze property has long been affected, if not determined, by tax considerations.

Economically speaking, it would be foolish to invest in real estate where the accounting income is zero or the investment results in a loss. However, as is apparent from basic study in the income tax field, a loss can be a valuable "asset," and this is not a *non-sequitur.* Obviously, a loss is valuable for its tax shelter. For example, if a $1,000 loss occurs, and the taxpayer is in the 28% bracket, by using the thousand dollars of loss to reduce other taxable income, the saving is $280; *i.e.,* $1,000 times the tax rate of 28% produces a $280 savings because there would be $280 fewer dollars owing for taxes.

Cash flow can result from the fact that property can generate cash in excess of cash needs. Possibly no tax will be owed, and in fact a loss may be generated; for example, where the depreciation deduction, which is a non-cash flow item (that is, it does not reduce the amount of cash available for spending) results in a deduction (expense) against income sufficient to produce a net loss. It is this concept that often results in real estate being identified as a "tax sheltered investment." This terminology is derived from the earlier mentioned example whereby a book net loss "shelters" other income in that the deduction allowed by the loss on one property offsets income from other sources. It is this tax shelter, combined with proper "tax planning" (euphemistic as it might seem when compared to "tax avoidance or evasion") that can produce great tax benefits to the investor.

¶¶¶¶ Some of the material in this Part Three was written by Author Levine in prior texts and was also reproduced in the text by Levine, Mark and Segev, Libbi, *Real Estate Transactions, Tax Planning,* published by Thomson/West (201).

B. Focus on Real Estate Securities— Often Influenced by Tax Issues

Although this text focuses on real estate securities issues, a basic understanding of Federal income tax in other areas is important to direct attention to the real estate tax issues that relate to syndications.

C. Calculation of Tax

In summary, when calculating taxable income, the taxpayer calculates all of the gross income, as required under 26 U.S.C.A. §61, or as otherwise required by the Code, and reduces that amount by allowed deductions. The deductions are those from gross income to reach adjusted gross income.

Once adjusted gross income amount has been calculated, the taxpayer claims a standard deduction or the taxpayer computes itemized deductions. If the itemized deductions are in excess of a minimum amount, referred to as the zero-bracket amount, the taxpayer will deduct the excess over this amount, subject to various limitations. Thus, in summary format, the basic tax calculator for federal income tax is:

- Gross Income (Code §61)
- minus deductions (above line) (Code §62)
- Adjusted Gross Income (Code §62)
- minus deductions (below line) (Code §63)
- minus exemptions (Code §151)
- Taxable Income (Code §63)
- times tax rate (Code §1)
- (Gr.) Tax Due (NET)
- minus Credits (Various Code sections)
- (net) Tax Due (NET)

D. Other Tax Issues

Additional tax issues related to syndications are discussed in subsequent chapters within this Work. For more information on federal income tax issues, especially related to real estate, see Levine, Mark and Segev, Libbi, *Real Estate Transactions, Tax Planning* published by Thomson/West (2017).

***

CHAPTER 2

Tax Classifications for Types of Property

A. CLASSIFICATIONS

Historically, the classifications of property for federal income tax purposes were usually made by dividing property into the following categories: (i) Capital assets (investment property); (ii) property that is used in the trade or business (§1231 property); (iii) personal (nonbusiness) property; and (iv) property for sale to customers (inventory and the like).

1. Capital asset (I.R.C. §1221)

A capital asset is defined in the negative sense in that it includes all property held by the taxpayer (whether or not connected with his trade or business) except *eight* classifications listed under 26 U.S.C.A. §1221 (I.R.C. 1986). The exclusions include: (i) stock in the trade or business of the taxpayer; (ii) property used in the trade or business; (iii) copyright, literary, musical, artistic composition, letter, or memorandum, or similar property; (iv) accounts or notes receivable acquired in the ordinary course of trade or business; (v) a publication of the United States Government received by the taxpayer without being purchased (gift, etc.) and held by the taxpayer or one who obtained it from the taxpayer without a purchase, *e.g.*, a gift; (vi) any commodities derivative financial instrument held by a commodities derivatives dealer (with a few exceptions); (vii) certain hedging transactions; and (viii) supplies of a type that are regularly consumed by the taxpayer in the ordinary trade or business of the taxpayer. All other property, unless otherwise decided by case law, is a capital asset under 26 U.S.C.A. §1221.

2. Business Property: Property used in the trade or business (I.R.C. §1231 property)

26 U.S.C.A. §1231 property used in the trade or business includes, among other items, (1) depreciable tangible property and (2) real estate, both used in the trade or business.

a. Property for personal use (non-business)

Property that is used for personal use, as opposed to business or investment use, whether it be real estate or personal, generally fits within the category of capital assets.

b. Property held for sale to customers

This classification results in ordinary income treatment with a gain on disposition. This is sometimes called inventory or dealer property.

B. CLASSIFICATIONS OF PROPERTY—TAX CLASSIFICATIONS FOR PROPERTY AS ACTIVE, PASSIVE OR PORTFOLIO TYPE INCOME

Although the historical classification of property is as noted above, there is also the Tax Reform Act of 1986 classification of property with three groups.

The essence of change in classifications or additions in classification includes what are referred to as passive income, active income, and portfolio income.

Passive activities are those businesses in which the individual does not materially participate in the activity on a regular, continuous and substantial basis. Other tests can also produce income for the passive category.

To the contrary, an active position is one where the taxpayer does materially participate in the activity or operations on a regular, continuous and substantial basis.

Portfolio income is income generated from sources involving non-business activities relative to dividends, interest, royalties, and sale of investment-type property. These groupings are in need of more discussion and differentiation.

Classification of property as active, passive or portfolio and the limitation on losses and credits from passive activities

The argument supporting the TRA of 1986 is that the use of losses causes increasing damage to the good faith position of the voluntary Federal income tax system. The loss of confidence in the tax system continued to be generated because of many reports in which individuals with very large gross or adjusted gross incomes paid little or no tax.

Reports by the Treasury supported the position that small amounts of tax were paid by many taxpayers, notwithstanding their very large incomes. The Senate Finance Committee took the position that major and decisive action was needed to curb expansion of tax shelters and to restore to the tax system the degree of equity that is necessary to support the system.

Obviously, one of the questions was how to undertake the limitation of these losses. The TRA of 1986 addressed this question by limiting passive losses in many circumstances.

The passive loss limitations provide that deductions for the passive trade or business activity, to the extent that they exceed the income from the passive activities of the taxpayer, exclusive of portfolio income (described below), *generally* cannot be deducted against other income. This is the essence of the limitation that has been invoked to curb the activity on loss shelter positions. (There is an exception, noted below, for real estate practitioners.)

There are three groupings or "baskets" under this concept:

- Active Income or Loss.
- Passive Income or Loss.
- Portfolio Income or Loss.

These are discussed below.

The unused losses and credits have been labeled as **suspended losses and credits**; they are carried forward and treated as deductions or credits in future years, as explained below. The losses that are suspended and are not used in future years against operating income are suspended until there is a disposition of the property by the taxpayer. They can be used at the time of disposition to offset the gain on the sale or to offset (reduce) other income of the taxpayer in the year of sale.

These rules apply to individuals in most circumstances, but also affect estates, trusts, Personal Service Corporation (PSC) positions, S Corporations and closely held corporations.

Interpretive questions have arisen as a result of these new rules. For example, rental activities must be classified; under the TRA of 1986 they are classified as passive activities. Losses from working interests in oil and gas properties are not limited, generally speaking, by the PLL rules.

Losses and tax credits to limited partners from limited partnership are generally treated as passive.

When a taxpayer incurs an interest expense to carry a passive activity, this passive interest is considered with regard to the passive loss computation.

As for taxes, relative to a passive activity, these are within the gamut of the passive loss rules, notwithstanding whether the taxpayer attempts to take the deduction from gross income or from adjusted gross income.

For 1986, there were transitional rules, which allowed losses to be deducted as they had been deducted, prior to the TRA of 1986.

The losses from passive activity can be applied against income for the taxable year from other passive activities, regardless of the transitional rules, as noted. They can also be applied against income subsequently generated by a passive activity.

The losses and credits that are passive in nature cannot be applied, aside from under the transitional rules, to offset or reduce income from active services, such as salary, commissions or other compensation for services. They cannot be applied against what is referred to as *portfolio income.* Portfolio income might also be thought, in a generic sense, to be "passive" income. Under the PLL rules, portfolio income is separated into another category, and such income is not considered passive for purposes of applying the rules as noted. Portfolio income consisting of dividends, interest, royalties, and gain from sale of investment-type property cannot be offset or reduced by shelter (losses) generated from passive loss-type property.

Portfolio income and salary income are in different categories, baskets or groupings. They are not part of the passive activity of losses and credits generated from the tax shelter-type activities.

The passive loss rules are designed to ensure that the active salary or commission-type income and the portfolio income, along with non-passive income, cannot be offset by the tax losses from the passive positions until the amount of the losses are determined upon disposition of the passive loss property.

The losses that cannot be applied from the passive loss activity, sometimes referred to as suspended losses attributable to passive trade or business activities, are allowed in full upon a taxable disposition of the taxpayer's entire interest in the property. If there is a partial transfer or recognition of gain in, passive activity or gain or boot generated on a partially tax-deferred transfer of an entire or partial interest in property, these are treated as passive activities. As such, gain on those transfers can be offset by losses and credits from passive activities, but the transfers are not treated as dispositions that would trigger all suspended losses from the activity to be used.

The amount of the gain or loss and the activity that can be determined can be applied when there is a total disposition of the property in question. To the extent that the taxpayer's basis in the activity has been reduced by the deductions that were suspended, thereby resulting in a gain on disposition because of a lower basis, the suspended losses that were not used can be claimed and would in many instances offset the gain that was generated because of the lower basis. There is no character change, *i.e.,* capital to ordinary, as a result of that position.

C. PASSIVE ACTIVITY

I. General

Under the TRA of 1986, an activity that is passive in nature is one that involves a trade or business *and* one where the taxpayer does not materially participate in the activity. Generally, a trade or business might generate an **active** activity. If it is not a trade or business, such as receiving interest or dividends as noted earlier, this could be portfolio income.

If the taxpayer is active and materially participates, the activity would generally not be passive because the positive passive test is at least two-fold: A trade or business *and* a situation where the taxpayer does *not* materially participate in the activity. (Even if this two-part positive test is met, the item could remain passive if other negative or overriding rules apply. See 26 U.S.C.A. §469.)

A taxpayer "materially participates" under the Senate Finance Committee position, where he is involved in the operations on a regular, continuous and substantial basis. Even if the taxpayer owns an interest in a trade or business or pass-through-type of activity, such as a general partnership or S Corporation, it nevertheless requires an involvement in the operations on a continuous, regular and substantial basis to meet the material participation test. The taxpayer does not materially participate if one is a limited partner.

If a partnership has income in the form of interest, and a partner receives his or her pro rata share of the interest, that portion is not passive it is portfolio income and is subject to the rules discussed earlier.

Guaranteed payments to a partner for services performed, possibly including a limited partner in some settings, is not passive in nature.

The TRA of 1986 does not include a working interest in oil or gas properties as passive activity. Therefore, an owner of such a working interest could deduct the losses attributable to the working interest whether or not there is a material participation in the activity.

Passive activity includes almost all real estate rental activity, even if the taxpayer materially participates; however, the Senate Finance Committee position supported the position that operating **a hotel or transient** lodging, consistent with prior positions before the TRA of 1986, is not considered passive, assuming substantial **services** are provided. There are other exceptions. See below as to real estate practitioners.

The activity of a **dealer** in real estate is not generally treated as rental activity.

The Treasury acknowledged that 26 U.S.C.A. §469, the Passive Loss and Credit Limitations, applies to only certain taxpayers and limits them only to certain activities. Therefore, it became imperative to know what constitutes an "activity." A passive activity is generally a trade or business in which the taxpayer does not materially participate. However, obviously, all rental activities, notwithstanding participation, are deemed to be passive. Certain other exceptions exist, such as oil and gas wells involving working interest, in which case they are not passive.

The activity in Regulations is codified under §1.469-4T. These Rules look to three main groups of discussion:

- Undertaking rules;
- Activity rules; and
- Special rules.

2. Undertaking rules

The undertaking consists of all the business and rental operations of the given taxpayer conducted at one location. This is true regardless whether the activities are similar or are diverse. This is the smallest unit in which an activity may be divided.

If all of the taxpayer's activities are conducted at one location, normally this is one activity, and one need not apply the activity rules or the special rules. In other words, most of the issue is solved. There are exceptions to this position, such as the involvement of real estate, as noted below.

Inasmuch as all rental real estate activities, except as noted below as to real estate practitioners, are deemed passive, or are not deemed to be a rental real estate activity, such as a short-term rental, special rules are needed with regard to the term activity, as noted.

Where an undertaking consists of both rental and non-rental operations, the general rule is that they must be treated as two separate undertakings and thereby divided. However, the basic undertaking will not be split if one type of operation dominates. If income dominates for purposes of the rule and represents greater than 80% of the basic undertaking's income, then this would be the dominant source. As such, the basic undertaking would not be split.

3. Activity rules

Unless there is another exception that applies, an undertaking by a taxpayer is a separate activity. As an example, under one of the activity rules, if there are similarly or commonly controlled trades or businesses, they are generally treated as the same activity. For purposes of interpreting this concept, undertakings are similar if greater than half, using a value test, of the operations, are in the same activity or business.

It is also considered a requirement by the taxpayer to aggregate, if there are commonly controlled trades or businesses under some integrated business.

Professional service undertakings can also be treated as one activity if they dominate relative to the services. The services in question on these are generally accounting, actuarial science, architecture, law, engineering, health, performing arts, consulting and certain other areas.

This aggregation rule may look to commonly controlled undertakings; this may be a "facts and circumstances" decision. However, if the same five or fewer people own substantial interest in the undertakings, there is a presumption, which could be rebutted, that they are commonly controlled.

As mentioned, the activity rules for a trade or business undertaking and for professional services must be followed. These are mandatory positions. However, taxpayers may decide whether to apply the rules relative to rental real estate in some settings; that is, taxpayers can treat a combination of rental real estate activities as a single activity or they may divide those rental real estate activities into separate activities. However, consistency is also necessary. The taxpayers cannot divide their rental real estate activities in a way that differs from the way they treated it in prior years.

Taxpayers may also not fragment the activity for the real estate in a way that differs from how the taxpayers' pass-through entities were treating such properties. On disposition, the taxpayer can treat a *non-rental* undertaking as a separate activity. This is true even if the undertaking would have been treated as part of a larger activity under some sort of aggregation approach.

Numerous examples are given within the Regulations that attempt to illustrate some of the rules noted earlier. Direct reference to these Regulations is necessary, as they are highly complex and are in a stage of development and comment. In addition, new Regulations will issue for additional questions that will arise and have arisen relative to passive losses and credits.

Even if one meets the requirements of the "at risk" rules to be considered active, this is not determinative of whether the activity is rental under the passive loss rules.

Long-term rentals or leases of property such as apartments or office equipment, are generally considered to be rental activities. In such case, losses are allowed only against passive activities, not other active income.

4. Active participation exception

There is a special rule under which an individual can deduct, annually, up to $25,000 of that individual's passive losses, to the extent that they exceed income from passive activities, where those losses are attributable to rental real estate activities, if the taxpayer is actively participating. The $25,000 rule is for individuals and not corporations. The taxpayer is not treated as actively participating in the rental real estate activity if he owns less than 10%.

Although the taxpayer can be disqualified from the $25,000 deduction if he does not own at least a 10% interest, he is not presumed to be actively participating simply if he has a 10% or greater interest. Also, as discussed subsequently, there is a distinction between "active participation" and "material participation." The active participation test does not produce as difficult a burden.

There is a limitation on the maximum that can be earned without losing the benefit of this $25,000 rule, similar to other phase-out concepts, such as those dealing with tax brackets and exemptions. The $25,000 is phased out ratably, as the taxpayer's adjusted gross income increases, as calculated without regard to the passive losses, from $100,000 to $150,000.

The $25,000 rental real estate rule applies, as a deduction, also to limit credits attributable to rental real estate.

The $25,000 applies to low-income housing credits, even if the taxpayer does not actively participate in the activity, including the case of the limited partner in such a setting.

The $25,000 amount and the phase-out rule apply to the aggregate basis of credits, including low-income housing credits and to deductions for other than low income housing, as opposed to $25,000 for each.

If the total net rental real estate losses and credits exceed the $25,000, the taxpayer must allocate, *pro rata*, first among all the losses, including rental real estate activity, losses suspended in prior years, and then apply credits, as to each separate activity, to determine the amount that applies.

5. Those who are subject to the Passive Loss Rules

The passive loss rules apply, as noted, generally to individuals, although there can be applications to estates and trusts, personal holding companies, S Corporations and closely held corporations.

To prevent the taxpayer from circumventing the rules, the passive loss limitation can apply to situations where there is a closely-held corporation. This is true where the taxpayer is subject to the at-risk rules, which generally means five or fewer individuals owning directly or indirectly more than 50% of the stock of the company. In such circumstances, such C Corporations cannot utilize losses or credits from the passive activities against **portfolio** income. (They **can** use the passive loss against (to reduce) **active** income.)

To determine the corporate activity to see if material participation exists, there is an examination of the activity of the corporate employees and owners.

6. Treatment of losses and credits—passive activities: losses

Losses that are generated from passive activity are deductible by an individual only against income from that or other passive activity, as indicated earlier. The suspended passive activity losses for the year are carried forward indefinitely. They are not carried back.

Suspended losses from an activity are allowed in full upon a taxable disposition of the property, as indicated earlier.

7. Passive losses and net operating losses

Passive losses are first considered (used by the taxpayer) before net operating loss carryovers are considered.

If any passive losses are not deductible in any year, the amount of the suspended losses from each activity is determined on a *pro rata* basis. With respect to each activity, the proportion of the loss that is suspended and carried forward is determined by the ratio of net losses from that activity to the total net losses from all passive activities for the year. This allocation is necessary to determine the suspended losses for the particular activity when they are allowed in full upon disposition of the property.

If the circumstance arises where the taxpayer could use up to the $25,000 amount, but the taxpayer has insufficient non-passive income against which to apply the losses, the otherwise allowable rental real estate losses are treated as a net operating loss arising that year and are carried forward and back in accordance with the net operating loss rules.

Net operating loss carryovers are allowed against any income of the taxpayer. In the case of individuals, estates, trusts and personal service corporations, the non-passive losses net operating losses ("NOLs") are considered only after reducing income from passive activities by current and suspended deductions from passive activities, but not below zero.

The passive loss is applied after the interest limitation and the at-risk rules. This is important since a loss that is not allowed for the year because the taxpayer is not at risk is suspended under the at-risk rules and not under the passive loss suspension rules. If an interest is disallowed under the interest deduction limitation, the suspension applies under it and not under the passive loss rules.

Once a loss has been disallowed under the investment interest limitation, as an example, that disallowed interest is not again disallowed under the passive loss rule. Only the remaining portion of interest, not disallowed due to the interest limitation, can be subject to disallowance under the phase-in and the passive loss rules.

Credits arising with respect to passive activities generally are treated in the same manner as the concept of deductions, as discussed earlier.

Generally speaking, credits that are generated from passive activities and that cannot be utilized on a current basis are carried forward for future use, but not back.

8. Passive losses, rehabilitation and low-income housing credits

The credit equivalent of the $25,000 deduction as provided earlier relative to passive losses is applicable with regard to the rehabilitation tax credit under 26 U.S.C.A. §48 and the low-income housing credit under 26 U.S.C.A. §42, even if the taxpayer is not "active." The taxpayer need not show any active participation to claim this credit.

9. Dispositions of property

If the taxpayer disposes of his entire interest in a property that falls within the passive rules, the actual economic gain or loss in the investment can be calculated. Upon a fully taxable disposition, any overall loss from the activity realized by the taxpayer is recognized and can be allowed against income, whether it is active, passive, or portfolio.

The theory is that the purpose of the passive loss limitation is to suspend losses because one cannot determine, in an economic sense, whether those losses have taken place. Once the property is disposed, in a total disposition, the purpose of the rule has been met, and the losses can be allowed.

If an interest is in the form of an ownership change and not a total disposition, generally the suspended losses are not allowed because the gain, in an economic sense, has not been realized. This may occur when the taxpayer transfers his property to an entity that the taxpayer controls.

There are special rules when property is transferred by gift, by death of a taxpayer, and other circumstances where the taxpayer is no longer subject to the passive loss limitations.

The taxpayer must dispose of his entire interest in the property including all entities that are engaged in the activity. If there is a disposition of less than the entire interest, the issue of ultimate economic gain or loss on the investment is still unresolved.

An installment sale of the taxpayer's entire interest in an activity, in a fully taxable transaction, triggers the allowance of suspended losses, even though the taxpayer will be reporting income over a period of time. The losses are allowed in each year of the installment obligation, in the ratio of the gain recognized in each year to the total gain on the sale.

The transfer of a taxpayer's interest in activity by reason of his death would cause the suspended losses to be allowed to the extent they *exceed* the amount, if any, by which the basis of the interest in the activity is increased at death, under 26 U.S.C.A. §1014. Suspended losses are eliminated to the extent of the amount of the basis increase. The losses allowed generally would be reported in the final return of the decedent-taxpayer. (There are many conflicts and unusual circumstances that must be treated with regard to the suspended losses and dispositions other than an outright sale.)

10. Other transfers, gift, etc.

A gift of all or part of the taxpayer's interest in a passive activity would not trigger the suspended losses. If the taxpayer gives away his entire interest, he cannot make a future taxable disposition of the property. Suspended losses are added to the basis of the property immediately before the gift; therefore, the donee would have a higher basis if the donee takes the donor's basis, which is often the case. If the taxpayer gives away less than all his interest, an allocable portion of suspended losses is added to the donee's basis.

Suspended losses are eliminated when added to the donee's basis, and the remainder of the losses that are not added to the basis of the donee continue to be suspended in the donor's hands.

The treatment of subsequent deductions from the activity, to the extent of the donee's interest in the property, depends on whether the activity is treated as passive or active in the donee's hands.

11. Tax-deferred exchanges

If there is an exchange of the taxpayer's interest in an activity in a non-recognition transaction, such as an exchange governed by 26 U.S.C.A. §351 for a tax-deferred creation of a corporation, Code §721, the tax-free creation of a partnership, or Code §1031, tax-deferred exchanges of like-kind property, again in which no gain or loss is recognized, suspended losses are not "triggered." That is, the suspended losses cannot be used to offset income.

Following the exchange, the taxpayer would retain an interest in the activity and, therefore, would not realize the ultimate economic gain or loss of the investment. The requirements of the passive loss limitations have not been met, since there was no realization and recognition of income.

To the extent the taxpayer does recognize gain on the transaction, such as boot in an otherwise tax-deferred exchange, the gain is treated as passive activity income from which passive losses can be deducted.

In tax-free or tax-deferred transactions, the suspended losses that are not allowed upon such non-recognition transaction will continue to be treated as passive activity losses. There are exceptions in some circumstances where the losses are applied against income from the property received in the tax-free exchange attributable to the original activity.

This rule would not apply to permit the offset of suspended passive losses against dividends or other income or gain otherwise treated as portfolio income. Following some transactions such as a 26 U.S.C.A. §1031 exchange, the taxpayer may no longer have an interest in the original activity. Therefore, there is no special rule permitting suspended losses from the prior interest to be offset by income from the new activity unless it, too, is a passive activity.

The suspended losses may not be applied against income from the property that is attributable to a **different activity** from the one that the taxpayer exchanged. Suspended passive activity losses cannot be applied against portfolio income from a pass-through entity (S Corporation or partnership).

Therefore, unless the taxpayer can show that income and gifts with suspended losses are offset clearly from the passive activity, the interest that he exchanged for a different form of ownership, does not allow for an offset. If a passive activity conducted by a general partnership is contributed to an S Corporation, followed by dissolution of the partnership, subsequent income from the activity may be offset by suspended losses from the activity of a shareholder who was formerly a general partner in the passive activity.

If the taxpayer disposes of his entire interest in the property received in tax-deferred exchange, the remaining suspended losses, if any, are allowed in full.

12. Dispositions and passive losses

When the taxpayer disposes of a passive loss property, the previously limited losses are now available for use. Another way of reaching this same conclusion is to simply say that the passive loss rules do not apply to this amount; therefore, the losses that were previously postponed can be applied. These are applied in the following order:

a.   apply it against income from the passive activity that was just disposed of in the applicable transaction;
b.   apply it against income from passive activities; and
c.   if any is left, as against the categories noted, apply it against any other income. This could be active source income or portfolio income; it is not restricted to passive income. See 26 U.S.C.A. §469(g).

A disposition to a related party would not cause the recognition of the losses noted above. Thus, if the taxpayer disposed of the property to a related party as provided under 26 U.S.C.A. §267, 26 U.S.C.A. §707(b), and as otherwise restricted under 26 U.S.C.A. §469(g)(1)(B), as explained earlier, the deductions would not be allowed.

26 U.S.C.A. §267 transactions refer to situations involving dispositions with family members and certain controlled entities. 26 U.S.C.A. §707(b) covers transactions between the taxpayer and certain partners or partnerships involving the taxpayer.

If the loss is denied currently because of the related party rules, the passive losses that are not currently deducted stay with the taxpayer who has made the transfer. See 26 U.S.C.A. §469(g)(1).

13. No longer treated as passive activity

Some events may arise that do not constitute a disposition, but would terminate the application of the passive loss rules to the taxpayer or to the taxpayer with respect to that particular activity. When taxpayer participation in an activity is material in any year, after one year or years during which he was not materially participating, previously suspended losses remain suspended and continue to be treated as passive activity losses. Such previously suspended losses, however, are allowed against income realized after the activity ceases to be passive with respect to that taxpayer.

As with tax-deferred exchanges of the taxpayer's entire interest in an activity, the taxpayer must be able to show that such income is from the same activity in which the taxpayer previously did not materially participate. A footnote in the Senate Finance Committee Reports in 1986 indicated that the reason for the treatment is that the taxpayer could have deducted the suspended losses against income from the activity had the change in his relation to the activity not occurred. Although the income from the activity may no longer be passive activity income, prior passive activity losses generated by that activity should continue to be deductible against income from the activity in question. The argument is that it would be unfair and inequitable to give less favorable treatment to a taxpayer whose income from an activity becomes active, than to one who continues to be merely a passive investor.

14. Treatment of portfolio income

Portfolio income is not treated as income from a passive activity. Passive losses and credits from passive activities cannot be applied to offset the portfolio income.

Portfolio income generally includes dividends, interest and royalties and also includes gain or loss attributable to disposition of property that is held for investment, not a passive activity, and property that normally produces the dividends, interest or royalty income.

Dividends from a C Corporation, Real Estate Investment Trust, and Real Estate Investment Company, and interest on debt obligations and royalties from the licensing of property are generally treated as portfolio income. Gains or losses from the sale of interests that normally produce such income are treated as portfolio income or losses.

With some exceptions, income from a general or limited partnership interest, income from an S Corporation, or from a grantor trust or from lease of property generally are not treated as portfolio income. These types of interests can generate losses that are applied to unrelated passive income of the taxpayer. Although such interests might otherwise (aside from the TRA basket rules) be considered as held for investment, the gains from the sale of those interests, when they are interests in passive activities, are not portfolio income except to the extent gain on sale of the interest is attributable to the portfolio income.

If a general partnership gains portfolio income from appreciated stocks and bonds and conducts a business activity, part of the sale of the partnership would be treated as portfolio income.

Portfolio income that is generated from an activity that is otherwise passive is taken into account separately from other items relating to that activity. Where a taxpayer has an interest in a passive activity, portfolio income from the activity is not taken into account in determining passive activity income or loss. The portfolio income is treated as non-passive income of the taxpayer.

The Senate Finance Committee noted that if a limited partnership publishes a magazine, and the partnership also holds a portfolio of dividend and interest-bearing securities, but the income from these is more than offset by tax losses from publishing the magazine, each limited partner must separately account for his share of the portfolio income and losses from the operation of the magazine. They may not offset them against each other in calculating tax liability. Portfolio income retains its character as income that is not income from a passive activity, even though the non-portfolio income or loss attributable to limited partnership interest is treated as passive activity income.

The rule treating portfolio income as not from a passive activity, as explained above, does not apply to the extent that the income, of the type generally regarded as portfolio income, is derived in the course of the trade or business of that activity, for example, bank interest income.

The Senate Finance Committee Reports also indicated that interest income may also arise in the course of a trade or business with respect to **installment sales** and interest charges on accounts receivable.

The argument is that the rationale for treating portfolio-type income as not from passive activity does not apply in this setting, as derivation of such income is what the business activity involves, and therefore, such interest, dividends or royalty income, derived in the ordinary course of a trade or business, is not treated, for purposes of the passive loss provision, as portfolio income.

If the taxpayer, directly or through a pass-through entity, owns an interest in an activity deriving income, the income is treated as part of the activity that may or may not be treated as passive, depending on whether the taxpayer materially participates.

The Senate Finance Committee Reports also indicated there is no exception for the treatment of portfolio income arising from working capital. Interest earned on funds set aside by a limited partnership to operate and expand its shopping mall is treated as portfolio income and cannot be taken into account in determining a limited partner's passive income or loss from the activity of the shopping mall.

The Secretary of the Treasury was given broad powers to prescribe regulations under which items of income from the limited partnership or other passive activity are treated as portfolio income. The thought is that this will prevent taxpayers from avoiding the passive loss rules.

15. Material participation

A taxpayer's interest in the trade or business activity is not treated as a passive interest if the taxpayer materially participates in the activity. This rule is applied by considering services provided, both by the taxpayer and by the taxpayer's spouse, whether or not such taxpayer and spouse file a joint return.

In some circumstances, material participation is not determinative, as indicated earlier. Working interests in oil and gas properties are treated as active, whether or not there is material participation. Interests in real estate activities are treated as passive, whether or not the taxpayer materially participates.

In the case of rental real estate, a separate standard, active participation, as opposed to material participation, is relevant to determine whether the taxpayer is permitted to use losses and credits up to the $25,000 limit of the rule, as discussed above.

Working as an employee or providing services as part of a personal services business, including professional activities, is not passive.

Material participation of a taxpayer in an activity is determined separately for **each** taxable year. In most cases, the material participation of a taxpayer in an activity is not expected to change from year to year, although it can.

16. Limited partnerships, LLCs, etc. and material participation

In the case of a limited partnership, it is generally presumed that the taxpayer has not materially participated in the activity if he is a limited partner.

The standard of material participation generally developed by relying on the concept developed for this issue under 26 U.S.C.A. §1402(a) (net earnings from self- employment) and §2032A relating to the estate tax valuation of farm property.

The issue has been raised as to whether an LLC might be classified as "active" and not "passive." Although a limited partnership interest quite often will be classified as a passive interest, if that limited partnership interest is also owned by a general partner, it could be active. That is, if one owns <u>both</u>

general and limited partnership positions, the interests could be active, if the general partner can show that he or she is generally active.

This same position now seems to apply to LLCs. See Proposed Regulation §1.469-5.

Case law has supported the position that simply because one is involved in an entity does not control the determination of whether the income is active or passive. Rather, if the taxpayer can show that the taxpayer meets the "active" test, as provided under Code §469(h), one could be classified as active.

The law for real estate people, to show participation of more than 750 hours per year and more than 50% of one's time in an active business are examples of such positions that might support an active posture, as stated in Treas. Reg. Under Code §469. But, these same arguments may help to show active participation in other, non-real estate areas. Thus, it might be significant participation for the individual and, thus, allow the avoidance of the passive loss rules under Code §469. A number of cases have supported this argument. See the Proposed Regulations under §1.469-5(e).

Since limited partners in limited partnerships and members in LLCs are now allowed much more participation in the activity of the entity, this seems to support the possibility of the argument that one can be active, as opposed to passive, even in an LLC.

The Senate Finance Committee Report of 1986 noted that a taxpayer is most likely to have materially participated in an activity for purposes of this rule where involvement in the activity is the taxpayer's principal business; however, the fact that an activity is or is not the individual's principal business is not conclusive in determining material participation.

For the taxpayer to materially participate, the taxpayer must be regularly, continuously and substantially involved in providing services integral to the activity. That a taxpayer has little knowledge or experience regarding the business is highly significant in determining whether the taxpayer's participation in management is likely to be deemed material.

17. Material participation by entities subject to the passive loss rule

An estate or trust is treated as materially participating in an activity if the executor or fiduciary, in his capacity, is materially participating.

A corporation subject to passive loss treatment is materially participating in the activity if one or more shareholders, owning in aggregate more than 50% of the outstanding stock of the corporation, materially participates.

There are other tests available for material participation by a corporation, and other entities.

18. Active participation in a rental real estate activity: allowance of $25,000 of loss and credit to reduce other income

For purposes of the passive loss provisions under the rental real estate activities, rental real estate activities are treated as passive without regard to whether the taxpayer materially participated, *except* as noted below.

There are exceptions. As indicated earlier, one relief provision for rental real estate is an individual who may offset up to $25,000 income that is not treated as passive, by using losses and credits from rental real estate activities with respect to which such individual is actively participating. For purposes of this material participation standard, services performed by the taxpayer and by the taxpayer's spouse are considered.

Low-income housing *credits* can be used as part of the $25,000 amount, even if the taxpayer does not actively participate in the rental real estate activities to which the *credits* relate. This $25,000 rule applies only if the individual does not have sufficient passive income for the year, after considering other passive deductions, to use the losses and credits from the rental real estate activities.

This $25,000 rule applies only to individuals and not to C Corporations of a type that are subject to passive loss limitations. To claim the loss, the active test applies in the year of the loss and the year it is used under this exception.

The $25,000 loss deduction rule amount is reduced, but not below zero, by 50% of the amount by which the taxpayer's adjusted gross income exceeds $100,000. In the case of a married individual not filing a joint return, and living apart at any time during the tax year, no more than $12,500 of relief is available, reduced by 50% of the amount by which the individual's adjusted gross income exceeds $50,000. If a married individual files separately from his spouse and they lived apart the entire year, the $25,000 rule cannot be used.

The adjusted gross income for this purpose is calculated without reference to *net* losses from passive activities, other than losses allowable solely by reason of a fully taxable disposition.

This special $25,000 rule applies to the rental of real estate and does not apply to other rentals, such as rentals of equipment or to activities such as an active operation of a hotel.

19. "Active participation"

The taxpayer is not treated as actively participating in rental real estate activity, as indicated earlier, if the taxpayer owns less than 10% of all interests in the activity. (Inasmuch as low-income housing *credits* are allowed without regard to active participation, they are unaffected by this requirement).

The 10% rule is designed to assist in restricting relief provided on the $25,000 rule to circumstances in which the taxpayer has a substantial interest. The active participation standard is designed to be less stringent than the material participation requirement.

The difference between active participation and material participation is that the former can be satisfied without regular, continuous and substantial involvement in the operation, so long as the taxpayer's participation is bona fide and significant, *e.g.,* in helping to make management decisions or arranging or providing other services.

A limited partner, to the extent of the limited partnership interest, is treated as not meeting the active participation standard. (However, the active participation rule does not apply with regard to low income housing **credits**.)

A lessor under a net lease is unlikely to have the degree of involvement that active participation entails, and therefore, would not, in most circumstances, meet the requirements of the active participation test. Services provided by an agent are not attributed to the principal in this setting. The Senate Finance Committee illustrated an instance of a taxpayer not meeting the active participation test by purchasing an undivided interest in a shopping mall from a promoter. The argument was that one of the taxpayer's principal interests in investing was tax shelter. He relied on professional management. This was said to hold even if formal letters might be sent indicating certain input by the investor.

D. Passive Activities and Overlap with Other Areas of the Law

I. Rental activity

The passive loss rule makes it clear that rental activity is generally treated as passive activity. This is true even if the taxpayer materially participates in the activity. Because it is passive, the deductions and credits from rental activity are applied to offset only other income from passive activity. If the taxpayer does actively participate, the special $25,000 limitation rule applies.

Some activities may not be treated as rental activities, even though payments may be made relative to tangible property. If significant services are rendered in connection with the payments, the rental may not be considered a rental activity. Payment for the use of rental property for short periods of time is not considered rental activity if significant services are rendered, for example, rental activities of a hotel or motel. This does not mean that the period for which the property is rented is determinative of whether the activity is a rental activity. A long-term rental period and low turnover of lessees does indicate that the activity is a rental activity in most circumstances.

Short-term leasing of a motor vehicle, with the lessor furnishing maintenance and other services, is not treated as a rental activity. On the other hand, chartering a boat can be a rental activity if the lessor does not supply substantial services.

Renting hotel rooms or similar space for lodging on a transient basis would not be considered a rental activity in most circumstances, because it is not passive in nature. Month-to-month renting of an apartment house would generally be treated as rental activity.

The Senate Finance Committee Report in 1986 stated that leasing property subject to a **net** lease is a rental activity under the investment rules of 26 U.S.C.A. 163. For purposes of the passive loss position, it is not relevant how long the taxpayer has owned the property.

Some businesses, indicated the Senate Finance Committee Reports, involve rental in association with other activities.

The Report indicated that other activities can immediately precede rental activity, be conducted at the same time, or take place in the same location and not be treated as part of the rental activity. This is because passive loss rental activities are considered passive activities without regard to the taxpayer's material participation.

Rental activities generally are treated as separate from non-rental activities. As an example, real estate construction and development is a different activity from renting a newly constructed building.

It is possible that ownership of a cooperative apartment in an apartment building generally would qualify as a separate activity, even though the ownership of the building may be shared with owners of other apartments. On the other hand, an undivided interest in the building or of an area too small to be rented as a separate unit does not qualify as a separate activity.

With commercial buildings rented to various tenants, in which different parties own different floors, it may be necessary to examine the degree of integration with which business relating to different floors is conducted.

2. Residence interest

Qualified residence interest is not subject to the passive loss rules.

3. Passive activity: real estate rentals in which taxpayer actively participates: proper sequence of rules

The Conference Committee Reports noted that the $25,000 rule of losses and credits for rental real estate activities in which the taxpayer actively participates is applied by first netting income and loss from all of the taxpayer's rental real estate activities in which he actively participates. If a net loss results from the activities for the year, net passive income, if any, from other activities, is applied against it to determine the amount eligible.

An example in the Committee Reports indicated that, if a taxpayer had $25,000 of losses from rental real estate activity in which he actively participated, and he also had $25,000 of gain in another rental real estate activity, resulting in no net loss from the rental real estate activities in which he actively participated, then no amount would be allowed under the $25,000 rule. This is true whether or not the taxpayer had net losses from other passive activities for the given year.

The Conference agreement also noted that a taxpayer is treated as not actively participating if at any time during the taxable year the taxpayer's interest in the activity is less than 10%. As to material participation, a change in the nature of the taxpayer's involvement does not trigger the allowance-of-deductions carryover from prior years with respect to active participation.

Under the TRA of 1986, if a taxpayer begins to actively participate in an activity in which he did not actively participate in prior years, the rule allowing up to $25,000 of losses from rental real estate activities against the non-passive income would not apply to losses from the activity carried over from the prior years. This also applies to credits, to the extent active participation is relevant.

When computing the phase-out on the $25,000 rule, adjusted gross income is calculated without regard to the net passive losses and also without regard to IRA contributions and taxable Social Security benefits.

If a taxpayer was actively participating in a rental activity, and the taxpayer died, the estate receives the benefit of this assumption and is deemed to be actively participating for the next two years following the death of the taxpayer.

A trust is not intended to qualify for the allowance of the $25,000 or the deduction-equivalent credits from rental real estate activity. This was designed to prevent individuals from circumventing the $25,000 allowance by creating multiple trusts in which to place rental real estate.

For married individuals, the amount of the $25,000 allowance and the adjusted gross income range for phasing out is halved where separate returns are filed and they did not live together for any part of the year. (No credit is allowed if they file separately and they had lived together any part of the year.)

4. Other credit limitations

Once a credit is allowed for a year under the passive loss rules, it is treated as an active credit arising in that year.

5. Passive losses: special dispositions

The Conference Committee Reports on the TRA of 1986 clarified that a transaction that is a sale or other taxable disposition, to the extent not treated as a taxable disposition under general tax rules, would not give rise to the allowance of the suspended deduction. Examples might be sham transactions, wash sales, or transfers not properly treated as sales because of a put, call or similar arrangement.

6. Related party transactions

The taxpayer is not treated as having disposed of an interest in a passive activity for purposes of triggering suspended losses if he disposes of property in an otherwise taxable transaction but transfers it to a related party within the meaning of 26 U.S.C.A. §§267(b) or 707(b)(1) (generally, family members or controlled entities). In that event, suspended losses are not triggered, but remain with the taxpayer. Those suspended losses can be offset by income from the passive activity in future years.

If the entire interest of the taxpayer and the passive interest transferred to the related party are transferred to a party who is not related within the rules noted, then to the extent that the transfer would otherwise qualify as a disposition to trigger the suspended losses, the taxpayer may deduct the suspended losses attributable to his interest in the passive activity.

7. Passive losses: disposition of activity of limited partnership

Under the passive loss rules, suspended deductions are allowed upon a taxable disposition of the taxpayer's entire interest in the activity because it becomes possible at that time to measure the taxpayer's gain or loss. A disposition of the taxpayer's entire interest in an activity conducted by a limited partnership, like a disposition of an activity conducted in any form, is a disposition that gives rise to the allowance of the suspended deductions from that activity.

To meet this special real estate exception, to avoid this passive loss limitation rule, there are eligibility tests. In essence, one must be in the real property trade or business. Under this change, under 26 U.S.C.A. §469, this real property trade or business means "... any real property development, redevelopment, construction, reconstruction, acquisition, conversion, rental, operation, management, leasing or broker trade or business."

To meet the requirements to avoid the passive loss rules and come within this special exception that removes this limitation of deducting passive losses against other income, the Joint Conference Committee, contrary to other more restricted provisions that were suggested, provided that a taxpayer can meet the eligibility requirements if more than half of the personal services rendered by the taxpayer as to this activity of real estate trade or business during the year in fact involved a real property trade or business, as defined, above. In addition, the taxpayer must materially participate in such activity.

The taxpayer must **also** show that the taxpayer performed more than 750 hours of service during the year in the real property business, *i.e.*, activities such as those outlined above. Although neither the House nor the Senate provisions initially contained this 750 hour rule, with regard to a spouse, there was concern that a taxpayer's spouse may "dabble" in real estate and thereby qualify to combine the income and losses of a husband and wife in the real estate activities and other activities, thereby avoiding the passive loss restriction. Therefore, under the RRA of 1993, the Conference Committee added the 750-hour rule to confront and avoid the problem of what was labeled as an "anti-dabbler" position.

The Conference Committee Report states:

> In the case of a joint return, the eligibility requirements are met only if either spouse separately satisfies both requirements. Thus, one of the spouses, separately, must satisfy the requirement with respect to the greater than half of each spouse's personal services in real estate, and the requirement of 750 hours or more of services, without regard to services performed by the other spouse.

(In determining "material participation," however, the Conference agreement did not change the prior law that participation of the spouse of the taxpayer is taken into account. Thus, although the 750-hour rule is present, such hour requirement is not necessary when testing for what is material.)

This change as to the passive loss rules is one of the more important provisions for real estate practitioners, under the RRA of 1993. The argument is that such change levels the playing field for those in real estate, or real property trade or business activities, as opposed to those who were in other activities. One who is in such real property trade or business may now utilize losses from such business to offset income from other businesses.

E. Capital Gains and Losses

I. Rates in General for Capital Gains

The Tax Reform Act of 1986 ("TRA") eliminated the capital gain **deduction**. However, the RR of 1990 reinstated some benefit to long-term capital gain by placing a ceiling tax rate on it of 28%. (However, the normal tax rate on long term capital gain, noted below is either 15% or 20%.)

Although the forerunners of the Revenue Reconciliation Act ("RRA") of 1990 contained a great deal of discussion as to changes in long-term capital gain, the final Act (Revenue Reconciliation Act of 1990) merely placed a ceiling on the rate of tax on such gain of 28%. It did not go back to the pre-1986 TRA rule of a capital gain *deduction*.

The RRA of 1993 increased the rate differential between capital gain (28%) and ordinary income (39.6%) on the high side. The EGTRR Act of 2001 reduced the tax rates. See *infra*, this Chapter.

The JGTRR Act of 2003 expanded this rate differential by reducing some capital gain rates to zero. That is, there may be no tax on some long-term capital gain. However, most long term capital gain is now taxed at 15%. Some taxpayers with larger taxable incomes may face a 20% rate under the changes by the ATRA of 2012.

2. Capital gain versus ordinary income

In transactions in real estate, it has been of particular importance to attempt, in most cases, to classify the sale or exchange, where a gain is produced as long term capital gain. This was due to tax benefits that attached to long term capital gain, and that were denied to other types of gain. The following discussion involves the basic classification of property as between ordinary income and capital gain property. It is important to determine the elements that affect or decide whether a given piece of property falls within the preferred capital gains group. A group, somewhat between ordinary income and capital gain property, is a hybrid group created in the tax law that is referred to under the Code as 26 U.S.C.A. §1231 property. The reader should keep in mind the crucial value of the distinction between the various groups.

The importance of the distinction of ordinary income, as opposed to capital gains, is reflected in part by the tax rates. The following is a summary of those rates.

Although the JGTRR Act of 2003 made many changes in the capital gain area, most notably a general capital gain rate of 15%, there are still tax rates for capital gains that move up to 28%. This 28% applies with collectibles.

3. Capital asset versus ordinary asset

To produce capital gain under the Code, the Code specifies that there must be a sale or exchange of a capital asset that was held in excess of a year. This topic and others related to the capital gains area was mentioned earlier. However, the essence is that when a taxpayer generates taxable income, the income is taxed as "ordinary income." As such, this means the income could be taxed under the Federal Income Tax Rates that are progressive. That is, the more that is earned, the higher the tax rate might be, up to the now maximum of 39.6%, absent other special additions, as noted earlier. However, if the gain is long term capital gain, the maximum is 20%, as explained earlier in this section. Clearly, if one has taxable income, such taxpayer would prefer to be taxed at the lowest rated allowed by law.

F. Depreciation

One of the most important tax benefits in owing real estate used in a trade or business, sometimes called Section 1231 Property (discussed earlier), is the possible depreciation of the property, for tax purposes, generating a tax deduction.

The focus in this area, and all of the tax discussion in this Work, generally, is for federal income tax rules. That is, there can be different rules for the states and for local governments.

Even the terminology employed for the concept of "depreciation" can vary. For example, one may call the deduction in this area as a "depreciation expense." Others may refer to this deduction as "Cost Recovery" or employ other terms. However, for purposes herein, the term "depreciation" will suffice to examine this area.

The rules for depreciation are fairly complex, since there are special laws as to when depreciation can be claimed, the amount of the depreciation that can be claimed, the method to use to claim the depreciation, the length of use or life employed when depreciating property, and much more.

Suffice to say at this point that if real property is depreciable, the deduction for the depreciation is generally an even amount each year, called the straight-line approach. The life for residential property (apartments, as an example) is 27.5 years and the life used to depreciate all other commercial real estate that is depreciable, with very few exceptions, is 39 years. Thus, 100% divided by 39 years is 2.564% per year. The 100% divided by the noted 27.5 years is 3.636% each year. Thus, if one multiplied this latter percent times the adjusted basis of an apartment building ("adjusted basis" would normally mean the cost, as modified for improvement, depreciation, etc.) of say $10,000,000, this would result in depreciation for the given year of $363,600 (rounded). Thus, the deductions from depreciation can be substantial.

There are many rules that impact the calculation for depreciation, when it is allowed, the difference on depreciating real estate as opposed to personal property, changes in tax results when property that was depreciated is sold, etc. These issues should be reviewed carefully for each proposed syndication.

And, as noted, there are also differences in the tax area as to state and local laws as compared to federal income tax rules, whether for depreciation or other areas within the tax field. For more on this topic, see Levine, Mark and Libbi, Segev, *Real Estate Transactions, Tax Planning* (Thomson/West, 2017).

G. Tax Deferred Exchanges

Taxpayers would clearly rather NOT be taxpayers, while still, of course, complying with the law. As mentioned earlier, Code Section 1031 is a part of the tax law that allows, for Federal income tax purposes, the taxpayer to avoid (defer) paying income taxes on a disposition of property by an exchange that falls within Code Section 1031.

The requirements, on a basic level, to meet this Section are fairly easy to state, assuming one is not discussing the exceptions or qualifications. Code Section 1031 provides:

> No gain or loss shall be recognized on the exchange of property held for productive use in a trade or business or for investment if such property is exchanged solely for property of like kind that is to be held either for productive use in a trade or business or for investment.

Some syndications are involved in undertaking exchanges of the property in the syndication. Such action has securities issues to review as well as tax issues. However, focusing on the tax issues, since some of the securities issues were reviewed earlier in Part One, the requirements for the 1031 treatment are well established on a fundamental level. That is, there must be no gain or loss recognized if there was an exchange meeting 1031(a), above. Thus, a sale does not fall within this rule. It takes an exchange. And, the exchange must be of property that is used in a trade or business or held for investment. (It does not include, for example, inventory property.)

Further the property exchanged must be real estate for real estate, not personal property for real estate, as an example.

If these items, noted above, are met, the exchange might fall within the 1031 language. But, Congress also excluded some property from the exchange rule, even if the above requirements were met. Congress provided the following exceptions under Code Section 1031 (a)(2), holding that:

This subsection shall not apply to any exchange of—

(A) stock in trade or other property held primarily for sale,
(B) stocks, bonds, or notes,
(C) other securities or evidences of indebtedness or interest,
(D) interests in a partnership,
(E) certificates of trust or beneficial interests, or
(F) choses in action.

The above six groups cannot be involved in a 1031 deferred exchange.

Further, Congress provided for exchanges that were not made at the same time; that is, the exchanges were not simultaneous. For example, if X transferred his property to Y, but X was not to receive replacement property for say 30 days after X transferred his interest, the transaction might nevertheless be considered an exchange if the following timing requirements were met:

(3) **Requirement that property be identified and that exchange be completed not more than 180 days after transfer of exchanged property**

For purposes of this subsection, any property received by the taxpayer shall be treated as property that is not like-kind property if—

(A) such property is not identified as property to be received in the exchange on or before the day that is 45 days after the date on which the taxpayer transfers the property relinquished in the exchange, or

(B) such property is received after the earlier of—

(i) the day that is 180 days after the date on which the taxpayer transfers the property relinquished in the exchange, or

(ii) the due date (determined with regard to extension) for the transferor's return of the tax imposed by this chapter for the taxable year in which the transfer of the relinquished property occurs.

Thus, the use of Section 1031 is advantageous in some settings, if one can qualify under this Section, to postpone (defer) paying tax on the gain that would otherwise be taxed on a disposition of property.

H. TAX ISSUES AND CROWDFUNDING:

Earlier in this Work we discussed the new concept of Crowdfunding under the Federal Securities Laws. Because this area has, under the JOBS Act, discussed earlier, gained more recent attention, some focus on the tax implications of Crowdfunding is worthwhile.

As discussed under various topics, *e.g.*, Rule 506 (c) as well as 4(6) and 4A, the term "Crowdfunding" was used. But, the term is in vogue and is being used in many settings today. It may arise in social settings, business settings, or in general reference. In this Work, it is important to distinguish such uses and to recognize that in most contexts in this Work the reference is in the formal, securities setting. However, not all those involved in discussions on the web, in the news, or otherwise take care to distinguish one form of "Crowdfunding" from another. And, the distinction may very much impact how expenditures in connection with Crowdfunding are treated from a tax position. Consider these points, below.

1. Crowdfunding for Help: It is common to see newspaper and web articles from an entrepreneur requesting help from members of the public. The help requested is often the solicitation of some financial input; it might be a small $10 check. After all, many small checks can create a good deal of funding. For example, a creator of a new computer type watch may request that those who believe in this idea and want to "help," should send ____dollars. These funds help provide the needed capital for the inventor/entrepreneur to develop a given proposal.

One tax issue in this setting, putting aside other issues, is to determine how the recipient of such funds treats the check, say $10, received from a contributor who, without any direct *quid pro quo*, sends the $10 check. Does the entrepreneur have taxable income? Is the payment a gift? Does it matter that the payor of the funds, the contributor, sends the check and attaches a note: "I hope that if this watch is a success, you will share the benefits with me."?

The Internal Revenue Code ("Code,") (26 USC Section 61)) clearly states that "income" is taxable. (See Code Section 61 (a).) But, is this income? If it was not intended to pay for something, such as an object (the watch), then arguably, it is not income. But, what is it?

The Code also provides in Code Section 102 that gifts are not taxable income. They are excluded from income. But, a gift takes the intent to not have a *quid pro quo*. It is often said that gifts are transfers for inadequate consideration (or no consideration). A gift is thought of as "detached and disinterested generosity," as often stated by the courts. But, was the contributor intending to make a gift?

And, how about the considerations for deductions of a payment made?

If one makes a payment to "invest," such as buying a partnership interest, such payment is normally not (currently) deductible. Rather, the payment is an investment, a capitalized expenditure that will be reviewed, later, to see if and when the "investor" receives or does not receive a return of the investment and on the investment.

Can the payor of the $10 in the example claim a deduction for the payment as a business expense? Code Section 162 states that ordinary and necessary business expenses are deductible. Would this $10 fit the setting for a deduction?

Maybe the payment was a gift, in which case the payment is **not** deductible by the payor. If the payment was intended to help and further the "hobby" of the recipient of the $10, clearly the Code would hold that no deduction would be allowed for the payor. (It was not, in the assumed setting, a business expense. It might have been a payment to further the "hobby" of inventing the special watch in the example given. However, in such instance, clearly the Code has said that "hobby expenses" are not deductible. See Code Section 183.)

Maybe the $10 was a "charitable" donation. Of course, it might be charitable in nature as to the payment by the contributor. However, the payment does not qualify for a charitable deduction for Federal income tax purposes, since charitable deductions must meet very specific requirements in the Code. The recipient must be a qualified charitable entity, etc. See Code Section 170 and Code Section 501 (c)(3). Thus, clearly no charitable deduction would be allowed in this setting for the payment of the $10.

The above payments in connection with "Crowdfunding" have tax implications. The above discussion focused on Federal Income tax issues. There could be other tax issues, such as whether some of the payments might be treated as payments subject to other taxes, such as employment taxes, sales taxes, etc. (What if the inventor/entrepreneur promised to allow the contributor of the $10 the benefit of buying a watch at a reduced price, if the watches come in to the market? What if there were other "possible" future benefits that would flow to a contributor?) The intent of this Work is not to examine tax issues in any detail; the idea is to at least recognize that many activities in the real estate securities field have tax implications involved. For more information on these tax issues, see the text cited earlier, Levine, Mark Lee and Segev, Libbi Levine, <u>Real Estate Transactions, Tax Planning</u>, (Thomson/West, 2017).

2. Crowdfunding for Web Sales—$1 Million Limit: As explained earlier in the text, the term "Crowdfunding" might be employed in the technical sense of complying with the new portal Crowdfunding that can arise under the new Sections 4(6) and 4A.

3. "Crowdfunding" and Rule 506(c): This term "Crowdfunding" can be employed to mean the broad public solicitation of sales, but not under the earlier discussed restricted Sections 4(6) and 4A and the $ 1 million cap. That is, if one was to use Rule 506(c), but the invested money was raised from many investors through Crowdfunding on the web, this use of the term "Crowdfunding" is a completely different use of the term as compared to the earlier two points, noted above, employing the term of "Crowdfunding."

***

CHAPTER 3

Accounting Tax Concepts Related to Parties Involved in Syndications

A. COMPUTATION OF TAXABLE INCOME—TAX YEAR

The Internal Revenue Code (Code), 26 U.S.C.A. §441(a), provides that taxable income shall be computed on the basis of the taxpayer's taxable year. 26 U.S.C.A. §441(b) provides the tax year means the taxpayer's annual accounting period, if it is a calendar or fiscal year. There are special provisions for unusual tax years under 26 U.S.C.A. §441(b) and the Regulations thereunder.

The "annual accounting period" referred to under 26 U.S.C.A. §441 means the annual period based on the method that the taxpayer regularly computes his income in keeping his books.

A calendar year has commonly been used. This means the period of twelve months, ending on December 31st of the current year. Any other period of time used to delineate a given period for accounting purposes is referred to as a *fiscal* year. By 26 U.S.C.A. §441(f)(4), the Secretary is given specific authority to prescribe regulations necessary for certain special accounting periods.

B. CHANGE OF ACCOUNTING PERIOD

Generally speaking, the right of a taxpayer to change the accounting period is conditioned on approval by the Secretary or his delegate. 26 U.S.C.A. §442, provides that, if the taxpayer changes his annual accounting period, the new accounting period shall become the taxpayer's taxable year only if the change is approved by the Secretary or his delegate. There are a great number of rulings, regulations, and other decisions that have interpreted what constitutes an "accounting period" and a "change" therein.

Under the TRA of 1986, there were limitations imposed on the election of the tax year. This special limitation applies in such instances as partnerships, S Corporations and personal service corporations, as provided under 26 U.S.C.A. §441(f)(3).

C. METHODS OF ACCOUNTING

1. Introduction

The method of accounting can make a great difference with regard to the amount of tax paid in a given year. It is crucial to understand the different methods of accounting.

The general rule is that taxable income, as that term is used in the Code, is computed according to the method of accounting on which the taxpayer regularly computes his income in keeping his books. A taxpayer might assume he has no method of accounting. However, the Code provides:

> If no method of accounting has been regularly used by the taxpayer or if the method used does not clearly reflect income, the computation of taxable income shall be made under such method as, in the opinion of the Secretary or his delegate, does clearly reflect income.

Most taxpayers use the cash method. This is discussed subsequently.

There are methods approved by the Code and the Service as clearly reflecting income. Under 26 U.S.C.A. §446(c), the taxpayer may use a cash method of accounting, an accrual method of accounting, any other method permitted by the Code, or any combination of the methods permitted by the Code, all required to "clearly reflect income."

2. Cash Method Taxpayer

The cash method requires the taxpayer to include in gross income all items of income actually or constructively received during the year. This includes not only cash, but all property, services, or items of value. The problem area for the cash method taxpayer is the use of the "constructive receipt" concept. The taxpayer must include monies in income when he receives it. The taxpayer cannot "turn his back" on income by refusing to accept payments until a time that is more beneficial for him. The law considers such income actually received, and therefore, it should be taxed in the year in which constructive receipt occurred.

Expenses are generally deductible in the year in which they are paid under the cash receipts and disbursements method, keeping in mind that any prepayments that result in a distortion of income, and, therefore, an accounting method that does not clearly reflect income, will not be allowed.

3. Accrual Method Taxpayer

Generally speaking, the accrual method of accounting provides that all items of income are included in gross income when earned. When the taxpayer has a *right* to such income, whether in fact it is physically received, is irrelevant. The general rule is that all events fixing the right to receive the income must have occurred to have the income included in the given year.

The earlier cited publication by the Treasury indicates an example where Mr. Smith, calendar year taxpayer, sold a radio on November 28, Year No. 1. He billed the customer two days later, but did not receive payment until February of Year No. 2. He would include the amount of the sale in his income for Year No. 1, because the income was earned in Year No. 1, and the taxpayer is on an accrual method. If the taxpayer was on a cash method, the income would not have been included in Year No. 1, but rather would have been included in Year No. 2.

Advance payments must also be included in income by the recipient, but are *not* necessarily deductible by the payor. Deferral is not permitted for amounts received as prepayment of rent, prepayment of interest and most other items; there are exceptions for advance payments received under service contracts.

Although an accrual basis taxpayer must normally accrue or determine the interest income on loans when earned, if it is questionable whether the loan can be collected, arguably, the interest need not be accrued.

4. Other Methods

In addition to the two basic methods mentioned, cash and accrual, there are also hybrid or other unusual methods. Many times these are used in conjunction with the general method of cash or accrual, or many times they are substitutes and overriding methods. Thus, there is the method of installment sales, deferred payment sales, open transactions, completed contract method, and other unusual methods to report income.

D. GENERAL RULE FOR TAXABLE YEAR

I. Inclusion

Under 26 U.S.C.A. §451(a), the amount of any item of gross income must be included in gross income for the taxable year in which it is received by the taxpayer, unless, under the method of accounting used by the taxpayer, such amount is properly reported in a different period. The general presumption is that gross income must be included in the year in which it is received by the taxpayer, unless a different method applies. A taxpayer using the accrual method may have included the income in a year prior to that of actual receipt. See the earlier discussion, above.

2. Deduction

Under 26 U.S.C.A. §461(a), similar to the rule under 26 U.S.C.A. §451, the amount of any deduction or credit must be taken in the year that is proper under the method of accounting used to compute taxable income. A cash basis taxpayer will generally take the deduction in the year in which he makes actual payment. An accrual basis taxpayer will take the deduction in the year in which the debt is *owing*, rather than the year in which the debt is physically paid, in the event they differ. This rule is subject to exceptions.

3. Constructive receipt

Although the various methods of accounting have been mentioned, the doctrine of constructive receipt is of importance in the tax law: where monies have "in effect" been received, but not physically received, the law will construe that the money is currently taxable. This is especially important to the cash basis taxpayer who intends to "turn his back" on money, *i.e.*, not receive a payment where he wishes to postpone it. Merely refusing to take a check when it is tendered, so that one might postpone the income until the next year, is not effective. The courts will treat it as though it is a "constructive" receipt of cash.

The general rule for taxable year of inclusion is provided by 26 U.S.C.A. §451(a). The Code states:

> The amount of any item of any gross income shall be included in the gross income for the taxpayer in which received by the taxpayer, unless, under the method of accounting used in computing taxable income, such amount is to be properly accounted for as of a different period.

In other words, the general rule is that the cash method is used unless another method, such as an accrual method, is used; however, again, where the cash method is used, one generally cannot simply refuse to take money simply to postpone income.

4. Assignment of Income

There has long been a doctrine in the tax law that prohibited the transferring of income from one taxpayer to another once the income had been earned. This is a general concept that is often labeled "assignment of income."

5. Alternative Minimum Tax: Individuals

Congress passed a law that in essence said that even if a taxpayer had a small amount of tax to pay under the normal or regular rules, Congress also requires taxpayers to calculate an Alternative Minimum Tax ("AMT"). And, if the AMT is greater than the Regular tax calculated, the taxpayer must, effectively, pay the greater of the two amounts, AMT or Regular Tax.

E. INSTALLMENT SALES

I. Overview

Under qualified circumstances, 26 U.S.C.A. §453 allows sales to be made and taxed on an installment basis. When the installment sale method is employed, it is possible for the taxpayer to reduce the amount of taxable income reportable in a given year by spreading the gain over a number of periods. 26 U.S.C.A. §453A allowed the installment sale method for dealers in personal property. (However, the TRA of 1986 and the RA of 1987 limited this position, as discussed below.)

State law will control whether an installment land contract by the Seller constitutes personal property or realty.

26 U.S.C.A. §453(a) states the general rule for the amount of income that is to be included. Under this Section the amount to be reported in a given taxable year is that proportion of the installment payment actually received in that year that the gross profit realized or to be realized when payment is completed, bears to the contract price. The contract price is defined subsequently.

26 U.S.C.A. §453 does not distinguish between tangible and intangible property.

As indicated earlier, the installment method can be used by a cash or accrual basis taxpayer, where the taxpayer otherwise qualifies. The installment election is unique: It can be applied to a number of pieces of property or simply one piece of property.

An installment method is defined under 26 U.S.C.A. §453(c), as a method in which the income recognized for any taxable year from a disposition is that proportion of the payments received in that year in which the gross profit (realized or to be realized when payment is completed) bears to the total contract price.

6 U.S.C.A. §453(a) provides the general rule that, except as otherwise provided, income from an installment sale shall be taken into account. In other words, the general proposition is that where the installment method applies, it is effective unless the taxpayer chooses *not* to make it effective.

Only one payment is necessary in any one year. Historically there was a requirement for two payments in two or more years. This requirement was eliminated, under the theory that it did not accomplish any major purpose, except to throw another pitfall in front of the taxpayer.

It is possible for a taxpayer to make an installment sale and transfer property in the current year, receiving no payments. All monies could be received in a subsequent year, and it would nevertheless qualify under the new rules.

There are exceptions to which the installment sale method will not apply, in addition to the electing out provision, noted subsequently.

2. Electing out of installment sales treatment

As mentioned, most transactions will qualify as installment sales, and 26 U.S.C.A. §453 will apply. 26 U.S.C.A. §453(d) specifically provides that the taxpayer need not use the installment sale method. The provision simply states: "Subsection (a) shall not apply to any disposition that the taxpayer elects to have Subsection (a) not apply." Thus, the taxpayer may elect out of the provision.

The election out provides that, with some exceptions, if the disposition falls within 26 U.S.C.A. §453, an election out of the rule can only be made on or before the due date prescribed by the law for filing the tax return, including extensions.

3. Limitations under Code §453

a. In general

Losses are not reported in installments.

The installment method does not affect the *character* of the gain realized. If the gain would normally be capital gain, it is still capital gain under the installment sale rule. The installment sale operates to affect the *time* period in which the gain is reported.

b. Disposition of installment obligations—Code §453B—Gain or Loss

Historically, the provisions for early dispositions of installment obligations have been provided under 26 U.S.C.A. §453(d). Provisions were added under 26 U.S.C.A. §453B to tax the taxpayer in question, where the taxpayer disposed of the installment obligation owing to the taxpayer.

Thus, if Taxpayer X sold a property and received 20% of the payment in the year of sale, with the balance owed to the taxpayer, and in a subsequent year, the taxpayer disposed of the obligation evidencing the indebtedness to the taxpayer, the balance of the unrecognized gain was recognized. This concept continues.

c. Related issues

As discussed, early dispositions of installment obligations generate the income previously postponed by the installment sale method.

d. Substituting

Substituting a new installment contract for an old installment contract will not generate realization and recognition where the parties are the same.

e. Pledging

Historically, the danger in improperly pledging installment obligations is that it might have been treated as a disposition. To this extent, it would cause immediate taxable income.

***

CHAPTER 4

Leases

A. INTRODUCTION

Not only do sales of real property generate tax consequences, but the leasing also has important tax implications. Rent deductions, depreciation, sale and lease-backs, security deposit questions, leasehold improvements, bonus payments, and other items must be considered.

B. IS IT A SALE OR LEASE?

One of the most important questions is whether a transaction constitutes a sale or a lease. The mere fact that the parties cast the transaction in a given light is not controlling if, in fact, it is a sale. A lease is an agreement whereby only the transfer of *possession* of the real property is made, with the intent that the property be returned, or transferred to a third party, after a given period of time. If the lessee acquires an equity interest in the property, as opposed to a mere leasing interest, this can result in a "sale" for tax purposes.

One of the most perplexing problems is determining whether a transaction constitutes a sale or a lease. The Service has held that it will make this decision case by case.

The Service has considered various items in determining whether to grant an advance ruling on this question. In dealing with personal property, the Courts seem to consider: (i) the term of the lease; (ii) the remaining useful life of the property after the expiration of the lease period; (iii) whether there are renewal options; (iv) the amount or the percentage of the property that is being financed; (v) whether there are any conditions upon the lessors ownership of the property after the termination of the lease; (vi) the possibility of terminating the lease; (vii) the treatment by the parties as to lease or sale conditions; (viii) accounting treatment used; (ix) whether the property is unique to the particular lessor-lessee; and (x) other items.

C. WHY LEASE?

Why would a lease be sought as opposed to a sale? Many times, a taxpayer wishes to purchase a property, but also wishes to have the present benefit of the deduction of the lease payments. For that reason, the transaction may be cast in the form of a lease, with an "option to buy" at the termination of the lease period. This would result, if not otherwise challenged by the Service, in the present deduction of the lease payments. Again, the substance of the matter will control.

D. Depreciation with Leases

1. Lessee

If the lessee makes the improvements on the property, the lessee claims the deductions over the useful life of the improvement. This is true even of the life of the asset exceeds the life of the lease.

2. Net-net-net lease

If the situation involves a net-net-net lease, that is, a lease where the lessee is to make not only lease payments to the lessor, but the lessee is to make all payments on the property, *and* otherwise to return the property in its *original condition, not* excluding ordinary wear and tear, the lessor may not take a depreciation deduction on the property. The theory supporting this result is that the property is in the same condition at the end of the lease as it was before the lease.

E. Improvements as Income

The improvements made by lessee do not generate income to the lessor, assuming the improvement is not a payment in *lieu of rent*. The same will not affect the basis of the property of the lessor, again, unless it constitutes an "in lieu of" rental payment.

F. Additional Payments

1. Lessor

If the lessor receives an additional payment from the lessee, either for an extension of the lease period, or an early cancellation, or for other reason under the lease, it will be treated as ordinary income.

2. Lessee

If the lessee receives payment from the lessor for an early cancellation of the lease, the payment is treated as a sale or exchange of the lease. This rule also applies with regard to modification of the lease.

Payments to the lessee for any other reasons, other than those indicated above, are generally treated as ordinary income. The lessor will treat payments he makes generally as capitalization of his cost and will amortize it over the remaining period of the cancelled lease.
***

CHAPTER 5

Mortgages Generally

A. In General

One of the most important benefits in owning most real property is the possibility of utilizing positive leverage. Leverage, simply stated, is the ability to apply a greater amount of debt as opposed to a lesser amount of equity when purchasing property.

Whether a property is purchased *subject to* a mortgage or the mortgage is *assumed* usually makes no difference in the *tax* law. In the first case, a "subject to" mortgage, only the realty is subject to the claim of the mortgage, as opposed to an individual. In the case of an assumption, individuals may be responsible for the debt in addition to the claim against the realty. There are some exceptions where the distinction between "subject to" and "assumed" can be important. See the discussion under the partnership area of the text where a "subject to" mortgage as opposed to an "assumed" mortgage can result in a step up of basis to the limited partners.

Mortgages are deemed part of cost, both for purposes of determining gain or loss, and for depreciation. This inclusion of the mortgage in the basis makes real estate even more attractive, since depreciation is computed on the basis.

There can be many implications to other alternative mortgage instruments. With shared-appreciation mortgages, there are several questions as to how the borrower and lender treat the tax implications.

B. Mortgages in Excess of Basis

If, after owning property X for a given period, A acquires a mortgage for $100,000 on the X property, which property has a basis of $90,000, excluding the new mortgage, the $10,000 difference between the basis and the loan is not taxable. If A was able to build an apartment house for $90,000 and then borrow $100,000 on the property, he would not only have his $90,000 in hand, but he would have an additional $10,000.

There are some limitations on the mortgage benefits: (i) as discussed under 26 U.S.C.A. §351 dealing with corporations, mortgages in excess of basis can result in tax liability; and (ii) also, as indicated in the text, if the mortgaged property is involved in an exchange, this may result in taxation where there is an assumption of a mortgage.

If the property subject to a mortgage is disposed of, the sales price would include the amount of the mortgage assumed by the purchaser; this is true even if the seller of the property is not personally liable for the property; that is, the property is purchased "subject to" a mortgage, as opposed to an "assumption" of the mortgage.

If there is a default on mortgaged property, there can be tax implications. If the mortgage is compromised, and part of the debt is cancelled as a result of a part pay-off by the debtor-mortgagor, this will produce taxable income. Generally, the cancellation of the mortgage amount will not constitute a gift. If property is only "subject to" a mortgage, and debt on the property is compromised or otherwise cancelled as noted above, ordinary income under 26 U.S.C.A. §61 might not be generated; the cancellation of the indebtedness may result only in a reduction of basis of the property.

C. Income can be Generated from the Discharge from Indebtedness, When the Basis is Less than FMV

Although it appeared fairly settled that income from discharge of indebtedness could be avoided by the use of 26 U.S.C.A. §108, where the taxpayer met the insolvency requirements.

Obviously, if the fair market value of the property is below the basis, the issue of generating gain in this setting is not relevant. In parts of the country where real estate values have substantially fallen, the issue in this Ruling would not be of concern. However, as in the example given, if the fair market value does exceed basis, but is less than the debt, the issue is present. [In such circumstances, informed taxpayers will obviously attempt to argue that the value of the property is equal to or less than the subject's basis. Certainly, additional legislation and/or case law will be reflective on this issue and for construing 26 U.S.C.A. §108.

D. Cancellation of Debt—Code §108(i)

The American Recovery and Reinvestment Act of 2009 (ARRA of 2009) provided for the potential of deferral of Cancellation of Debt (COD) income. Cancellation of Debt income is generated under Code §61(12), where such cancellation can result in taxable income. However, under Code §108(i), if one can fit the requirements, the income can be postponed.

E. Character of Payments Made on Mortgages

Payments made on a mortgage or deed of trust usually include principal, interest, insurance, and/or taxes. The payments made on principal, so far as the purchaser is concerned, have no effect on basis because the mortgage is a part of his basis and, for accounting purposes, the net effect is to reduce debt, and to increase equity.

F. Income and Mortgages

The placing of a mortgage on real property is not itself a taxable transaction for income tax purposes. This does not mean, however, that a mortgage on property does not have tax implications. Placing a mortgage on property, and then transferring the property in a "Tax Deferred Exchange" or transferring it to a corporation or other transfers to outside parties where there is an assumption of the loan, can result in a taxable event.

G. Corporations and Partnerships

Where there is a transfer of property to a corporation or a partnership and the property is encumbered by a mortgage on the property with the mortgage in excess of the adjusted basis of the transferor, under both corporation and partnership sections in the Code, taxable gain can result to the transferor.

H. Mortgage and Basis

As stated, a mortgage on property is generally considered part of the basis. If A purchases property for $40,000 cash and assumes an existing mortgage on the property for $60,000 or takes subject to it, the basis for the purchaser is $100,000. The $60,000 loan is deemed part of the cost. Therefore, it is apparent that a loan affects basis. It is this concept of a loan or encumbrance-mortgage being included as part of the basis that results in the tax benefits under the leverage principle. If B was to purchase an apartment house with no money down, but merely agreed to "take over" (assume) the obligations existing or encumbering the property being purchased, the basis to the purchaser is equal to the mortgage assumed. The purchaser will be able to take depreciation on the building equal to the amount of the mortgage attributable to the building, even though there is no out of pocket cash placed into the building by the purchaser.

If one purchases a building or other property and *subsequently* borrows money by putting a mortgage or deed of trust on the property, this will not increase the basis of the property. If the money is put into the property through improvements, such action will increase the basis of the property.

I. Prepayment Penalty

It is the current practice for lenders to provide for prepayment penalties. The prepayment penalty is the additional fee, beyond the normal interest provided for in the instrument, for the "privilege" of being allowed to prepay an amount that was otherwise payable over a longer period of time. It may be deductible as a business expense. Carried to an extreme, however, it is possible that such payments would be disallowed due to an improper tax motive. An extreme case might arise where there is some relationship between the mortgagee and the mortgagor. In such case, it might prove most advantageous to allow a current deduction of a large amount for the mortgagor by allowing the mortgagee to charge a prepayment penalty. If the mortgagee is the son of the mortgagor, and in a much lower tax bracket, it might be advisable to "refinance" by allowing a new mortgage to be issued and to charge a prepayment penalty against the mortgagor. The mortgagor would take the current deduction of the prepayment penalty and the mortgagee would pay the tax on that amount, but in a much lower tax bracket. A court might consider such action to be for tax avoidance purposes and it might disallow the deduction.

J. Debt and Income

As mentioned above, there can be income generated as a result of a discharge of debt, especially where there is a mortgage in excess of basis.

Generally speaking, income is generated when debt is eliminated, discharged, or cancelled.

There are situations where income will not be generated, even with debt relief. These are unusual. 26 U.S.C.A. §108 previously allowed for the exclusion of income where there was an adjustment to basis as provided under 26 U.S.C.A. §1017. In many cases such basis adjustment is not allowed. 26 U.S.C.A. §108 was modified by the TRA of 1986. It provided for a limitation on the exclusion from income from a discharge of indebtedness. The possibility of reducing basis, while still solvent, as a result of discharge of indebtedness, was repealed by the TRA of 1986. However, it was reinstated by the RRA of 1993.

Under RRA of 1993, 26 U.S.C.A. §108 was modified to allow the taxpayer to elect, assuming they were not a C Corporation, to exclude from gross income any amount if there was a discharge of debt and the taxpayer otherwise qualified within 26 U.S.C.A. §108. *(The taxpayer need not show he or she is insolvent or bankrupt to come within the rule.)*

There are many situations in between those outlined above. For example, does an adjustment of the purchase price by the debtor and the creditor generate taxable income? There seems to be some authority indicating it will not generate taxable income. There are some authorities that indicate that it is currently taxable and will generate income.

K. Repossessions and Foreclosures

Assuming the purchaser was unable to meet his commitments, the seller often has the security of a mortgage or deed of trust. If this is the case, the questions arise as to how the seller is to foreclose the property and the tax implications of this act. The procedural steps are a matter of local law and will not be discussed. The tax implications of such repossession, however, will be reviewed. They have an important effect in the real estate and tax field.

There are many tax aspects that must be reviewed when discussing mortgage foreclosures, repossessions, reacquisitions, and the like. As is the case in many areas in the tax field, it is important to determine which party is being examined, *e.g.*, creditor or the debtor.

* * *

CHAPTER 6

Entities in Syndications

Legal Principles for Entities and Tax Characteristics

A. Corporations—Corporate Organizations and Reorganizations—Property Transferred to Controlled Corporation in Exchange for Other Property—Non-Recognition of Gain or Loss to Transferor

1. Introduction

The following material is intended only to highlight the main areas of entity ownership and corporate and partnership tax law as they relate to real estate tax.

A corporation is an artificial entity, existing only in contemplation of law. That is, the entity exists because the state law allows, under a statute, the creation of the entity.

The choice of which entity to use, as discussed in this Part Three, normally is focused on two major areas of concern:

- Liability: The use of the corporation-type entity often protects the shareholders from being personally liable for the activities of the entity. Thus, a corporation might be formed when running a restaurant or bar. This helps to insulate the shareholders from personal liability for claims against issues connected with the business.
- Taxation: Some corporations were historically formed because the rate of tax at the corporate level was less than the individual rate. However, many of the tax laws in this area have changed, making the corporate entity a poor choice because of the need to pay a corporate tax AND an individual tax when dividends are distributed to the shareholder. It is for this reason, that is, the double tax, that most syndications do not favor the use of a corporation for the syndication. Further, the corporation, if it has losses and/or deductions cannot pass through the deductions to the shareholders. As such, given these tax disadvantages, again, the corporate form of entity is not often used in syndications. This topic is examined in detail later in this Part III of the text.

Certainly, investors would like to have both of the above benefits, *i.e.*, insulation from liability and tax benefits. Thus, as discussed subsequently in this material, promoters in syndications of real estate, among others, often choose an entity that will provide both of the above noted benefits, *i.e.*, limited liability and tax benefits. These two benefits can often be structured very favorably in syndications by using an LLC, among other entities. This matter will be examined in detail, later in this Part Three.

Under Federal income tax laws, 26 U.S.C.A. §351, there may be a transfer of property to a corporation, controlled by the transferor, and generally it will not result in any gain or loss on said transfer. For tax purposes, a general corporation is often referred to in the Federal Tax Laws as a "C" corporation. (It is under the "C" area of the Code that the corporate laws are generally located; hence, the name: "C Corporation.")

26 U.S.C.A. §351(a) provides that no gain or loss shall be recognized if *property* is transferred to a corporation by one or more persons solely in exchange for stock or securities in the corporation, and immediately after the exchange, such person or persons are in *control* of the corporation as defined under 26 U.S.C.A. §368(c). Notice the emphasis on the transfer of *property* (not services) and *solely* in exchange for *stock or securities* of this corporation, as opposed to other items.

2. Distributions of Property and Dividends by Corporations—Code §301

26 U.S.C.A. §301 provides the language to control distributions by corporations.

26 U.S.C.A. §301(b) provides for what is deemed to be the "amount distributed:"

(1) If property is distributed and the shareholder is not a corporation, the amount of money received plus the fair market value of the other property received is deemed to be the amount of distribution.

(2) If the shareholder is a corporation, with some exceptions, the amount of money received plus the *lesser* of the fair market value of the property received, or the adjusted basis in the hands of the distributing corporation, immediately before the distribution of the other property received, increased by the amount of gain to the distributing corporation that is recognized under 26 U.S.C.A. §311, and other sections, is the "amount distributed."

There are other modifications regarding the distribution rules, but in essence, the above rules state the amount of distribution.

3. Distributions and Redemption of Stock

Under 26 U.S.C.A. §302(a), the general rule is that if a corporation "redeems" (see 26 U.S.C.A. §317(b)) its own stock, the redemption payments are treated as a *distribution* in part or full payment in exchange for the stock. The character of such payments depends upon the subsections under 26 U.S.C.A. §302.

In summary, the character of the redemption is partially determined by 26 U.S.C.A. §301(c), *supra*, and the following, under 26 U.S.C.A. §302:

- Under 26 U.S.C.A. §302(b) (1), redemptions *not equivalent to dividends* receive the "exchange treatment" under 26 U.S.C.A. § 302(a). (If they are capital assets, it then follows that capital gain, as opposed to ordinary income, will result.)
- Under 26 U.S.C.A. § 302(b) (2), redemptions that are *substantially disproportionate* redemptions of stock, as defined under that section, are also treated as "exchanges" (not as ordinary dividends).
- Under 26 U.S.C.A. §302(b) (3), a complete termination of a shareholder's interest within the meaning of the Section, will result in an "exchange" treatment.

- Under 26 U.S.C.A. §302(b) (4), a redemption applies to a distribution if the distribution is:
  - in redemption of stock held by the shareholder who is not a corporation, and
  - in partial liquidation of the distributing corporation.

There are also other special sections under 26 U.S.C.A. §302(b) that allow for an "exchange treatment."

In the alternative, if the exchange rules under 26 U.S.C.A. §302(b) are not met, the distribution will be treated as a distribution under 26 U.S.C.A. § 301. 26 U.S.C.A. §302(d). That is, ordinary income may be the result.

4. Distributions of Stock and Stock Rights—Code § 305

Like the reasoning behind 26 U.S.C.A. §304, 26 U.S.C.A. §305 was enacted to prevent distributions of stock and stock rights to effectively avoid the dividend treatment under 26 U.S.C.A. §301.

5. Dispositions of Certain Stock—Code §306

A corporation is subject to having its distributions treated as dividends, under 26 U.S.C.A. §301, as mentioned, unless a special exception applies. One disadvantage with dividend treatment is taxation to the shareholder and additional taxation at the corporate level (double tax). Taxpayers generally favor the use of a corporation, but they do not favor the commonly referred to problem of "double taxation," as noted.

6. Corporate Reorganizations—Code §368

26 U.S.C.A. §368 defines the types of reorganizations. The overall key to most types of reorganizations is an attempt to undergo transformations without the recognition of taxable income. Whether this is possible depends on whether the requirements are met under 26 U.S.C.A. §368 and related sections.

In summary, the types and characteristics of 26 U.S.C.A. §368 reorganizations are:

a. 26 U.S.C.A. §368—A Reorganization

An "A" type reorganization (merger or consolidation) has its advantages in that it does not limit itself to the use of only stock in an exchange, as does a B reorganization, nor is it limited to an exchange of assets for stock, as in the case in a C reorganization. An A reorganization is usually easier to accomplish than a B reorganization.

b. 26 U.S.C.A. §368-B Reorganization

This type of reorganization involves an exchange of stock of one company for stock of another company. It is highly restricted as to the type of stock that may be used; it further limits the amount of boot, *i.e.*, non-stock, that may be received. It is hampered by the requirement of an 80% approval by the seller's shareholders.

c. 26 U.S.C.A. § 368—C Reorganization

A "C" reorganization allows an exchange of stock for assets. In effect, it is much the same as an "A" reorganization. There is also a requirement for a transfer of "substantially all the assets" of the acquired company. This requirement is sometimes difficult to meet. There is also a problem with boot, *i.e.,* where the assets are not exchanged solely for stock.

d. 26 U.S.C.A. §368D Reorganization.

Concerns itself with split-offs and spin-offs and basic divisive reorganizations.

e. 26 U.S.C.A. §368—E Reorganization

A recapitalization type of reorganization.

f. 26 U.S.C.A. §368—F Reorganization

A mere change in identity, form, or place of organization of one corporation. This is more of a technical reorganization.

g. 26 U.S.C.A. §368—G Reorganization

A transfer by a corporation of all or part of its orders to another corporation in a title 11 or similar bankruptcy matter.

7. Miscellaneous sections under corporate rules

a. Other Corporate Issues

There are many other sections of the corporate Code that must be discussed to properly fill the picture. However, most of these are outside the scope of this Work. The above discussion was intended as an overview; certainly, it did not discuss the details under the above provisions.

b. Foreign Corporations

There are also special rules for foreign companies. Foreign Corporations and foreign taxes in general are beyond the scope of this text.

c. Corporate Tax Rates

Regular C Corporations can be taxed, for federal income tax purposes at a rate of 15% on the low side to 39.6% on the high side.

B. PARTNERSHIPS AND LIMITED LIABILITY COMPANIES

1. Definitions—Code §761

A *partnership* is defined under 26 U.S.C.A. §761(a). It includes a syndicate, group, pool, joint venture, or other unincorporated organization.

Under the laws of the given state where the partnership might be created, the normal definition of a partnership involves two or more parties carrying on a business for profit. That is, unless otherwise agreed by the parties, when two or more parties create a business, and they have not otherwise created a vehicle in which to operate the business, the state law normally defers to the entity of a partnership. (This is a general partnership, since state law requires certain filings in most instances to create a limited partnership; thus, the failure to act to properly create a limited partnership, which normally requires at least one general partner and one limited partner, is that the entity will be treated as a general partnership.)

26 U.S.C.A. §761(c) provides that the partnership agreement includes "any modifications of the partnership agreement made prior to or at the time described by law for the filing of the partnership return for the taxable year."

2. Entity Election

The Treasury issued Proposed Regulation PS 43-95, and approved them under T.D. 8697. The rules address the question of the use of an election to determine the type of tax entity that exists.

In general, the rule allowed the entity to elect the type of treatment, basically corporation or partnership, for tax purposes.

Assuming there is a separate entity, in most instances the entity will be allowed to determine by its choice whether it will be treated as a corporation or a partnership for tax purposes. In some instances, there are default provisions that apply, absent an election to the contrary. That is, in general the determination will apply in a general way as a default provision. This supposedly is based on the expectation, normally, by parties. For example, if an organization has members that have personal liability, the expectation is that the entity would be classified as a partnership. If there is no liability, normally the default classification is as an association (corporation). [However, under these rules, an entity may file an election to obtain a chosen classification and avoid the default provision, at least in most instances.]

3. Partners subject to taxation

Under 26 U.S.C.A. §701, the basic principle of partnership taxation is stated: The partners, and not the partnership, are subject to tax. The partnership is a *conduit* for taxation purposes in the sense that no partnership bears tax, but the individual partners pick up their proportionate share of income or loss. The proportionate share rules and the other allocations that may be made are discussed subsequently. 26 U.S.C.A. §701 states:

> A partnership as such shall not be subject to the income tax imposed by this chapter. Persons carrying on business as partners shall be liable for income tax only in their separate or individual capacities.

4. Elections by partnerships

The determination of *character* of income is normally made at the *partnership* level. Most decisions as to elections affecting partners are made at the partnership level. 26 U.S.C.A. §703(b) specifically provides for elections affecting the computation of taxable income derived from the partnership to be made at the partnership level, with certain exceptions, *e.g.,* 26 U.S.C.A. §108 relating to the definition of discharge of debt. This is made at each partner's level, not the partnership level.

5. Computing partnership income

Under 26 U.S.C.A. §703, the taxable income of a partnership is computed in the same manner as an individual's income, with some exceptions. The exceptions basically provide exclusion from a double benefit. A partnership cannot take personal exemptions under 26 U.S.C.A. §151 or similar items, simply because the individual partner will claim these on his *own* personal return, when he also picks up his income from the partnership.

6. Distributive share of a partner

26 U.S.C.A. §702 provides for the individual accounting of income and credits of a partner. 26 U.S.C.A. §704 provides that a partner's distributive share of income, gain, loss, deduction, or credit is to be determined, except as otherwise provided in the Code, by the partnership agreement. (See 26 U.S.C.A. §761 for a definition of the "partnership agreement.")

Generally speaking, 26 U.S.C.A. § 704(b) provides that a partner's distributive share of any of the items, noted above (income, gain, loss, *etc.*) are determined in accord with his distributive share of taxable income or loss of the partnership (as determined by the partnership agreement), with two exceptions:

- the partnership agreement does not provide, as to the partner's distributive share, for another allocation; or
- the allocation to a partner does not have substantial economic effect.

Thus, 26 U.S.C.A. §704(b) provides that if partners distribute a share of income, gain, loss, deduction, or credit (or item thereof), it is determined in accord with the partner's interest in the partnership, taking into account all facts and circumstances, *if* the partnership agreement does not provide as to the partner's distributive share of these items or the allocation under the agreement does not have "substantial economic effect."

A special allocation (dividing the profit among the partners, not necessarily equal to the percentage of ownership in the partnership) is allowable, providing it has "substantial economic effect," and the partnership agreement provides for the same. See also 26 U.S.C.A. §737.

7. Deficit Reduction Act (DRA) and Timing to Report Income

The DRA provided that the Secretary has authority to require items of income, gain, loss, and deduction with respect to the contributed property to be shared among the partners to take into account the variations between the basis of the property and the fair market value of the property at the time of the contribution. The theory is this would allow a proper adjustment for the gain or loss that might be present that might otherwise be shifted or shared among the partners. 26 U.S.C.A. §704(c)(2)(A).

Congress intended to address situations in which a partner on the cash receipts and disbursements method of accounting contributes accounts receivable, accounts payable, or other accrued items, but unpaid items, to a partnership that uses the same method of accounting. Thus, if a cash method taxpayer contributes accounts payable to a cash method partnership, the deductions attributable to those items would be allocated to the contributing partner, if possible.

Likewise, such changes are made to reflect accrued items, but unpaid, so as not to be treated as partnership liabilities under 26 U.S.C.A. §752.

The Secretary of the Treasury may decide to require the taxpayers to allocate only certain gain or loss on contributed property under 26 U.S.C.A. §704(c) and permit allocations of depreciation and other items to be governed by 26 U.S.C.A. §704(b).

8. Tax year partner and partnership

Under 26 U.S.C.A. §706, the partnership's taxable year is determined almost as though the partnership were, in effect, an individual. This rule is an overgeneralization. However, most partnerships use a calendar tax year.

The tax law has imposed additional restrictions on the use of tax years for partnerships, S Corporations and personal service corporations, in addition to the existing special restrictions. In general, partnerships, S Corporations and personal service corporations must conform their tax years to the taxable years of their owners. It is possible to have an exception to this if the entity can show, to the satisfaction of the Secretary of the Treasury, that there is a business purpose for having a different tax year.

(An S Corporation, as discussed later in this material, is the same as a C Corporation for many purposes, but it does not normally have to pay a corporate tax. Again, this topic is discussed later in this Part Three.)

Although the rules before the TRA of 1986 provided that partnerships generally must adopt the tax year of its majority partners, there have been questions if partners owning a majority of the partnership profits and capital did not have the same taxable year.

Under the provisions of the 1986 TRA, partnerships were required to adopt the same tax year as the partners owning a majority interest in the partnership's profits and capital. If the partners owning a majority interest do not have the same tax year, the partnership would adopt the same tax year as all of its principal partners. If the partners owning a majority of partnership profits and capital or all of the partnership's principal partners have different years, the partnership would adopt a calendar year. 26 U.S.C.A. §706(b)(1).

S Corporations and personal service corporations (such as law firms) would generally be forced into use of a calendar year.

9. Partnership—Continuity

Under 26 U.S.C.A. §706, the taxable year of the partner in a partnership was mentioned. 26 U.S.C.A. §708 deals with *continuation* of a partnership. A partnership, tax wise, continues unless there is a specific rule providing for its termination. Termination rules are provided under 26 U.S.C.A. §708(b). A partnership is considered terminated if:

(a) no part of any business, financial operation or venture of the partnership continues to be carried on by any of the partners in the partnership, *or*

(b) within a 12-month period, there is a sale or exchange of *50% or more* of the total interests in the partnership capital and profits. Under a Ruling, the partnership will not terminate if there is cash paid to the partnership by new partners and the new partners acquire more than a 50% interest in the partnership.

If A and B were to build a new building and owned it in partnership, and subsequently A transferred his 50% interest to Mr. C, this is a transfer of "50% or more" within the language mentioned. There is a termination of the tax year of the partnership. This is true, notwithstanding the fact that the partnership may have a clause that allows the partnership to be continued by B and C.

The Service has held that where there are payments by new partners in exchange for more than 50% of the capital and profits interest, there would not be a 26 U.S.C.A. §708(b)(1) termination in that there was not a sale or exchange of partnership interests by or between members of that partnership.

There may be very adverse tax implications to termination of a partnership. Those adverse events may mean that taxable income is generated!

10. Losses in partnerships

One of the limits on deducting losses from a partnership is provided under 26 U.S.C.A. §704(d). A partner's distributive share of partnership loss, including capital loss, is only allowed to the extent of the partner's adjusted basis in the partnership at the end of the partnership year in which the loss was incurred. Any excess of such loss over the adjusted basis is allowed as a deduction at the end of the partnership year in which such excess is repaid to the partnership. To the extent that one partner has heavy leverage, with no basis by debt, it could be that although the partnership may generate a loss, that partner will not be allowed to deduct his proportionate share of that loss until his basis is at least equal to that amount of loss.

26 U.S.C.A. §704(d) was amended to provide that a partner may deduct losses, under the general rule, up to the amount of his adjusted basis and to the extent of any items for which he has liability. A partner's adjusted basis will *not* generally include that *portion* of the partnership liability where the partner has no personal liability. (There are exceptions to this rule, such as the case where no partner is liable.)

11. Tax free creation of partnership

26 U.S.C.A. §721, one of the simplest, but powerful, rules of partnership law, states: "No gain or loss shall be recognized to a partnership or to any of its partners upon a contribution of property to the partnership in exchange for an interest in the partnership." Therefore, where A, B, and C combine their interests by forming a partnership, there is no gain or loss recognized on such contributions if the general rule under 26 U.S.C.A. §721 is applicable. There are exceptions. See 26 U.S.C.A. §721(b).

12. Basis of partner's interest in partnership—§ 705

26 U.S.C.A. §705 determines *basis* of a partner's interest. This section operates in conjunction with 26 U.S.C.A. § 722, which relates to *contributions to a partnership* and 26 U.S.C.A. §742 that relates to *transfers of partnership interests.*

In essence, the basis of a partner's interest in a partnership is: (i) his adjusted basis (for example, $20,000) of property transferred to the partnership; (ii) increased by the sum of his distributive share for the taxable year and prior years of (a) taxable income (assume $10,000) of the partnership, (b) income of the partnership exempt from tax, and (c) the excess of the deductions for depletion over the basis of the property subject to the depletion; and (iii) decreased, but not below zero, by distributions by the partnership (assume $5,000) and the sum of that partner's distributive share for the taxable year and prior years of (a) losses of the partnership, and (b) expenditures of the partnership not deductible in computing taxable income and not properly chargeable to capital account. [In summary, $20,000 + $10,000 - $5,000 = $25,000]. (There is an alternative rule under 26 U.S.C.A. §705(b) for determining basis.)

26 U.S.C.A. §722 provides that the *basis of a contributing partner's interest* in the partnership is the amount of money contributed and the *adjusted basis* of such property to the contributing partner at the time of the contribution to the partnership.

In essence, basis in the partnership interest is the basis in the property contributed, adjusted as noted.

13. Basis of distributed property other than money

Under 26 U.S.C.A. §732, distributions, *other than in liquidation* of a partner's interest, of property results in a basis of that property, other than money distributed by a partnership to a partner, in an amount equal to the adjusted basis *to the partnership* of the distributed property, immediately before the distribution. If the partnership was to distribute an apartment building with an adjusted basis of $2 million, and a fair market value of $3 million, and it was *not a distribution in liquidation,* the adjusted basis to the partnership would carry over to the partner-distributee. There are exceptions: The basis to the distributee partner in property to which the above rule is applicable cannot exceed the adjusted basis of the partner's interest in the partnership, reduced by any money the partner receives. In the above example, if the partner's basis in the partnership was $1,500,000, his basis in the distributed apartment house would be limited to $1,500,000, reduced by any money distributed to the partner at the same time.

14. Basis of distributee partner's interest—Code §733

Where there is a distribution by the partnership to a partner, and there is *not a liquidation,* there must be an adjustment to the partner's basis. The adjusted basis to the partner of his *interest in the partnership* must be reduced, but not below zero, by the amount of any money distributed to the partner and any amount of the basis to such partner of the distributed property, as determined under the above rules.

If the partner's basis, prior to distribution, was $100,000, and $20,000 cash and property, with an adjusted basis of $15,000, was distributed—the partner's new adjusted basis is $100,000-$35,000, or $65,000.

15. Basis to the partnership of property contributed to a partnership

To turn the matter around, the basis of property contributed to a *partnership,* as far as the *partnership* is concerned, is the adjusted basis of the property to the contributing partner. The basis is *transferred* from the partner to the partnership. 26 U.S.C.A. §723.

There are also some very unusual and somewhat complicated rules for *optional adjustments to basis* of partnership property. Under 26 U.S.C.A. §743(a), the basis of partnership property is generally not adjusted as a result of a *transfer of an interest* in a partnership by sale or exchange or on the death of a partner, unless a *special election* is made as provided under 26 U.S.C.A. §754 of the Code. [This relates to an optional adjustment to the basis of partnership property. However, for an exception, see 26 U.S.C.A. §743(d).]

16. Distributions—Recognition of gain or loss

Because partnerships are not taxable entities, there is generally no gain or loss recognized on distributions from the partnership to the partners. Gain or loss, as indicated, is recognized by the individual partners, by picking up their proportionate share of the gain or loss.

Where there are distributions from the partnership, adjustments are required. 26 U.S.C.A. §731(a) provides that where there is a distribution by a partnership to a partner, *gain* is not recognized to such partner, except to the extent that any *money distributed exceeds the adjusted basis of the partner's interest in the partnership* immediately before the distribution.

Losses are generally not recognized by a partner where there is a distribution. Where there is a *liquidating* distribution of a partner's interest in a partnership and the only property distributed is: (i) money; and (ii) the basis to the distributee, as determined under 26 U.S.C.A. §732, as to unrealized receivables and inventory (see subsequent discussion), the loss is recognized to the extent of the excess of the adjusted basis of such partner's interest in the partnership, over the amount of the items mentioned, that is, the money distributed and the basis to the distributee under 26 U.S.C.A. §732 of the unrealized receivables and inventory.

Aside from certain overriding rules as mentioned subsequently under 26 U.S.C.A. §751, any gain or loss recognized on the distribution is considered as gain or loss from the sale or exchange of the partnership interest of the distributee. (These rules affect the treatment to the *partners*).

As to the *partnership*, no gain or loss is recognized on a distribution to a partner of property, including any money distributions. See 26 U.S.C.A. §731(b).

The above rules are subject to exceptions. There is the exception mentioned under 26 U.S.C.A. §751, relating to unrealized receivables and inventory. (See *infra*.) 26 U.S.C.A. §731(c) provides an exception whereby, if 26 U.S.C.A. §736 applies, which deals with payments to a *retiring* partner or *deceased* partner, 26 U.S.C.A. §736 overrides the provisions discussed above under 26 U.S.C.A. §731. There are other exceptions.

17. Unrealized receivables and inventory items—Ordinary income property

26 U.S.C.A. §751 provides for an overriding treatment to *change what would have been capital gain into ordinary income.* It operates on a theory much like the application of 26 U.S.C.A. §§1245 and 1250. Those sections also function to change what would have been capital gain into ordinary income. It stops the collapsible partnership.

26 U.S.C.A. §751 provides that the amount of any money, or fair market value of any property, received by a transferor partner in exchange for all or part of his interest in a partnership, where that transfer is attributable to: (i) unrealized receivables of the partnership, or (ii) inventory, is considered as amounts realized from the sale or exchange of property that is *not* from the sale or exchange of a capital asset. In other words, it will not generate capital gain or loss.

18. Transactions between partner and partnership—Guaranteed payments

26 U.S.C.A. §707(c) provides that

> to the extent determined without regard to the income of the partnership, payments to a partner for services or the use of capital shall be considered as made to one who is not a member of the partnership, but only for the purpose of 26 U.S.C.A. §61(a) (relating to gross income) and 26 U.S.C.A. § 162(a) (relating to trade or business expense).

19. Entities: Limited liability type companies

A Limited Liability Company ("LLC") and other types of limited entities are normally structures created by state laws, with tax related issues. However, in summary form, most of these types of limited entities, from the Federal Tax point of view, are treated as partnerships.

Although the focus of this material is in the area of real estate tax, and in this area on partnerships, additional entities have appeared on the horizon, namely limited liability companies (LLC), Limited Liability Partnerships (LLP), Limited Liability Limited Partnerships (LLLP), Limited Partnership Associations (LPA), and other similar vehicles. As noted, this issue is placed in this area as it appears that the Federal tax law will treat many of these types of entities, herein labeled as LLE (limited liability entity) as a partnership for most tax purposes.

20. The LLE is a creation of statute

From a tax standpoint, these LLEs are generally treated similar to partnerships, in that the tax law generally allows a flow-through of gains and losses to the owners, labeled as "members" in the LLC/LLC statutes.

The LLC/LLE seemingly has the advantages of the corporation for limited liability and the tax advantages of a partnership, for most purposes.

An LLC is generally thought to have more favorable advantages than an S Corporation, from a tax standpoint. (This assumes it will be respected as a partnership for tax purposes, consistent with the Federal Government's position and the position of most of the states.)

Although S corporations are limited (see later in this Part Three) as to who can be shareholders and limited to a maximum of 100 shareholders, there are no similar limitations on LLCs.

Certainly, they have associates and carry on a business for profit. In other words, they have the characteristics in common with most partnerships and corporations. However, quite often they do not have the characteristics of continuity of life and free transferability of shares. Therefore, for Federal tax purposes they are normally treated as a partnership. (Some states are also treating the entity in the same fashion. Other states have not ruled on this position. In addition, other states might treat the entity as a corporation for both tax and liability purposes. However, most states are treating a LLC as a partnership.)

C. Contrast of Corporations and Partnerships/LLCs

1. Corporation versus partnership

One of the most important business tax planning determinations is the type of legal entity to use. This area discusses the advantages and disadvantages of using the corporate form of organization as opposed to a partnership/LLC form. Obviously this problem is very complex; therefore, only some of those items that appear most important in resolving the above question of choosing the structure or form are analyzed in the following sections.

2. Corporations and partnerships in general—Historical position

A corporation has been referred to as an "artificial being, intangible, invisible, and existing only in contemplation of law." A corporation is created under statute. The corporation is composed of shareholders who hold stock and operate under a common name. A corporation has associates, it is organized to carry on a business, it usually also has the characteristics of continuity of life, centralized management, limited liability and free transferability of shares. These characteristics are discussed, *infra*.

CAVEAT: As mentioned above, the Treasury approved Regulations under T.D. 8697, allowing entities to file a form to choose the type of tax structure that is desired.

The Service issued PS 43-95, which involved Proposed Regulations to undertake the prior Announcement in Notice N95-14, 1995-1 C.B. 297, which Notice allows for an elective position to select or choose the type of entity, in many cases, that would exist, *vis-à-vis*, a corporation or partnership in most instances. These were made final under T.D. 8697.

The basic rule allows for the taxpayer, with certain exceptions, to avoid some of the uncertainties that previously existed under the Regulations (§301.7701-2). These prior Regulations normally focused on six corporate characteristics. "Associates" (two or more), and "carrying on a business for profit" are common to partnerships and corporations. Therefore, the main focus over the last number of years, to determine for Federal tax purposes whether there is an Association (corporation) or partnership was to look to see if a dominant number of the remaining four characteristics exist. Thus, if three of the four or all of the four of the following characteristics are present, corporate or association treatment would be present. These characteristics are Centralized management, continuity of existence, limited liability and transferability of shares.

These tests have for the most part been eliminated under the check-the-box test. Under this test, taxpayers will **elect** to be a corporation or a partnership by **filing a form with a service center.** The form would also be included with the taxpayer's tax return. The form could be undertaken by all of the members in the entity or by the person or parties who are delegated to act for the entity.

Although there are some exceptions to this option to elect, such as some corporations that, for Federal tax purposes, are automatically classified as corporations, and a single individual cannot be a partnership, most entities may choose between corporate or partnership tax treatment. (If one is an individual, the individual may act as a corporation or as a sole proprietorship. It cannot be a partnership.)

For tax purposes, a corporation might not be treated as a corporation, notwithstanding any agreements or local law. When creating the business entity, investors must be careful to comply not only with state law, but also with federal requirements under the Internal Revenue Code. For tax purposes, historically, *prior to the Check-the-Box Regs.*, an organization would be treated as a corporation only if the corporate characteristics, noted subsequently, outnumbered the non-corporate characteristics.

A partnership is an association of two or more people who carry on a business, for profit. (For most purposes, tax wise, it is likely that an LLC will be treated the same as a partnership.)

For tax purposes, the Code defines a partnership as including any unincorporated organization carrying on a business for profit that is not a trust or an estate. It could include a syndicate, pool, joint venture, group, or other combination not otherwise included in the grouping of a corporation, trust, or estate.

Not only should the businessman, investor, etc., be concerned with *choosing* the type of entity structure, but he must be sure that the structure will be treated in the manner elected.

Assuming there can be compliance as required for both state and tax purposes, to assure the treatment desired, what are the factors to consider when choosing the *modus operandi?*

There are many other variables when choosing the structure for a business. The previous discussion is sufficient to warn the reader there are many considerations that must be weighed when making this determination.

3. "Check-the-Box" Regulations Allow for Selection of an Entity

Aside from new Regulations, noted below, for practically the history of the Federal income tax law, once entities were considered, there has been the issue as to how one knows, for tax purposes, whether the entity in question would be taxed as a "flow through" to the individual, or partnership, or taxed as a corporation or other entity or hybrid. As noted, this issue has been addressed over the years by numerous cases, Internal Revenue Service authority, Treasury Releases and interpretations, all to determine the tax entity at the local, state and Federal levels.

D. Hybrid Forms of Corporations and Partnerships

Before proceeding to the characteristics that might apply to a "general" corporation or a general partnership, the reader should note there are special types of corporations and special types of partnerships. For example, there can be tax option corporations, sometimes referred to as Subchapter S Corporations or S Corporations. See below. There are also special types of partnerships that are modified forms of a general partnership.

1. Corporation versus partnership—Taxes in general

One of the basic tax differences between a corporation and a partnership is entity taxation. A corporation is taxed on its income, as are the shareholders when they receive dividends (assuming there are earnings and profits). There is the exception for an S Corporation. The S shareholders are required to report the income, whether distributed or retained by the corporation. A partnership is required to file an information return, but it is not taxed on its income directly; the partners report their pro rata share of income on their individual returns, even if there is no partnership distribution.

A partnership is referred to as a "conduit" for tax purposes, not as a separate taxpayer. The "regular" corporation is a separate entity for many local law purposes and also for tax purposes.

The subsequent discussion analyzes considerations when owning property as: (i) an individual; (ii) a trust or estate; (iii) a corporation or other association taxed as a corporation; and (iv) a partnership or other joint venture. The characteristics of these types of ownership are reviewed, along with certain non-tax factors.

Smaller real estate investments are *usually* not owned by corporations. This is true because of a desire to avoid double taxation and to pass through current losses generated by depreciation and other "write offs." A corporation cannot pass losses through to shareholders. Usually a partnership allows more flexibility for distributions.

2. Character of income

For partnership purposes, income or deductions of a partnership retain their same character when passed through to the partners. They are reported by them on their individual returns. In contrast, distributions from corporations are taxed as ordinary income, notwithstanding whether the income generated when the corporation earned the money was capital gain or of any other character other than ordinary income.

The conduit principle is important and should be considered when choosing the form of ownership. If a corporation earned interest from municipal bonds, the corporation might not pay federal income tax on this interest, but a distribution from the corporation, to the extent there are earnings and profits, could result in taxation to the shareholder. By contrast, a distribution of the municipal interest by a partnership would result in no federal tax to the partners because the income retains its tax exempt character.

3. Partnerships—Character of Gain or Loss on Contributed Property

In some instances, there has been a conversion of what would be ordinary income into capital gain where dealer status might exist at a partner level but not at a partnership level through the dealer/partner contributing property to a partnership, which then sells it.

To prevent this gain from being changed from ordinary income to capital gain, the Federal tax law provides that if a partnership disposes of property that was inventory property in the hands of the partner prior to the contribution, any gain or loss recognized by the partnership on the disposition of that property within a given time frame in the Code is ordinary income or loss.

Gain or loss on the disposition of unrealized receivables by a partner is treated as ordinary income or loss regardless of the date of disposition.

Losses on capital assets retain their character as capital losses, within the above rule, but only to the extent of pre-contribution unrealized losses.

There are special carryover rules with regard to distribution of property. For example, if property subject to 26 U.S.C.A. §735 (character of gain or loss on disposition of distributed property) is disposed of in a non-recognition transaction, the treatment for the transferred property will carry over to any substitute basis property resulting from that transaction. 26 U.S.C.A. §§704(c), 743(b), and 613A(c) (7)(D).

The conduit concept similarly applies to corporation deductions. Where a charitable contribution is made by a corporation, only the corporation can take the deduction, to the extent it is allowed. With partnership contributions, the partners will each receive a pro rata benefit, based on percentage of their ownership interest, unless a different valid allocation is made.

4. Corporation tax rates

A corporation has different tax rates from those applied to individuals. Where the corporation will pay a standard rate on gain, based on its tax rates, a partnership, via the partners, will have different rates applied to the same type of gain; these rates will depend upon the individual partners' tax brackets. Again, the conduit principle has important consequences.

5. Time period for reporting

Partnership earnings for the partnership's taxable year are taxable to the partners whether or not the profits from the partnership are actually distributed.

Corporate earnings (absent an S election) are taxed to the corporate shareholders only when they are actually or constructively distributed to the shareholders. Without distribution, only the corporation will pay tax on the profits.

When the S election is made, not to be taxed as a regular corporation, the corporation will pay no tax, but the shareholders must report the taxable income for the year in which the corporate tax year ends.

An S Corporation is not identical to a partnership, as discussed as the S Corporation is only a partial conduit, *i.e.*, there is only a partial retention of the character of income. Specifically, long term capital gain will retain its character; the other items will generally lose their special character.

6. Losses

Losses of a partnership are reported by the partners (within limits as noted subsequently) whether or not there is an actual distribution. The loss can be a "valuable asset" as it can offset other income. By contrast, a corporation (except an S Corporation) can only deduct its losses with regard to *its* income; individual shareholders will not directly obtain a benefit by a pass-through of the losses.

7. Tax rates—Corporations

Generally speaking, pay federal income tax rates on their income of between 15% to 39.6%.

8. Termination of corporations and partnerships

There can be many adverse tax implications on the unplanned termination of a corporation or partnership. The scope of liquidations and reorganizations of corporations and partnerships is beyond the intent of the text.

9. Partnership losses—Limited partners

A partner is limited to a maximum of his adjusted basis in the partnership and his share of partnership debt when deducting his share of losses from the partnership. The Regulations provide the limited partner's share of partnership liabilities cannot exceed the actual contribution and the additional contributions that the limited partner is obligated to pay under the limited partnership agreement.

Under the Uniform Limited Partnership Act ("ULPA") (adopted by many states) and the Revised ULPA, as adopted by most states, a limited partner is liable to the partnership for the difference between his actual contributions and the total contribution he agreed to make if required under conditions of the partnership agreement.

10. Subchapter S Corporations and S Corporations

Some years ago, strong feelings were expressed by a number of influential parties that there was no reason to treat differently, for tax purposes, shareholders of a closely held corporation and those involved in a partnership. The thought was that the corporation should be relieved from paying taxes, and to allow individual shareholders to report the gain or loss produced from the "corporation." In 1954, such a position was approved by the Senate. The 1954 position by the Senate died in the Conference Committee. The same concept was later passed in 1958, and was referred to as Subchapter S of the Internal Revenue Code, which consisted of 26 U.S.C.A. §§1371 to 1379.

Often there is the concern as to whether it is best to elect this S Corporation form.

If a corporation was a Subchapter S Corporation, it was as much a corporation as what might be referred to as the "normal" or C Corporation. The Subchapter S Corporation had unique features, discussed subsequently. S Corporations should also be contrasted with LLCs.

11. C Corporation

A C Corporation means with respect to any taxable year a corporation that is not an S Corporation for that year.

12. S Corporation defined

26 U.S.C.A. §1361(a)(1) provides that the term an "S Corporation" means with respect to any taxable year a small business corporation for which an election under 26 U.S.C.A. §1362(a) is in effect for such year. The benefits of S Corporation have been elected.

26 U.S.C.A. §1361(b)(1) provides that the term "small business corporation" means a domestic corporation that is not otherwise ineligible. It also does not include a corporation that:

- has more than 100 shareholders (the prior rule, before this change to 100 shareholders, was 75 shareholders);
- has a shareholder as a person, other than an estate and other than a trust described below, one who is not an individual or one who is not otherwise a qualified shareholder;
- has a non-resident alien as a shareholder; and
- has more than one class of stock. In other words, any of the four items noted above would eliminate the S treatment.

26 U.S.C.A. §1361 defines an ineligible corporation as any corporation that is:

- a member of an affiliated group, determined under 26 U.S.C.A. §1504, without regard to exceptions as provided under 26 U.S.C.A. §1504(b);
- certain types of financial institutions;
- types of insurance companies;
- a corporation to which an election applies as to a Puerto Rico entity; or
- a Domestic International Sales Corporation (DISC).

13. Election—26 U.S.C.A. §1362: Election of S Treatment

26 U.S.C.A. §1362(a) provides for an election to be treated as an S Corporation.

The rule provides that an election is valid only if all persons who are shareholders in the corporation on the day on which the election is made consent to that election.

14. Major Features of S Election: Effect of Election of a Corporation

Under 26 U.S.C.A. §1363, with some exceptions, an S Corporation is not subject to tax imposed by the normal corporate rules. This is the effect of making the Subchapter S election.

The taxable income of an S Corporation is computed in the same manner as in the case of an individual, with a few exceptions.

15. Tax treatment to shareholders—Pass-Through of Items to Shareholders

Except as noted below, under 26 U.S.C.A. §1366(a), in determining the tax for a shareholder for the shareholder's taxable year in which this S Corporation ends, or for the final taxable year of a shareholder who dies before the end of the corporation's taxable year, there is considered the shareholder's pro rata share of the corporation's:

- Income, including tax-exempt income, losses, deductions, or credits, the separate treatment of which could affect the liability of any tax for any shareholder; and
- Non-separately computed income or loss.

16. Real Estate Investment Trusts and Other Entities

a. REITs in general

The real estate investment trust, hereinafter referred to as REIT, is allowed through the medium of 26 U.S.C.A. §§856 to 859. These sections were passed in 1960. In recent years the use of the REIT has, again, gained favor.

The purpose of the REIT is to allow a small investor, in theory, to invest in a diversified portfolio of real estate investments.

The beneficial ownership of the REIT shares must generally be held by *100* persons or more during at least 335 days of the taxable year of 12 months or during a proportionate part of a taxable year if it is a tax year of less than 12 months. 26 U.S.C.A. §§ 856(a) and (b).

26 U.S.C.A. §857(a) provides that for a REIT to avoid taxation at the entity level, it must distribute 90% or more of its taxable income.

b. REIT Taxation

REITs must meet the requirements under 26 U.S.C.A. §4981, requiring the payment of excise tax on *undistributed* income of Real Estate Investment Trusts. (Some of these technical rules were modified by the TRA of 1997.)

There are other adjustments and considerations under the provisions for distribution. However, in general, REITs must be aware of these requirements and meet the requirements to avoid an additional excise tax burden and possibly lose their REIT status.

As explained, a REIT generally receives its income from real estate activities of a properly qualified nature. If the REIT qualifies for REIT treatment, the income distributed to the investors is taxed to the investors, and there is no entity or REIT tax. The REIT will be subject to the corporate tax rates on the income that it does not distribute, and on certain foreclosure income from property.

17. TIC—Tenants in Common—the "Non-Entity"

As discussed in Part One, a tenancy in common ("TIC"), is a group of investors that own together, but not as a partnership or other entity. It is as undivided owners.

This issue, as stated in Part One, can be important to help determine if there is or is not a security involved. It may also be important to determine, for tax purposes, if the group calling themselves a "TIC" will be treated for tax purposes as a non-entity or as an entity, often defaulting to the position of a general partnership.

Recall that Part One, stated the following as to the Government's tax position as to whether a TIC would be considered a non-entity or a partnership.

In its Rev. Proc. (RP) 2002-22 ("2002-22"), regarding the issue to determine if the given TIC is an entity (*e.g.*, a partnership) for tax purposes, the RP listed 15 conditions. If all these conditions were present, the Taxpayers could apply for a Private Letter Ruling to see if the Treasury would conclude that the TIC would in fact be treated as a TIC and not as a legal entity, such as a partnership. This conclusion is very important, since the interests held by a TIC owner possibly could be exchanged under Code Section 1031 (see *supra*, Part Three for taxes) for other qualified property in an exchange. On the other hand, if the Treasury concluded that the TIC does not exist as individual owners, but the group investing is a Partnership, such interests are NOT allowed to be exchanged, tax deferred, under Code Section 1031.

***

PART FOUR

A POTPOURRI OF PRACTICAL ISSUES IN SYNDICATION OF REAL ESTATE

CHAPTER 1

Introduction

In this Part, we are focused on the myriad of practical issues that arise when one is involved in syndication. We are not concerned with the regulatory positions as the main focus at this time. Many of the state and Federal rules in the securities area have been addressed. However, in addition to following all the statutes and other controlling authorities, there are many practical issues that occupy the time and energies of the syndicator/sponsor/issuer. This Part addresses many of these concerns and issues that must be tackled, successfully, to undertake, with success, the syndication of real estate.

***

CHAPTER 2

What Did You Say is a "Syndication"?

Although we have learned that there are formal definitions that must be examined in this area, including the basic definition of what is a syndication, there are many generic uses of the term "syndication."

When using the term "syndication" in the context of this Work, the term is referring to putting together a group of people/entities that might be involved in the acquisition and development of real estate. Such "group" might consist of only two people and/or entities. One may be the individual or entity directing the day to day activity; or, one might be the passive investor. (In a general partnership and in an LLC, both parties can be involved in the active, day-to-day activities of the investment/syndication in question. However, in an LP, the General Partner has all the management power and responsibility; the limited partners are not supposed to participate in management as a matter of law.)

In most real estate circles, the term "syndication" means the involvement of two or more people or entities involved in real estate, with, normally, one or more persons undertaking the daily activity and one or more other parties supplying the capital. The latter such parties are normally the passive investors in the syndication.

Having studied some of the rules and implications of dealing in securities, there remain many issues that must be addressed as to dealing with the investment. The issue as to who makes the decisions must be addressed. Who will handle the daily and the unusual questions that will arise with the investment in the syndication? What happens if a party to the group/syndication can no longer function with the syndication and/or no longer chooses to function with the group? After all, death, disability, bankruptcy, and other intervening events must be considered as part of the "real world" in syndicating. "Things Happen" and these and related issues must be anticipated. Of course, well drafted documents that cover the syndication, such as the Operating Agreement for an LLC, might cover some or all of these factors. But, the key is that the syndicator and counsel try to anticipate and craft solutions for as many of these unknown and known issues that might impact the operation and future of the syndication. (Additional "practical" issues are addressed later in this Part Four.)

***

CHAPTER 3

Why Syndicate?

A good syndicator will anticipate the concerns, needs and idiosyncrasies of each property and syndication. That is, for example, if the property in question is located further away from the manager of the property, this difference, among many must be considered.

If many of the investors are older, the concern with transfer of interests in the syndication on death and/or disability of an investor must be considered. (Of course, all potential future transfers must be considered in the syndication.)

If the nature of the syndication is susceptible to many changes in the marketplace, political issues, financial concerns in the marketplace, etc., these and many other issues must be well-thought-out. For example, if the property in question is an apartment building that was syndicated, what impact might there be on the investment group if rent controls are suddenly imposed, impacting the rental stream of the property in question?

Is the property/syndication substantially dependent on one or more key people to make it successful? What if those key people are no longer involved with the project, possibly because of death, disability, change of economic circumstances, etc.?

If the above issues, and many more, are not anticipated on the front end of the syndication, it is likely that many investors will hesitate to join the group; or, it is possible, that if the syndication goes forward, there will be huge issues to address at a later time when some of these unforeseen and/or unaddressed issues arise. This is not always a legal matter. But, it is a real world, practical matter that must be examined on a timely basis!

* * *

CHAPTER 4

Is Syndicating for Everyone?

Why does one syndicate? The most fundamental answer is that one syndicates to make a profit. But, one can also, potentially, earn a profit by buying, operating and selling the property in question. Thus, the issue: Why syndicate?

Of course, the answer may be a traditional response: OPM. That is, use "Other Peoples' Money." Although funding is one of the factors that should be considered when syndicating, that certainly should NOT be THE reason to syndicate. That is, merely having money available from other parties is NOT the reason to syndicate.

Another very compelling question is who should be in the business of syndication? It is not for everyone. Even in the most one-sided, manager friendly operating agreements, investor members will be empowered with certain rights. The syndicator will not be free to do anything he or she wants. The responsibilities of being entrusted with other people's money are not to be taken lightly.

Further, the property to be syndicated must be "right" for the syndication. Many issues must be addressed. For example, consider:

1. Does the syndicator want to be involved with others?
2. Is the property one that the syndicator should buy with others?
3. Does the syndicator know and understand the property that is being considered for the syndication? (Sometime people know one area of the real property spectrum, *e.g.*, residential real estate, but they know very little about other areas of real property investment. In such situation, it would not normally be wise for the syndicator to attempt to syndicate property of a type that is not well understood by the syndicator. In the example given, it would not normally make sense for this syndicator to suddenly try to syndicate a retail property, when the key manager/syndicator has only a knowledge base in residential real estate.)
4. Later in this Part Four, the issue of "suitability" will be addressed. For now, one can consider whether the property in question for syndication is the "right" property, an appropriate investment, for the investors. This is often labeled as "suitable." For example, if there is a property where the syndicator might fit nicely with the type of property, but the investor (for example, an investor that is in a zero-tax bracket—a tax exempt entity) does not fit as to the property being syndicated. (Assume the property being syndicated is one that has as a major facet the "benefit" of large tax deductions for depreciation, etc.)

If the property in question is one that the syndicator cannot reasonably manage, this person should not be syndicating this property or the syndicator needs to make arrangements ahead of time for the management of the property. Can the syndicator also manage and deal with the investors?

If the given potential manager prefers to act quickly, independently, and for his own interests, syndicating for the interests of many would probably not be a good idea.

And, even if the syndicator may have the ability to function for this given property, it may be that the syndication should be for a smaller group, a group that involves very financially strong investors, etc. That is, all syndications are NOT the same.

* * *

CHAPTER 5

Steps in the Syndication Process

A. INTRODUCTION

When addressing the many areas of concern that might arise in syndications, it is often convenient to break the areas of focus in to at least three groups or steps. (This approach to grouping or organizing the steps was often used by many early syndicators that were involved in a group called the Real Estate Securities and Syndications Institute ("RESSI"). RESSI was a part of the National Association of Realtors ("NAR") but RESSI no longer exists. However, the need to address areas of the syndication continues.

These three steps are functional in nature. They normally are broken into the following:

1.   the Organizational Phase;
2.   the Operation Phase; and
3.   the Completion/Termination/ and/or Disposition Phase

There is no law that requires these three phases. Rather, the practical, real world examination of this area normally results in these three divisions.

The authors are both attorneys, so forgive us a little professional puffery here. Real estate syndicators will be well served to consult with competent securities counsel (and CPAs for that matter) in undertaking a syndication. We understand there are all sorts of examples of private placement memoranda, operating agreements and subscription agreements available on line, and lots of "DIY" materials out there. If you are planning to raise, say, $10 million from 50 investors, that results in approximately 500 million reasons to consult with counsel beforehand! Securities law is neither easy nor intuitive. The penalties for securities mistakes can be career threatening.

In preparing to consult with counsel, a few pointers are worth noting. First, *do not draft your own documents and ask the attorney to review them for you in an attempt to save money.* It will take the attorney twice as long to dissect your documents to make sure they are complete as compared to allowing the attorney to use his own matrix. That said, think through the essential elements of the deal and commit them to a term sheet. What's the deal? How much money will you need? What's the investment outlook for return? How will investors and you be paid? Are there any unique risks, like environmental, zoning, etc.? Competition? This does not mean you cannot think about the items and information that would be placed in the materials used for the offering of the securities (also known as the Private

Placement Memorandum—PPM); but you are not trying to draft the document, *i.e.*, the PPM. Leave this to your attorney.

Finally, temper your entrepreneurial zeal for a moment and face some cold, hard facts. Where are you going to raise the money? The best ideas in the world for the syndication are worthless, if you do not have a viable sources or sources of capital. Finding investors is the hardest, practical aspect of real estate syndication, particularly if you are only starting out in the field of syndication and you do not have a cache of prior investors that want to work with you.

B. Organizational Phase—Structuring the Deal

1. What's the Project?

a. The Basics

This phase is certainly tied to its label of "organizing" the syndication. There are two main steps in this Phase:

1.   locate the property to be syndicated; and
2.   locate the investors for the syndication.

Many real estate investors are familiar with the first step—finding the property. However, unlike an investment not involving others, the syndicator/promoter must determine that not only is the property acceptable within the criteria determined by the syndicator, but the property must also be acceptable to those that will be the investors.

b. One payment?

The syndicator must decide if the project is to be accomplished at one time or if it will be undertaken in phases, through one or separate investments. Will there be a separate offering later for Phase 2? Will investors be asked to invest now for a project to be undertaken in the future? Or, will investors be asked to invest in Project 1 today, but pledge to participate in the future for Project 2, perhaps with a letter of credit or some similar arrangement? Some caution is warranted. Relying on promises to pay in the future, without some means of securing such payment, can lead to scrambled dreams. Things change with time; and, circumstances that are rosy today may not be as favorable down the road.

c. More than one project—Integration

Syndicators might have more than one project in mind at a given time. There are a number of considerations to keep in mind. In a project with different phases, for instance, a housing development with a second phase recreational facility, might generate questions as to whether it is one offering or two. (This was covered more completely in Part One, Chapter 3.)

d. More than one project—Conflict of Interest

Most conflicts of interest are *not* irreconcilable. In other words, while a conflict of interest may be present, disclosing both the conflict and how you intend to deal with it often resolves the problem.

Potential investors may be wary if the syndicator has what they perceive to be "too many irons in the fire." In other words, a prospective investor may wonder how much time the syndicator can spend on the given investor's project, if the syndicator is also involved in two other projects across town or that otherwise draw down the time available for the syndicator to function.

The conflict issue can also arise when the syndicator has elected to conduct business through use of "blind pools (non-specified property)." If you are running two blind pools, you are strongly advised to make sure the parameters for acquisition are markedly different. For instance, one blind pool may be focused on commercial warehouses, while the other pool is focused on motels. If there is some overlap, the operating agreements should be drafted to include preset means for describing and defining which of the pools will be given priority over which properties. Designating the solutions to problems *before* they happen is a surefire way to lessen dissent and confusion at a later time.

e. More conflicts—wearing more than one "Hat"

It is not uncommon at all for the syndicator to serve in more capacities than LLC Manager alone. The Manager may also be positioned to serve as realtor, construction company, management company and more to the LLC. These relationships all pose potential conflicts of interest because, through these affiliated entities, the Manager will be serving both his own interest as well as that of the LLC at the same time. With no one independent third party to make sure LLC business conducted with these Manager affiliates is performed at a fair price and competently, the LLC is somewhat at the mercy of the Manager to proceed in good faith.

As we noted previously, most conflicts of interest are resolved by disclosure in advance followed by dealing in good faith, good recordkeeping and timely reporting. If the Manager's realtor affiliate is to handle the purchase and sale of real estate for commission, the Manager should disclose in the offering materials that the commission rate will be at or below the customary rate charged in the community. Any departure higher than customary rate must be disclosed, explained and justified in the disclosures. The same goes for construction and management services.

Generally, when affiliates are to be retained to provide services, the Manager can support the decision to use them with the claim that "keeping everything in house will save time and money" and will back that up by charging rates below those prevailing in the marketplace. These can be strong selling points and should be attractive to investors when treated properly.

It should be abundantly clear by now that going in the opposite direction, *i.e.*, failing to disclose beforehand that a vendor the Manager hires to do work for the LLC is affiliated with the Manager, is both bad business and likely to be deemed a violation of the securities disclosure requirements.

f. Series LLC

If considering multiple projects, one other form of organization may be of interest, the Series LLC. This form originated in Delaware, expressly designed to deal with serial real estate promoters. Instead of operating separate LLCs with all the accounting costs and complications, what might be separate LLCs under traditional LLC law can become independent series under one umbrella LLC, with one single, bundled, netted reporting burden. The series can all be created at once, or over time. (See your attorney for more details on this approach.)

2. Which laws will apply?

As mentioned in this Work as to licensing of those undertaking syndications, clearly another element that impacts syndications is to determine what laws and rules apply to the syndication. For example, although one might be syndicating, there may be a question as to "who will raise the capital for the syndication?" It may be that the syndicator should not be one of those raising capital; or, it may be that the syndicator is well positioned to raise capital in a given structure, such as a Private Offering under Regulation D.

It has already been established, earlier in this text, that under SEC Release 5347 (sale of condominiums, etc.) and elsewhere under federal and state securities laws, real estate can be marketed in such a way that the activity will be deemed to be the offer and sale of securities. In such instance, there are, as discussed earlier, many federal and state laws that must be addressed.

Because of these concerns, when one is selling real estate that constitutes a security as a result of how the security/real estate is being marketed, to whom it is marketed, who undertakes the marketing of the real estate, who operates the real estate, etc., all of these issues must all be examined; and, these items must be examined in light of the securities issue, not simple by considering the rules and laws that apply to the sale of real estate.

Please refer to the earlier discussion in Part One, Chapter 2 as to this issue of when real estate is a security and the implications to the same.

3. How will we raise the funds?

a. Who can sell?

As discussed, real estate can be marketed in such a manner that the offer and/or sale of the same can constitute a security.

One approach, as discussed in Part One, Chapter 4, to avoiding problems with the person selling the security, is to become licensed for the sale of securities. This means complying with the 34 Act, other Federal laws impacting licensing, and meeting the state laws where the sale of the securities will take place.

Although the earlier discussion in the text addressed how one might be exempt from the requirement to be licensed, *if* one is not exempt, what other options exist to raise capital?

1. Again, one can become licensed. But, as explained earlier in Part One, Chapter 4, the cost, time and headaches to be licensed and to maintain the license must be considered. If a substantial amount of capital is regularly being raised, it may make economic sense to become licensed.

2. It is possible to pay other firms that are licensed to raise the capital for your investments. However, although this sounds reasonable, it is often not reasonable for smaller syndicators. Why? Because there are many concerns when having others raise the capital for your syndication. Consider these issues:
   a. The firm raising the capital may have little interest in dealing with you as you might not raise enough money to warrant their time.
   b. The firm raising your capital may charge you a fee that is so substantial that it makes no economic sense for you to deal with them. That fee is negotiable; but, do not be surprised that the fee is in the 15 to 20% range, or more, of the capital raised.
   c. There are other items to negotiate with the firm raising capital. For example, how long will it take to raise the capital? What other support will the firm that is raising the capital require of you? What guarantee will there be that the capital will be raised? And there are many more issues that must be addressed!

3. Consider raising capital under the new Reg. D, 506(c) rules and/or crowdfunding rules as discussed in Part One, Chapter 3.

4. And more…!

b. Who and what are "Finders"?

Please refer to the earlier discussion in Part One, Chapter 4 as to "finders" or others that help direct capital to a given person and receive a "finder's fee." As mentioned, the investors, be they accredited or non-accredited investors, must be suitable for the investment.

c. To whom can we sell?

For which investors will the interests be "suitable?" This term, "suitability," generally means that there is match in the desired positions of the investor and the syndicator. The term is borrowed from the realm of broker-dealer and investment adviser regulation where, for an investment professional to recommend a security to a client, the professional must first ascertain whether the security in question would be a suitable (proper) investment for them considering the investors' financial circumstances and experience, their risk tolerance, investment strategy and time horizon, among other issues. It is not enough to say that the investor has the money and the syndicator is willing to take the money for a share in the investment. Rather, suitability requires that one consider the needs of the investor.

As mentioned, for an example, if the nature of the investment/syndication is heavily dependent and focused on tax benefits, *e.g.*, tax exempt interest, and the investor, a charitable organization, does not need and cannot gain any benefits from the tax exempt interest, it is likely that the investor is not suitable for this investment.

The SEC determined in 1982 that Rule 506 private placements could be sold to no more than 35 "sophisticated investors" and an unlimited number of "accredited investors." We discussed "accredited investors" in Part One, Chapter 3. Recall that, as currently set, individuals generally qualify as "accredited investors" if they have at least $1 million in assets or have earned $200,000 a year for the last two years, or $300,000 with their spouse (expecting the same for the coming year). It is not unusual at all for promoters to limit their deals to accredited investors alone, deciding not to risk selling to too many sophisticated but not accredited investors, or a finding after the fact that the investors are not in fact "sophisticated."

In addition to limiting sales to accredited investors, many syndicators set the minimum investment at a very high number, for at least two reasons. First, they do not wish to spend all their time searching for dozens of investors. Second, they only want people involved who know what they are doing as investors and can accept the risk for the investment; and, people who can invest $100,000 to $1 million are presumed to be able to conduct themselves as sophisticated professionals, and not someone who calls every day wondering what is happening to their $25,000 investment.

It is likely that, for example, an investor who is elderly (90 years old) would have less interest in property investments where the focus is long term investment. Of course, this is not always true; but, in the main, this type of investor is probably more focused on security and cash flow.

On the other hand, an investor (Doctor?) who is earning say $500,000 per year might be less concerned with equity build up and more concerned with tax deductions and appreciation. Again this is not always the case, but the generalization is probably valid in most cases as to the issue of suitability.

Another issue that arises from time to time is the foreign investor. Can a syndicator sell a real estate syndication, LLC membership interest to an investor in Germany or Japan? While the answer is, "of course," it comes with some complicating bells and whistles, particularly when real estate is concerned. Suffice to say here that if considering sales to non-U.S. investors, consult with counsel on, at a minimum, the Foreign Investment in Real Property Tax Act ("FIRPTA").

4. When is the best time to syndicate the property?

This answer to this question might seem obvious. However, on reflection, one must consider the position of the syndicator, the investors, the property market, and many other factors.

For example, if the syndicator wants to move quickly to buy a property, possible rehab the property and sell it, what happens if things do not go as smoothly as anticipated? If the syndicator needs to be in and out of the subject property within a short window, it may not be the best time for the syndicator to act; the timing may prove to be faulty.

And, sometimes it is simply not a good time to syndicate in the first place. If, for example, X is in a given business, and the market slows, maybe X should also slow down and/or stop activity in a given area. If X was a home builder, and there was an overbuilding of homes, the logical position would be to say that X should stop building homes—or at least slow the building activity.

Applying the same point to syndications, if X has as his/her major source of business the syndication of properties, but the business is now slowing, it would be expected that X would also slow or stop this activity. But, is this reasonable for X, who only makes money by syndicating? The answer to the question is that if the market is slow, one should slow and/or stop syndicating. But, similar to some home builders, sometimes when one makes a living in a given area, it is difficult to stop doing it.

Therefore, in summary, syndicators should not syndicate unless the market indicates that the timing is correct. And, since such position is reasonable, it is also reasonable for those who syndicate to consider various activities, not only syndication. One might be a real estate broker, property manager, appraiser AND syndicator. And, the use of the syndication should only be a tool, applied when the market supports such activity. This is an obvious paradigm, but one that is often overlooked by many in the syndication business.

5. When do we acquire the property?

There are some types of properties that are more easily syndicated than is true with other types of properties. Properties that are better understood by the average investor are often much easier to present to an investor. Apartment buildings, as an example, are more easily presented to investors than would be a golf club. Why? People live in and/or deal with those in apartments. Most investors have no idea what are reasonable numbers to expect from income and expenses at a golf club.

How property will be acquired is another related issue. Will it be financed? Will the seller of the property be willing to accept payments over time (called a "carry back")? This "owner carry back" often has many advantages over new financing, if the terms are reasonable. Why would it be an advantage? Because the syndicator does not have to worry about making the syndication conditional on obtaining financing. This often saves time and money. And, it often allows the transaction to go forward, since this piece of the Origination Phase, the financing, is already solved.

Often it is difficult for a syndicator to "tie up" a property with a seller, go out and obtain financing AND obtain investors for the syndication. Thus, these issues of financing and having investors must be considered as one works to also acquire a property.

As mentioned, if the seller of the property would be willing to carry back (take payments form the buyer), the issue of financing may be solved or partially solved.

But, how does the syndicator solve the issue of finding investors, since the syndicator cannot present the property to investors until the property is at least under contract, when it is difficult to place the property under contract without having investors? This common Catch 22 situation, where the syndicator is trying to cover both sides of the concern, vis-à-vis, tie up the property and gain investors, has a couple of solutions. First, the syndicator can acquire the property with his own funds, to be reimbursed to the syndicator, later, when investors come in to the picture. However, the syndicator often lacks the funds to so act. Secondly, perhaps the syndicator has the wherewithal to at least secure the property through an option to purchase, but there are resource and timing issues there as well.

A third possibility is through use of a "blind pool." (See Part One, Chapter 3) The start-up syndicator may have more of a problem selling such an offering to investors than a more seasoned developer.

Essentially, in a blind pool offering, the syndicator describes the type of properties the syndicator will look to acquire, the potential locations and other parameters or minimum qualifications, although the specific properties cannot be identified at the time of the offering. If investors are willing to rely on the investment parameters and the skills of the promoter in acquiring the properties, the syndicator will have a pool of money to draw on when the right opportunity presents itself. Such offerings usually include timeframes in which properties must be acquired or investments refunded.

6. What are investors looking for?

a. Are they interested in a real estate investment?

As mentioned in this Work, the promoter/issuer/syndicator often enters this field of syndication because he/she has determined there is a wonderful opportunity to gain a substantial profit. Of course, such profit does not always come to fruition.

But, why does an investor invest in a syndication?

Certainly there are many reasons an investor may consider investing in a syndication. Consider the investor may:

1. not have the expertise to buy and handle the property in question that is syndicated, such as a retail piece of real estate;
2. not have the time to undertake the steps necessary to acquire a good piece of real estate;
3. have little desire to devote the time and energy to the investment;
4. not want to manage the investment property and make all of the decisions that are concomitant with the investment;
5. gain economies of scale by investing with others; and
6. have other motivations that encourage group investing as opposed to the investor locating and buying a separate property.

b. RESSI's Four Points

The earlier mentioned RESSI body (REAL ESTATE SECURITIES AND SYNDICATIONS INSTITUTE) under the NAR (National Association of Realtors) proposed, as did many other groups, a demarcation as to factors of concern or interest when investing in property with a group.

Their four-part demarcation included:

i. Appreciation;
ii. Equity buildup;
iii. Cash Flow; and
iv. Tax benefits.

That is, the thinking was (and is today) that investors buy property for at least one or more of the above four reasons.

i. Appreciation

This is simply the hoped-for position that the real estate investment, individually made or undertaken via a group, will appreciate or increase in value. Raw ground is normally purchased with this benefit in mind, since there is normally no income from the vacant land.

This practical issue is one that has no set answer, yet the issue must be addressed.

That is, assuming that the given investor is comfortable with group investing and with you as the syndicator, one additional question is to state the rate of return that would interest the investor. In other words, if the investment property is attractive, and you, the promoter, have a good track record, the investor still needs to know the potential, reasonable return on the investment.

The question is now to address what return will the investor require to attract the investor to invest in the syndication?

It was discussed in this material that there are different types of financial investment considerations, such as appreciation, cash flow, equity build up and tax benefits.

But, to be specific, what level of return is necessary to encourage the investment? If the combination of appreciation and subsequent sale benefits, even after tax issues, results in a return on the investment of 8%, 10%, 12%, 20%, etc., what amount will be required to cause the investor to be willing to place his or her money in the investment?

And, again, there is no set answer. Certainly the SEC and State law cannot require a given return. And, assuming a pure equity position, not a given, stated return for investing in a bond, what return will be "acceptable."

This percentage return is subject to many factors, such as the time of the investment, the nature of the investment, the risks involved with the investment, the term of the investment, etc.

To examine these points in more detail, clearly if there are other factors, beyond the percent of return, this may influence the investor to accept an investment that might likely return less on a percentage basis than is true with other investments.

If the timing for the investment is one in which the investor has few alternatives to gain a similar return, such assumption is important. For example, if the investor knows that the return on cash in a bank is only 1/10th of 1%, yet a Treasury Bond will return 3%, it makes the Treasury attractive, between the two investments. But, if a real estate investment looks to return 6% per annum return, the real estate investment is more attractive, on its face, given the better return. However, clearly there appears to be more risk with the real estate investment as compared to the Treasury Bond.

If the return for the investor is NOT solely dependent on the financial considerations, but there are other issues, such as investing and gaining a visa to enter the USA, the percentage of return may not be a key factor.*****

If the risk is substantial, but the return is also substantial, this may influence the willingness of an investor to enter the investment group.

Thus, there is no clear answer as to the return necessary to attract capital. And, such return varies with the timing in the market, the risk involved, the potential of large returns, etc.

ii. Equity Buildup

If a building or other property is financed, with a loan that is amortized over time with the regular payments being made, the idea is that as the loan is paid down and the balance of debt is reduced, the effective equity is increased. As an example, if there is a $10 million purchase with an $8 million loan, there is $2 million of equity or net value. However, if all things remain the same, aside from the balance of the loan, and the loan is reduced to $7 million, there is now $3 million of equity.

Thus, this increase in equity is another goal that is desired by many investors.

***** See the website regarding the EB-5 program where certain people may immigrate to the United States provided they make a substantial investment in an American business that will create jobs for people in the U.S. http://www.uscis.gov/working-united-states/permanent-workers/employment-based-immigration-fifth-preference-eb-5/eb-5-immigrant-investor

iii. Cash Flow

It is the desire by most investors to have more cash coming in than being paid out to third parties. Thus, if one receives, monthly, $300,000 of cash and pays out $250,000, the $50,000 per month cash flow to the positive, which is $600,000 per year, is the net, positive Cash Flow that investors normally seek.

iv. Tax Benefits

This category of benefit is what improves the taxpayer's position because of a lessening of tax obligations. That is, if Taxpayer X receives a $500,000 deduction from the investment, by a group or individually, the deduction translates into tax savings that can entice an investor. If X is assumed to be in the 40% marginal tax bracket, that is, for each $1 of taxable income, X must pay local, state and federal taxes of 40%, this means that .40 cents of each dollar is lost (paid in) to the government.

In turn, this means that a deduction of $500,000, for the 40% tax bracket taxpayer, is saving X $200,000 in current taxes.

Hence, taxpayers often seek tax benefits when investing.

Thus, taxpayers would like to have benefits in all four of the areas noted above. Of course, many investments do not provide benefits in all four of the above areas; but, clearly, when syndicating, if the investment can produce benefits in the four areas noted, this may be attractive to the investor. (It was judiciously stated that such investment "may" be attractive to an investor who would gain in all four of the areas noted; however, most investors seek or lean toward one or two of the four factors noted; they normally are not focused on all four benefits. For example, if the investor is not a taxable entity, the production of tax benefits from deductions is of little interest to that type of investor. Another investor who is paying a substantial amount of income taxes each year might be more favorably attracted to an investment that generates sizeable tax deductions, tax exempt interest and/or other tax benefits.

It should also be noted that, no matter how well thought out the syndicator believes his deal is before presenting it to potential investors, the investors will inevitably come up with some point that has not been contemplated, or with a request that one term or another be changed if they are to invest. Rule 506 offerings are well suited to such give and take, and it is not unusual at all for a private placement offering to be changed several times in the course of the offering process.

c. Escrow

Investors may also require that their investment funds be placed in escrow at an independent bank pursuant to an escrow agreement until all or a stated percentage of the total investment is raised. The reasons should be obvious. It is the rare venture that can commence meaningful operations with just the first investment. A minimum level is necessary to do so. However, if the Manager is free to use the first funds in and does, if the minimum remaining funds are not raised and operations never really commence, unless the Manager has independent resources, he will be unable to refund the first investments.

d. Use of proceeds

Among the most elemental of disclosures required under securities law and by reasonable investors is how their funds are to be used. The question should be addressed in both the private placement memorandum and the operating agreement. It should also be specified in the operating agreement as to how idle funds, if any, will be held. A simple and common answer to the question is the use of an insured bank account or money market fund.

e. Access to records and reporting to investors

There are few more surefire ways for a syndicator to upset his investors than to restrict their access to records and to keep them in the dark as to what is going on with their investments. Although communicating with people may not be every syndicator's strong suit, it is essential that it be done. If the manager cannot or will not communicate himself, he should hire someone who will communicate with investors. Both access to records and frequency of reporting are points that should be disclosed in the private placement memorandum and addressed in the operating agreement or other relevant documents.

7. Operations—Who will be the Manager and how will the company be managed?

Before deciding the form for the company, *i.e.*, an LLC, LP or some other form of entity, one of the first steps in organizing a syndication will be to organize the syndicator. If there is more than one principal, it is very common for the principals to form their own member managed LLC or other entity to govern their duties and responsibilities, how they will be compensated, and what will happen if one or more principals wants to leave the operation. This issue can be among the most difficult steps of all, because all the principals are there to work with each other. It is not all that different from drafting a pre-nuptial agreement relative to a couple getting married. The couple is anxious to get started on their honeymoon, while the evil lawyer is there working out the terms of what will happen if there is a divorce. As uncomfortable as it may be, it is crucial for the principals to pay attention to these points from the outset, as later discovered problems, without predetermined means of resolution, can doom any business association. As an aside, we generally refuse to prepare operating agreements for two principals who will share in everything, management and income, on a 50%/50% basis. It is a meaningless effort, unless there is some independent way to break a tie.

Again, the label for the operations phase directs attention to much of what will take place in this part of the syndication. The property that is syndicated, such as an apartment building, shopping center, warehouse, or office building, must be handled, *i.e.*, operated, on a daily basis. This is not unlike any ownership of realty.

However, when working with a group of owners, other issues in the operation must be addressed, such as:

- Who makes the operational decisions?
- When will the property be positioned for a disposition?
- What participation will the investors have, if any?
- What conflicts of interest might be present between the syndicator/general partner of the company and the investors?
- Is refinancing needed? If so, who determines the terms for the same?
- And much more….

Of course, many of the above issues should have been addressed in the ownership/investment documents, such as the LLC Operating Agreement. However, note that failing to account for foreseeable events, such as disputes, sudden death of a key person, change in circumstances as to the property, special financing events, etc., can be devastating to the health of the venture.

8. Completion/Termination Phase—Exit Strategy

This Phase, too, appears to be self-defining, at least at first blush. However, there may be many intervening events that create issues on this phase, too. For example, consider:

- it is probable the intent was to sell the subject property in about five years. However, what if the market is not in a good position for such sale? How much longer is the property held?
- might the Termination phase be accelerated if the key Manager of the syndication is no longer available to handle the group?
- what if laws have changed that impact the investment? For example, what if capital gain rates are to be raised? What if depreciation rates are adversely impacted by new laws requiring a longer depreciation period?
- what if financing is or is not available? and
- what if the group is suddenly faced with an offer made by a third party to acquire the subject property of the syndication?

Certainly, there are many issues that may change the direction for the group as to when the termination phase occurs and how the phase is handled. If some of the investors and/or the operating partner suddenly have major financial problems, this may or may not impact when and how the termination phase is undertaken.

A well advised, experienced syndicator will try to anticipate many of the above problems and many other issues. However, not every issue can be addressed ahead of time. As such, the timing and approach to the Completion phase can be uncertain.

As mentioned, the three Phases stated above simply provide a skeletal outline of some of the major pieces to consider over the life of a syndication. There are many, many other issues that will not fit neatly into the three divisions stated. However, recognizing at least these three major divisions will help plan the syndication and provide a greater opportunity for success.

9. Syndicator Compensation

a. The Basics

One of the most basic questions anyone can ask in considering entering the syndication business is about the fees and other benefits that might be obtained by syndicating real estate. If one is willing to undertake the effort to create a group of investors, to acquire "good" real estate, manage the same, dispose of the real estate and windup the investment group, what is the compensation that one earns in this setting? Simply stated, the syndicator asks: "What's in it for me?"

The benefits and fees that can be earned in syndicating can be substantial. Many of these benefits and fees are what one might earn from undertaking brokerage work and/or owning a property as an individual. However, many of the benefits in the syndication involve the combination of these benefits. Consider the following economic gains one might obtain through syndication.

It is worth noting that, although the sorts of private offerings being discussed are not normally subject to state merit standards applicable to some registered offerings, those merit standards can be a valuable source of reference. For instance, a merit state would not normally permit a promoter to receive all his compensation before the investors received a return of all or part of their investment. A promoter willing to structure a syndication in a way that it at least appears it would be merit compliant may be able to use that position as a selling point.

b. Compensation on Acquisition

The syndicator/promoter might gain fees and other payments when property is acquired. There might be real estate brokerage commissions that the syndicator might obtain by being licensed in real estate and cooperating (sharing) the real estate commission with others.

Certainly, there can be fees paid to one who helps acquire the financing for the syndicated project. Thus, if the syndicator helps on the financing, there may be mortgage brokerage fees that could be obtained. (It is assumed that one is licensed, if this is required in the given state.)

There can be other fees earned when acquiring the property, including consulting fees, etc.

c. Compensation as to the Operation Phase

The syndicator may charge a property management fee for operating the property in question. If there are additional tasks, such as remodeling office space for new tenants, etc., other construction fees may be earned.

Placing insurance on the property may generate fees for the syndicator/insurance agent. (Again, throughout this discussion, it is assumed that all necessary licenses are present to allow the fees to be legally paid.)

It takes time and money to manage the entity, such as the LLC, partnership, etc. Thus, there can be fees stated that will be paid for this management of the Entity.

There can be other fees earned during the operation, *e.g.*, brokerage fees for leasing space in the subject property, etc.

d. Compensation on Disposition/Termination

When the property is sold, there can be fees paid for brokerage work.

Of course, some of the largest fees or interests paid to a syndicator involve work for putting together the property, the entity/partnership/LLC, etc. Such fees may be those paid in the Acquisition phase (front end fees) and/or those paid on Disposition (back end fees).

These fees are often a percentage of cash raised, cash paid in during the operation, cash generated from re-financing, cash generated on the sale of the property, etc.

Although the amount of the fees earned is sometimes influenced or regulated by state law, this is fairly rare. That is, normally the fees charged are negotiated by the parties to the syndication. The important point for the syndicator is to be certain that the fees and compensation to the syndicator are properly disclosed in the offering memorandum (See Part One, Chapter 3). These fee settings are made under the assumption that there is full disclosure, no breach of fiduciary duties, and full compliance with the applicable law.

There are also many tax implications to the fees being charged and when and if the same are taxed. For more on this, see Part Three.

10. Reserves

The concept of having a "reserve" is not new to most people. A reserve is simple having something set aside—for the "rainy day." That is, the Reserve amounts to funds to help provide for some unknowns (as to time and/or amount). In the syndication field, it is said that a smart syndicator will have reserves put aside for the protection of the syndication and the syndicator.

OK. Given this position as to the benefit of having reserves, how much is the "right" amount of reserves? Again, at least for exempt offerings, neither federal nor state securities laws dictate whether reserves are required and/or how much is required. There is an old adage: the amount of reserves is the distance between you and your investors! That is, the more you have in reserves, the better off/safer you are as the syndicator.

That makes sense. But, if it makes so much sense, why is this such a problem? Why would we not see all syndicators putting aside a large amount of funds to cover unknowns? After all, if you as an owner faced a sudden need for funds, such as the need to put on a new roof on your apartment building, you would either go into your savings and/or borrow the funds, if possible.

Now, put yourself in the place of the syndicator. You need a new roof for the apartment. You do not have the funds available or you have the funds, but you do not want to expend your funds for the whole group. What do you do? You could:

- do nothing; but, that will not work as the roof is leaking!
- loan the money yourself; but, that does not make much sense (even though it is undertaken sometimes!);
- try to borrow the funds for the group, but, you need authority to do this; it costs your time and money to try and obtain a good loan for the group; and, there could be other problems to obtain the loan;
- "call" the investors and ask them to send in their share of the cost of the roof. But, what if they do not send their share to you? (Look at your operating agreements!); or
- consider other approaches.

Clearly, if you had the funds in the reserve, this could answer the problem. Thus, again, why not have BIG reserves? Some of the concerns are:

- the larger the reserve, the more you have money sitting and not earning very much, thus reducing the return on investment (IRR, etc.).
- to have big reserves, you must raise big money.
- how much is "Big"?
- if you can raise this much extra money, you might be tempted to say that the money should be used to do ANOTHER syndication!

And there are many other concerns we can all think about as to retaining a large amount of reserves.

The amount for reserves is influenced by the nature of the syndication. For example, if you have a syndication that is acquiring an old building and remodeling it, there are many more unknowns and uncertainties as compared to a syndication that owns raw ground, with no activity on the ground. Thus, the amount of the reserve should be tempered by what you are doing in the syndication.

Again, a raw ground investment that is sitting, waiting for a future sale, needs a good deal less in reserves than an operating real estate activity, such as remodeling property or owning a shopping center.

*****

APPENDIX

APPENDIX

Some General Web Addresses

- **Financial Industry Regulatory Authority ("FINRA")**
  http://www.finra.org/
- **North American Securities Administrators Association ("NASAA")**
  http://www.nasaa.org/
- **Securities and Exchange Commission ("SEC")**
  http://www.sec.gov/
- **Securities Act of 1933 ("'33 Act")**
  http://www.sec.gov/about/laws/sa33.pdf
- **Securities Exchange Act of 1934 ("'34 Act")**
  http://www.sec.gov/about/laws/sea34.pdf
- **SEC Rules and Regulations**
  http://www.sec.gov/about/laws/secrulesregs.htm
- **Uniform Securities Act 2002**
  http://www.uniformlaws.org/shared/docs/securities/securities_final_05.pdf

Case Citations and Reference Addresses

SEC v. Edwards	540 U.S. 389 (2004)
Reves v. Ernst & Young	494 U.S. 1092 (1990)
TSC Industries, Inc. v. Northway	426 U.S. 438 at 449 (1976)
United Housing v. Forman	421 U.S. 837 (1975)
SEC v. Ralston Purina Co.	346 U.S. 119 (1953)
SEC v. W.J. Howey Co.	328 U.S. 293 (1946)
SEC v. Glenn Turner Enterprises	474 F.2d 476 (9th Cir. 1973)
Lowery v. Ford Hill Inv. Co.	37 Colo. App. 260, 548 P.2d 127 (1976)
Silver Hills Country Club v. Sobieski	361 P.2d 903 (Ca. 1961)

IRC § 1031	http://www.law.cornell.edu/uscode/text_26/1031
Rev. Proc. 2002-22	http://www.irs.gov/pub/irs-drop/rp-02-22.pdf
Guidelines as to the Applicability of the Federal Securities Laws to Offers and Sales of Condominiums or Units in a Real Estate Development	http://www.sec.gov/rules/interp/1973/33-5347.pdf
SEC Guide to Broker-Dealer Registration	http://www.sec.gov/divisions/marketreg/bdguide.htm
SEC Regulation A	https://www.ecfr.gov/cgi-bin/text-idx?node=17:3.0.1.1.12&rgn=div5#sg17.3.230_1240.sg2
SEC Regulation D	http://www.ecfr.gov/cgi-bin/text-idx?node=17:3.0.1.1.12&rgn=div5#sg17.3.230_1498.sg11
SEC Rule 147	https://www.ecfr.gov/cgi-bin/text-idx?node=17:3.0.1.1.12&rgn=div5#se17.3.230_1147
SEC Rule 147A	https://www.ecfr.gov/cgi-bin/text-idx?node=17:3.0.1.1.12&rgn=div5#se17.3.230_1147a
Form D	http://www.sec.gov/about/forms/formd.pdf
Guide 5-Disclosures	https://www.google.com/search?q=SEC+guide+5+Real+Estate+&ie=utf-8&oe=utf-8&aq=t&rls=org.mozilla:en-US:official&client=firefox-a&channel=np&source=hp#channel=np&q=sec+industry+guide&rls=org.mozilla:en-US:official

SEC Division of Corporation Finance
Guidance on Intrastate Crowdfunding

SEC Division of Corporation Finance
Compliance and Disclosure Interpretations
http://www.sec.gov/divisions/corpfin/guidance/securitiesactrules-interps.htm
Securities Act
Rules
Last Update: July 3, 2014

These Compliance and Disclosure Interpretations ("C&DIs") comprise the Division's interpretations of the rules adopted under the Securities Act. Some of these C&DIs were first published in prior Division publications and have been revised in some cases. The bracketed date following each C&DI is the latest date of publication or revision.

QUESTION 141.03

Question: If an issuer plans to conduct an intrastate offering pursuant to the Section 3(a)(11) exemption, may the issuer engage in general advertising or a general solicitation?

Answer: Securities Act Rule 147 does not prohibit general advertising or general solicitation. Any such general advertising or solicitation, however, must be conducted in a manner consistent with the requirement that offers made in reliance on Section 3(a)(11) and Rule 147 be made only to persons resident within the state or territory of which the issuer is a resident. [April 10, 2014]

QUESTION 141.04

Question: An issuer plans to use a third-party Internet portal to promote an offering to residents of a single state in accordance with a state statute or regulation intended to enable securities crowdfunding within that state. Assuming the issuer met the other conditions of Rule 147, could it rely on Rule 147 for an exemption from Securities Act registration for the offering, or would use of an Internet portal necessarily entail making offers to persons outside the relevant state or territory?

Answer: Use of the Internet would not be incompatible with a claim of exemption under Rule 147 if the portal implements adequate measures so that offers of securities are made only to persons resident in the relevant state or territory. In the context of an offering conducted in accordance with state crowdfunding requirements, such measures would include, at a minimum, disclaimers and restrictive legends making it clear that the offering is limited to residents of the relevant state under applicable law, and limiting access to information about specific investment opportunities to persons who confirm they are residents of the relevant state (for example, by providing a representation as to residence or in-state residence information, such as a zip code or residence address). Of course, any issuer seeking to rely on Rule 147 for the offering also would have to meet all the other conditions of Rule 147. [April 10, 2014]

QUESTION 141.05

Question: Can an issuer use its own website or social media presence to offer securities in a manner consistent with Rule 147?

Answer: Issuers generally use their websites and social media presence to advertise their market presence in a broad, indiscriminate manner. Although whether a particular communication is an "offer" of securities will depend on all of the facts and circumstances, using such established Internet presence to convey information about specific investment opportunities would likely involve offers to residents outside the particular state in which the issuer did business. [April 10, 2014]

++
The following materials are a few of the key documents and authorities that have been referenced in this Text. Of course, also included are web citations to these and other materials. The following materials have been abridged in many cases. Where materials have been omitted, the reader will see four asterisks (****), signaling the deletions.

++

U.S. Supreme Court
SECURITIES AND EXCHANGE COMMISSION V. W. J. HOWEY CO. ET AL.

328 U.S. 293 (66 S.Ct. 1100, 90 L.Ed. 1244) (1946)

****

Mr. Justice MURPHY delivered the opinion of the Court.

This case involves the application of § 2(1) of the Securities Act of 1933[1] to an offering of units of a citrus grove development coupled with a contract for cultivating, marketing and remitting the net proceeds to the investor.

The Securities and Exchange Commission instituted this action to restrain the respondents from using the mails and instrumentalities of interstate commerce in the offer and sale of unregistered and nonexempt securities in violation of § 5(a) of the Act, 15 U.S.C.A. § 77e(a). The District Court denied the injunction, 60 F.Supp. 440, and the Fifth Circuit Court of Appeals affirmed the judgment, 151 F.2d 714. We granted certiorari, 327 U.S. 773, 66 S.Ct. 821, on a petition alleging that the ruling of the Circuit Court of Appeals conflicted with other federal and state decisions and that it introduced a novel and unwarranted test under the statute which the Commission regarded as administratively impractical.

Most of the facts are stipulated. The respondents, W. J. Howey Company and Howey-in-the-Hills Service Inc., are Florida corporations under direct common control and management. The Howey Company owns large tracts of citrus acreage in Lake County, Florida. During the past several years it has planted about 500 acres annually, keeping half of the groves itself and offering the other half to the public 'to help us finance additional development.' Howey-in-the-Hills Service, Inc., is a service company engaged in cultivating and developing many of these groves, including the harvesting and marketing of the crops.

Each prospective customer is offered both a land sales contract and a service contract, after having been told that it is not feasible to invest in a grove unless service arrangements are made. While the purchaser is free to make arrangements with other service companies, the superiority of Howey-in-the-Hills Service, Inc., is stressed. Indeed, 85% of the acreage sold during the 3-year period ending May 31, 1943, was covered by service contracts with Howey-in-the-Hills Service, Inc.

The land sales contract with the Howey Company provides for a uniform purchase price per acre or fraction thereof, varying in amount only in accordance with the number of years the particular plot has been planted with citrus trees. Upon full payment of the purchase price the land is conveyed to the purchaser by warranty deed. Purchases are usually made in narrow strips of land arranged so that an acre consists of a row of 48 trees. During the period between February 1, 1941, and May 31, 1943, 31 of the 42 persons making purchases bought less than 5 acres each. The average holding of these 31 persons was 1.33 acres and sales of as little as 0.65, 0.7 and 0.73 of an acre were made. These tracts are not separately fenced and the sole indication of several ownership is found in small land marks intelligible only through a plat book record.

The service contract, generally of a 10-year duration without option of cancellation, gives Howey-in-the-Hills Service, Inc., a leasehold interest and 'full and complete' possession of the acreage. For a specified fee plus the cost of labor and materials, the company is given full discretion and authority over the cultivation of the groves and the harvest and marketing of the crops. The company is well established in the citrus business and maintains a large force of skilled personnel and a great deal of equipment, including 75 tractors, sprayer wagons, fertilizer trucks and the like. Without the consent of the company, the land owner or purchaser has no right of entry to market the crop;[2] thus there is ordinarily no right to specific fruit. The company is accountable only for an allocation of the net profits based upon a check made at the time of picking. All the produce is pooled by the respondent companies, which do business under their own names.

APPENDIX

The purchasers for the most part are non-residents of Florida. They are predominantly business and professional people who lack the knowledge, skill and equipment necessary for the care and cultivation of citrus trees. They are attracted by the expectation of substantial profits. It was represented, for example, that profits during the 1943—1944 season amounted to 20% and that even greater profits might be expected during the 1944 1945 season, although only a 10% annual return was to be expected over a 10-year period. Many of these purchasers are patrons of a resort hotel owned and operated by the Howey Company in a scenic section adjacent to the groves. The hotel's advertising mentions the fine groves in the vicinity and the attention of the patrons is drawn to the groves as they are being escorted about the surrounding countryside. They are told that the groves are for sale; if they indicate an interest in the matter they are then given a sales talk.

It is admitted that the mails and instrumentalities of interstate commerce are used in the sale of the land and service contracts and that no registration statement or letter of notification has ever been filed with the Commission in accordance with the Securities Act of 1933 and the rules and regulations thereunder. ****

Section 2(1) of the Act defines the term 'security' to include the commonly known documents traded for speculation or investment.[3] This definition also includes 'securities' of a more variable character, designated by such descriptive terms as 'certificate of interest or participation in any profit-sharing agreement,' 'investment contract' and 'in general, any interest or instrument commonly known as a 'security." The legal issue in this case turns upon a determination of whether, under the circumstances, the land sales contract, the warranty deed and the service contract together constitute an 'investment contract' within the meaning of § 2(1). An affirmative answer brings into operation the registration requirements of § 5(a), unless the security is granted an exemption under § 3(b), 15 U.S.C.A. § 77c(b). The lower courts, in reaching a negative answer to this problem, treated the contracts and deeds as separate transactions involving no more than an ordinary real estate sale and an agreement by the seller to manage the property for the buyer.

The term 'investment contract' is undefined by the Securities Act or by relevant legislative reports. But the term was common in many state 'blue sky' laws in existence prior to the adoption of the federal statute and, although the term was also undefined by the state laws, it had been broadly construed by state courts so as to afford the investing public a full measure of protection. Form was disregarded for substance and emphasis was placed upon economic reality. An investment contract thus came to mean a contract or scheme for 'the placing of capital or laying out of money in a way intended to secure income or profit from its employment.' State v. Gopher Tire & Rubber Co., 146 Minn. 52, 56, 177 N.W. 937, 938. This definition was uniformly applied by state courts to a variety of situations where individuals were led to invest money in a common enterprise with the expectation that they would earn a profit solely through the efforts of the promoter or of someone other than themselves.[4]

By including an investment contract within the scope of § 2(1) of the Securities Act, Congress was using a term the meaning of which had been crystallized by this prior judicial interpretation. It is therefore reasonable to attach that meaning to the term as used by Congress, especially since such a definition is consistent with the statutory aims. In other words, an investment contract for purposes of the Securities Act means a contract, transaction or scheme whereby a person invests his money in a common enterprise and is led to expect profits solely from the efforts of the promoter or a third party, it being immaterial whether the shares in the enterprise are evidenced by formal certificates or by nominal interests in the physical assets employed in the enterprise. Such a definition necessarily underlies this Court's decision in Securities Exch. Commission v. C. M. Joiner Leasing Corp., 320 U.S. 344, 64 S.Ct. 120, 88 L.Ed. 88, and has been enunciated and applied many times by lower federal courts.****

The transactions in this case clearly involve investment contracts as so defined. The respondent companies are offering something more than fee simple interests in land, something different from a farm or orchard coupled with management services. They are offering an opportunity to contribute money and to share in the profits of a large citrus fruit enterprise managed and partly owned by respondents. They are offering this opportunity to persons who reside in distant localities and who lack the equipment and experience requisite to the cultivation, harvesting and marketing of the citrus products. Such persons have no desire to occupy the land or to develop it themselves; they are attracted solely by the prospects of a return on their investment. Indeed, individual development of the plots of land that are offered and sold would seldom be economically feasible due to their small size. Such tracts gain utility as citrus groves only when cultivated and developed as component parts of a larger area. A common enterprise managed by respondents or third parties with adequate personnel and equipment is therefore essential if the investors are to achieve their paramount aim of a return on their investments. Their respective shares in this enterprise are evidenced by land sales contracts and warranty deeds, which serve as a convenient method of determining the investors' allocable shares of the profits. The resulting transfer of rights in land is purely incidental.

Thus all the elements of a profit-seeking business venture are present here. The investors provide the capital and share in the earnings and profits; the promoters manage, control and operate the enterprise. It follows that the arrangements whereby the investors' interests are made manifest involve investment contracts, regardless of the legal terminology in which such contracts are clothed. The investment contracts in this instance take the form of land sales contracts, warranty deeds and service contracts which respondents offer to prospective investors. And respondents' failure to abide by the statutory and administrative rules in making such offerings, even though the failure result from a bona fide mistake as to the law, cannot be sanctioned under the Act.

This conclusion is unaffected by the fact that some purchasers choose not to accept the full offer of an investment contract by declining to enter into a service contract with the respondents. The Securities Act prohibits the offer as well as the sale of unregistered, non-exempt securities.[6] Hence it is enough that the respondents merely offer the essential ingredients f an investment contract.

We reject the suggestion of the Circuit Court of Appeals, 151 F.2d at page 717, that an investment contract is necessarily missing where the enterprise is not speculative or promotional in character and where the tangible interest which is sold has intrinsic value independent of the success of the enterprise as a whole. The test is whether the scheme involves an investment of money in a common enterprise with profits to come solely from the efforts of others. If that test be satisfied, it is immaterial whether the enterprise is speculative or non-speculative or whether there is a sale of property with or without intrinsic value. See S.E.C. v. C. M. Joiner Leasing Corp., supra, 320 U.S. 352, 64 S.Ct. 124, 88 L.Ed. 88. The statutory policy of affording broad protection to investors is not to be thwarted by unrealistic and irrelevant formulae.

REVERSED ****

APPENDIX

U.S. SUPREME COURT
UNITED HOUSING FOUNDATION, INC. V. FORMAN

421 U.S. 837 (1975)
****

CERTIORARI TO THE UNITED STATES COURT OF APPEALS
FOR THE SECOND CIRCUIT

Syllabus

Respondents are 57 residents of Co-op City, a massive cooperative housing project in New York City, organized, financed, and constructed under the New York Private Housing Finance Law (Mitchell-Lama Act). They brought this action on behalf of all the apartment owners and derivatively on behalf of the housing corporation, alleging, inter alia, violations of the antifraud provisions of the Securities Act of 1933 and of the Securities Exchange Act of 1934 (hereafter collectively Securities Acts), in connection with the sale to respondents of shares of the common stock of the cooperative housing corporation. Citing substantial increases in the tenants' monthly rental charges as a result of higher construction costs, respondents' claim centered on a Co-op City Information Bulletin issued in the project's initial stages, which allegedly misrepresented that the developers would absorb future cost increases due to such factors as inflation. Under the Mitchell-Lama Act, which was designed to encourage private developers to build low-cost cooperative housing, the State provides large, long-term low-interest mortgage loans and substantial tax exemptions, conditioned on step-by-step state supervision of the cooperative's development. Developers must agree to operate the facilities "on a nonprofit basis," and may lease apartments to only state-approved lessees whose incomes are below a certain level. The corporate petitioners in this case built, promoted, and presently control Co-op City: United Housing Foundation (UHF), a nonprofit membership corporation, initiated and sponsored the project; Riverbay, a nonprofit cooperative housing corporation, was organized by UHF to own and operate the land and buildings and issue the stock that is the subject of the instant action; and Community Securities, Inc. (CSI), UHF's wholly owned subsidiary, was the project's general [838] contractor and sales agent. To acquire a Co-op City apartment, a prospective purchaser must buy 18 shares of Riverbay stock for each room desired at $25 per share. The shares cannot be transferred to a nontenant, pledged, encumbered, or bequeathed (except to a surviving spouse), and do not convey voting rights based on the number owned (each apartment having one vote). On termination of occupancy, a tenant must offer his stock to Riverbay at $25 per share, and, in the unlikely event that Riverbay does not repurchase, the tenant cannot sell his shares for more than their original price, plus a fraction of the mortgage amortization that he has paid during his tenancy, and then only to a prospective tenant satisfying the statutory income eligibility requirements. Under the Co-op City Lease arrangement, the resident is committed to make monthly rental payments in accordance with the size, nature, and location of the apartment. The Securities Acts define a "security" as "any . . . stock, . . . investment contract, . . . or, in general, any interest or instrument commonly known as a security.'" Petitioners moved to dismiss the complaint for lack of federal jurisdiction, maintaining that the Riverbay stock did not constitute securities as thus defined. The District Court granted the motion to dismiss. The Court of Appeals reversed, holding that (1) since the shares purchased were called "stock," the definitional sections of the Securities Acts were literally applicable, and (2) the transaction was an investment contract under the Securities Acts, there being a profit expectation from rental reductions resulting from (i) the income produced by commercial facilities established for the use of Co-op City tenants; (ii) tax deductions for the portion of monthly rental charges allocable to interest payments on the mortgage; and (iii) savings based on the fact that Co-op City apartments cost substantially less than comparable nonsubsidized housing.

Held: The shares of stock involved in this Litigation do not constitute "securities" within the purview of the Securities Acts, and since respondents' claims are not cognizable in federal court, the District Court properly dismissed their complaint. Pp. 421 U. S. 847-858.

(a) When viewed, as they must be, in terms of their substance (the economic realities of the transaction), rather than their form, the instruments involved here were not shares of stock in the ordinary sense of conferring the right to receive "dividends contingent upon an apportionment of profits," Tcherepnin v. Knight,389 U. S. 332, 389 U. S. 339, with the traditional characteristics of being [839] negotiable, subject to pledge or hypothecation, conferring voting rights proportional to the number of shares owned, and possibility of appreciating in value. On the contrary, these instruments were purchased not for making a profit, but for acquiring subsidized low-cost. housing. Pp. 421 U. S. 848-851.

(b) A share in Riverbay does not constitute an "investment contract" as defined by the Securities Acts, a term which, like the term "any . . . instrument commonly known as a security,'" involves investment in a common venture premised on a reasonable expectation of profits to be derived from the entrepreneurial or managerial efforts of others. Here, neither of the kinds of profits traditionally associated with securities were offered to respondents; instead, as indicated in the Information Bulletin, which stressed the "non-profit" nature of the project, the focus was upon the acquisition of a place to live. Pp. 421 U. S. 851-854.

(c) Although deductible for tax purposes, the portion of rental charges applied to interest on the mortgage (benefits generally available to home mortgagors) does not constitute "profits," and, in any event, does not derive from the efforts of third parties. Pp. 421 U. S. 854-855.

(d) Low rent attributable to state financial subsidies no more embodies income or profit attributes than other types of government subsidies. P. 421 U. S. 855.

(e) Such income as might derive from Co-op City's leasing of commercial facilities within the housing project to be used to reduce tenant rentals (the prospect of which was never mentioned in the Information Bulletin) is too speculative and insubstantial to bring the entire transaction within the Securities Acts. These facilities were established not for profit purposes, but to make essential services available to residents of the huge complex. Pp. 421 U. S. 855-857.

500 F.2d 1246, reversed.

POWELL, J., delivered the opinion of the Court, in which BURGER, C.J., and STEWART, MARSHALL, BLACKMUN, and REHNQUIST, JJ., joined. BRENNAN, J., filed a dissenting opinion, in which DOUGLAS and WHITE, JJ., joined, post, p. 421 U. S. 860.

[840]

MR. JUSTICE POWELL delivered the opinion of the Court.

The issue in these cases is whether shares of stock entitling a purchaser to lease an apartment in Co-op City, a state subsidized and supervised nonprofit housing cooperative, are "securities" within the purview of the Securities Act of 1933 and the Securities Exchange Act of 1934.

I

****

In view of the importance of the issues presented, we granted certiorari. 419 U.S. 1120 (1975). As we conclude that the disputed transactions are not purchases of securities within the contemplation of the federal statutes, we reverse.

II

Section 2(1) of the Securities Act of 1933, 15 U.S.C. § 77b(1), defines a "security" as

"any note, stock, treasury stock, bond, debenture, evidence of indebtedness, certificate of interest or participation in any profit-sharing agreement, collateral trust certificate, preorganization certificate or subscription, transferable share, investment contract, voting-trust certificate, certificate of deposit for a security, fractional undivided interest in oil, gas, or other mineral rights, or, in general, any interest or instrument commonly known as a 'security,' or any certificate of interest or participation in, temporary or interim certificate for, receipt for, guarantee of, or warrant or right to subscribe to or purchase, any of the foregoing.[12]

In providing this definition, Congress did not attempt to articulate the relevant economic criteria for distinguishing "securities" from "non-securities." Rather, it sought to define

"the term 'security' in sufficiently broad and general terms so as to include within that definition the many types of instruments that, in our commercial world [848] fall within the ordinary concept of a security."

H.R.Rep. No. 85, 73d Cong., 1st Sess., 11 (1933). The task has fallen to the Securities and Exchange Commission (SEC), the body charged with administering the Securities Acts, and ultimately to the federal courts to decide which of the myriad financial transactions in our society come within the coverage of these statutes.

In making this determination in the present case, we do not write on a clean slate. Well-settled principles enunciated by this Court establish that the shares purchased by respondents do not represent any of the "countless and variable scheme devised by those who seek the use of the money of others on the promise of profits," Howey, 328 U.S. at 328 U. S. 299, and therefore do not fall within "the ordinary concept of a security."

A

We reject at the outset any suggestion that the present transaction, evidenced by the sale of shares called "stock,"[13] must be considered a security transaction simply because the statutory definition of a security includes the words "any . . . stock." Rather, we adhere to the basic principle that has guided all of the Court's decisions in this area:

"[I]n searching for the meaning and scope of the word 'security' in the Act[s], form should be disregarded for substance and the emphasis should be on economic reality."

Tcherepnin v. Knight,389 U. S. 332, 389 U. S. 336 (1967). See also Howey, supra, at 328 U. S. 298. [849]

The primary purpose of the Acts of 1933 and 1934 was to eliminate serious abuses in a largely unregulated securities market. The focus of the Acts is on the capital market of the enterprise system: the sale of securities to raise capital for profit-making purposes, the exchanges on which securities are traded, and the need for regulation to prevent fraud and to protect the interest of investors. Because securities transactions are economic in character, Congress intended the application of these statutes to turn on the economic realities underlying a transaction, and not on the name appended thereto. Thus, in construing these Acts against the background of their purpose, we are guided by a traditional canon of statutory construction:

"[A] thing may be within the letter of the statute and yet not within the statute, because not within its spirit, nor within the intention of its makers."

Church of the Holy Trinity v. United States,143 U. S. 457, 143 U. S. 459 (1892). See also United States v. American Trucking Assns.,310 U. S. 534, 310 U. S. 543 (1940).[14] Respondents' reliance on Joiner as support for a "literal approach" to defining a security is misplaced. The issue in Joiner was whether assignments of interests in oil leases, coupled with the promoters' offer to drill an exploratory well, were securities. Looking to the economic [850] inducement provided by the proposed exploratory well, the Court concluded that these leases were securities even though "leases" as such were not included in the list of instruments mentioned in the statutory definition. In dictum, the Court noted that

"[i]nstruments may be included within [the definition of a security], as [a] matter of law, if on their face they answer to the name or description."

320 U.S. at 320 U. S. 351 (emphasis supplied). And later, again in dictum, the Court stated that a security "might" be shown "by proving the document itself, which, on its face, would be a note, a bond, or a share of stock." Id. at 320 U. S. 355 (emphasis supplied). By using the conditional words "may" and "might" in these dicta the Court made clear that it was not establishing an inflexible rule barring inquiry into the economic realities underlying a transaction. On the contrary, the Court intended only to make the rather obvious point that, in contrast to the instrument before it which was not included within the explicit statutory terms, most instruments bearing these traditional titles are likely to be covered by the statutes.[15]

In holding that the name given to an instrument is not dispositive, we do not suggest that the name is wholly irrelevant to the decision whether it is a security. There may be occasions when the use of a traditional name such as "stocks" or "bonds" will lead a purchaser justifiably to assume that the federal securities laws apply. [851] This would clearly be the case when the underlying transaction embodies some of the significant characteristics typically associated with the named instrument.

In the present case, respondents do not contend, nor could they, that they were misled by use of the word "stock" into believing that the federal securities laws governed their purchase. Common sense suggests that people who intend to acquire only a residential apartment in a state-subsidized cooperative, for their personal use, are not likely to believe that, in reality they are purchasing investment securities simply because the transaction is evidenced by something called a share of stock. These shares have none of the characteristics "that, in our commercial world fall within the ordinary concept of a security." H.R.Rep. No. 85, supra, at 11. Despite their name, they lack what the Court in Tcherepnin deemed the most common feature of stock: the right to receive "dividends contingent upon an apportionment of profits." 389 U.S. at 389 U. S. 339. Nor do they possess the other characteristics traditionally associated with stock: they are not negotiable; they cannot be pledged or hypothecated; they confer no voting rights in proportion to the number of shares owned; and they cannot appreciate in value. In short, the inducement to purchase was solely to acquire subsidized low-cost living space; it was not to invest for profit.

B

The Court of Appeals, as an alternative ground for its decision, concluded that a share in Riverbay was also an "investment contract" as defined by the Securities Acts. Respondents further argue that, in any event, what they agreed to purchase is "commonly known as a security'" within the meaning of these laws. In considering these claims, we again must examine the substance -- the economic realities of the transaction -- rather than the [852] names that may have been employed by the parties. We perceive no distinction, for present purposes, between an "investment contract" and an "instrument commonly known as a 'security.'" In either case, the basic test for distinguishing the transaction from other commercial dealings is

"whether the scheme involves an investment of money in a common enterprise with profits to come solely from the efforts of others."

Howey, 328 U.S. at 328 U. S. 301. [Footnote 16] This test, in shorthand form, embodies the essential attributes that run through all of the Court's decisions defining a security. The touchstone is the presence of an investment in a common venture premised on a reasonable expectation of profits to be derived from the entrepreneurial or managerial efforts of others. By profits, the Court has meant either capital appreciation resulting from the development of the initial investment, as in Joiner, supra, (sale of oil leases conditioned on promoters' agreement to drill exploratory well), or a participation in earnings resulting from the use of investors' funds, as in Tcherepnin v. Knight, supra (dividends on the investment based on savings and loan association's profits). In such cases, the investor is "attracted solely by the prospects of a return" on his investment. Howey, supra, at 328 U. S. 300. By contrast, when a purchaser is motivated by a [853] desire to use or consume the item purchased -- "to occupy the land or to develop it themselves," as the Howey Court put it, ibid. -- the securities laws do not apply. [Footnote 17] See also Joiner, supra.[18]

In the present case, there can be no doubt that investors were attracted solely by the prospect of acquiring a place to live, and not by financial returns on their investments. The Information Bulletin distributed to prospective residents emphasized the fundamental nature and purpose of the undertaking:

"A cooperative is a non-profit enterprise owned and controlled democratically by its members -- the people who are using its services. . . ."
"* * * *"

"People find living in a cooperative community enjoyable for more than one reason. Most people join, however, for the simple reason that it is a way to obtain decent housing at a reasonable price.

However, there are other advantages. The purpose of a cooperative is to provide home ownership, not just apartments to rent. The community is designed to provide a favorable environment for family and community living. . . ."

"The common bond of collective ownership which you share makes living in a cooperative different. It is a community of neighbors. Home ownership, common interest, and the community atmosphere make living in a cooperative like living in a small town. As a rule, there is very little turnover in a cooperative."

App. 162a, 166a. Nowhere does the Bulletin seek to attract investors by the prospect of profits resulting from the efforts of the promoters or third parties. On the contrary, the Bulletin repeatedly emphasizes the "nonprofit" nature of the endeavor. It explains that, if rental charges exceed expenses, the difference will be returned as a rebate, not invested for profit. It also informs purchasers that they will be unable to resell their apartments at a profit, since the apartment must first be offered back to Riverbay "at the price . . . paid for it."[19] Id. at 163a. In short, neither of the kinds of profits traditionally associated with securities was offered to respondents.

The Court of Appeals recognized that there must be an expectation of profits for these shares to be securities, and conceded that there is "no possible profit on a resale of [this] stock." 500 F.2d at 1254. The court correctly noted, however, that profit may be derived from the income yielded by an investment as well as from capital appreciation, and then proceeded to find "a expectation of income' in at least three ways." Ibid. Two of these supposed sources of income or profits may be disposed of summarily. We turn first to the Court of Appeals' reliance on the deductibility for tax purposes of the portion of the monthly rental charge applied to interest on the mortgage. We know of no basis in law for the view that the payment of interest, with its consequent deductibility for tax purposes, constitutes income or profits.[20] These tax benefits are nothing more than that which is available to any homeowner who pays interest on his mortgage. See § 216 of Internal Revenue Code, 26 U.S.C. § 216; Eckstein v. United States, 196 Ct.Cl. 644, 452 F.2d 1036 (1971).

The Court of Appeals also found support for its concept of profits in the fact that Co-op City offered space at a cost substantially below the going rental charges for comparable housing. Again, this is an inappropriate theory of "profits" that we cannot accept. The low rent derives from the substantial financial subsidies provided by the State of New York. This benefit cannot be liquidated into cash; nor does it result from the managerial efforts of others. In a real sense, it no more embodies the attributes of income or profits than do welfare benefits, food stamps, or other government subsidies.

The final source of profit relied on by the Court of Appeals was the possibility of net income derived from the leasing by Co-op City of commercial facilities, professional [856] offices and parking spaces, and its operation of community washing machines. The income, if any, from these conveniences, all located within the common areas of the housing project, is to be used to reduce tenant rental costs. Conceptually, one might readily agree that net income from the leasing of commercial and professional facilities is the kind of profit traditionally associated with a security investment.[21] See Tcherepnin v. Knight, supra. But in the present case, this income -- if indeed there is any -- is far too speculative and insubstantial to bring the entire transaction within the Securities Acts.

Initially we note that the prospect of such income as a means of offsetting rental costs is never mentioned in the Information Bulletin. Thus, it is clear that investors were not attracted to Co-op City by the offer of these potential rental reductions. See Joiner, 320 U.S. at 320 U. S. 353. Moreover, nothing in the record suggests that the facilities, in fact, return a profit in the sense that the leasing fees are greater than the actual cost to Co-op City of the space rented.[22] The short of the matter is that the stores and services in question were established not as a means of returning profits to tenant, but for the purpose of making essential services available for the residents of this enormous complex.[23] By statute, these facilities can only be "incidental and appurtenant" to the housing project. N.Y.Priv.Hous. Fin.Law § 12(5) (Supp. 1974-1975). Undoubtedly they make Co-op City a more attractive housing opportunity, but the possibility of some rental reduction is not an "expectation of profit" in the sense found necessary in Howey.[24] [858]

There is no doubt that purchasers in this housing cooperative sought to obtain a decent home at an attractive price. But that type of economic interest characterizes every form of commercial dealing. What distinguishes a security transaction -- and what is absent here -- is an investment where one parts with his money in the hope of receiving profits from the efforts of others, and not where he purchases a commodity for personal consumption or living quarters for personal use.

III

In holding that there is no federal jurisdiction, we do not address the merits of respondents' allegations of fraud. Nor do we indicate any view as to whether the type of claims here involved should be protected by federal regulation.[26] We decide only that the type of transaction before us, in which the purchasers were interested in acquiring housing, rather than making an investment for profit, is not within the scope of the federal securities laws.

Since respondents' claims are not cognizable in federal court, the District Court properly dismissed their complaint.[27] The judgment below is therefore

Reversed.

****

MR JUSTICE BRENNAN, with whom MR. JUSTICE DOUGLAS and MR. JUSTICE WHITE join, dissenting.

I dissent. The property interests here are "securities," in my view, both because they are shares of "stock" and because they are "investment contracts."

APPENDIX

Release No. 5347 (S.E.C. Release No.), Release No. 33-5347, 1973 WL 158443
Securities Act of 1933

SECURITIES AND EXCHANGE COMMISSION (S.E.C.)
GUIDELINES AS TO THE APPLICABILITY OF THE FEDERAL SECURITIES LAWS TO OFFERS AND SALES OF CONDOMINIUMS OR UNITS IN A REAL ESTATE DEVELOPMENT

January 4, 1973

The Securities and Exchange Commission today called attention to the applicability of the federal securities laws to the offer and sale of condominium units, or other units in a real estate development, coupled with an offer or agreement to perform or arrange certain rental or other services for the purchaser. The Commission noted that such offerings may involve the offering of a security in the form of an investment contract or a participation in a profit sharing arrangement within the meaning of the Securities Act of 1933 and the Securities Exchange Act of 1934.[1] Where this is the case any offering of any such securities must comply with the registration and prospectus delivery requirements of the Securities Act, unless an exemption therefrom is available, and must comply with the anti-fraud provisions of the Securities Act and the Securities Exchange Act and the regulations thereunder. In addition, persons engaged in the business of buying or selling investment contracts or participations in profit sharing agreements of this type as agents for others, or as principal for their own account, may be brokers or dealers within the meaning of the Securities Exchange Act, and therefore may be required to be registered as such with the Commission under the provisions of Section 15 of that Act.

The Commission is aware that there is uncertainty about when offerings of condominiums and other types of similar units may be considered to be offerings of securities that should be registered pursuant to the Securities Act. The purpose of this release is to alert persons engaged in the business of building and selling condominiums and similar types of real estate developments to their responsibilities under the Securities Act and to provide guidelines for a determination of when an offering of condominiums or other units may be viewed as an offering of securities. Resort condominiums are one of the more common interests in real estate the offer of which may involve an offering of securities. However, other types of units that are part of a development or project present analogous questions under the federal securities laws. Although this release speaks in terms of condominiums, it applies to offerings of all types of units in real estate developments which have characteristics similar to those described herein.

The offer of real estate as such, without any collateral arrangements with the seller or others, does not involve the offer of a security. When the real estate is offered in conjunction with certain services, a security, in the form of an investment contract, may be present. The Supreme Court in <u>Securities and Exchange Commission</u> v. <u>W. J. Howey Co.</u>, 328 U.S. 293 (1946) set forth what has become a generally accepted definition of an investment contract:

> "a contract, transaction or scheme whereby a person invests his money in a common enterprise and is led to expect profits solely from the efforts of the promoter or a third party, it being immaterial whether the shares in the enterprise are evidenced by formal certificates or by nominal interests in the physical assets employed in the enterprise."(298)

The <u>Howey</u> case involved the sale and operation of orange groves. The reasoning, however, is applicable to condominiums.

As the Court noted in <u>Howey</u> substance should not be disregarded for form, and the fundamental statutory policy of affording broad protection to investors should be heeded. Recent interpretations have indicated that the expected return need not be <u>solely</u> from the efforts of others, as the holding in <u>Howey</u> appears to indicate.[2] For this reason, an investment contract may be present in situations where an investor is not wholly inactive, but even participates to a limited degree in the operations of the business. The "profits" that the purchaser is led to expect may consist of revenues received from rental of the unit; these revenues and any tax benefits resulting from rental of the unit are the economic inducements held out to the purchaser.

The existence of various kinds of collateral arrangements may cause an offering of condominium units to involve an offering of investment contracts or interests in a profit sharing agreement. The presence of such arrangements indicates that the offeror is offering an opportunity through which the purchaser may earn a return on his investment through the managerial efforts of the promoters or a third party in their operation of the enterprise.

For example, some public offerings of condominium units involve rental pool arrangements. Typically, the rental pool is a device whereby the promoter or a third party undertakes to rent the unit on behalf of the actual owner during that period of time when the unit is not in use by the owner. The rents received and the expenses attributable to rental of all the units in the project are combined and the individual owner receives a ratable share of the rental proceeds regardless of whether his individual unit was actually rented. The offer of the unit together with the offer of an opportunity to participate in such a rental pool involves the offer of investment contracts which must be registered unless an exemption is available.

Also, the condominium units may be offered with a contract or agreement that places restrictions, such as required use of an exclusive rental agent or limitations on the period of time the owner may occupy the unit, on the purchaser's occupancy or rental of the property purchased. Such restrictions suggest that the purchaser is in fact investing in a business enterprise, the return from which will be substantially dependent on the success of the managerial efforts of other persons. In such cases, registration of the resulting investment contract would be required.

In any situation where collateral arrangements are coupled with the offering of condominiums, whether or not specifically of the types discussed above, the manner of offering and economic inducements held out to the prospective purchaser play an important role in determining whether the offerings involve securities. In this connection, see Securities and Exchange Commission v. C. M. Joiner Leasing Corp., 320 U.S. 344 (1943). In Joiner, the Supreme Court also noted that:

> "In enforcement of [the Securities Act], it is not inappropriate that promoters' offerings be judged as being what they were represented to be." (353)

In other words, condominiums, coupled with a rental arrangement, will be deemed to be securities if they are offered and sold through advertising, sales literature, promotional schemes or oral representations which emphasize the economic benefits to the purchaser to be derived from the managerial efforts of the promoter, or a third party designated or arranged for by the promoter, in renting the units.

In summary, the offering of condominium units in conjunction with any one of the following will cause the offering to be viewed as an offering of securities in the form of investment contracts:

1. The condominiums, with any rental arrangement or other similar service, are offered and sold with emphasis on the economic benefits to the purchaser to be derived from the managerial efforts of the promoter, or a third party designated or arranged for by the promoter, from rental of the units.
2. The offering of participation in a rental pool arrangement; and
3. The offering of a rental or similar arrangement whereby the purchaser must hold his unit available for rental for any part of the year, must use an exclusive rental agent or is otherwise materially restricted in his occupancy or rental of his unit.

In all of the above situations, investor protection requires the application of the federal securities laws.

If the condominiums are not offered and sold with emphasis on the economic benefits to the purchaser to be derived from the managerial efforts of others, and assuming that no plan to avoid the registration requirements of the Securities Act is involved, an owner of a condominium unit may, after purchasing his unit, enter into a non-pooled rental arrangement with an agent not designated or required to be used as a condition to the purchase, whether or not such agent is affiliated with the offeror, without causing a sale of a security to be involved in the sale of the unit. Further a continuing affiliation between the developers or promoters of a project and the project by reason of maintenance arrangements does not make the unit a security.

In situations where commercial facilities are a part of the common elements of a residential project, no registration would be required under the investment contract theory where (a) the income from such facilities is used only to offset common area expenses and (b) the operation of such facilities is incidental to the project as a whole and are not established as a primary income source for the individual owners of a condominium or cooperative unit.

The Commission recognizes the need for a degree of certainty in the real estate offering area and believes that the above guidelines will be helpful in assisting persons to comply with the securities laws. It is difficult, however, to anticipate the variety of arrangements that may accompany the offering of condominium projects. The Commission, therefore, would like to remind those engaged in the offering of condominiums or other interests in real estate with similar features that there may be situations, not referred to in this release, in which the offering of the interests constitutes an offering of securities. Whether an offering of securities is involved necessarily depends on the facts and circumstances of each particular case. The staff of the Commission will be available to respond to written inquiries on such matters.

By the Commission.

Ronald F. Hunt

Secretary

FOOTNOTES

[1] It should be noted that where an investment contract is present, it consists of the agreement offered and the condominium itself.

[2] SEC v. Glenn W. Turner Enterprises, Inc. CCH Fed Sec L. Rep. ¶93, 605 (D.C. Ore. No. 72-390, May 25, 1972) See also State v. Hawaii Market Center, Inc., 485 P. 2d 105 (1971) (cited in Securities Act Release No. 5211 (1971); and Securities Act Release No. 5018 (1969) regarding the applicability of the federal securities laws to the sale and distribution of whiskey warehouse receipts.

Release No. 5347 (S.E.C. Release No.), Release No. 33-5347, 1973 WL 158443

Rev. Proc. 2002-22
Covering Undivided Fractional Interests

SECTION 1. PURPOSE

This revenue procedure specifies the conditions under which the Internal Revenue Service will consider a request for a ruling that an undivided fractional interest in rental real property (other than a mineral property as defined in section 614) is not an interest in a business entity, within the meaning of § 301.7701-2(a) of the Procedure and Administration Regulations.

This revenue procedure supersedes Rev. Proc. 2000-46, 2002-2 C.B. 438, which provides that the Service will not issue advance rulings or determination letters on the questions of whether an undivided fractional interest in real property is an interest in an entity that is not eligible for tax-free exchange under § 1031(a)(1) of the Internal Revenue Code and whether arrangements where taxpayers acquire undivided fractional interests in real property constitute separate entities for federal tax purposes under § 7701. This revenue procedure also modifies Rev. Proc. 2002-3, 2002-1 I.R.B. 117, by removing these issues from the list of subjects on which the Service will not rule. Requests for advance rulings described in Rev. Proc. 2000-46 that are not covered by this revenue procedure, such as rulings concerning mineral property, will be considered under procedures set forth in Rev. Proc. 2002-1, 2002-1 I.R.B. 1 (or its successor).

SECTION 2. BACKGROUND

Section 301.7701-1(a)(1) provides that whether an organization is an entity separate from its owners for federal tax purposes is a matter of federal law and does not depend on whether the entity is recognized as an entity under local law. Section 301.7701-1(a)(2) provides that a joint venture or other contractual arrangement may create a separate entity for federal tax purposes if the participants carry on a trade, business, financial operation, or venture and divide the profits therefrom, but the mere co- ownership of property that is maintained, kept in repair, and rented or leased does not constitute a separate entity for federal tax purposes.

Section 301.7701-2(a) provides that a business entity is any entity recognized for federal tax purposes (including an entity with a single owner that may be disregarded as an entity separate from its owner under § 301.7701-3) that is not properly classified as a trust under § 301.7701-4 or otherwise subject to special treatment under the Internal Revenue Code. A business entity with two or more members is classified for federal tax purposes as either a corporation or a partnership.

Section 761(a) provides that the term "partnership" includes a syndicate, group, pool, joint venture, or other unincorporated organization through or by means of which any business, financial operation, or venture is carried on, and that is not a corporation or a trust or estate. Section 1.761-1(a) of the Income Tax Regulations provides that the term "partnership" means a partnership as determined under §§ 301.7701-1, 301.7701-2, and 301.7701-3.

The central characteristic of a tenancy in common, one of the traditional concurrent estates in land, is that each owner is deemed to own individually a physically undivided part of the entire parcel of property. Each tenant in common is entitled to share with the other tenants the possession of the whole parcel and has the associated rights to a proportionate share of rents or profits from the property, to transfer the interest, and to demand a partition of the property. These rights generally provide a tenant in common the benefits of ownership of the property within the constraint that no rights may be exercised to the detriment of the other tenants in common. 7 Richard R. Powell, Powell on Real Property §§ 50.01-50.07 (Michael Allan Wolf ed., 2000).

Rev. Rul. 75-374, 1975-2 C.B. 261, concludes that a two-person co-ownership of an apartment building that was rented to tenants did not constitute a partnership for federal tax purposes. In the revenue ruling, the co-owners employed an agent to manage the apartments on their behalf; the agent collected rents, paid property taxes, insurance premiums, repair and maintenance expenses, and provided the tenants with customary services, such as heat, air conditioning, trash removal, unattended parking, and maintenance of public areas. The ruling concludes that the agent's activities in providing customary services to the tenants, although imputed to the co-owners, were not sufficiently extensive to cause the co-ownership to be characterized as a partnership. See also Rev. Rul. 79-77, 1979-1 C.B. 448, which did not find a business entity where three individuals transferred ownership of a commercial building subject to a net lease to a trust with the three individuals as beneficiaries.

Where a sponsor packages co-ownership interests for sale by acquiring property, negotiating a master lease on the property, and arranging for financing, the courts have looked at the relationships not only among the co-owners, but also between the sponsor (or persons related to the sponsor) and the co-owners in determining whether the co- ownership gives rise to a partnership. For example, in Bergford v. Commissioner, 12 F.3d 166 (9th Cir. 1993), seventy-eight investors purchased "co-ownership" interests in computer equipment that was subject to a 7-year net lease. As part of the purchase, the co-owners authorized the manager to arrange financing and refinancing, purchase and lease the equipment, collect rents and apply those rents to the notes used to finance the equipment, prepare statements, and advance funds to participants on an interest-free basis to meet cash flow. The agreement allowed the co-owners to decide by majority vote whether to sell or lease the equipment at the end of the lease. Absent a majority vote, the manager could make that decision. In addition, the manager was entitled to a remarketing fee of 10 percent of the equipment's selling price or lease rental whether or not a co-owner terminated the agreement or the manager performed any remarketing. A co-owner could assign an interest in the co-ownership only after fulfilling numerous conditions and obtaining the manager's consent.

The court held that the co-ownership arrangement constituted a partnership for federal tax purposes. Among the factors that influenced the court's decision were the limitations on the co-owners' ability to sell, lease, or encumber either the co-ownership interest or the underlying property, and the manager's effective participation in both profits (through the remarketing fee) and losses (through the advances). Bergford, 12 F.3d at 169-170. Accord Bussing v. Commissioner, 88 T.C. 449 (1987), aff'd on reh'g, 89 T.C. 1050 (1987); Alhouse v. Commissioner, T.C. Memo. 1991-652.

Under § 1.761-1(a) and §§ 301.7701-1 through 301.7701-3, a federal tax partnership does not include mere co-ownership of property where the owners' activities are limited to keeping the property maintained, in repair, rented or leased. However, as the above authorities demonstrate, a partnership for federal tax purposes is broader in scope than the common law meaning of partnership and may include groups not classified by state law as partnerships. Bergford, 12 F.3d at 169. Where the parties to a venture join together capital or services with the intent of conducting a business or enterprise and of sharing the profits and losses from the venture, a partnership (or other business entity) is created. Bussing, 88 T.C. at 460. Furthermore, where the economic benefits to the individual participants are not derivative of their co-ownership, but rather come from their joint relationship toward a common goal, the co-ownership arrangement will be characterized as a partnership (or other business entity) for federal tax purposes. Bergford, 12 F.3d at 169.

SECTION 3. SCOPE

This revenue procedure applies to co-ownership of rental real property (other than mineral interests) (the Property) in an arrangement classified under local law as a tenancy-in-common. This revenue procedure provides guidelines for requesting advance rulings solely to assist taxpayers in preparing ruling requests and the Service in issuing advance ruling letters as promptly as practicable. The guidelines set forth in this revenue procedure are not intended to be substantive rules and are not to be used for audit purposes.

SECTION 4. GUIDELINES FOR SUBMITTING RULING REQUESTS

The Service ordinarily will not consider a request for a ruling under this revenue procedure unless the information described in section 5 of this revenue procedure is included in the ruling request and the conditions described in section 6 of this revenue procedure are satisfied. Even if sections 5 and 6 of this revenue procedure are satisfied, however, the Service may decline to issue a ruling under this revenue procedure whenever warranted by the facts and circumstances of a particular case and whenever appropriate in the interest of sound tax administration.

Where multiple parcels of property owned by the co-owners are leased to a single tenant pursuant to a single lease agreement and any debt of one or more co-owners is secured by all of the parcels, the Service will generally treat all of the parcels as a single "Property." In such a case, the Service will generally not consider a ruling request under this revenue procedure unless: (1) each co-owner's percentage interest in each parcel is identical to that co-owner's percentage interest in every other parcel, (2) each co-owner's percentage interests in the parcels cannot be separated and traded independently, and (3) the parcels of property are properly viewed as a single business unit. The Service will generally treat contiguous parcels as comprising a single business unit. Even if the parcels are not contiguous, however, the Service may treat multiple parcels as comprising a single business unit where there is a close connection between the business use of one parcel and the business use of another parcel. For example, an office building and a garage that services the tenants of the office building may be treated as a single business unit even if the office building and the garage are not contiguous.

For purposes of this revenue procedure, the following definitions apply. The term "co-owner" means any person that owns an interest in the Property as a tenant in common. The term "sponsor" means any person who divides a single interest in the Property into multiple co-ownership interests for the purpose of offering those interests for sale. The term "related person" means a person bearing a relationship described in § 267(b) or 707(b)(1), except that in applying § 267(b) or 707(b)(1), the co-ownership will be treated as a partnership and each co-owner will be treated as a partner. The term "disregarded entity" means an entity that is disregarded as an entity separate from its owner for federal tax purposes. Examples of disregarded entities include qualified REIT subsidiaries (within the meaning of § 856(i)(2)), qualified subchapter S subsidiaries (within the meaning of § 1361(b)(3)(B)), and business entities that have only one owner and do not elect to be classified as corporations. The term "blanket lien" means any mortgage or trust deed that is recorded against the Property as a whole.

SECTION 5. INFORMATION TO BE SUBMITTED

.01 Section 8 of Rev. Proc. 2002-1 outlines general requirements concerning the information to be submitted as part of a ruling request, including advance rulings under this revenue procedure. For example, any ruling request must contain a complete statement of all facts relating to the co-ownership, including those relating to promoting, financing, and managing the Property. Among the information to be included are the items of information specified in this revenue procedure; therefore, the ruling request must provide all items of information and conditions specified below and in section 6 of this revenue procedure, or at least account for all of the items. For example, if a co- ownership arrangement has no brokerage agreement permitted in section 6.12 of this revenue procedure, the ruling request should so state. Furthermore, merely submitting documents and supplementary materials required by section 5.02 of this revenue procedure does not satisfy all of the information requirements contained in section 5.02 of this revenue procedure or in section 8 of Rev. Proc. 2002-1; all material facts in the documents submitted must be explained in the ruling request and may not be merely incorporated by reference. All submitted documents and supplementary materials must contain applicable exhibits, attachments, and amendments. The ruling request must identify and explain any information or documents required in section 5 of this revenue procedure that are not included and any conditions in section 6 of this revenue procedure that are or are not satisfied.

.02 <u>Required General Information and Copies of Documents and Supplementary Materials</u>. Generally the following information and copies of documents and materials must be submitted with the ruling request:

(1) The name, taxpayer identification number, and percentage fractional interest in Property of each co-owner;

(2) The name, taxpayer identification number, ownership of, and any relationship among, all persons involved in the acquisition, sale, lease and other use of Property, including the sponsor, lessee, manager, and lender;

(3) A full description of the Property;

(4) A representation that each of the co-owners holds title to the Property (including each of multiple parcels of property treated as a single Property under this revenue procedure) as a tenant in common under local law;

(5) All promotional documents relating to the sale of fractional interests in the Property;

(6) All lending agreements relating to the Property;

(7) All agreements among the co-owners relating to the Property;

(8) Any lease agreement relating to the Property;

(9) Any purchase and sale agreement relating to the Property;

(10) Any property management or brokerage agreement relating to the Property; and

(11) Any other agreement relating to the Property not specified in this section, including agreements relating to any debt secured by the Property (such as guarantees or indemnity agreements) and any call and put options relating to the Property.

SECTION 6. CONDITIONS FOR OBTAINING RULINGS

The Service ordinarily will not consider a request for a ruling under this revenue procedure unless the conditions described below are satisfied. Nevertheless, where the conditions described below are not satisfied, the Service may consider a request for a ruling under this revenue procedure where the facts and circumstances clearly establish that such a ruling is appropriate.

.01 <u>Tenancy in Common Ownership</u>. Each of the co-owners must hold title to the Property (either directly or through a disregarded entity) as a tenant in common under local law. Thus, title to the Property as a whole may not be held by an entity recognized under local law.

.02 <u>Number of Co-Owners</u>. The number of co-owners must be limited to no more than 35 persons. For this purpose, "person" is defined as in § 7701(a)(1), except that a husband and wife are treated as a single person and all persons who acquire interests from a co-owner by inheritance are treated as a single person.

.03 <u>No Treatment of Co-Ownership as an Entity</u>. The co-ownership may not file a partnership or corporate tax return, conduct business under a common name, execute an agreement identifying any or all of the co-owners as partners, shareholders, or members of a business entity, or otherwise hold itself out as a partnership or other form of business entity (nor may the co-owners hold themselves out as partners, shareholders, or members of a business entity). The Service generally will not issue a ruling under this revenue procedure if the co-owners held interests in the Property through a partnership or corporation immediately prior to the formation of the co-ownership.

.04 <u>Co-Ownership Agreement</u>. The co-owners may enter into a limited co-ownership agreement that may run with the land. For example, a co-ownership agreement may provide that a co-owner must offer the co-ownership interest for sale to the other co-owners, the sponsor, or the lessee at fair market value (determined as of the time the partition right is exercised) before exercising any right to partition (see section 6.06 of this revenue procedure for conditions relating to restrictions on alienation); or that certain actions on behalf of the co-ownership require the vote of co-owners holding more than 50 percent of the undivided interests in the Property (see section 6.05 of this revenue procedure for conditions relating to voting).

.05 <u>Voting</u>. The co-owners must retain the right to approve the hiring of any manager, the sale or other disposition of the Property, any leases of a portion or all of the Property, or the creation or modification of a blanket lien. Any sale, lease, or re-lease of a portion or all of the Property, any negotiation or renegotiation of indebtedness secured by a blanket lien, the hiring of any manager, or the negotiation of any management contract (or any extension or renewal of such contract) must be by unanimous approval of the co- owners. For all other actions on behalf of the co-ownership, the co-owners may agree to be bound by the vote of those holding more than 50 percent of the undivided interests in the Property. A co-owner who has consented to an action in conformance with this section 6.05 may provide the manager or other person a power of attorney to execute a specific document with respect to that action, but may not provide the manager or other person with a global power of attorney.

.06 <u>Restrictions on Alienation</u>. In general, each co-owner must have the rights to transfer, partition, and encumber the co-owner's undivided interest in the Property without the agreement or approval of any person. However, restrictions on the right to transfer, partition, or encumber interests in the Property that are required by a lender and that are consistent with customary commercial lending practices are not prohibited. See section 6.14 of this revenue procedure for restrictions on who may be a lender. Moreover, the co-owners, the sponsor, or the lessee may have a right of first offer (the right to have the first opportunity to offer to purchase the co-ownership interest) with respect to any co-owner's exercise of the right to transfer the co-ownership interest in the Property. In addition, a co-owner may agree to offer the co-ownership interest for sale to the other co-owners, the sponsor, or the lessee at fair market value (determined as of the time the partition right is exercised) before exercising any right to partition.

.07 <u>Sharing Proceeds and Liabilities upon Sale of Property</u>. If the Property is sold, any debt secured by a blanket lien must be satisfied and the remaining sales proceeds must be distributed to the co-owners.

.08 <u>Proportionate Sharing of Profits and Losses</u>. Each co-owner must share in all revenues generated by the Property and all costs associated with the Property in proportion to the co-owner's undivided interest in the Property. Neither the other co- owners, nor the sponsor, nor the manager may advance funds to a co-owner to meet expenses associated with the co-ownership interest, unless the advance is recourse to the co-owner (and, where the co-owner is a disregarded entity, the owner of the co-owner) and is not for a period exceeding 31 days.

.09 <u>Proportionate Sharing of Debt</u>. The co-owners must share in any indebtedness secured by a blanket lien in proportion to their undivided interests.

.10 <u>Options</u>. A co-owner may issue an option to purchase the co-owner's undivided interest (call option), provided that the exercise price for the call option reflects the fair market value of the Property determined as of the time the option is exercised. For this purpose, the fair market value of an undivided interest in the Property is equal to the co-owner's percentage interest in the Property multiplied by the fair market value of the Property as a whole. A co-owner may not acquire an option to sell the co-owner's undivided interest (put option) to the sponsor, the lessee, another co-owner, or the lender, or any person related to the sponsor, the lessee, another co-owner, or the lender.

.11 <u>No Business Activities</u>. The co-owners' activities must be limited to those customarily performed in connection with the maintenance and repair of rental real property (customary activities). See Rev. Rul. 75-374, 1975-2 C.B. 261. Activities will be treated as customary activities for this purpose if the activities would not prevent an amount received by an organization described in § 511(a)(2) from qualifying as rent under § 512(b)(3)(A) and the regulations thereunder. In determining the co-owners' activities, all activities of the co-owners, their agents, and any persons related to the co- owners with respect to the Property will be taken into account, whether or not those activities are performed by the co-owners in their capacities as co-owners. For example, if the sponsor or a lessee is a co-owner, then all of the activities of the sponsor or lessee (or any person related to the sponsor or lessee) with respect to the Property will be taken into account in determining whether the co-owners' activities are customary activities. However, activities of a co-owner or a related person with respect to the Property (other than in the co-owner's capacity as a co-owner) will not be taken into account if the co-owner owns an undivided interest in the Property for less than 6 months.

.12 <u>Management and Brokerage Agreements</u>. The co-owners may enter into management or brokerage agreements, which must be renewable no less frequently than annually, with an agent, who may be the sponsor or a co-owner (or any person related to the sponsor or a co-owner), but who may not be a lessee. The management agreement may authorize the manager to maintain a common bank account for the collection and deposit of rents and to offset expenses associated with the Property against any revenues before disbursing each co-owner's share of net revenues. In all events, however, the manager must disburse to the co-owners their shares of net revenues within 3 months from the date of receipt of those revenues. The management agreement may also authorize the manager to prepare statements for the co-owners showing their shares of revenue and costs from the Property. In addition, the management agreement may authorize the manager to obtain or modify insurance on the Property, and to negotiate modifications of the terms of any lease or any indebtedness encumbering the Property, subject to the approval of the co-owners. (See section 6.05 of this revenue procedure for conditions relating to the approval of lease and debt modifications.) The determination of any fees paid by the co-ownership to the manager must not depend in whole or in part on the income or profits derived by any person from the Property and may not exceed the fair market value of the manager's services. Any fee paid by the co-ownership to a broker must be comparable to fees paid by unrelated parties to brokers for similar services.

.13 <u>Leasing Agreements</u>. All leasing arrangements must be bona fide leases for federal tax purposes. Rents paid by a lessee must reflect the fair market value for the use of the Property. The determination of the amount of the rent must not depend, in whole or in part, on the income or profits derived by any person from the Property leased (other than an amount based on a fixed percentage or percentages of receipts or sales). See section 856(d)(2)(A) and the regulations thereunder. Thus, for example, the amount of rent paid by a lessee may not be based on a percentage of net income from the Property, cash flow, increases in equity, or similar arrangements.

.14 <u>Loan Agreements</u>. The lender with respect to any debt that encumbers the Property or with respect to any debt incurred to acquire an undivided interest in the Property may not be a related person to any co-owner, the sponsor, the manager, or any lessee of the Property.

.15 <u>Payments to Sponsor</u>. Except as otherwise provided in this revenue procedure, the amount of any payment to the sponsor for the acquisition of the co- ownership interest (and the amount of any fees paid to the sponsor for services) must reflect the fair market value of the acquired co-ownership interest (or the services rendered) and may not depend, in whole or in part, on the income or profits derived by any person from the Property.

Regulation D—Rules Governing the Limited Offer and Sale of Securities Without Registration Under the Securities Act of 1933

Source: Sections 230.501 through 230.506 appear at 47 FR 11262, Mar. 16, 1982, unless otherwise noted.

§230.500 Use of Regulation D.

Users of Regulation D (§§230.500 *et seq.*) should note the following:

(a) Regulation D relates to transactions exempted from the registration requirements of section 5 of the Securities Act of 1933 (the Act) (15 U.S.C.77a *et seq.*, as amended). Such transactions are not exempt from the antifraud, civil liability, or other provisions of the federal securities laws. Issuers are reminded of their obligation to provide such further material information, if any, as may be necessary to make the information required under Regulation D, in light of the circumstances under which it is furnished, not misleading.

(b) Nothing in Regulation D obviates the need to comply with any applicable state law relating to the offer and sale of securities. Regulation D is intended to be a basic element in a uniform system of federal-state limited offering exemptions consistent with the provisions of sections 18 and 19(c) of the Act (15 U.S.C. 77r and 77(s)(c)). In those states that have adopted Regulation D, or any version of Regulation D, special attention should be directed to the applicable state laws and regulations, including those relating to registration of persons who receive remuneration in connection with the offer and sale of securities, to disqualification of issuers and other persons associated with offerings based on state administrative orders or judgments, and to requirements for filings of notices of sales.

(c) Attempted compliance with any rule in Regulation D does not act as an exclusive election; the issuer can also claim the availability of any other applicable exemption. For instance, an issuer's failure to satisfy all the terms and conditions of rule 506(b) (§230.506(b)) shall not raise any presumption that the exemption provided by section 4(a)(2) of the Act (15 U.S.C. 77d(2)) is not available.

(d) Regulation D is available only to the issuer of the securities and not to any affiliate of that issuer or to any other person for resales of the issuer's securities. Regulation D provides an exemption only for the transactions in which the securities are offered or sold by the issuer, not for the securities themselves.

(e) Regulation D may be used for business combinations that involve sales by virtue of rule 145(a) (§230.145(a)) or otherwise.

(f) In view of the objectives of Regulation D and the policies underlying the Act, Regulation D is not available to any issuer for any transaction or chain of transactions that, although in technical compliance with Regulation D, is part of a plan or scheme to evade the registration provisions of the Act. In such cases, registration under the Act is required.

(g) Securities offered and sold outside the United States in accordance with Regulation S (§230.901 through 905) need not be registered under the Act. See Release No. 33-6863. Regulation S may be relied upon for such offers and sales even if coincident offers and sales are made in accordance with Regulation D inside the United States. Thus, for example, persons who are offered and sold securities in accordance with Regulation S would not be counted in the calculation of the number of purchasers under Regulation D. Similarly, proceeds from such sales would not be included in the aggregate offering price. The provisions of this paragraph (g), however, do not apply if the issuer elects to rely solely on Regulation D for offers or sales to persons made outside the United States.

[77 FR 18684, Mar. 28, 2012, as amended at 78 FR 44804, July 24, 2013]

APPENDIX

§230.501 Definitions and terms used in Regulation D.

As used in Regulation D (§230.500 *et seq.* of this chapter), the following terms shall have the meaning indicated:

(a) *Accredited investor. Accredited investor* shall mean any person who comes within any of the following categories, or who the issuer reasonably believes comes within any of the following categories, at the time of the sale of the securities to that person:

   (1) Any bank as defined in section 3(a)(2) of the Act, or any savings and loan association or other institution as defined in section 3(a)(5)(A) of the Act whether acting in its individual or fiduciary capacity; any broker or dealer registered pursuant to section 15 of the Securities Exchange Act of 1934; any insurance company as defined in section 2(a)(13) of the Act; any investment company registered under the Investment Company Act of 1940 or a business development company as defined in section 2(a)(48) of that Act; any Small Business Investment Company licensed by the U.S. Small Business Administration under section 301(c) or (d) of the Small Business Investment Act of 1958; any plan established and maintained by a state, its political subdivisions, or any agency or instrumentality of a state or its political subdivisions, for the benefit of its employees, if such plan has total assets in excess of $5,000,000; any employee benefit plan within the meaning of the Employee Retirement Income Security Act of 1974 if the investment decision is made by a plan fiduciary, as defined in section 3(21) of such act, which is either a bank, savings and loan association, insurance company, or registered investment adviser, or if the employee benefit plan has total assets in excess of $5,000,000 or, if a self-directed plan, with investment decisions made solely by persons that are accredited investors;

   (2) Any private business development company as defined in section 202(a)(22) of the Investment Advisers Act of 1940;

   (3) Any organization described in section 501(c)(3) of the Internal Revenue Code, corporation, Massachusetts or similar business trust, or partnership, not formed for the specific purpose of acquiring the securities offered, with total assets in excess of $5,000,000;

   (4) Any director, executive officer, or general partner of the issuer of the securities being offered or sold, or any director, executive officer, or general partner of a general partner of that issuer;

   (5) Any natural person whose individual net worth, or joint net worth with that person's spouse, exceeds $1,000,000.

      (i) Except as provided in paragraph (a)(5)(ii) of this section, for purposes of calculating net worth under this paragraph (a)(5):

         (A) The person's primary residence shall not be included as an asset;

         (B) Indebtedness that is secured by the person's primary residence, up to the estimated fair market value of the primary residence at the time of the sale of securities, shall not be included as a liability (except that if the amount of such indebtedness outstanding at the time of sale of securities exceeds the amount outstanding 60 days before such time, other than as a result of the acquisition of the primary residence, the amount of such excess shall be included as a liability); and

         (C) Indebtedness that is secured by the person's primary residence in excess of the estimated fair market value of the primary residence at the time of the sale of securities shall be included as a liability;

(ii) Paragraph (a)(5)(i) of this section will not apply to any calculation of a person's net worth made in connection with a purchase of securities in accordance with a right to purchase such securities, provided that:

- (A) Such right was held by the person on July 20, 2010;
- (B) The person qualified as an accredited investor on the basis of net worth at the time the person acquired such right; and
- (C) The person held securities of the same issuer, other than such right, on July 20, 2010.

(6) Any natural person who had an individual income in excess of $200,000 in each of the two most recent years or joint income with that person's spouse in excess of $300,000 in each of those years and has a reasonable expectation of reaching the same income level in the current year;

(7) Any trust, with total assets in excess of $5,000,000, not formed for the specific purpose of acquiring the securities offered, whose purchase is directed by a sophisticated person as described in §230.506(b)(2)(ii); and

(8) Any entity in which all of the equity owners are accredited investors.

(b) *Affiliate.* An *affiliate* of, or person *affiliated* with, a specified person shall mean a person that directly, or indirectly through one or more intermediaries, controls or is controlled by, or is under common control with, the person specified.

(c) *Aggregate offering price. Aggregate offering price* shall mean the sum of all cash, services, property, notes, cancellation of debt, or other consideration to be received by an issuer for issuance of its securities. Where securities are being offered for both cash and non-cash consideration, the aggregate offering price shall be based on the price at which the securities are offered for cash. Any portion of the aggregate offering price attributable to cash received in a foreign currency shall be translated into United States currency at the currency exchange rate in effect at a reasonable time prior to or on the date of the sale of the securities. If securities are not offered for cash, the aggregate offering price shall be based on the value of the consideration as established by bona fide sales of that consideration made within a reasonable time, or, in the absence of sales, on the fair value as determined by an accepted standard. Such valuations of non-cash consideration must be reasonable at the time made.

(d) *Business combination. Business combination* shall mean any transaction of the type specified in paragraph (a) of Rule 145 under the Act (17 CFR 230.145) and any transaction involving the acquisition by one issuer, in exchange for all or a part of its own or its parent's stock, of stock of another issuer if, immediately after the acquisition, the acquiring issuer has control of the other issuer (whether or not it had control before the acquisition).

(e) *Calculation of number of purchasers.* For purposes of calculating the number of purchasers under § §230.506(b) and 230.506(b) only, the following shall apply:

(1) The following purchasers shall be excluded:

- (i) Any relative, spouse or relative of the spouse of a purchaser who has the same primary residence as the purchaser;
- (ii) Any trust or estate in which a purchaser and any of the persons related to him as specified in paragraph (e)(1)(i) or (e)(1)(iii) of this section collectively have more than 50 percent of the beneficial interest (excluding contingent interests);
- (iii) Any corporation or other organization of which a purchaser and any of the persons related to him as specified in paragraph (e)(1)(i) or (e)(1)(ii) of this section collectively are beneficial owners of more than 50 percent of the equity securities (excluding directors' qualifying shares) or equity interests; and
- (iv) Any accredited investor.

(2) A corporation, partnership or other entity shall be counted as one purchaser. If, however, that entity is organized for the specific purpose of acquiring the securities offered and is not an accredited investor under paragraph (a)(8) of this section, then each beneficial owner of equity securities or equity interests in the entity shall count as a separate purchaser for all provisions of Regulation D (§§230.501-230.508), except to the extent provided in paragraph (e)(1) of this section.

(3) A non-contributory employee benefit plan within the meaning of Title I of the Employee Retirement Income Security Act of 1974 shall be counted as one purchaser where the trustee makes all investment decisions for the plan.

NOTE: The issuer must satisfy all the other provisions of Regulation D for all purchasers whether or not they are included in calculating the number of purchasers. Clients of an investment adviser or customers of a broker or dealer shall be considered the "purchasers" under Regulation D regardless of the amount of discretion given to the investment adviser or broker or dealer to act on behalf of the client or customer.

(f) *Executive officer. Executive officer* shall mean the president, any vice president in charge of a principal business unit, division or function (such as sales, administration or finance), any other officer who performs a policy making function, or any other person who performs similar policy making functions for the issuer. Executive officers of subsidiaries may be deemed executive officers of the issuer if they perform such policy making functions for the issuer.

(g) *Final order. Final order* shall mean a written directive or declaratory statement issued by a federal or state agency described in §230.506(d)(1)(iii) under applicable statutory authority that provides for notice and an opportunity for hearing, which constitutes a final disposition or action by that federal or state agency.

(h) *Issuer.* The definition of the term *issuer* in section 2(a)(4) of the Act shall apply, except that in the case of a proceeding under the Federal Bankruptcy Code (11 U.S.C. 101 *et seq.*), the trustee or debtor in possession shall be considered the issuer in an offering under a plan or reorganization, if the securities are to be issued under the plan.

(i) *Purchaser representative. Purchaser representative* shall mean any person who satisfies all of the following conditions or who the issuer reasonably believes satisfies all of the following conditions:

    (1) Is not an affiliate, director, officer or other employee of the issuer, or beneficial owner of 10 percent or more of any class of the equity securities or 10 percent or more of the equity interest in the issuer, except where the purchaser is:

        (i) A relative of the purchaser representative by blood, marriage or adoption and not more remote than a first cousin;

        (ii) A trust or estate in which the purchaser representative and any persons related to him as specified in paragraph (h)(1)(i) or (h)(1)(iii) of this section collectively have more than 50 percent of the beneficial interest (excluding contingent interest) or of which the purchaser representative serves as trustee, executor, or in any similar capacity; or

        (iii) A corporation or other organization of which the purchaser representative and any persons related to him as specified in paragraph (h)(1)(i) or (h)(1)(ii) of this section collectively are the beneficial owners of more than 50 percent of the equity securities (excluding directors' qualifying shares) or equity interests;

    (2) Has such knowledge and experience in financial and business matters that he is capable of evaluating, alone, or together with other purchaser representatives of the purchaser, or together with the purchaser, the merits and risks of the prospective investment;

(3)   Is acknowledged by the purchaser in writing, during the course of the transaction, to be his purchaser representative in connection with evaluating the merits and risks of the prospective investment; and

(4)   Discloses to the purchaser in writing a reasonable time prior to the sale of securities to that purchaser any material relationship between himself or his affiliates and the issuer or its affiliates that then exists, that is mutually understood to be contemplated, or that has existed at any time during the previous two years, and any compensation received or to be received as a result of such relationship.

NOTE 1 TO §230.501: A person acting as a purchaser representative should consider the applicability of the registration and antifraud provisions relating to brokers and dealers under the Securities Exchange Act of 1934 (*Exchange Act*) (15 U.S.C. 78a *et seq.*, as amended) and relating to investment advisers under the Investment Advisers Act of 1940.

NOTE 2 TO §230.501: The acknowledgment required by paragraph (h)(3) and the disclosure required by paragraph (h)(4) of this section must be made with specific reference to each prospective investment. Advance blanket acknowledgment, such as for *all securities transactions* or *all private placements,* is not sufficient.

NOTE 3 TO §230.501: Disclosure of any material relationships between the purchaser representative or his affiliates and the issuer or its affiliates does not relieve the purchaser representative of his obligation to act in the interest of the purchaser.

[47 FR 11262, Mar. 16, 1982, as amended at 53 FR 7868, Mar. 10, 1988; 54 FR 11372, Mar. 20, 1989; 76 FR 81806, Dec. 29, 2011; 77 FR 18685, Mar. 28, 2012; 78 FR 44770, 44804, July 24, 2013; 81 FR 83553, Nov. 21, 2016]

§230.502 GENERAL CONDITIONS TO BE MET.

The following conditions shall be applicable to offers and sales made under Regulation D (§230.500 *et seq.* of this chapter):

(a) *Integration.* All sales that are part of the same Regulation D offering must meet all of the terms and conditions of Regulation D. Offers and sales that are made more than six months before the start of a Regulation D offering or are made more than six months after completion of a Regulation D offering will not be considered part of that Regulation D offering, so long as during those six month periods there are no offers or sales of securities by or for the issuer that are of the same or a similar class as those offered or sold under Regulation D, other than those offers or sales of securities under an employee benefit plan as defined in rule 405 under the Act (17 CFR 230.405).

NOTE: The term *offering* is not defined in the Act or in Regulation D. If the issuer offers or sells securities for which the safe harbor rule in paragraph (a) of this §230.502 is unavailable, the determination as to whether separate sales of securities are part of the same offering (*i.e.,* are considered *integrated*) depends on the particular facts and circumstances. Generally, transactions otherwise meeting the requirements of an exemption will not be integrated with simultaneous offerings being made outside the United States in compliance with Regulation S. See Release No. 33-6863.

The following factors should be considered in determining whether offers and sales should be integrated for purposes of the exemptions under Regulation D:
(a)   Whether the sales are part of a single plan of financing;
(b)   Whether the sales involve issuance of the same class of securities;
(c)   Whether the sales have been made at or about the same time;

(d) Whether the same type of consideration is being received; and

(e) Whether the sales are made for the same general purpose.

See Release 33-4552 (November 6, 1962) [27 FR 11316].

(b) *Information requirements—*(1) *When information must be furnished.* If the issuer sells securities under §230.506(b) to any purchaser that is not an accredited investor, the issuer shall furnish the information specified in paragraph (b)(2) of this section to such purchaser a reasonable time prior to sale. The issuer is not required to furnish the specified information to purchasers when it sells securities under §230.504, or to any accredited investor.

Note: When an issuer provides information to investors pursuant to paragraph (b)(1), it should consider providing such information to accredited investors as well, in view of the anti-fraud provisions of the federal securities laws.

(2) *Type of information to be furnished.* (i) If the issuer is not subject to the reporting requirements of section 13 or 15(d) of the Exchange Act, at a reasonable time prior to the sale of securities the issuer shall furnish to the purchaser, to the extent material to an understanding of the issuer, its business and the securities being offered:

(A) *Non-financial statement information.* If the issuer is eligible to use Regulation A (§230.251-263), the same kind of information as would be required in Part II of Form 1-A (§239.90 of this chapter). If the issuer is not eligible to use Regulation A, the same kind of information as required in Part I of a registration statement filed under the Securities Act on the form that the issuer would be entitled to use.

(B) *Financial statement information—*(1) *Offerings up to $2,000,000.* The information required in Article 8 of Regulation S-X (§210.8 of this chapter), except that only the issuer's balance sheet, which shall be dated within 120 days of the start of the offering, must be audited.

(2) *Offerings up to $7,500,000.* The financial statement information required in Form S-1 (§239.10 of this chapter) for smaller reporting companies. If an issuer, other than a limited partnership, cannot obtain audited financial statements without unreasonable effort or expense, then only the issuer's balance sheet, which shall be dated within 120 days of the start of the offering, must be audited. If the issuer is a limited partnership and cannot obtain the required financial statements without unreasonable effort or expense, it may furnish financial statements that have been prepared on the basis of Federal income tax requirements and examined and reported on in accordance with generally accepted auditing standards by an independent public or certified accountant.

(3) *Offerings over $7,500,000.* The financial statement as would be required in a registration statement filed under the Act on the form that the issuer would be entitled to use. If an issuer, other than a limited partnership, cannot obtain audited financial statements without unreasonable effort or expense, then only the issuer's balance sheet, which shall be dated within 120 days of the start of the offering, must be audited. If the issuer is a limited partnership and cannot obtain the required financial statements without unreasonable effort or expense, it may furnish financial statements that have been prepared on the basis of Federal income tax requirements and examined and reported on in accordance with generally accepted auditing standards by an independent public or certified accountant.

(C) If the issuer is a foreign private issuer eligible to use Form 20-F (§249.220f of this chapter), the issuer shall disclose the same kind of information required to be included in a registration statement filed under the Act on the form that the issuer would be entitled to use. The financial statements need be certified only to the extent required by paragraph (b)(2)(i) (B) (*1*), (*2*) or (*3*) of this section, as appropriate.

(ii) If the issuer is subject to the reporting requirements of section 13 or 15(d) of the Exchange Act, at a reasonable time prior to the sale of securities the issuer shall furnish to the purchaser the information specified in paragraph (b)(2)(ii)(A) or (B) of this section, and in either event the information specified in paragraph (b)(2)(ii)(C) of this section:

(A) The issuer's annual report to shareholders for the most recent fiscal year, if such annual report meets the requirements of Rules 14a-3 or 14c-3 under the Exchange Act (§240.14a-3 or §240.14c-3 of this chapter), the definitive proxy statement filed in connection with that annual report, and if requested by the purchaser in writing, a copy of the issuer's most recent Form 10-K (§249.310 of this chapter) under the Exchange Act.

(B) The information contained in an annual report on Form 10-K (§249.310 of this chapter) under the Exchange Act or in a registration statement on Form S-1 (§239.11 of this chapter) or S-11 (§239.18 of this chapter) under the Act or on Form 10 (§249.210 of this chapter) under the Exchange Act, whichever filing is the most recent required to be filed.

(C) The information contained in any reports or documents required to be filed by the issuer under sections 13(a), 14(a), 14(c), and 15(d) of the Exchange Act since the distribution or filing of the report or registration statement specified in paragraphs (b)(2)(ii) (A) or (B), and a brief description of the securities being offered, the use of the proceeds from the offering, and any material changes in the issuer's affairs that are not disclosed in the documents furnished.

(D) If the issuer is a foreign private issuer, the issuer may provide in lieu of the information specified in paragraph (b)(2)(ii) (A) or (B) of this section, the information contained in its most recent filing on Form 20-F or Form F-1 (§239.31 of the chapter).

(iii) Exhibits required to be filed with the Commission as part of a registration statement or report, other than an annual report to shareholders or parts of that report incorporated by reference in a Form 10-K report, need not be furnished to each purchaser that is not an accredited investor if the contents of material exhibits are identified and such exhibits are made available to a purchaser, upon his or her written request, a reasonable time before his or her purchase.

(iv) At a reasonable time prior to the sale of securities to any purchaser that is not an accredited investor in a transaction under §230.506(b), the issuer shall furnish to the purchaser a brief description in writing of any material written information concerning the offering that has been provided by the issuer to any accredited investor but not previously delivered to such unaccredited purchaser. The issuer shall furnish any portion or all of this information to the purchaser, upon his written request a reasonable time prior to his purchase.

(v) The issuer shall also make available to each purchaser at a reasonable time prior to his purchase of securities in a transaction under §230.506(b) the opportunity to ask questions and receive answers concerning the terms and conditions of the offering and to obtain any additional information which the issuer possesses or can acquire without unreasonable effort or expense that is necessary to verify the accuracy of information furnished under paragraph (b)(2) (i) or (ii) of this section.

(vi) For business combinations or exchange offers, in addition to information required by Form S-4 (17 CFR 239.25), the issuer shall provide to each purchaser at the time the plan is submitted to security holders, or, with an exchange, during the course of the transaction and prior to sale, written information about any terms or arrangements of the proposed transactions that are materially different from those for all other security holders. For purposes of this subsection, an issuer which is not subject to the reporting requirements of section 13 or 15(d) of the Exchange Act may satisfy the requirements of Part I.B. or C. of Form S-4 by compliance with paragraph (b)(2)(i) of this §230.502.

(vii) At a reasonable time prior to the sale of securities to any purchaser that is not an accredited investor in a transaction under §230.506(b), the issuer shall advise the purchaser of the limitations on resale in the manner contained in paragraph (d)(2) of this section. Such disclosure may be contained in other materials required to be provided by this paragraph.

(c) *Limitation on manner of offering.* Except as provided in §230.504(b)(1) or §230.506(c), neither the issuer nor any person acting on its behalf shall offer or sell the securities by any form of general solicitation or general advertising, including, but not limited to, the following:

(1) Any advertisement, article, notice or other communication published in any newspaper, magazine, or similar media or broadcast over television or radio; and

(2) Any seminar or meeting whose attendees have been invited by any general solicitation or general advertising; *Provided, however,* that publication by an issuer of a notice in accordance with §230.135c or filing with the Commission by an issuer of a notice of sales on Form D (17 CFR 239.500) in which the issuer has made a good faith and reasonable attempt to comply with the requirements of such form, shall not be deemed to constitute general solicitation or general advertising for purposes of this section; *Provided further,* that, if the requirements of §230.135e are satisfied, providing any journalist with access to press conferences held outside of the United States, to meetings with issuer or selling security holder representatives conducted outside of the United States, or to written press-related materials released outside the United States, at or in which a present or proposed offering of securities is discussed, will not be deemed to constitute general solicitation or general advertising for purposes of this section.

(d) *Limitations on resale.* Except as provided in §230.504(b)(1), securities acquired in a transaction under Regulation D shall have the status of securities acquired in a transaction under section 4(a)(2) of the Act and cannot be resold without registration under the Act or an exemption therefrom. The issuer shall exercise reasonable care to assure that the purchasers of the securities are not underwriters within the meaning of section 2(a)(11) of the Act, which reasonable care may be demonstrated by the following:

(1) Reasonable inquiry to determine if the purchaser is acquiring the securities for himself or for other persons;

(2) Written disclosure to each purchaser prior to sale that the securities have not been registered under the Act and, therefore, cannot be resold unless they are registered under the Act or unless an exemption from registration is available; and

(3) Placement of a legend on the certificate or other document that evidences the securities stating that the securities have not been registered under the Act and setting forth or referring to the restrictions on transferability and sale of the securities.

While taking these actions will establish the requisite reasonable care, it is not the exclusive method to demonstrate such care. Other actions by the issuer may satisfy this provision. In addition, §230.502(b)(2)(vii) requires the delivery of written disclosure of the limitations on resale to investors in certain instances.

[47 FR 11262, Mar. 16, 1982, as amended at 47 FR 54771, Dec. 6, 1982; 53 FR 7869, Mar. 11, 1988; 54 FR 11372, Mar. 20, 1989; 55 FR 18322, May 2, 1990; 56 FR 30054, 30055, July 1, 1991; 57 FR 47409, Oct. 16, 1992; 58 FR 26514, May 4, 1993; 59 FR 21650, Apr. 26, 1994; 62 FR 53954, Oct. 17, 1997; 73

FR 969, Jan. 4, 2008; 73 FR 10615, Feb. 27, 2008; 77 FR 18685, Mar. 28, 2012; 78 FR 44804, July 24, 2013; 81 FR 83553, Nov. 21, 2016]

§230.503 FILING OF NOTICE OF SALES.

(a) *When notice of sales on Form D is required and permitted to be filed.* (1) An issuer offering or selling securities in reliance on §230.504 or §230.506 must file with the Commission a notice of sales containing the information required by Form D (17 CFR 239.500) for each new offering of securities no later than 15 calendar days after the first sale of securities in the offering, unless the end of that period falls on a Saturday, Sunday or holiday, in which case the due date would be the first business day following.

(2) An issuer may file an amendment to a previously filed notice of sales on Form D at any time.

(3) An issuer must file an amendment to a previously filed notice of sales on Form D for an offering:

   (i) To correct a material mistake of fact or error in the previously filed notice of sales on Form D, as soon as practicable after discovery of the mistake or error;

   (ii) To reflect a change in the information provided in the previously filed notice of sales on Form D, as soon as practicable after the change, except that no amendment is required to reflect a change that occurs after the offering terminates or a change that occurs solely in the following information:

      (A) The address or relationship to the issuer of a related person identified in response to Item 3 of the notice of sales on Form D;

      (B) An issuer's revenues or aggregate net asset value;

      (C) The minimum investment amount, if the change is an increase, or if the change, together with all other changes in that amount since the previously filed notice of sales on Form D, does not result in a decrease of more than 10%;

      (D) Any address or state(s) of solicitation shown in response to Item 12 of the notice of sales on Form D;

      (E) The total offering amount, if the change is a decrease, or if the change, together with all other changes in that amount since the previously filed notice of sales on Form D, does not result in an increase of more than 10%;

      (F) The amount of securities sold in the offering or the amount remaining to be sold;

      (G) The number of non-accredited investors who have invested in the offering, as long as the change does not increase the number to more than 35;

      (H) The total number of investors who have invested in the offering; or

      (I) The amount of sales commissions, finders' fees or use of proceeds for payments to executive officers, directors or promoters, if the change is a decrease, or if the change, together with all other changes in that amount since the previously filed notice of sales on Form D, does not result in an increase of more than 10%; and

   (iii) Annually, on or before the first anniversary of the filing of the notice of sales on Form D or the filing of the most recent amendment to the notice of sales on Form D, if the offering is continuing at that time.

(4) An issuer that files an amendment to a previously filed notice of sales on Form D must provide current information in response to all requirements of the notice of sales on Form D regardless of why the amendment is filed.

(b) *How notice of sales on Form D must be filed and signed.* (1) A notice of sales on Form D must be filed with the Commission in electronic format by means of the Commission's Electronic Data Gathering, Analysis, and Retrieval System (EDGAR) in accordance with EDGAR rules set forth in Regulation S-T (17 CFR Part 232).

   (2) Every notice of sales on Form D must be signed by a person duly authorized by the issuer.

[73 FR 10615, Feb. 27, 2008, as amended at 81 FR 83553, Nov. 21, 2016]

§230.504 EXEMPTION FOR LIMITED OFFERINGS AND SALES OF SECURITIES NOT EXCEEDING $5,000,000.

(a) *Exemption.* Offers and sales of securities that satisfy the conditions in paragraph (b) of this §230.504 by an issuer that is not:

   (1) Subject to the reporting requirements of section 13 or 15(d) of the Exchange Act,;

   (2) An investment company; or

   (3) A development stage company that either has no specific business plan or purpose or has indicated that its business plan is to engage in a merger or acquisition with an unidentified company or companies, or other entity or person, shall be exempt from the provision of section 5 of the Act under section 3(b) of the Act.

(b) *Conditions to be met*—(1) *General conditions.* To qualify for exemption under this §230.504, offers and sales must satisfy the terms and conditions of §§230.501 and 230.502 (a), (c) and (d), except that the provisions of §230.502 (c) and (d) will not apply to offers and sales of securities under this §230.504 that are made:

   (i) Exclusively in one or more states that provide for the registration of the securities, and require the public filing and delivery to investors of a substantive disclosure document before sale, and are made in accordance with those state provisions;

   (ii) In one or more states that have no provision for the registration of the securities or the public filing or delivery of a disclosure document before sale, if the securities have been registered in at least one state that provides for such registration, public filing and delivery before sale, offers and sales are made in that state in accordance with such provisions, and the disclosure document is delivered before sale to all purchasers (including those in the states that have no such procedure); or

   (iii) Exclusively according to state law exemptions from registration that permit general solicitation and general advertising so long as sales are made only to "accredited investors" as defined in §230.501(a).

   (2) The aggregate offering price for an offering of securities under this §230.504, as defined in §230.501(c), shall not exceed $5,000,000, less the aggregate offering price for all securities sold within the twelve months before the start of and during the offering of securities under this §230.504 or in violation of section 5(a) of the Securities Act.

Instruction to paragraph (b)(2): If a transaction under §230.504 fails to meet the limitation on the aggregate offering price, it does not affect the availability of this §230.504 for the other transactions considered in applying such limitation. For example, if an issuer sold $5,000,000 of its securities on January 1, 2014 under this §230.504 and an additional $500,000 of its securities on July 1, 2014, this §230.504 would not be available for the later sale, but would still be applicable to the January 1, 2014 sale.

   (3) *Disqualifications.* No exemption under this section shall be available for the securities of any issuer if such issuer would be subject to disqualification under §230.506(d) on or after January 20, 2017; provided that disclosure of prior "bad actor" events shall be required in accordance with §230.506(e).

Instruction to paragraph (b)(3): For purposes of disclosure of prior "bad actor" events pursuant to §230.506(e), an issuer shall furnish to each purchaser, a reasonable time prior to sale, a description in writing of any matters that would have triggered disqualification under this paragraph (b)(3) but occurred before January 20, 2017.

§230.505 [RESERVED]

§230.506 EXEMPTION FOR LIMITED OFFERS AND SALES WITHOUT REGARD TO DOLLAR AMOUNT OF OFFERING.

(a) *Exemption.* Offers and sales of securities by an issuer that satisfy the conditions in paragraph (b) or (c) of this section shall be deemed to be transactions not involving any public offering within the meaning of section 4(a)(2) of the Act.

(b) *Conditions to be met in offerings subject to limitation on manner of offering*—(1) *General conditions.* To qualify for an exemption under this section, offers and sales must satisfy all the terms and conditions of §§230.501 and 230.502.

   (2) *Specific conditions*—(i) *Limitation on number of purchasers.* There are no more than or the issuer reasonably believes that there are no more than 35 purchasers of securities from the issuer in any offering under this section.

NOTE TO PARAGRAPH (b)(2)(i): See §230.501(e) for the calculation of the number of purchasers and §230.502(a) for what may or may not constitute an offering under paragraph (b) of this section.

     (ii) *Nature of purchasers.* Each purchaser who is not an accredited investor either alone or with his purchaser representative(s) has such knowledge and experience in financial and business matters that he is capable of evaluating the merits and risks of the prospective investment, or the issuer reasonably believes immediately prior to making any sale that such purchaser comes within this description.

(c) *Conditions to be met in offerings not subject to limitation on manner of offering*—(1) *General conditions.* To qualify for exemption under this section, sales must satisfy all the terms and conditions of §§230.501 and 230.502(a) and (d).

   (2) *Specific conditions*—(i) *Nature of purchasers.* All purchasers of securities sold in any offering under paragraph (c) of this section are accredited investors.

     (ii) *Verification of accredited investor status.* The issuer shall take reasonable steps to verify that purchasers of securities sold in any offering under paragraph (c) of this section are accredited investors. The issuer shall be deemed to take reasonable steps to verify if the issuer uses, at its option, one of the following non-exclusive and non-mandatory methods of verifying that a natural person who purchases securities in such offering is an accredited investor; provided, however, that the issuer does not have knowledge that such person is not an accredited investor:

       (A) In regard to whether the purchaser is an accredited investor on the basis of income, reviewing any Internal Revenue Service form that reports the purchaser's income for the two most recent years (including, but not limited to, Form W-2, Form 1099, Schedule K-1 to Form 1065, and Form 1040) and obtaining a written representation from the purchaser that he or she has a reasonable expectation of reaching the income level necessary to qualify as an accredited investor during the current year;

       (B) In regard to whether the purchaser is an accredited investor on the basis of net worth, reviewing one or more of the following types of documentation dated within the prior three months and obtaining a written representation from the purchaser that all liabilities necessary to make a determination of net worth have been disclosed:

        (*1*)   With respect to assets: Bank statements, brokerage statements and other statements of securities holdings, certificates of deposit, tax assessments, and appraisal reports issued by independent third parties; and

        (*2*)   With respect to liabilities: A consumer report from at least one of the nationwide consumer reporting agencies; or

    (C) Obtaining a written confirmation from one of the following persons or entities that such person or entity has taken reasonable steps to verify that the purchaser is an accredited investor within the prior three months and has determined that such purchaser is an accredited investor:

        (*1*)   A registered broker-dealer;

        (*2*)   An investment adviser registered with the Securities and Exchange Commission;

        (*3*)   A licensed attorney who is in good standing under the laws of the jurisdictions in which he or she is admitted to practice law; or

        (*4*)   A certified public accountant who is duly registered and in good standing under the laws of the place of his or her residence or principal office.

    (D) In regard to any person who purchased securities in an issuer's Rule 506(b) offering as an accredited investor prior to September 23, 2013 and continues to hold such securities, for the same issuer's Rule 506(c) offering, obtaining a certification by such person at the time of sale that he or she qualifies as an accredited investor.

Instructions to paragraph (c)(2)(ii)(A) through (D) of this section:

1. The issuer is not required to use any of these methods in verifying the accredited investor status of natural persons who are purchasers. These methods are examples of the types of non-exclusive and non-mandatory methods that satisfy the verification requirement in §230.506(c)(2)(ii).

2. In the case of a person who qualifies as an accredited investor based on joint income with that person's spouse, the issuer would be deemed to satisfy the verification requirement in §230.506(c)(2)(ii)(A) by reviewing copies of Internal Revenue Service forms that report income for the two most recent years in regard to, and obtaining written representations from, both the person and the spouse.

3. In the case of a person who qualifies as an accredited investor based on joint net worth with that person's spouse, the issuer would be deemed to satisfy the verification requirement in §230.506(c)(2)(ii)(B) by reviewing such documentation in regard to, and obtaining written representations from, both the person and the spouse.

(d)   *"Bad Actor" disqualification.* (1) No exemption under this section shall be available for a sale of securities if the issuer; any predecessor of the issuer; any affiliated issuer; any director, executive officer, other officer participating in the offering, general partner or managing member of the issuer; any beneficial owner of 20% or more of the issuer's outstanding voting equity securities, calculated on the basis of voting power; any promoter connected with the issuer in any capacity at the time of such sale; any investment manager of an issuer that is a pooled investment fund; any person that has been or will be paid (directly or indirectly) remuneration for solicitation of purchasers in connection with such sale of securities; any general partner or managing member of any such investment manager or solicitor; or any director, executive officer or other officer participating in the offering of any such investment manager or solicitor or general partner or managing member of such investment manager or solicitor:

(i)   Has been convicted, within ten years before such sale (or five years, in the case of issuers, their predecessors and affiliated issuers), of any felony or misdemeanor:

    (A)   In connection with the purchase or sale of any security;

    (B)   Involving the making of any false filing with the Commission; or

    (C)   Arising out of the conduct of the business of an underwriter, broker, dealer, municipal securities dealer, investment adviser or paid solicitor of purchasers of securities;

(ii)   Is subject to any order, judgment or decree of any court of competent jurisdiction, entered within five years before such sale, that, at the time of such sale, restrains or enjoins such person from engaging or continuing to engage in any conduct or practice:

    (A)   In connection with the purchase or sale of any security;

    (B)   Involving the making of any false filing with the Commission; or

    (C)   Arising out of the conduct of the business of an underwriter, broker, dealer, municipal securities dealer, investment adviser or paid solicitor of purchasers of securities;

(iii)   Is subject to a final order of a state securities commission (or an agency or officer of a state performing like functions); a state authority that supervises or examines banks, savings associations, or credit unions; a state insurance commission (or an agency or officer of a state performing like functions); an appropriate federal banking agency; the U.S. Commodity Futures Trading Commission; or the National Credit Union Administration that:

    (A)   At the time of such sale, bars the person from:

        (1)   Association with an entity regulated by such commission, authority, agency, or officer;

        (2)   Engaging in the business of securities, insurance or banking; or

        (3)   Engaging in savings association or credit union activities; or

    (B)   Constitutes a final order based on a violation of any law or regulation that prohibits fraudulent, manipulative, or deceptive conduct entered within ten years before such sale;

(iv)   Is subject to an order of the Commission entered pursuant to section 15(b) or 15B(c) of the Securities Exchange Act of 1934 (15 U.S.C. 78o(b) or 78o-4(c)) or section 203(e) or (f) of the Investment Advisers Act of 1940 (15 U.S.C. 80b-3(e) or (f)) that, at the time of such sale:

    (A)   Suspends or revokes such person's registration as a broker, dealer, municipal securities dealer or investment adviser;

    (B)   Places limitations on the activities, functions or operations of such person; or

    (C)   Bars such person from being associated with any entity or from participating in the offering of any penny stock;

(v)   Is subject to any order of the Commission entered within five years before such sale that, at the time of such sale, orders the person to cease and desist from committing or causing a violation or future violation of:

    (A)   Any scienter-based anti-fraud provision of the federal securities laws, including without limitation section 17(a)(1) of the Securities Act of 1933 (15 U.S.C. 77q(a)(1)), section 10(b) of the Securities Exchange Act of 1934 (15 U.S.C. 78j(b)) and 17 CFR 240.10b-5, section 15(c)(1) of the Securities Exchange Act of 1934 (15 U.S.C. 78*o*(c)(1)) and section 206(1) of the Investment Advisers Act of 1940 (15 U.S.C. 80b-6(1)), or any other rule or regulation thereunder; or

(B)   Section 5 of the Securities Act of 1933 (15 U.S.C. 77e).

(vi)   Is suspended or expelled from membership in, or suspended or barred from association with a member of, a registered national securities exchange or a registered national or affiliated securities association for any act or omission to act constituting conduct inconsistent with just and equitable principles of trade;

(vii)   Has filed (as a registrant or issuer), or was or was named as an underwriter in, any registration statement or Regulation A offering statement filed with the Commission that, within five years before such sale, was the subject of a refusal order, stop order, or order suspending the Regulation A exemption, or is, at the time of such sale, the subject of an investigation or proceeding to determine whether a stop order or suspension order should be issued; or

(viii) Is subject to a United States Postal Service false representation order entered within five years before such sale, or is, at the time of such sale, subject to a temporary restraining order or preliminary injunction with respect to conduct alleged by the United States Postal Service to constitute a scheme or device for obtaining money or property through the mail by means of false representations.

(2)   Paragraph (d)(1) of this section shall not apply:

(i)   With respect to any conviction, order, judgment, decree, suspension, expulsion or bar that occurred or was issued before September 23, 2013;

(ii)   Upon a showing of good cause and without prejudice to any other action by the Commission, if the Commission determines that it is not necessary under the circumstances that an exemption be denied;

(iii)   If, before the relevant sale, the court or regulatory authority that entered the relevant order, judgment or decree advises in writing (whether contained in the relevant judgment, order or decree or separately to the Commission or its staff) that disqualification under paragraph (d)(1) of this section should not arise as a consequence of such order, judgment or decree; or

(iv)   If the issuer establishes that it did not know and, in the exercise of reasonable care, could not have known that a disqualification existed under paragraph (d)(1) of this section.

Instruction to paragraph (d)(2)(iv). An issuer will not be able to establish that it has exercised reasonable care unless it has made, in light of the circumstances, factual inquiry into whether any disqualifications exist. The nature and scope of the factual inquiry will vary based on the facts and circumstances concerning, among other things, the issuer and the other offering participants.

(3)   For purposes of paragraph (d)(1) of this section, events relating to any affiliated issuer that occurred before the affiliation arose will be not considered disqualifying if the affiliated entity is not:

(i)   In control of the issuer; or

(ii)   Under common control with the issuer by a third party that was in control of the affiliated entity at the time of such events.

(e)   *Disclosure of prior "bad actor" events.* The issuer shall furnish to each purchaser, a reasonable time prior to sale, a description in writing of any matters that would have triggered disqualification under paragraph (d)(1) of this section but occurred before September 23, 2013. The failure to furnish such information timely shall not prevent an issuer from relying on this section if the issuer establishes that it did not know and, in the exercise of reasonable care, could not have known of the existence of the undisclosed matter or matters.

Instruction to paragraph (e). An issuer will not be able to establish that it has exercised reasonable care unless it has made, in light of the circumstances, factual inquiry into whether any disqualifications exist. The nature and scope of the factual inquiry will vary based on the facts and circumstances concerning, among other things, the issuer and the other offering participants.

[47 FR 11262, Mar. 6, 1982, as amended at 54 FR 11373, Mar. 20, 1989; 78 FR 44770, 44804, July 24, 2013]

§230.507 DISQUALIFYING PROVISION RELATING TO EXEMPTIONS UNDER §§230.504 AND 230.506.

(a) No exemption under §230.504 or §230.506 shall be available for an issuer if such issuer, any of its predecessors or affiliates have been subject to any order, judgment, or decree of any court of competent jurisdiction temporarily, preliminary or permanently enjoining such person for failure to comply with §230.503.

(b) Paragraph (a) of this section shall not apply if the Commission determines, upon a showing of good cause, that it is not necessary under the circumstances that the exemption be denied.

[54 FR 11374, Mar. 20, 1989, as amended at 81 FR 83553, Nov. 21, 2016]

§230.508 INSIGNIFICANT DEVIATIONS FROM A TERM, CONDITION OR REQUIREMENT OF REGULATION D.

(a) A failure to comply with a term, condition or requirement of §230.504 or §230.506 will not result in the loss of the exemption from the requirements of section 5 of the Act for any offer or sale to a particular individual or entity, if the person relying on the exemption shows:

(1) The failure to comply did not pertain to a term, condition or requirement directly intended to protect that particular individual or entity; and

(2) The failure to comply was insignificant with respect to the offering as a whole, provided that any failure to comply with paragraph (c) of §230.502, paragraph (b)(2) of §230.504 and paragraph (b)(2)(i) of §230.506 shall be deemed to be significant to the offering as a whole; and

(3) A good faith and reasonable attempt was made to comply with all applicable terms, conditions and requirements of §230.504 or §230.506.

(b) A transaction made in reliance on §230.504 or §230.506 shall comply with all applicable terms, conditions and requirements of Regulation D. Where an exemption is established only through reliance upon paragraph (a) of this section, the failure to comply shall nonetheless be actionable by the Commission under section 20 of the Act.

[54 FR 11374, Mar. 20, 1989, as amended at 57 FR 36473, Aug. 13, 1992; 81 FR 83553, Nov. 21, 2016]

APPENDIX

§230.147 INTRASTATE OFFERS AND SALES.

[Practice Note: Federal statutes, rules and regulations are notoriously difficult to follow because, no matter how long and complex the text may be, they are not indented. When I will be using a particular provision in depth, I take the time to indent, as shown below, to aid understanding.]

(a) This section shall not raise any presumption that the exemption provided by section 3(a)(11) of the Act (15 U.S.C. 77c(a)(11)) is not available for transactions by an issuer which do not satisfy all of the provisions of this section.

(b) *Manner of offers and sales.* An issuer, or any person acting on behalf of the issuer, shall be deemed to conduct an offering in compliance with section 3(a)(11) of the Act (15 U.S.C. 77c(a)(11)), where offers and sales are made only to persons resident within the same state or territory in which the issuer is resident and doing business, within the meaning of section 3(a)(11) of the Act, so long as the issuer complies with the provisions of paragraphs (c), (d), and (f) through (h) of this section.

(c) *Nature of the issuer.* The issuer of the securities shall at the time of any offers and sales be a person resident and doing business within the state or territory in which all of the offers and sales are made.

    (1) The issuer shall be deemed to be a resident of the state or territory in which:

        (i) It is incorporated or organized, and it has its principal place of business, if a corporation, limited partnership, trust or other form of business organization that is organized under state or territorial law. The issuer shall be deemed to have its principal place of business in a state or territory in which the officers, partners or managers of the issuer primarily direct, control and coordinate the activities of the issuer;

        (ii) It has its principal place of business, as defined in paragraph (c)(1)(i) of this section, if a general partnership or other form of business organization that is not organized under any state or territorial law;

        (iii) Such person's principal residence is located, if an individual.

Instruction to paragraph (c)(1): An issuer that has previously conducted an intrastate offering pursuant to this section (§230.147) or Rule 147A (§230.147A) may not conduct another intrastate offering pursuant to this section (§230.147) in a different state or territory, until the expiration of the time period specified in paragraph (e) of this section (§230.147(e)) or paragraph (e) of Rule 147A (§230.147A(e)), calculated on the basis of the date of the last sale in such offering.

    (2) The issuer shall be deemed to be doing business within a state or territory if the issuer satisfies at least one of the following requirements:

        (i) The issuer derived at least 80% of its consolidated gross revenues from the operation of a business or of real property located in or from the rendering of services within such state or territory;

Instruction to paragraph (c)(2)(i): Revenues must be calculated based on the issuer's most recent fiscal year, if the first offer of securities pursuant to this section is made during the first six months of the issuer's current fiscal year, and based on the first six months of the issuer's current fiscal year or during the twelve-month fiscal period ending with such six-month period, if the first offer of securities pursuant to this section is made during the last six months of the issuer's current fiscal year.

        (ii) The issuer had at the end of its most recent semi-annual fiscal period prior to an initial offer of securities in any offering or subsequent offering pursuant to this section, at least 80% of its assets and those of its subsidiaries on a consolidated basis located within such state or territory;

        (iii) The issuer intends to use and uses at least 80% of the net proceeds to the issuer from sales made pursuant to this section (§230.147) in connection with the operation of a business or of real property, the purchase of real property located in, or the rendering of services within such state or territory; or

    (iv)   A majority of the issuer's employees are based in such state or territory.

(d)   *Residence of offerees and purchasers.* Offers and sales of securities pursuant to this section (§230.147) shall be made only to residents of the state or territory in which the issuer is resident, as determined pursuant to paragraph (c) of this section, or who the issuer reasonably believes, at the time of the offer and sale, are residents of the state or territory in which the issuer is resident. For purposes of determining the residence of offerees and purchasers:

    (1)   A corporation, partnership, limited liability company, trust or other form of business organization shall be deemed to be a resident of a state or territory if, at the time of the offer and sale to it, it has its principal place of business, as defined in paragraph (c)(1)(i) of this section, within such state or territory.

Instruction to paragraph (d)(1): A trust that is not deemed by the law of the state or territory of its creation to be a separate legal entity is deemed to be a resident of each state or territory in which its trustee is, or trustees are, resident.

    (2)   Individuals shall be deemed to be residents of a state or territory if such individuals have, at the time of the offer and sale to them, their principal residence in the state or territory.

    (3)   A corporation, partnership, trust or other form of business organization, which is organized for the specific purpose of acquiring securities offered pursuant to this section (§230.147), shall not be a resident of a state or territory unless all of the beneficial owners of such organization are residents of such state or territory.

Instruction to paragraph (d): Obtaining a written representation from purchasers of in-state residency status will not, without more, be sufficient to establish a reasonable belief that such purchasers are in-state residents.

(e)   *Limitation on resales.* For a period of six months from the date of the sale by the issuer of a security pursuant to this section (§230.147), any resale of such security shall be made only to persons resident within the state or territory in which the issuer was resident, as determined pursuant to paragraph (c) of this section, at the time of the sale of the security by the issuer.

Instruction to paragraph (e): In the case of convertible securities, resales of either the convertible security, or if it is converted, the underlying security, could be made during the period described in paragraph (e) only to persons resident within such state or territory. For purposes of this paragraph (e), a conversion in reliance on section 3(a)(9) of the Act (15 U.S.C. 77c(a)(9)) does not begin a new period.

(f)   *Precautions against interstate sales.*

    (1)   The issuer shall, in connection with any securities sold by it pursuant to this section:

        (i)   Place a prominent legend on the certificate or other document evidencing the security stating that: "Offers and sales of these securities were made under an exemption from registration and have not been registered under the Securities Act of 1933. For a period of six months from the date of the sale by the issuer of these securities, any resale of these securities (or the underlying securities in the case of convertible securities) shall be made only to persons resident within the state or territory of [identify the name of the state or territory in which the issuer was resident at the time of the sale of the securities by the issuer].";

        (ii)   Issue stop transfer instructions to the issuer's transfer agent, if any, with respect to the securities, or, if the issuer transfers its own securities, make a notation in the appropriate records of the issuer; and

        (iii)   Obtain a written representation from each purchaser as to his or her residence.

    (2)   The issuer shall, in connection with the issuance of new certificates for any of the securities that are sold pursuant to this section (§230.147) that are presented for transfer

during the time period specified in paragraph (e), take the steps required by paragraphs (f)(1)(i) and (ii) of this section.

(3) The issuer shall, at the time of any offer or sale by it of a security pursuant to this section (§230.147), prominently disclose to each offeree in the manner in which any such offer is communicated and to each purchaser of such security in writing a reasonable period of time before the date of sale, the following: "Sales will be made only to residents of [identify the name of the state or territory in which the issuer was resident at the time of the sale of the securities by the issuer]. Offers and sales of these securities are made under an exemption from registration and have not been registered under the Securities Act of 1933. For a period of six months from the date of the sale by the issuer of the securities, any resale of the securities (or the underlying securities in the case of convertible securities) shall be made only to persons resident within the state or territory of [identify the name of the state or territory in which the issuer was resident at the time of the sale of the securities by the issuer]."

(g) *Integration with other offerings.* Offers or sales made in reliance on this section will not be integrated with:

(1) Offers or sales of securities made prior to the commencement of offers and sales of securities pursuant to this section (§230.147); or

(2) Offers or sales made after completion of offers and sales of securities pursuant to this section (§230.147) that are:

(i) Registered under the Act, except as provided in paragraph (h) of this section (§230.147);

(ii) Exempt from registration under Regulation A (§§230.251 through 230.263);

(iii) Exempt from registration under Rule 701 (§230.701);

(iv) Made pursuant to an employee benefit plan;

(v) Exempt from registration under Regulation S (§§230.901 through 230.905);

(vi) Exempt from registration under section 4(a)(6) of the Act (15 U.S.C. 77d(a)(6)); or

(vii) Made more than six months after the completion of an offering conducted pursuant to this section (§230.147).

Instruction to paragraph (g): If none of the safe harbors applies, whether subsequent offers and sales of securities will be integrated with any securities offered or sold pursuant to this section (§230.147) will depend on the particular facts and circumstances.

(h) *Offerings limited to qualified institutional buyers and institutional accredited investors.* Where an issuer decides to register an offering under the Act after making offers in reliance on this section (§230.147) limited only to qualified institutional buyers and institutional accredited investors referenced in section 5(d) of the Act, such offers will not be subject to integration with any subsequent registered offering. If the issuer makes offers in reliance on this section (§230.147) to persons other than qualified institutional buyers and institutional accredited investors referenced in section 5(d) of the Act, such offers will not be subject to integration if the issuer (and any underwriter, broker, dealer, or agent used by the issuer in connection with the proposed offering) waits at least 30 calendar days between the last such offer made in reliance on this section (§230.147) and the filing of the registration statement with the Commission.

[81 FR 83550, Nov. 21, 2016]

§230.147A INTRASTATE SALES EXEMPTION.

(a) *Scope of the exemption.* Offers and sales by or on behalf of an issuer of its securities made in accordance with this section (§230.147A) are exempt from section 5 of the Act (15 U.S.C.

77e). This exemption is not available to an issuer that is an investment company registered or required to be registered under the Investment Company Act of 1940 (15 U.S.C. 80a-1 *et seq.*).

(b)   *Manner of offers and sales.* An issuer, or any person acting on behalf of the issuer, may rely on this exemption to make offers and sales using any form of general solicitation and general advertising, so long as the issuer complies with the provisions of paragraphs (c), (d), and (f) through (h) of this section.

(c)   *Nature of the issuer.* The issuer of the securities shall at the time of any offers and sales be a person resident and doing business within the state or territory in which all of the sales are made.

    (1)   The issuer shall be deemed to be a resident of the state or territory in which it has its principal place of business. The issuer shall be deemed to have its principal place of business in a state or territory in which the officers, partners or managers of the issuer primarily direct, control and coordinate the activities of the issuer.

    (2)   The issuer shall be deemed to be doing business within a state or territory if the issuer satisfies at least one of the following requirements:

        (i)   The issuer derived at least 80% of its consolidated gross revenues from the operation of a business or of real property located in or from the rendering of services within such state or territory;

Instruction to paragraph (c)(2)(i): Revenues must be calculated based on the issuer's most recent fiscal year, if the first offer of securities pursuant to this section is made during the first six months of the issuer's current fiscal year, and based on the first six months of the issuer's current fiscal year or during the twelve-month fiscal period ending with such six-month period, if the first offer of securities pursuant to this section is made during the last six months of the issuer's current fiscal year.

        (ii)   The issuer had at the end of its most recent semi-annual fiscal period prior to an initial offer of securities in any offering or subsequent offering pursuant to this section, at least 80% of its assets and those of its subsidiaries on a consolidated basis located within such state or territory;

        (iii)   The issuer intends to use and uses at least 80% of the net proceeds to the issuer from sales made pursuant to this section (§230.147A) in connection with the operation of a business or of real property, the purchase of real property located in, or the rendering of services within such state or territory; or

        (iv)   A majority of the issuer's employees are based in such state or territory.

Instruction to paragraph (c): An issuer that has previously conducted an intrastate offering pursuant to this section (§230.147A) or Rule 147 (§230.147) may not conduct another intrastate offering pursuant to this section (§230.147A) in a different state or territory, until the expiration of the time period specified in paragraph (e) of this section (§230.147A(e)) or paragraph (e) of Rule 147 (§230.147(e)), calculated on the basis of the date of the last sale in such offering.

(d)   *Residence of purchasers.* Sales of securities pursuant to this section (§230.147A) shall be made only to residents of the state or territory in which the issuer is resident, as determined pursuant to paragraph (c) of this section, or who the issuer reasonably believes, at the time of sale, are residents of the state or territory in which the issuer is resident. For purposes of determining the residence of purchasers:

    (1)   A corporation, partnership, limited liability company, trust or other form of business organization shall be deemed to be a resident of a state or territory if, at the time of sale to it, it has its principal place of business, as defined in paragraph (c)(1) of this section, within such state or territory.

Instruction to paragraph (d)(1): A trust that is not deemed by the law of the state or territory of its creation to be a separate legal entity is deemed to be a resident of each state or territory in which its trustee is, or trustees are, resident.

(2) Individuals shall be deemed to be residents of a state or territory if such individuals have, at the time of sale to them, their principal residence in the state or territory.

(3) A corporation, partnership, trust or other form of business organization, which is organized for the specific purpose of acquiring securities offered pursuant to this section (§230.147A), shall not be a resident of a state or territory unless all of the beneficial owners of such organization are residents of such state or territory.

Instruction to paragraph (d): Obtaining a written representation from purchasers of in-state residency status will not, without more, be sufficient to establish a reasonable belief that such purchasers are in-state residents.

(e) *Limitation on resales.* For a period of six months from the date of the sale by the issuer of a security pursuant to this section (§230.147A), any resale of such security shall be made only to persons resident within the state or territory in which the issuer was resident, as determined pursuant to paragraph (c) of this section, at the time of the sale of the security by the issuer.

Instruction to paragraph (e): In the case of convertible securities, resales of either the convertible security, or if it is converted, the underlying security, could be made during the period described in paragraph (e) only to persons resident within such state or territory. For purposes of this paragraph (e), a conversion in reliance on section 3(a)(9) of the Act (15 U.S.C. 77c(a)(9)) does not begin a new period.

(f) *Precautions against interstate sales.* (1) The issuer shall, in connection with any securities sold by it pursuant to this section:

    (i) Place a prominent legend on the certificate or other document evidencing the security stating that: "Offers and sales of these securities were made under an exemption from registration and have not been registered under the Securities Act of 1933. For a period of six months from the date of the sale by the issuer of these securities, any resale of these securities (or the underlying securities in the case of convertible securities) shall be made only to persons resident within the state or territory of [identify the name of the state or territory in which the issuer was resident at the time of the sale of the securities by the issuer].";

    (ii) Issue stop transfer instructions to the issuer's transfer agent, if any, with respect to the securities, or, if the issuer transfers its own securities, make a notation in the appropriate records of the issuer; and

    (iii) Obtain a written representation from each purchaser as to his or her residence.

(2) The issuer shall, in connection with the issuance of new certificates for any of the securities that are sold pursuant to this section (§230.147A) that are presented for transfer during the time period specified in paragraph (e), take the steps required by paragraphs (f)(1)(i) and (ii) of this section.

(3) The issuer shall, at the time of any offer or sale by it of a security pursuant to this section (§230.147A), prominently disclose to each offeree in the manner in which any such offer is communicated and to each purchaser of such security in writing a reasonable period of time before the date of sale, the following: "Sales will be made only to residents of the state or territory of [identify the name of the state or territory in which the issuer was resident at the time of the sale of the securities by the issuer]. Offers and sales of these securities are made under an exemption from registration and have not been registered under the Securities Act of 1933. For a period of six months from the date of the sale by the issuer of the securities, any resale of the securities (or the underlying securities in the case of convertible securities) shall be made only to persons resident within the state or territory of [identify the name of the state or territory in which the issuer was resident at the time of the sale of the securities by the issuer]."

(g) *Integration with other offerings.* Offers or sales made in reliance on this section will not be integrated with:

(1) Offers or sales of securities made prior to the commencement of offers and sales of securities pursuant to this section (§230.147A); or

(2) Offers or sales of securities made after completion of offers and sales of securities pursuant to this section (§230.147A) that are:

    (i) Registered under the Act, except as provided in paragraph (h) of this section (§230.147A);

    (ii) Exempt from registration under Regulation A (§§230.251 through 230.263);

    (iii) Exempt from registration under Rule 701 (§230.701);

    (iv) Made pursuant to an employee benefit plan;

    (v) Exempt from registration under Regulation S (§§230.901 through 230.905);

    (vi) Exempt from registration under section 4(a)(6) of the Act (15 U.S.C. 77d(a)(6)); or

    (vii) Made more than six months after the completion of an offering conducted pursuant to this section (§230.147A).

Instruction to paragraph (g): If none of the safe harbors applies, whether subsequent offers and sales of securities will be integrated with any securities offered or sold pursuant to this section (§230.147A) will depend on the particular facts and circumstances.

(h) *Offerings limited to qualified institutional buyers and institutional accredited investors.* Where an issuer decides to register an offering under the Act after making offers in reliance on this section (§230.147A) limited only to qualified institutional buyers and institutional accredited investors referenced in section 5(d) of the Act, such offers will not be subject to integration with any subsequent registered offering. If the issuer makes offers in reliance on this section (§230.147A) to persons other than qualified institutional buyers and institutional accredited investors referenced in section 5(d) of the Act, such offers will not be subject to integration if the issuer (and any underwriter, broker, dealer, or agent used by the issuer in connection with the proposed offering) waits at least 30 calendar days between the last such offer made in reliance on this section (§230.147A) and the filing of the registration statement with the Commission.

[81 FR 83551, Nov. 21, 2016]

APPENDIX

Regulation A
Conditional Small Issues Exemption

AUTHORITY: Secs. 230.251 to 230.263 issued under 15 U.S.C. 77c, 77s.
SOURCE: 57 FR 36468, Aug. 13, 1992, unless otherwise noted.

§230.251 SCOPE OF EXEMPTION.

(a) *Tier 1 and Tier 2.* A public offer or sale of eligible securities, as defined in Rule 261 (§230.261), pursuant to Regulation A shall be exempt under section 3(b) from the registration requirements of the Securities Act of 1933 (the "Securities Act") (15 U.S.C. 77a *et seq.*).

   (1) *Tier 1.* Offerings pursuant to Regulation A in which the sum of all cash and other consideration to be received for the securities being offered ("aggregate offering price") plus the gross proceeds for all securities sold pursuant to other offering statements within the 12 months before the start of and during the current offering of securities ("aggregate sales") does not exceed $20,000,000, including not more than $6,000,000 offered by all selling securityholders that are affiliates of the issuer ("Tier 1 offerings").

   (2) *Tier 2.* Offerings pursuant to Regulation A in which the sum of the aggregate offering price and aggregate sales does not exceed $50,000,000, including not more than $15,000,000 offered by all selling securityholders that are affiliates of the issuer ("Tier 2 offerings").

   (3) *Additional limitation on secondary sales in first year.* The portion of the aggregate offering price attributable to the securities of selling securityholders shall not exceed 30% of the aggregate offering price of a particular offering in:

      (i) The issuer's first offering pursuant to Regulation A; or

      (ii) Any subsequent Regulation A offering that is qualified within one year of the qualification date of the issuer's first offering.

Note to paragraph (a). Where a mixture of cash and non-cash consideration is to be received, the aggregate offering price must be based on the price at which the securities are offered for cash. Any portion of the aggregate offering price or aggregate sales attributable to cash received in a foreign currency must be translated into United States currency at a currency exchange rate in effect on, or at a reasonable time before, the date of the sale of the securities. If securities are not offered for cash, the aggregate offering price or aggregate sales must be based on the value of the consideration as established by bona fide sales of that consideration made within a reasonable time, or, in the absence of sales, on the fair value as determined by an accepted standard. Valuations of non-cash consideration must be reasonable at the time made. If convertible securities or warrants are being offered and such securities are convertible, exercisable, or exchangeable within one year of the offering statement's qualification or at the discretion of the issuer, the underlying securities must also be qualified and the aggregate offering price must include the actual or maximum estimated conversion, exercise, or exchange price of such securities.

(b) *Issuer.* The issuer of the securities:

   (1) Is an entity organized under the laws of the United States or Canada, or any State, Province, Territory or possession thereof, or the District of Columbia, with its principal place of business in the United States or Canada;

   (2) Is not subject to section 13 or 15(d) of the Securities Exchange Act of 1934 (the "Exchange Act") (15 U.S.C. 78a *et seq.*) immediately before the offering;

   (3) Is not a development stage company that either has no specific business plan or purpose, or has indicated that its business plan is to merge with or acquire an unidentified company or companies;

   (4) Is not an investment company registered or required to be registered under the Investment Company Act of 1940 (15 U.S.C. 80a-1 *et seq.*) or a business development company

as defined in section 2(a)(48) of the Investment Company Act of 1940 (15 U.S.C. 80a-2(a)(48));

(5) Is not issuing fractional undivided interests in oil or gas rights, or a similar interest in other mineral rights;

(6) Is not, and has not been, subject to any order of the Commission entered pursuant to Section 12(j) of the Exchange Act (15 U.S.C. 78*l*(j)) within five years before the filing of the offering statement;

(7) Has filed with the Commission all reports required to be filed, if any, pursuant to Rule 257 (§230.257) during the two years before the filing of the offering statement (or for such shorter period that the issuer was required to file such reports); and

(8) Is not disqualified under Rule 262 (§230.262).

(c) *Integration with other offerings.* Offers or sales made in reliance on this Regulation A will not be integrated with:

(1) Prior offers or sales of securities; or

(2) Subsequent offers or sales of securities that are:

(i) Registered under the Securities Act, except as provided in Rule 255(e) (§230.255(e));

(ii) Exempt from registration under Rule 701 (§230.701);

(iii) Made pursuant to an employee benefit plan;

(iv) Exempt from registration under Regulation S (§§230.901 through 203.905);

(v) Made more than six months after the completion of the Regulation A offering; or

(vi) Exempt from registration under Section 4(a)(6) of the Securities Act (15 U.S.C. 77d(a)(6)).

Note to paragraph (c). If these safe harbors do not apply, whether subsequent offers and sales of securities will be integrated with the Regulation A offering will depend on the particular facts and circumstances.

(d) *Offering conditions—*

(1) *Offers.*

(i) Except as allowed by Rule 255 (§230.255), no offer of securities may be made unless an offering statement has been filed with the Commission.

(ii) After the offering statement has been filed, but before it is qualified:

(A) Oral offers may be made;

(B) Written offers pursuant to Rule 254 (§230.254) may be made; and

(C) Solicitations of interest and other communications pursuant to Rule 255 (§230.255) may be made.

(iii) Offers may be made after the offering statement has been qualified, but any written offers must be accompanied with or preceded by the most recent offering circular filed with the Commission for such offering.

(2) *Sales.*

(i) No sale of securities may be made:

(A) Until the offering statement has been qualified;

(B) By issuers that are not currently required to file reports pursuant to Rule 257(b) (§230.257(b)), until a Preliminary Offering Circular is delivered at least 48 hours before the sale to any person that before qualification of the offering statement had indicated an interest in purchasing securities in the offering, including those persons that responded to an issuer's solicitation of interest materials; and

(C) In a Tier 2 offering of securities that are not listed on a registered national securities exchange upon qualification, unless the purchaser is either an accredited investor (as defined in Rule 501 (§230.501)) or the aggregate purchase price to be paid by the purchaser for the securities (including the actual or maximum estimated conversion, exercise, or exchange price for any under-lying securities that have been qualified) is no more than ten percent (10%) of the greater of such purchaser's:

(1) Annual income or net worth if a natural person (with annual income and net worth for such natural person purchasers determined as pro-vided in Rule 501 (§230.501)); or

(2) Revenue or net assets for such purchaser's most recently completed fiscal year end if a non-natural person.

Note to paragraph (d)(2)(i)(C). When securities underlying warrants or convertible securities are being qualified pursuant to Tier 2 of Regulation A one year or more after the qualification of an offering for which investment limitations previously applied, purchasers of the underlying securities for which investment limita-tions would apply at that later date may determine compliance with the ten percent (10%) investment limitation using the conversion, exercise, or exchange price to acquire the underlying securities at that later time without aggregating such price with the price of the overlying warrants or convertible securities.

(D) The issuer may rely on a representation of the purchaser when determining compliance with the ten percent (10%) investment limitation in this para-graph (d)(2)(i)(C), provided that the issuer does not know at the time of sale that any such representation is untrue.

(ii) In a transaction that represents a sale by the issuer or an underwriter, or a sale by a dealer within 90 calendar days after qualification of the offering statement, each underwriter or dealer selling in such transaction must deliver to each purchaser from it, not later than two business days following the completion of such sale, a copy of the Final Offering Circular, subject to the following provisions:

(A) If the sale was by the issuer and was not effected by or through an underwriter or dealer, the issuer is responsible for delivering the Final Offering Circular as if the issuer were an underwriter;

(B) For continuous or delayed offerings pursuant to paragraph (d)(3) of this sec-tion, the 90 calendar day period for dealers shall commence on the day of the first bona fide offering of securities under such offering statement;

(C) If the security is listed on a registered national securities exchange, no offer-ing circular need be delivered by a dealer more than 25 calendar days after the later of the qualification date of the offering statement or the first date on which the security was bona fide offered to the public;

(D) No offering circular need be delivered by a dealer if the issuer is subject, immediately prior to the time of the filing of the offering statement, to the reporting requirements of Rule 257(b) (§230.257(b)); and

(E) The Final Offering Circular delivery requirements set forth in paragraph (d)(2)(ii) of this section may be satisfied by delivering a notice to the effect that the sale was made pursuant to a qualified offering statement that includes the uniform resource locator ("URL"), which, in the case of an electronic-only offering, must be an active hyperlink, where the Final Offering Circu-lar, or the offering statement of which such Final Offering Circular is part, may be obtained on the Commission's Electronic Data Gathering, Analysis and Retrieval System ("EDGAR") and contact information sufficient to notify a purchaser where a request for a Final Offering Circular can be sent and received in response.

(3) *Continuous or delayed offerings.*

(i) Continuous or delayed offerings may be made under this Regulation A, so long as the offering statement pertains only to:

(A) Securities that are to be offered or sold solely by or on behalf of a person or persons other than the issuer, a subsidiary of the issuer, or a person of which the issuer is a subsidiary;

(B) Securities that are to be offered and sold pursuant to a dividend or interest reinvestment plan or an employee benefit plan of the issuer;

(C) Securities that are to be issued upon the exercise of outstanding options, warrants, or rights;

(D) Securities that are to be issued upon conversion of other outstanding securities;

(E) Securities that are pledged as collateral; or

(F) Securities the offering of which will be commenced within two calendar days after the qualification date, will be made on a continuous basis, may continue for a period in excess of 30 calendar days from the date of initial qualification, and will be offered in an amount that, at the time the offering statement is qualified, is reasonably expected to be offered and sold within two years from the initial qualification date. These securities may be offered and sold only if not more than three years have elapsed since the initial qualification date of the offering statement under which they are being offered and sold; provided, however, that if a new offering statement has been filed pursuant to this paragraph (d)(3)(i)(F), securities covered by the prior offering statement may continue to be offered and sold until the earlier of the qualification date of the new offering statement or 180 calendar days after the third anniversary of the initial qualification date of the prior offering statement. Before the end of such three-year period, an issuer may file a new offering statement covering the securities. The new offering statement must include all the information that would be required at that time in an offering statement relating to all offerings that it covers. Before the qualification date of the new offering statement, the issuer may include as part of such new offering statement any unsold securities covered by the earlier offering statement by identifying on the cover page of the new offering circular, or the latest amendment, the amount of such unsold securities being included. The offering of securities on the earlier offering statement will be deemed terminated as of the date of qualification of the new offering statement. Securities may be sold pursuant to this paragraph (d)(3)(i)(F) only if the issuer is current in its annual and semiannual filings pursuant to Rule 257(b) (§230.257(b)), at the time of such sale.

(ii) At the market offerings, by or on behalf of the issuer or otherwise, are not permitted under this Regulation A. As used in this paragraph (d)(3)(ii), the term *at the market offering* means an offering of equity securities into an existing trading market for outstanding shares of the same class at other than a fixed price.

(e) *Confidential treatment.* A request for confidential treatment may be made under Rule 406 (§230.406) for information required to be filed, and Rule 83 (§200.83) for information not required to be filed.

(f) *Electronic filing.* Documents filed or otherwise provided to the Commission pursuant to this Regulation A must be submitted in electronic format by means of EDGAR in accordance with the EDGAR rules set forth in Regulation S-T (17 CFR part 232).

[80 FR 21895, Apr. 20, 2015]

APPENDIX

§230.252 OFFERING STATEMENT.

(a) *Documents to be included.* The offering statement consists of the contents required by Form 1-A (§239.90 of this chapter) and any other material information necessary to make the required statements, in light of the circumstances under which they are made, not misleading.

(b) *Paper, printing, language and pagination.* Except as otherwise specified in this rule, the requirements for offering statements are the same as those specified in Rule 403 (§230.403) for registration statements under the Act. No fee is payable to the Commission upon either the submission or filing of an offering statement on Form 1-A, or any amendment to an offering statement.

(c) *Signatures.* The issuer, its principal executive officer, principal financial officer, principal accounting officer, and a majority of the members of its board of directors or other governing body, must sign the offering statement in the manner prescribed by Form 1-A. If a signature is by a person on behalf of any other person, evidence of authority to sign must be filed, except where an executive officer signs for the issuer.

(d) *Non-public submission.* An issuer whose securities have not been previously sold pursuant to a qualified offering statement under this Regulation A or an effective registration statement under the Securities Act may submit a draft offering statement to the Commission for non-public review by the staff of the Commission before public filing, provided that the offering statement shall not be qualified less than 21 calendar days after the public filing with the Commission of:

(1) The initial non-public submission;

(2) All non-public amendments; and

(3) All non-public correspondence submitted by or on behalf of the issuer to the Commission staff regarding such submissions (subject to any separately approved confidential treatment request under Rule 251(e) (§230.251(e)).

(e) *Qualification.* An offering statement and any amendment thereto can be qualified only at such date and time as the Commission may determine.

(f) *Amendments.*

(1) (i) Amendments to an offering statement must be signed and filed with the Commission in the same manner as the initial filing. Amendments to an offering statement must be filed under cover of Form 1-A and must be numbered consecutively in the order in which filed.

(ii) Every amendment that includes amended audited financial statements must include the consent of the certifying accountant to the use of such accountant's certification in connection with the amended financial statements in the offering statement or offering circular and to being named as having audited such financial statements.

(iii) Amendments solely relating to Part III of Form 1-A must comply with the requirements of paragraph (f)(1)(i) of this section, except that such amendments may be limited to Part I of Form 1-A, an explanatory note, and all of the information required by Part III of Form 1-A.

(2) Post-qualification amendments must be filed in the following circumstances for ongoing offerings:

(i) At least every 12 months after the qualification date to include the financial statements that would be required by Form 1-A as of such date; or

(ii) To reflect any facts or events arising after the qualification date of the offering statement (or the most recent post-qualification amendment thereof) which, individually or in the aggregate, represent a fundamental change in the information set forth in the offering statement.

[80 FR 21895, Apr. 20, 2015]

§230.253 OFFERING CIRCULAR.

(a) *Contents.* An offering circular must include the information required by Form 1-A for offering circulars.

(b) *Information that may be omitted.* Notwithstanding paragraph (a) of this section, a qualified offering circular may omit information with respect to the public offering price, underwriting syndicate (including any material relationships between the issuer or selling securityholders and the unnamed underwriters, brokers or dealers), underwriting discounts or commissions, discounts or commissions to dealers, amount of proceeds, conversion rates, call prices and other items dependent upon the offering price, delivery dates, and terms of the securities dependent upon the offering date; provided, that the following conditions are met:

(1) The securities to be qualified are offered for cash.

(2) The outside front cover page of the offering circular includes a bona fide estimate of the range of the maximum offering price and the maximum number of shares or other units of securities to be offered or a bona fide estimate of the principal amount of debt securities offered, subject to the following conditions:

(i) The range must not exceed $2 for offerings where the upper end of the range is $10 or less or 20% if the upper end of the price range is over $10; and

(ii) The upper end of the range must be used in determining the aggregate offering price under Rule 251(a) (§230.251(a)).

(3) The offering statement does not relate to securities to be offered by competitive bidding.

(4) The volume of securities (the number of equity securities or aggregate principal amount of debt securities) to be offered may not be omitted in reliance on this paragraph (b).

Note to paragraph (b). A decrease in the volume of securities offered or a change in the bona fide estimate of the offering price range from that indicated in the offering circular filed as part of a qualified offering statement may be disclosed in the offering circular filed with the Commission pursuant to Rule 253(g) (§230.253(g)), so long as the decrease in the volume of securities offered or change in the price range would not materially change the disclosure contained in the offering statement at qualification. Notwithstanding the foregoing, any decrease in the volume of securities offered and any deviation from the low or high end of the price range may be reflected in the offering circular supplement filed with the Commission pursuant to Rule 253(g)(1) or (3) (§230.253(g)(1) or (3)) if, in the aggregate, the decrease in volume and/or change in price represent no more than a 20% change from the maximum aggregate offering price calculable using the information in the qualified offering statement. In no circumstances may this paragraph be used to offer securities where the maximum aggregate offering price would result in the offering exceeding the limit set forth in Rule 251(a) (§230.251(a)) or if the change would result in a Tier 1 offering becoming a Tier 2 offering. An offering circular supplement may not be used to increase the volume of securities being offered. Additional securities may only be offered pursuant to a new offering statement or post-qualification amendment qualified by the Commission.

(c) *Filing of omitted information.* The information omitted from the offering circular in reliance upon paragraph (b) of this section must be contained in an offering circular filed with the Commission pursuant to paragraph (g) of this section; except that if such offering circular is not so filed by the later of 15 business days after the qualification date of the offering statement or 15 business days after the qualification of a post-qualification amendment thereto that contains an offering circular, the information omitted in reliance upon paragraph (b) of this section must be contained in a qualified post-qualification amendment to the offering statement.

(d) *Presentation of information.*

(1) Information in the offering circular must be presented in a clear, concise and understandable manner and in a type size that is easily readable. Repetition of information should be avoided; cross-referencing of information within the document is permitted.

(2) Where an offering circular is distributed through an electronic medium, issuers may satisfy legibility requirements applicable to printed documents by presenting all required information in a format readily communicated to investors.

(e) *Date.* An offering circular must be dated approximately as of the date it was filed with the Commission.

(f) *Cover page legend.* The cover page of every offering circular must display the following statement highlighted by prominent type or in another manner:

The United States Securities and Exchange Commission does not pass upon the merits of or give its approval to any securities offered or the terms of the offering, nor does it pass upon the accuracy or completeness of any offering circular or other solicitation materials. These securities are offered pursuant to an exemption from registration with the Commission; however, the Commission has not made an independent determination that the securities offered are exempt from registration.

(g) *Offering circular supplements.*

(1) An offering circular that discloses information previously omitted from the offering circular in reliance upon Rule 253(b) (§230.253(b)) must be filed with the Commission no later than two business days following the earlier of the date of determination of the offering price or the date such offering circular is first used after qualification in connection with a public offering or sale.

(2) An offering circular that reflects information other than that covered in paragraph (g)(1) of this section that constitutes a substantive change from or addition to the information set forth in the last offering circular filed with the Commission must be filed with the Commission no later than five business days after the date it is first used after qualification in connection with a public offering or sale. If an offering circular filed pursuant to this paragraph (g)(2) consists of an offering circular supplement attached to an offering circular that previously had been filed or was not required to be filed pursuant to paragraph (g) of this section because it did not contain substantive changes from an offering circular that previously was filed, only the offering circular supplement need be filed under paragraph (g) of this section, provided that the cover page of the offering circular supplement identifies the date(s) of the related offering circular and any offering circular supplements thereto that together constitute the offering circular with respect to the securities currently being offered or sold.

(3) An offering circular that discloses information, facts or events covered in both paragraphs (g)(1) and (2) of this section must be filed with the Commission no later than two business days following the earlier of the date of the determination of the offering price or the date it is first used after qualification in connection with a public offering or sale.

(4) An offering circular required to be filed pursuant to paragraph (g) of this section that is not filed within the time frames specified in paragraphs (g)(1) through (3) of this section, as applicable, must be filed pursuant to this paragraph (g)(4) as soon as practicable after the discovery of such failure to file.

(5) Each offering circular filed under this section must contain in the upper right corner of the cover page the paragraphs of paragraphs (g)(1) through (4) of this section under which the filing is made, and the file number of the offering statement to which the offering circular relates.

[80 FR 21895, Apr. 20, 2015]

§230.254 PRELIMINARY OFFERING CIRCULAR.

After the filing of an offering statement, but before its qualification, written offers of securities may be made if they meet the following requirements:

(a) *Outside front cover page.* The outside front cover page of the material bears the caption *Preliminary Offering Circular,* the date of issuance, and the following legend, which must be highlighted by prominent type or in another manner:

An offering statement pursuant to Regulation A relating to these securities has been filed with the Securities and Exchange Commission. Information contained in this Preliminary Offering Circular is subject to completion or amendment. These securities may not be sold nor may offers to buy be accepted before the offering statement filed with the Commission is qualified. This Preliminary Offering Circular shall not constitute an offer to sell or the solicitation of an offer to buy nor may there be any sales of these securities in any state in which such offer, solicitation or sale would be unlawful before registration or qualification under the laws of any such state. We may elect to satisfy our obligation to deliver a Final Offering Circular by sending you a notice within two business days after the completion of our sale to you that contains the URL where the Final Offering Circular or the offering statement in which such Final Offering Circular was filed may be obtained.

(b) *Other contents.* The Preliminary Offering Circular contains substantially the information required to be in an offering circular by Form 1-A (§239.90 of this chapter), except that certain information may be omitted under Rule 253(b) (§230.253(b)) subject to the conditions set forth in such rule.

(c) *Filing.* The Preliminary Offering Circular is filed as a part of the offering statement.

[80 FR 21895, Apr. 20, 2015]

§230.255 SOLICITATIONS OF INTEREST AND OTHER COMMUNICATIONS.

(a) *Solicitation of interest.* At any time before the qualification of an offering statement, including before the non-public submission or public filing of such offering statement, an issuer or any person authorized to act on behalf of an issuer may communicate orally or in writing to determine whether there is any interest in a contemplated securities offering. Such communications are deemed to be an offer of a security for sale for purposes of the antifraud provisions of the federal securities laws. No solicitation or acceptance of money or other consideration, nor of any commitment, binding or otherwise, from any person is permitted until qualification of the offering statement.

(b) *Conditions.* The communications must:

(1) State that no money or other consideration is being solicited, and if sent in response, will not be accepted;

(2) State that no offer to buy the securities can be accepted and no part of the purchase price can be received until the offering statement is qualified, and any such offer may be withdrawn or revoked, without obligation or commitment of any kind, at any time before notice of its acceptance given after the qualification date;

(3) State that a person's indication of interest involves no obligation or commitment of any kind; and

(4) After the public filing of the offering statement:

(i) State from whom a copy of the most recent version of the Preliminary Offering Circular may be obtained, including a phone number and address of such person;

      (ii)   Provide the URL where such Preliminary Offering Circular, or the offering statement in which such Preliminary Offering Circular was filed, may be obtained; or

      (iii) Include a complete copy of the Preliminary Offering Circular.

(c)   *Indications of interest.* Any written communication under this rule may include a means by which a person may indicate to the issuer that such person is interested in a potential offering. This issuer may require the name, address, telephone number, and/or email address in any response form included pursuant to this paragraph (c).

(d)   *Revised solicitations of interest.* If solicitation of interest materials are used after the public filing of the offering statement and such solicitation of interest materials contain information that is inaccurate or inadequate in any material respect, revised solicitation of interest materials must be redistributed in a substantially similar manner as such materials were originally distributed. Notwithstanding the foregoing in this paragraph (d), if the only information that is inaccurate or inadequate is contained in a Preliminary Offering Circular provided with the solicitation of interest materials pursuant to paragraphs (b)(4)(i) or (ii) of this section, no such redistribution is required in the following circumstances:

    (1)   in the case of paragraph (b)(4)(i) of this section, the revised Preliminary Offering Circular will be provided to any persons making new inquiries and will be recirculated to any persons making any previous inquiries; or

    (2)   in the case of paragraph (b)(4)(ii) of this section, the URL continues to link directly to the most recent Preliminary Offering Circular or to the offering statement in which such revised Preliminary Offering Circular was filed.

(e)   *Abandoned offerings.* Where an issuer decides to register an offering under the Securities Act after soliciting interest in a contemplated, but subsequently abandoned, Regulation A offering, the abandoned Regulation A offering would not be subject to integration with the registered offering if the issuer engaged in solicitations of interest pursuant to this rule only to qualified institutional buyers and institutional accredited investors permitted by Section 5(d) of the Securities Act. If the issuer engaged in solicitations of interest to persons other than qualified institutional buyers and institutional accredited investors, an abandoned Regulation A offering would not be subject to integration if the issuer (and any underwriter, broker, dealer, or agent used by the issuer in connection with the proposed offering) waits at least 30 calendar days between the last such solicitation of interest in the Regulation A offering and the filing of the registration statement with the Commission.

[80 FR 21895, Apr. 20, 2015]

§230.256 DEFINITION OF "QUALIFIED PURCHASER".

For purposes of Section 18(b)(3) of the Securities Act [15 U.S.C. 77r(b)(3)], a "qualified purchaser" means any person to whom securities are offered or sold pursuant to a Tier 2 offering of this Regulation A.

[80 FR 21895, Apr. 20, 2015]

§230.257 PERIODIC AND CURRENT REPORTING; EXIT REPORT.

(a)   *Tier 1: Exit report.* Each issuer that has filed an offering statement for a Tier 1 offering that has been qualified pursuant to this Regulation A must file an exit report on Form 1-Z (§239.94 of this chapter) not later than 30 calendar days after the termination or completion of the offering.

(b) *Tier 2: Periodic and current reporting.* Each issuer that has filed an offering statement for a Tier 2 offering that has been qualified pursuant to this Regulation A must file with the Commission the following periodic and current reports:

(1) *Annual reports.* An annual report on Form 1-K (§239.91 of this chapter) for the fiscal year in which the offering statement became qualified and for any fiscal year thereafter, unless the issuer's obligation to file such annual report is suspended under paragraph (d) of this section. Annual reports must be filed within the period specified in Form 1-K.

(2) *Special financial report.*

(i) A special financial report on Form 1-K or Form 1-SA if the offering statement did not contain the following:

(A) Audited financial statements for the issuer's most recent fiscal year (or for the life of the issuer if less than a full fiscal year) preceding the fiscal year in which the issuer's offering statement became qualified; or

(B) unaudited financial statements covering the first six months of the issuer's current fiscal year if the offering statement was qualified during the last six months of that fiscal year.

(ii) The special financial report described in paragraph (b)(2)(i)(A) of this section must be filed under cover of Form 1-K within 120 calendar days after the qualification date of the offering statement and must include audited financial statements for such fiscal year or other period specified in that paragraph, as the case may be. The special financial report described in paragraph (b)(2)(i)(B) of this section must be filed under cover of Form 1-SA within 90 calendar days after the qualification date of the offering statement and must include the semiannual financial statements for the first six months of the issuer's fiscal year, which may be unaudited.

(iii) A special financial report must be signed in accordance with the requirements of the form on which it is filed.

(3) *Semiannual report.* A semiannual report on Form 1-SA (§239.92 of this chapter) within the period specified in Form 1-SA. Semiannual reports must cover the first six months of each fiscal year of the issuer, commencing with the first six months of the fiscal year immediately following the most recent fiscal year for which full financial statements were included in the offering statement, or, if the offering statement included financial statements for the first six months of the fiscal year following the most recent full fiscal year, for the first six months of the following fiscal year.

(4) *Current reports.* Current reports on Form 1-U (§239.93 of this chapter) with respect to the matters and within the period specified in that form, unless substantially the same information has been previously reported to the Commission by the issuer under cover of Form 1-K or Form 1-SA.

(5) *Reporting by successor issuers.* Where in connection with a succession by merger, consolidation, exchange of securities, acquisition of assets or otherwise, securities of any issuer that is not required to file reports pursuant to paragraph (b) of this section are issued to the holders of any class of securities of another issuer that is required to file such reports, the duty to file reports pursuant to paragraph (b) of this section shall be deemed to have been assumed by the issuer of the class of securities so issued. The successor issuer must, after the consummation of the succession, file reports in accordance with paragraph (b) of this section, unless that issuer is exempt from filing such reports or the duty to file such reports is terminated or suspended under paragraph (d) of this section.

(c) *Amendments.* All amendments to the reports described in paragraphs (a) and (b) of this section must be filed under cover of the form amended, marked with the letter *A* to designate the document as an amendment, e.g., "1-K/A," and in compliance with pertinent requirements applicable to such reports. Amendments filed pursuant to this paragraph (c) must set forth the complete text of each item as amended, but need not include any items that were not amended. Amendments must be numbered sequentially and be filed separately for each report amended. Amendments must be signed on behalf of the issuer by a duly authorized representative of the issuer. An amendment to any report required to include certifications as specified in the applicable form must include new certifications by the appropriate persons.

(d) *Suspension of duty to file reports.*

    (1) The duty to file reports under this rule shall be automatically suspended if and so long as the issuer is subject to the duty to file reports required by section 13 or 15(d) of the Exchange Act (15 U.S.C. 78m or 15 U.S.C. 78o).

    (2) The duty to file reports under paragraph (b) of this section with respect to a class of securities held of record (as defined in Rule 12g5-1 (§240.12g5-1 of this chapter)) by less than 300 persons, or less than 1,200 persons for a bank (as defined in Section 3(a)(6) of the Exchange Act (15 U.S.C. 78c(a)(6)), or a bank holding company (as defined in section 2 of the Bank Holding Company Act of 1956 (12 U.S.C. 1841)), shall be suspended for such class of securities immediately upon filing with the Commission an exit report on Form 1-Z (§239.94 of this chapter) if the issuer of such class has filed all reports due pursuant to this rule before the date of such Form 1-Z filing for the shorter of:

        (i) The period since the issuer became subject to such reporting obligation; or

        (ii) Its most recent three fiscal years and the portion of the current year preceding the date of filing Form 1-Z.

    (3) For the purposes of paragraph (d)(2) of this section, the term *class* shall be construed to include all securities of an issuer that are of substantially similar character and the holders of which enjoy substantially similar rights and privileges. If the Form 1-Z is subsequently withdrawn or if it is denied because the issuer was ineligible to use the form, the issuer must, within 60 calendar days, file with the Commission all reports which would have been required if such exit report had not been filed. If the suspension resulted from the issuer's merger into, or consolidation with, another issuer or issuers, the notice must be filed by the successor issuer.

    (4) The ability to suspend reporting, as described in paragraph (d)(2) of this section, is not available for any class of securities if:

        (i) During that fiscal year a Tier 2 offering statement was qualified;

        (ii) The issuer has not filed an annual report under this rule or the Exchange Act for the fiscal year in which a Tier 2 offering statement was qualified; or

        (iii) Offers or sales of securities of that class are being made pursuant to a Tier 2 Regulation A offering.

(e) *Termination of duty to file reports.* If the duty to file reports is suspended pursuant to paragraph (d)(1) of this section and such suspension ends because the issuer terminates or suspends its duty to file reports under the Exchange Act, the issuer's obligation to file reports under paragraph (b) of this section shall:

    (1) Automatically terminate if the issuer is eligible to suspend its duty to file reports under paragraphs (d)(2) and (3) of this section; or

    (2) Recommence with the report covering the most recent financial period after that included in any effective registration statement or filed Exchange Act report.

[80 FR 21895, Apr. 20, 2015]

§230.258 SUSPENSION OF THE EXEMPTION.

   (a)   *Suspension.* The Commission may at any time enter an order temporarily suspending a Regulation A exemption if it has reason to believe that:

      (1)   No exemption is available or any of the terms, conditions or requirements of Regulation A have not been complied with;

      (2)   The offering statement, any sales or solicitation of interest material, or any report filed pursuant to Rule 257 (§230.257) contains any untrue statement of a material fact or omits to state a material fact necessary in order to make the statements made, in light of the circumstances under which they are made, not misleading;

      (3)   The offering is being made or would be made in violation of section 17 of the Securities Act;

      (4)   An event has occurred after the filing of the offering statement that would have rendered the exemption hereunder unavailable if it had occurred before such filing;

      (5)   Any person specified in Rule 262(a) (§230.262(a)) has been indicted for any crime or offense of the character specified in Rule 262(a)(1) (§230.262(a)(1)), or any proceeding has been initiated for the purpose of enjoining any such person from engaging in or continuing any conduct or practice of the character specified in Rule 262(a)(2) (§230.262(a)(2)), or any proceeding has been initiated for the purposes of Rule 262(a)(3)-(8) (§230.262(a)(3) through (8)); or

      (6)   The issuer or any promoter, officer, director, or underwriter has failed to cooperate, or has obstructed or refused to permit the making of an investigation by the Commission in connection with any offering made or proposed to be made in reliance on Regulation A.

   (b)   *Notice and hearing.* Upon the entry of an order under paragraph (a) of this section, the Commission will promptly give notice to the issuer, any underwriter, and any selling securityholder:

      (1)   That such order has been entered, together with a brief statement of the reasons for the entry of the order; and

      (2)   That the Commission, upon receipt of a written request within 30 calendar days after the entry of the order, will, within 20 calendar days after receiving the request, order a hearing at a place to be designated by the Commission.

   (c)   *Suspension order.* If no hearing is requested and none is ordered by the Commission, an order entered under paragraph (a) of this section shall become permanent on the 30th calendar day after its entry and shall remain in effect unless or until it is modified or vacated by the Commission. Where a hearing is requested or is ordered by the Commission, the Commission will, after notice of and opportunity for such hearing, either vacate the order or enter an order permanently suspending the exemption.

   (d)   *Permanent suspension.* The Commission may, at any time after notice of and opportunity for hearing, enter an order permanently suspending the exemption for any reason upon which it could have entered a temporary suspension order under paragraph (a) of this section. Any such order shall remain in effect until vacated by the Commission.

   (e)   *Notice procedures.* All notices required by this rule must be given by personal service, registered or certified mail to the addresses given by the issuer, any underwriter and any selling securityholder in the offering statement.

[80 FR 21895, Apr. 20, 2015]

§230.259 WITHDRAWAL OR ABANDONMENT OF OFFERING STATEMENTS.

(a) *Withdrawal.* If none of the securities that are the subject of an offering statement has been sold and such offering statement is not the subject of a proceeding under Rule 258 (§230.258), the offering statement may be withdrawn with the Commission's consent. The application for withdrawal must state the reason the offering statement is to be withdrawn and must be signed by an authorized representative of the issuer. Any withdrawn document will remain in the Commission's files, as well as the related request for withdrawal.

(b) *Abandonment.* When an offering statement has been on file with the Commission for nine months without amendment and has not become qualified, the Commission may, in its discretion, declare the offering statement abandoned. If the offering statement has been amended, the nine-month period shall be computed from the date of the latest amendment.

[80 FR 21895, Apr. 20, 2015]

§230.260 INSIGNIFICANT DEVIATIONS FROM A TERM, CONDITION OR REQUIREMENT OF REGULATION A.

(a) *Failure to comply.* A failure to comply with a term, condition or requirement of Regulation A will not result in the loss of the exemption from the requirements of section 5 of the Securities Act for any offer or sale to a particular individual or entity, if the person relying on the exemption establishes that:

    (1) The failure to comply did not pertain to a term, condition or requirement directly intended to protect that particular individual or entity;

    (2) The failure to comply was insignificant with respect to the offering as a whole, provided that any failure to comply with Rule 251(a), (b), and (d)(1) and (3) (§230.251(a), (b), and (d)(1) and (3)) shall be deemed to be significant to the offering as a whole; and

    (3) A good faith and reasonable attempt was made to comply with all applicable terms, conditions and requirements of Regulation A.

(b) *Action by Commission.* A transaction made in reliance upon Regulation A must comply with all applicable terms, conditions and requirements of the regulation. Where an exemption is established only through reliance upon paragraph (a) of this section, the failure to comply shall nonetheless be actionable by the Commission under section 20 of the Securities Act.

(c) *Suspension.* This provision provides no relief or protection from a proceeding under Rule 258 (§230.258).

[80 FR 21895, Apr. 20, 2015]

§230.261 DEFINITIONS.

As used in this Regulation A, all terms have the same meanings as in Rule 405 (§230.405), except that all references to *registrant* in those definitions shall refer to the issuer of the securities to be offered and sold under Regulation A. In addition, these terms have the following meanings:

(a) *Affiliated issuer.* An affiliate (as defined in Rule 501 (§230.501)) of the issuer that is issuing securities in the same offering.

(b) *Business day.* Any day except Saturdays, Sundays or United States federal holidays.

(c) *Eligible securities.* Equity securities, debt securities, and securities convertible or exchangeable to equity interests, including any guarantees of such securities, but not including asset-backed securities as such term is defined in Item 1101(c) of Regulation AB.

(d) *Final order.* A written directive or declaratory statement issued by a federal or state agency described in Rule 262(a)(3) (§230.262(a)(3)) under applicable statutory authority that provides for notice and an opportunity for hearing, which constitutes a final disposition or action by that federal or state agency.

(e) *Final offering circular.* The more recent of: the current offering circular contained in a qualified offering statement; and any offering circular filed pursuant to Rule 253(g) (§230.253(g)). If, however, the issuer is relying on Rule 253(b) ((§230.253(b)), the Final Offering Circular is the most recent of the offering circular filed pursuant to Rule 253(g)(1) or (3) (§230.253(g)(1) or (3)) and any subsequent offering circular filed pursuant to Rule 253(g) (§230.253(g)).

(f) *Offering statement.* An offering statement prepared pursuant to Regulation A.

(g) *Preliminary offering circular.* The offering circular described in Rule 254 (§230.254).

[80 FR 21895, Apr. 20, 2015]

§230.262 DISQUALIFICATION PROVISIONS.

(a) *Disqualification events.* No exemption under this Regulation A shall be available for a sale of securities if the issuer; any predecessor of the issuer; any affiliated issuer; any director, executive officer, other officer participating in the offering, general partner or managing member of the issuer; any beneficial owner of 20% or more of the issuer's outstanding voting equity securities, calculated on the basis of voting power; any promoter connected with the issuer in any capacity at the time of filing, any offer after qualification, or such sale; any person that has been or will be paid (directly or indirectly) remuneration for solicitation of purchasers in connection with such sale of securities; any general partner or managing member of any such solicitor; or any director, executive officer or other officer participating in the offering of any such solicitor or general partner or managing member of such solicitor:

(1) Has been convicted, within ten years before the filing of the offering statement (or five years, in the case of issuers, their predecessors and affiliated issuers), of any felony or misdemeanor:

   (i) In connection with the purchase or sale of any security;

   (ii) Involving the making of any false filing with the Commission; or

   (iii) Arising out of the conduct of the business of an underwriter, broker, dealer, municipal securities dealer, investment adviser or paid solicitor of purchasers of securities;

(2) Is subject to any order, judgment or decree of any court of competent jurisdiction, entered within five years before the filing of the offering statement, that, at the time of such filing, restrains or enjoins such person from engaging or continuing to engage in any conduct or practice:

   (i) In connection with the purchase or sale of any security;

   (ii) Involving the making of any false filing with the Commission; or

   (iii) Arising out of the conduct of the business of an underwriter, broker, dealer, municipal securities dealer, investment adviser or paid solicitor of purchasers of securities;

(3) Is subject to a final order (as defined in Rule 261 (§230.261)) of a state securities commission (or an agency or officer of a state performing like functions); a state authority that supervises or examines banks, savings associations, or credit unions; a state insurance commission (or an agency or officer of a state performing like functions); an appropriate federal banking agency; the U.S. Commodity Futures Trading Commission; or the National Credit Union Administration that:

   (i) At the time of the filing of the offering statement, bars the person from:

      (A) Association with an entity regulated by such commission, authority, agency, or officer;

      (B) Engaging in the business of securities, insurance or banking; or

(C)   Engaging in savings association or credit union activities; or

(ii)   Constitutes a final order based on a violation of any law or regulation that prohibits fraudulent, manipulative, or deceptive conduct entered within ten years before such filing of the offering statement;

(4)   Is subject to an order of the Commission entered pursuant to section 15(b) or 15B(c) of the Securities Exchange Act of 1934 (15 U.S.C. 78*o*(b) or 78*o*-4(c)) or section 203(e) or (f) of the Investment Advisers Act of 1940 (15 U.S.C. 80b-3(e) or (f)) that, at the time of the filing of the offering statement:

(i)   Suspends or revokes such person's registration as a broker, dealer, municipal securities dealer or investment adviser;

(ii)   Places limitations on the activities, functions or operations of such person; or

(iii)   Bars such person from being associated with any entity or from participating in the offering of any penny stock;

(5)   Is subject to any order of the Commission entered within five years before the filing of the offering statement that, at the time of such filing, orders the person to cease and desist from committing or causing a violation or future violation of:

(i)   Any scienter-based anti-fraud provision of the federal securities laws, including without limitation section 17(a)(1) of the Securities Act of 1933 (15 U.S.C. 77q(a)(1)), section 10(b) of the Securities Exchange Act of 1934 (15 U.S.C. 78j(b)) and 17 CFR 240.10b-5, section 15(c)(1) of the Securities Exchange Act of 1934 (15 U.S.C. 78*o*(c)(1)) and section 206(1) of the Investment Advisers Act of 1940 (15 U.S.C. 80b-6(1)), or any other rule or regulation thereunder; or

(ii)   Section 5 of the Securities Act of 1933 (15 U.S.C. 77e).

(6)   Is suspended or expelled from membership in, or suspended or barred from association with a member of, a registered national securities exchange or a registered national or affiliated securities association for any act or omission to act constituting conduct inconsistent with just and equitable principles of trade;

(7)   Has filed (as a registrant or issuer), or was or was named as an underwriter in, any registration statement or offering statement filed with the Commission that, within five years before the filing of the offering statement, was the subject of a refusal order, stop order, or order suspending the Regulation A exemption, or is, at the time of such filing, the subject of an investigation or proceeding to determine whether a stop order or suspension order should be issued; or

(8)   Is subject to a United States Postal Service false representation order entered within five years before the filing of the offering statement, or is, at the time of such filing, subject to a temporary restraining order or preliminary injunction with respect to conduct alleged by the United States Postal Service to constitute a scheme or device for obtaining money or property through the mail by means of false representations.

(b)   *Transition, waivers, reasonable care exception.* Paragraph (a) of this section shall not apply:

(1)   With respect to any order under §230.262(a)(3) or (5) that occurred or was issued before June 19, 2015;

(2)   Upon a showing of good cause and without prejudice to any other action by the Commission, if the Commission determines that it is not necessary under the circumstances that an exemption be denied;

(3)   If, before the filing of the offering statement, the court or regulatory authority that entered the relevant order, judgment or decree advises in writing (whether contained in the relevant judgment, order or decree or separately to the Commission or its staff) that disqualification under paragraph (a) of this section should not arise as a consequence of such order, judgment or decree; or

(4)   If the issuer establishes that it did not know and, in the exercise of reasonable care, could not have known that a disqualification existed under paragraph (a) of this section.

Note to paragraph (b)(4). An issuer will not be able to establish that it has exercised reasonable care unless it has made, in light of the circumstances, factual inquiry into whether any disqualifications exist. The nature and scope of the factual inquiry will vary based on the facts and circumstances concerning, among other things, the issuer and the other offering participants.

(c)   *Affiliated issuers.* For purposes of paragraph (a) of this section, events relating to any affiliated issuer that occurred before the affiliation arose will be not considered disqualifying if the affiliated entity is not:

(1)   In control of the issuer; or

(2)   Under common control with the issuer by a third party that was in control of the affiliated entity at the time of such events.

(d)   *Disclosure of prior "bad actor" events.* The issuer must include in the offering circular a description of any matters that would have triggered disqualification under paragraphs (a)(3) and (5) of this section but occurred before June 19, 2015. The failure to provide such information shall not prevent an issuer from relying on Regulation A if the issuer establishes that it did not know and, in the exercise of reasonable care, could not have known of the existence of the undisclosed matter or matters.

[80 FR 21895, Apr. 20, 2015]

§230.263 Consent to service of process.

(a)   If the issuer is not organized under the laws of any of the states or territories of the United States of America, it shall furnish to the Commission a written irrevocable consent and power of attorney on Form F-X (§239.42 of this chapter) at the time of filing the offering statement required by Rule 252 (§230.252).

(b)   Any change to the name or address of the agent for service of the issuer shall be communicated promptly to the Commission through amendment of the requisite form and referencing the file number of the relevant offering statement.

[80 FR 21895, Apr. 20, 2015]

*****

SAMPLE: OFFERING MEMORANDUM—PPM

ABC APARTMENTS, LLLP
* * * CONFIDENTIAL * * *

THE DELIVERY OF THIS PRIVATE OFFERING MEMORANDUM ("MEMORANDUM") SHALL NOT CONSTITUTE AN OFFER OR SOLICITATION TO ANY PERSON IN ANY JURISDICTION IN WHICH SUCH AN OFFER OR SOLICITATION IS UNLAWFUL, AND SHALL CONSTITUTE AN OFFER ONLY TO THE OFFEREE WHOSE NAME APPEARS IN THE SPACE BELOW. EACH OFFEREE AGREES BY ACCEPTING THIS MEMORANDUM THAT HE/SHE WILL NOT DISCLOSE ITS CONTENTS TO ANY OTHER PERSON, EXCEPT WITH THE CONSENT OF THE GENERAL PARTNER AND WILL RETURN IT PROMPTLY UPON REACHING A DECISION NOT TO INVEST IN THE INVESTMENT OFFERED HEREUNDER.

_____
Print Name of Offeree

_____
Signature of Offeree

_____
Number of Memorandum

_____
Date Delivered

* * * THESE ARE SPECULATIVE SECURITIES * * *

THIS MEMORANDUM SUPERSEDES PRIOR WRITTEN OR ORAL INFORMATION OR MATERIAL RELATING TO THE PARTNERSHIP

THE EFFECTIVE DATE OF THIS MEMORANDUM IS [DATE]

* * * CONFIDENTIAL * * *

ABC APARTMENTS, LLLP
(an Arizona limited liability limited partnership)

Thirty-three (33) limited partnership interests ("Units") of ABC Apartments, LP, a Colorado limited partnership ("Partnership"), are hereby offered ("Offering") at a price per Unit of $100,000, payable in cash upon subscription. The minimum subscription generally will be one Unit. Units will be sold by the Partnership solely to "accredited investors" as defined in Regulation D as promulgated under the Securities Act of 1933, as amended ("Securities Act").

The Partnership has been formed for the purpose of acquiring the ABC Building, an apartment community located in [CITY], [STATE] ("Property"), and operating, holding for appreciation, improving, refinancing, and ultimately selling the Property. The general partner of the Partnership is ABC

Investments, LLC, a Colorado limited liability company ("General Partner"). All persons subscribing for Units will hereinafter be referred to as a "Limited Partner" or "Limited Partners."

THESE SECURITIES HAVE NOT BEEN REGISTERED UNDER THE SECURITIES ACT OR ANY STATE SECURITIES LAWS AND ARE BEING OFFERED AND SOLD IN RELIANCE ON EXEMPTIONS FROM THE REGISTRATION REQUIREMENTS OF THE SECURITIES ACT AND STATE LAWS. THESE SECURITIES ARE SUBJECT TO RESTRICTION ON TRANSFERABILITY AND RESALE AND MAY NOT BE TRANSFERRED OR RESOLD EXCEPT AS PERMITTED UNDER THE SECURITIES ACT AND SUCH LAWS PURSUANT TO REGISTRATION OR EXEMPTION THEREFROM. THESE SECURITIES HAVE NOT BEEN APPROVED OR DISAPPROVED BY THE SECURITIES AND EXCHANGE COMMISSION OR ANY OTHER FEDERAL OR STATE REGULATORY AUTHORITIES NOR HAVE ANY FEDERAL OR STATE AUTHORITIES PASSED UPON OR ENDORSED THE MERITS OF THIS OFFERING, THESE SECURITIES, OR THE ACCURACY OR ADEQUACY OF THIS MEMORANDUM. ANY REPRESENTATION TO THE CONTRARY IS A CRIMINAL OFFENSE.

Until all Units are sold, investors' funds will be held in a segregated, non-interest-bearing account established in the Partnership's name ("Special Account"). The Partnership is not required to and may not accept subscriptions in the order received. Subscriptions for Units may be accepted or rejected in whole or in part by the Partnership for any reason. Unless terminated earlier by the Partnership, this Offering will terminate on [DATE] unless extended by the General Partner ("Termination Date"). If all Units are sold, the Partnership will transfer the proceeds from the Special Account to the Partnership, issue Units, and admit persons acquiring Units as Limited Partners of the Partnership. The General Partner or its Affiliates may acquire Units to allow the Offering to close. If all Units are not subscribed and paid for prior to the Termination Date, all proceeds will be returned to subscribers. See "Terms of Offering." The Units are offered by the General Partner on behalf of the Partnership on a best efforts basis. The Partnership will not pay commissions or finders' fees. The Partnership will reimburse the General Partner or pay for legal, accounting, and filing fees and printing, or other organization and syndication costs, which the General Partner estimates will be approximately $25,000. The General Partner will receive the Acquisition Fee upon the Partnership's acquisition of the Property.

This Offering involves a high degree of risk. See "Risk Factors" herein. The risk factors include, among others, the following factors, which are not exhaustive but are merely illustrative.

1. The Limited Partners will have no voice in decisions relating to the business of the Partnership, including such matters as to whether, when, and under what terms the Property will be sold or refinanced.
2. The contributions of the Limited Partners are sufficient for the Partnership to purchase the Property on a leveraged basis. If cash flow from the Property is insufficient to pay debt secured by the Property, the Property could be lost through foreclosure.
3. Any appreciation in value of the Property acquired by the Partnership will be dependent upon national and local economic conditions and other factors beyond the control of the Partnership. There can be no assurance that the Property will generate cash flow for regular distributions or appreciate or can be operated or sold on terms satisfactory to the Partnership.

Neither the delivery of this Memorandum nor any sale hereunder shall, under any circumstances, create any implication that there has been no change in the prospects of the Partnership since the date hereof, however, if material changes occur, this Memorandum will be amended or supplemented as necessary.

No dealer, salesman or any other person has been authorized to give any information or to make any representations or warranties, either express or implied, other than those contained in this Memorandum or the documents attached hereto as exhibits, and, if given or made, such information, representations and warranties must not be relied upon as having been authorized by the General Partner.

In making an investment decision, investors must rely on their own examination of the Partnership and the terms of this Offering, including the merits and risks involved. Prospective investors are not to construe the contents of this Memorandum as legal, tax, investment, or accounting advice. if a prospective investor does not understand all aspects of the Partnership and this Offering, he/she is urged to consult with his/her own counsel, accountant, or business advisor as to the legal, tax, regulatory, financial, and accounting consequences of an investment in the Partnership and related matters involved with respect to his/her investment herein.

The distribution of this Memorandum and the offer and sale of the Units in certain jurisdictions may be restricted by law. This Memorandum does not constitute an offer to sell or the solicitation of an offer to buy in any state or other jurisdiction to any person to whom it is unlawful to make such offer or solicitation in such state or jurisdiction. Units of the Partnership that are acquired by persons not entitled to hold them will be compulsorily redeemed.

Any distribution of this Memorandum other than by the General Partner or its agents is unauthorized.

Each prospective investor agrees not to reproduce this Memorandum, in whole or in part, or to deliver it to, or permit its use by, any other person and agrees to return it to the General Partner if he/she does not intend to enter into this investment.

This investment is illiquid, involves a high degree of risk and is suitable generally for persons of substantial financial means who have no need for liquidity in this investment. furthermore, the Partnership should not be considered as a "tax shelter" investment.

This Memorandum is qualified in its entirety by reference to the Limited Partnership Agreement ("LPA"), which is attached to this Memorandum and should be reviewed prior to purchasing an interest in the Partnership. In the event that the descriptions in or terms of this Memorandum are inconsistent with or contrary to the descriptions in or terms of the LPA, the LPA shall control.

In considering any investment performance information contained in this Memorandum or as otherwise provided by the General Partner or its Affiliates, prospective investors should bear in mind that past performances are not necessarily indicative of future results and there can be no assurance that the Partnership will achieve comparable results, that the Preferred Return will be met, or that the Partnership will be able to implement its investment strategy and investment approach or achieve its investment objectives.

Certain information contained in this Memorandum and the Business Plan attached as Exhibit "E" to this Memorandum constitutes "forward-looking statements," which can be identified by the use of forward-looking terminology, such as "may," "will," "seek," "should," "expect," "anticipate," "project," "estimate," "intend," "continue," or "believe" or the negatives thereof or other variations thereon or comparable terminology. Due to various risks and uncertainties, including those set forth under "Risk Factors" and "Potential Conflicts of Interest," actual events or results or the actual performance of the Partnership may differ materially from those reflected or contemplated in such forward-looking statements. The Partnership and the General Partner believe that such statements and information are based upon reasonable estimates and assumptions. However, forward-looking statements and information are inherently uncertain and actual events or results can and will differ from those projected.

All time sensitive representations herein are made as of the date of this Memorandum unless stated otherwise. Neither the delivery of this Memorandum at any time, nor any sale hereunder, shall under any circumstances create an implication that the information contained herein is correct as of any other time subsequent to such dates.

This Memorandum contains what the General Partner considers to be fair summaries of certain provisions of the documents that will govern this investment, including the Partnership's LPA;

however, these summaries do not purport to be complete and are qualified in their entirety by reference to the texts of the original documents.

Copies of the Partnership's LPA and the Certificate of Limited Partnership of the Partnership are included herewith. Any prospective investor or his/her representative will be accorded the opportunity to obtain any additional information he/she may request that may be necessary to verify the accuracy of the contents of this Memorandum. Each prospective investor is invited to meet with representatives of the Partnership and to discuss with, ask questions of, and receive answers from such representatives concerning the terms and conditions of this Offering and to obtain any additional information concerning this investment, to the extent that such representatives possess such information or can acquire it without unreasonable effort or expense. To obtain any additional information, please contact the offices of the general partner, ABC Investments, LLC, at (999) 999-9999.

TABLE OF CONTENTS

APPENDIX

WHO CAN INVEST?

A purchase of the Units offered hereby involves a high degree of risk. There will be no public market for the Units and the sale or transfer thereof will be subject to substantial restrictions and limitations. Accordingly, the Units are suitable only for a person who: (i) does not anticipate that he/she will be required to sell his/her Unit(s) in the foreseeable future; and (ii) has sufficient net worth to sustain a complete loss with respect to his/her investment. In addition, a purchaser must possess such background and experience in business and financial matters that he/she is capable of evaluating the merits and risks and fully appreciates the speculative nature of this investment or be represented by someone who does. Units will be sold only to an investor who represents in writing that he or she meets one of the following criteria for being an "accredited investor" as defined in Regulation D as promulgated under the Securities Act of 1933 ("Securities Act").

1. Is a natural person whose:
   (i) net worth, along with the net worth of his/her spouse, exceeds $1,000,000;[†††††] (excluding the value of the principal residence); or (ii) individual annual income exceeds $200,000, or with his/her spouse has a joint income in excess of $300,000, for each of the past two years and who expects to have income in excess of such levels for the current year.

[†††††] For purposes of calculating "net worth, excluded are ":

(i) the investor's primary residence as an asset;

(ii) any indebtedness that is secured by the investors primary residence, up to the estimated fair market value of the primary residence at the time of the purchase of Units, as a liability (Note that special rules apply if the primary residence of the investor has been refinanced within the last 60 days); and

(iii) any indebtedness that is secured by the investor's primary residence in excess of the estimated fair market value of the primary residence at the time of the purchase of Units must be included as a liability.

2. Is a corporation, partnership, tax-exempt entity (as described in Section 501(c)(3) of the Internal Revenue Code of 1986, as amended) or business trust with assets greater than $5,000,000 that was not formed for the purpose of making this investment.

3. Is a trust with assets greater than $5,000,000 that was not formed for the purpose of investing in the Corporation and that is being directed by a sophisticated person.

4. Is an employee benefit plan under ERISA that meets one of the following criteria: (i) the plan fiduciary makes the investment decision and is either a bank, savings and loan, or registered investment adviser; (ii) the plan has total assets in excess of $5,000,000; or (iii) the plan is self-directed, the investment decisions are made only by, and the investment is only for the benefit of, accredited investors.

5. Is an entity all of the owners of which are accredited under any of the above-listed categories.

SUMMARY OF THE OFFERING

THIS SUMMARY IS INTENDED FOR REFERENCE ONLY AND IS NOT INTENDED TO BE COMPLETE. THIS MEMORANDUM DESCRIBES IN DETAIL NUMEROUS ASPECTS OF THE TRANSACTION THAT ARE MATERIAL TO INVESTORS, INCLUDING THOSE SUMMARIZED BELOW, AND THIS MEMORANDUM AND THE ACCOMPANYING EXHIBITS SHOULD BE REVIEWED IN THEIR ENTIRETY BY PROSPECTIVE INVESTORS.

Partnership Purpose:	The Partnership is being formed for the purpose of acquiring the ABC Building ("Property"). The Partnership expects to close the purchase of the Property on approximately [DATE]. See "Description of Proposed Activities" herein and the Business Plan attached as Exhibit "E" to this Memorandum.
The Property:	The ABC Building was constructed in 2005 on approximately [xyz] acres, is an apartment community located at 1234 Main Street in [CITY], [STATE]. It is a [xyz]-unit, multifamily community, having approximately [xyz] rentable square feet in XY two-story wings. The Property offers xyz floor plans consisting of [descriptions]. The units range in size from XYZ square feet to ZYX square feet with an average unit size of over XYZ square feet. The Property is located just off Highway 1, and is situated on XYZ acres. The current occupancy of the Property is 95%. See "Description of the Property" below.
Purchase of the Property:	The purchase price of the Property, not including renovations, will be $15,000,000. Closing costs and renovation costs are anticipated to be $1,000,000, which includes renovation costs of $500,000. It is anticipated that the closing of the purchase of the Property will be approximately [DATE].
Equity Raising:	The Partnership is offering ("Offering") a total of QQ limited partnership interests ("Units") to investors at a price of $100,000 per Unit payable upon subscription. Units are being offered solely to accredited investors. No Units will be accepted unless all QQ Units are subscribed and sold. The Partnership will keep all funds received from the sale of Units in a non-interest bearing escrow account established in the Partnership's name ("Special Account") until the Partnership has received paid subscriptions for QQ Units. Upon the sale of QQ Units and the deposit of the proceeds in the Special Account, the Offering will close, the persons subscribing for Units will be admitted as Limited Partners, and the General Partner will transfer the proceeds from the Special Account to the Partnership. The General Partner or its Affiliates may acquire Units to allow the Offering to close.

For a subscription for Units to be deemed received, the investor must deliver to the Partnership a completed and signed Subscription Agreement and a signed Limited Partnership Agreement and the Partnership must have received the purchase price for the Units subscribed.

See "Terms of the Offering" and "Summary of the Limited Partnership Agreement - Interests of Limited Partners" herein.

Financing: The General Partner anticipates obtaining a loan from BBBB in the amount of $7,000,000. The interest rate will be approximately X% with 24 months of interest-only payments. At the expiration of the 24-month period, the loan will be amortized based on a 30-year amortization. The loan will be due after 10 years. See "Description of Proposed Activities - Financing" herein.

General Partner's Ownership: The General Partner is ABC Investments, LLC. The General Partner is owned by ...... See "General Partner" herein.

General Partner's Experience: The General Partner was formed on or about [DATE], and is managed by ......

Net Cash Flow: The Limited Partners will receive all Net Cash Flow until they have received an annual, non-compounded Preferred Return of 7%, commencing from the later of the date the Partnership closes on the purchase of the Property or the date that each Limited Partner contributes capital to the Partnership. Cash flows in excess of the Preferred Return will be distributed 67% to the Limited Partners and 33% to the General Partner. See "Summary of the Limited Partnership Agreement - Net Cash Flow" herein.

Major Capital Event Proceeds: Major Capital Event Proceeds will be distributed 100% to the Limited Partners until they have received all of their accrued but unpaid Preferred Return; next, to the Limited Partners until they have received amount equal to their Capital Contribution; and thereafter 67% to the Limited Partners and 33% to the General Partner. See "Summary of the Limited Partnership Agreement - Major Capital Event Proceeds" herein.

Compensation of General Partner: In addition to General Partner's interest in the Partnership, the General Partner or its Affiliates will receive:

- an Acquisition Fee in the amount of 2% of the purchase price of the Property when the purchase of the Property is closed;
- a Due Diligence Fee in the amount of $15,000;
- a Refinancing Fee in the amount of 1% of the principal amount of the loan when the Property is refinanced;
- a Disposition Fee in the amount of 1% of the sales price if and when the Property is sold; and
- a Construction Management Fee equal to 5% of the cost of any capital improvements to the Property.

In addition, ABC Realty, LLC, a property management company owned by ABC Investments, LLC, will receive a Property Management Fee in the amount of 5% of gross revenue for the on-going property management of the Property.

See "Compensation of General Partner and Affiliates" herein.

Acquisition and Offering Fees and Expenses:	The Units are being offered on a best efforts basis. The Partnership will reimburse the General Partner for fees and expenses related to acquiring the Property. The Partnership will also pay fees and expenses for forming the Partnership and related to this Offering in the amount of approximately $25,000. See "Terms of the Offering" and "Compensation of General Partner and Affiliates" herein.
Risk Factors:	This Offering involves certain risks. See "Risk Factors" herein.
Competition:	The Property is located in a metropolitan area that includes other apartment complexes. The number of competitive apartment properties in the area of the Property could have a material affect on the Partnership's ability to lease sites at the Property and on the rents charged. Although the Partnership believes this Offering will provide it with adequate capital resources to accomplish the purpose of the Partnership and the General Partner has significant experience, the Partnership will be competing with others who may have greater resources than the Partnership and whose management may have more expertise and greater resources than the General Partner. In addition, other forms of multi-family residential properties and single-family housing may provide housing alternatives to potential residents of the Property.
Conflicts of Interest:	The General Partner will not be required to devote any fixed amount of time to the affairs of the Partnership. The General Partner may, and Affiliates of the General Partner will continue to, engage in business activities; apartment complex investment, ownership, management, and development; and other real estate activities that may involve a conflict of interest with the proposed activities of the Partnership. See "Conflicts of Interest" herein.
Allocation of Income and Losses:	Income will generally be allocated to the Limited Partner and General Partner to the extent of Losses previously allocated to the Limited Partner and General Partner, next to the Limited Partners in the amount of their Preferred Return, and thereafter 67% to the Limited Partners and 33% to the General Partner. Losses will generally be allocated to the Limited Partners and the General Partner to the extent of Income previously allocated to the Limited Partners or General Partner less any distributions associated with such Income, next to the Limited Partners to the extent their Capital Contributions exceed distributions associated with the Capital Contributions, next, to the Limited Partners and General Partner to the extent of the positive balances of their Capital Accounts, and thereafter, to the Limited Partners. See "Summary of the Limited Partnership Agreement - Allocation of Income and Losses" herein.
Termination Date of the Offering:	The Offering will terminate on [DATE] unless extended in the sole discretion of the General Partner with notice to the persons who have tendered subscriptions for Units (the "Termination Date"). If QQ Units are not subscribed to and paid for on or before the Termination Date, all proceeds from the sale of the Units will be returned to subscribers. See "Terms of the Offering" herein.
Glossary of Terms:	For the definitions of certain terms used in this Memorandum, see "Glossary of Terms" herein.

Description of Proposed Activities

General

The Partnership is being formed to acquire an apartment complex known as The ABC Building located at 1234 Main Street, [CITY], [STATE].

Description of the Property

The ABC Building was constructed in 2005 on approximately [xyz] acres, is an apartment community. It is a [xyz]-unit, multifamily community, having approximately [xyz] rentable square feet in XY two-story wings.

The Property offers xyz floor plans consisting of [descriptions]. The units range in size from XYZ square feet to ZYX square feet with an average unit size of over XYZ square feet. The Property is located just off Highway 1, and is situated on XYZ acres. The current occupancy of the Property is 95%. For additional detail regarding the Property and its features and amenities, see the Business Plan attached as Exhibit "E" to this Memorandum.

Location

The Property is situated within one mile of Highway 1 and approximately two miles east of Eden. These transportation corridors provide access to nearby employers, health care, and retail centers connecting residents to virtually all points in the [CITY] metropolitan area. Additionally, the LMNO International Airport (LMN0 is less than 10 miles south of the Property.

The Best Medical Center, which includes the Even Better Hospital, is located less than five miles east of the Property. Several shopping options are located within a short distance of the Property, including a major regional mall, power centers with big box retail, pharmacies and a brand new grocery option. A short drive north on Highway 99 is the Gross Mall, a 1.5 million square foot enclosed mall, anchored by blah, blah, blah.

[CITY] Area Market

The Property is located in the [CITY], [STATE] metropolitan area. Apartment complexes similar to the Property and located within a one mile radius and built between 2002-2012 average 95.1% occupancy, an average effective rent of $982.96, and an average unit size of 1,500 square feet.

Purchase of the Property

The purchase price of the Property, not including renovations, will be $15,000,000. Closing costs and renovation costs are anticipated to be $1,000,000, which includes renovation costs of $500,000. The General Partner anticipates borrowing a total of $7,000,000. It is anticipated that the closing date for the purchase of the Property will be approximately [DATE].

Occupancy and Rents

The Property currently averages 95% occupancy versus 95.1% occupancy for the immediate submarket. The Property is in line with competition. Monthly market rents at the Property are currently $1.00 per square foot. See the Business Plan attached as Exhibit "E" of this Memorandum.

Financing

The General Partner anticipates obtaining a loan from BBBB in the amount of $7,000,000. The interest rate will be approximately X% with 24 months of interest-only payments. At the expiration of the 24-month period, the loan will be amortized based on a 30-year amortization. The loan will be due after 10 years.

Partnership Goals

The Partnership's primary goal is to provide each investor with sustainable long- term distributions of Net Cash Flow while protecting the investor's principal and to make distributions of Major Capital Event Proceeds upon the sale or refinance of the Property. Due to the overall macro-economic environment in Houston, the Partnership believes it will be able to increase rents as a result of the healthy employment growth and the lack of new apartment supply over the past two years. See the Business Plan attached as Exhibit "E" of this Memorandum.

Competition

The Property is located in a metropolitan area that includes other apartment properties. The number of competitive apartment properties in the area could have a material effect on the Partnership's ability to lease units at the Property and on the rents charged. Although the Partnership believes this Offering will provide it with adequate capital resources to accomplish the purpose of the Offering and the General Partner has significant experience, the Partnership will be competing with others who may have greater resources than the Partnership and whose management may have more expertise and greater resources than the General Partner. In addition, other forms of multi-family residential properties and single-family housing provide housing alternatives to potential residents of the Property.

RISK FACTORS

The purchase of Units involves a high degree of risk. Adverse economic conditions and other factors could negatively affect the economic performance and value of the Partnership and the Property and amounts available for distribution to Limited Partners. In addition to the factors set forth elsewhere in this Memorandum, prospective purchasers should carefully consider the following:

Investment and Strategy Risk Considerations

Investments in Real Estate

Investments in real estate, including indirect investment in the Property through the purchase of Units, are subject to various risks, including:

- adverse changes in national or international economic conditions;
- changes in fiscal policies and tax laws (including rent controls and local property taxes);
- adverse local market conditions, population trends, and community conditions;
- tendency of real estate values to undergo cyclical change;
- uncertainty of cash flow to meet fixed and other obligations;
- changes in operating expenses;
- the financial condition of tenants, buyers, and sellers of properties;

- adverse use of adjacent or neighboring real estate (including overbuilding that causes an excess supply of similar available space for lease);
- inability to obtain adequate insurance;
- decrease in local employment;
- changes in the demand for or supply of competing properties;
- change in environmental laws and regulations;
- zoning laws and other governmental rules;
- environmental claims arising in respect of real estate acquired with undisclosed or unknown environmental problems or as to which inadequate reserves had been established; and
- uninsurable losses, acts of God, and other factors beyond the control of the General Partner or the Partnership.

There can be no assurance of profitable operations because the cost of owning the Property may exceed the income produced, particularly since certain expenses related to real estate and its owner-ship, such as property taxes, utility costs, maintenance costs, and insurance, tend to increase over time and are largely beyond the control of the owner. Although casualty and general liability insurance will be obtained for the Property, there is no assurance that such coverage will cover all losses that may be incurred. No insurance will be available to cover cash deficits from ongoing operations.

Investments in Multifamily Real Estate Properties

The Partnership intends to invest in the Property, which is a multifamily apartment complex. Invest-ments in apartments involve certain special risks. Apartments are particularly vulnerable to the risks that the population levels, economic conditions, or employment conditions may decline in the sur-rounding geographic area. Any of these developments likely would have an adverse impact on the size or affluence of the tenant population in the area and a negative impact on the occupancy rates, rent levels, and property values of apartment complexes in the area. Unlike many other types of real estate investments, apartment complexes do not have tenants occupying large portions of the property whose lease payments provide reliable sources of income for extended lease terms. Instead, multifam-ily properties typically have individual residential tenants with very limited net worth and with lease terms that are typically one year or less. Apartments generally experience frequent tenant turnover due to factors such as transient populations, new competition in the area, and changes in the tenants' economic status. In addition to continuously needing to replace vacating tenants, tenant turnover at apartment complexes causes the property owner to incur significant rehabilitation and maintenance costs in order to prepare units for new tenants.

Additional factors that may adversely affect the operation of the Property include, but are not limited to:

- inability to increase rents as expenses increase;
- unanticipated expenses or expense increases;
- necessity to make more or more costly capital improvements than projected;
- inability to obtain and maintain projected occupancy levels; and
- inability to sell the Property for the projected sales price.

No assurances can be given that any anticipated results will occur.

Financing; Balloon Payment

The financing on the Property provides for interest-only payments during the first two years of the term of the loan and payments based on a 30-year amortization thereafter, with the payment of the entire principal balance due 10 years from the date of the acquisition of the Property. The General Partner will attempt to arrange the refinancing of the Property during this period, however, the availability of financing and lending standards have tightened considerably in the past few years. There can be no assurance that the Partnership will able to refinance the Property. If, for any reason, the Partnership is unable to refinance or sell the Property during the 10-year loan term period, the Partnership could lose the Property through foreclosure.

Lack of Liquidity

Liquidity refers to the ability of an asset to readily be converted into cash. The Partnership's sole asset will consist of the Property, which is considered an asset that is illiquid or for which a secondary market is not readily available. Unlike publicly traded stocks and other liquid investments, it takes considerable time and effort to market and sell multifamily properties. This illiquidity increases the Partnership's risk that an investment in the Property will not be converted into cash within an acceptable period of time.

Occupancy

The occupancy of the Property may fluctuate. The Property is currently approximately 95% occupied. Most of the leases are on a 6-month or one-year basis. While the General Partner will seek to renew the leases with the tenants and/or to lease the Property to others, there can be no assurance that the General Partner will be successful. Moreover, dependent on local market factors, leasing of apartments may only be achievable at unfavorable rental rates.

Management of the Partnership

The responsibility for the management and business affairs of the Partnership is vested solely in the General Partner. No Limited Partner in his/her capacity as such will have the right to participate in the management of the Partnership. Under the Partnership's Limited Partnership Agreement, the General Partner shall have authority to manage the Partnership. See "Summary of the Limited Partnership Agreement" below.

Economic Conditions

The Partnership's ability to achieve its goals is dependent upon economic conditions in the United States generally and, more specifically, in the geographic area in which the Property is located. Further adverse changes in national economic conditions and in the economic conditions in [CITY] may have an adverse effect on the ability of the Property to generate revenue, the Property's value and the Partnership's short- and long- term financial performance and value. Changes in local economic conditions, zoning laws, transportation patterns, environmental laws, interest rates, and other business conditions will also affect the ultimate success and profitability of the Partnership.

Downturn in Market

The real estate market is subject to great cyclical changes. Numerous events could occur that may have a negative effect on the market and that are beyond the control of the General Partner. Such conditions include the continuing slowdown in general or local economic growth and a longer than normal recovery period from the current economic downturn, a decline in population growth in [STATE], and a decline in the popularity of apartments. For the past several years, there has been a serious economic downturn in the United States that has severely affected real estate. The widespread availability of foreclosed and otherwise distressed single-family and multi-family housing and decreased interest rates have also contributed to the increase in vacancies by making site- built housing more attractive and affordable.

Increased Interest Rates

Many commercial loans in the present market require variable as opposed to fixed interest rates. In a variable rate loan the debt service can increase substantially if interest rates rise. The General Partner has no control over interest rates and there can be no assurance that a substantial rise in interest rates will not occur. A rise in interest rates may adversely affect the market value of the Property and the ability of prospective purchasers to finance any acquisition of the Property from the Partnership.

Additionally, in a rising interest rate environment, investors typically require higher yields from investment vehicles like the Partnership, which may result in downward pressure on the value of Limited Partners' Units, reflecting the higher yields available on alternatives, such as bonds. Higher interest rates on mortgages would increase refinancing costs or the costs of purchase financing for new buyers of the Property. Higher mortgage interest rates would decrease the cash flow of the Property, which in turn would decrease the amount of money available through a refinancing, and, in the case of a sale of the Property, put downward pressure on the percentage return on investment each year and the ultimate sales price (value) of the Property.

Leverage

The Property will be highly leveraged and this degree of leverage could increase the risk of foreclosure. As a result, a decrease in rental revenues of the Property may materially and adversely affect the Property's cash flow and, in turn, the Partnership's ability to make distributions. No assurance can be given that future cash flow will be sufficient to make the debt service payments on any borrowed funds and also cover operating expenses. If the revenue from the Property is insufficient to pay debt service and operating expenses, the Partnership would be required to use working capital or seek additional funds. There can be no assurance that additional funds would be available, if needed, or, if such funds were available, that they would be available on terms acceptable to the General Partner. If the Partnership is unable to pay debt service, the lender could foreclose on the Property and the Limited Partners would be likely to lose their entire investment in the Property.

Property Tax Increase

[STATE] property taxes are based upon each property's assessed value and can increase or decrease annually depending upon the value established by the local county assessor and the applicable tax rate (which is subject to change).

Rent Control

The [STATE] and the [CITY] do not presently impose rent control. The General Partner does not anticipate that rent control will be imposed in the future, however, there can be no assurance that the political jurisdictions that govern the Property will not impose rent control.

No Guarantee of Return

The Partnership and the Property could fail to perform as expected. The Units offered hereby should be considered as speculative investment for which there is no guarantee of income or return of all or any of the amounts invested.

Fees to General Partner and Affiliates

The General Partner and certain Affiliates will receive certain fees and payments from the Partnership. The General Partner and its Affiliates will profit from such fees and payments regardless of the profitability of the Partnership or the return, if any, to the Limited Partners holding Units. See "Compensation of General Partner and Affiliates" below.

Return of Distributions

In the Colorado Limited Partnership Act, it is provided that, even though a Limited Partner has rightfully received a return of his/her Capital Contribution, he/she is nevertheless liable to the Partnership or to creditors thereof, up to the amount of the capital returned together with interest, for any liability or claim arising before the return of such capital.

Priority of Creditors

In the event of a dissolution or termination of the Partnership, the proceeds realized from the liquidation of assets, if any, will be distributed to the holders of Units but only after the satisfaction of claims of creditors. Accordingly, the ability of the Limited Partners to recover all or any portion of their investment under such circumstances will depend on the amount of funds so realized and claims to be satisfied therefrom.

Property Purchased "As Is"

The physical condition of the Property will not be guaranteed by the seller to the Partnership. The Property will be acquired by the Partnership from the seller on an "as is" basis, with only limited representations and warranties.

Property Condition

Although the Partnership has reviewed inspections of the condition of the Property, certain conditions, including subsurface conditions, cannot be easily evaluated. There can be no assurance that there will not be some undetected physical condition of the Property, particularly in connection with underground utilities, which exists and could require very expensive repairs or replacements, and significantly decrease the Property's value and Partnership's cash flow after purchase of the Property.

Environmental Regulation of Real Property

Under various federal, state, and local environmental laws and regulations, a current or previous owner or operator of real estate may be required to investigate and clean up hazardous or toxic substances or wastes, or petroleum products or other pollutants or regulated materials, or threatened releases of such materials, at such property (collectively, "Contamination") and may be held liable to a government entity or to third parties for property damage and for investigation, clean up, and monitoring (collectively "Response") costs incurred by such parties in connection with the Contamination. Such laws may impose clean up responsibility and liability without regard to fault, or whether or not the owner knew of or caused the presence of the Contamination. The liability under such laws may be joint and several for the full amount of the Response costs incurred or to be incurred or Response actions to be undertaken, although a party held jointly and severally liable may be able to obtain contributions from other identified, solvent, responsible parties for their fair share toward these costs. The Response costs may be substantial and can exceed the value of the Property. In connection with its ownership and operation of the Property, the Partnership may be liable for such costs. The presence of Contamination, or the failure to properly remediate Contamination, on the Property may adversely affect the Partnership's ability to sell or rent the Property or to borrow using the Property as collateral.

Federal regulations require building owners and those exercising control over a building's management to identify and warn, via signs and labels, of potential hazards posed by workplace exposure to installed asbestos-containing materials ("ACM") and potentially asbestos-containing materials ("PACM") in their buildings. The regulations also set forth employee training, record keeping, and due diligence requirements pertaining to ACM and PACM. Significant fines can be assessed for violation of these regulations. Building owners and those exercising control over a building's management may be subject to an increased risk of personal injury lawsuits by workers and others exposed to ACM as a result of the regulations. Certain federal, state, and local laws and regulations also govern the removal, encapsulation, disturbance, handling, and disposal of ACM when such materials are in poor condition or in the event of remodeling, renovation, construction, or demolition of a building containing these materials. Such laws provide for liability for improper handling or a release to the environment of ACM and for fines to, and for third parties to seek recovery from, owners or operators of real properties for personal injury or improper exposure or notices associated with ACM.

In addition, recent studies have linked radon, a naturally occurring substance, to an increased risk of lung cancer. While there are currently no state or federal requirements regarding the monitoring for, presence of, or exposure to, radon in indoor air, the United States Environmental Protection Agency ("EPA") and the Surgeon General recommend testing residential and other buildings for the presence of radon in indoor air, and the EPA further recommends that concentrations of radon in indoor air be limited to less than four picocuries per liter of air (the "Recommended Action Level"). The presence of radon in concentrations equal to or greater than the Recommended Action Level in the Property may adversely affect the owner's ability to lease the Property and the market value of the Property. The EPA as well as state and local environmental agencies are increasingly concerned about indoor air quality and if certain conditions are met may require an owner or property manager to conduct indoor air quality testing. Based on the results of that testing, remedial measures to improve indoor air quality may be required.

Federal legislation requires owners and landlords of residential housing constructed prior to 1978 to disclose to potential tenants or purchasers, and to real estate brokers, any known presence of lead paint and lead paint hazards and allows for treble damages, fines, and attorneys' fees for failure to so notify. In addition, ABC could be held liable under state laws for any injuries caused by ingestion of lead-based paint by tenants, or of dust or particles from lead-based paint, by children or others living at or using the properties. Under some state laws, the liability is without regard to fault, and may also require ABC to remediate soil and groundwater contaminated with lead in and around the subject multifamily housing.

Mold is a fungus that may grow within buildings if sufficient moisture is present, for instance as a result of leaking roofs or pipes, flooding, or poor insulation in bathrooms. Certain molds are allergenic to certain tenants and capable of producing toxins that can be harmful. Mold can injure other living things and damage property. It is customary practice to promptly remediate water damage, which can result in mold, and any damage from mold growth, to prevent personal injury and property damage, and unsafe living conditions. If mold grows in the Property, the Partnership may be liable for any personal injury and property damage that results. Under state or local laws pertaining to health, housing, building standards, and consumer protection, the Partnership may be required to remediate mold and may be fined due to the presence of mold in a building, its tenants may be evicted, it may be liable for rent during the period when mold was present in the building, and the building may be condemned and razed. Mold remediation may be difficult and expensive. It is difficult and expensive to obtain insurance to protect against liability, remediation costs, or other damages pertaining to mold, and there may be no insurance coverage under policies obtained by the Partnership on the Property. State and federal legislation pertaining to mold, including its remediation and disclosure, may be enacted in the next few years, and it is unknown what economic impact such legislation could have on building owners and operators.

The General Partner will obtain, or cause to be obtained, and review a Phase I environmental report for the Property. If any hazardous materials are found within the Property in violation of law at any time, the Partnership may be jointly and severally liable for all cleanup costs, fines, penalties and other costs. This potential liability will continue after the Partnership sells the Property and may apply to hazardous materials present within the Property before the Partnership acquired the Property. If losses arise from hazardous substance contamination that cannot be recovered from a responsible party, the financial viability of the Property may be substantially affected. In addition, hazardous substance contamination on the Property could adversely affect the cash flow from the Property. In extreme cases, the Property may be rendered worthless, or worse, where the Partnership is obligated to pay cleanup costs, in excess of the value of the Property. The Partnership could lose its entire investment in the Property.

Americans with Disabilities Act

The Property may not comply with the Americans with Disabilities Act. Under the Americans with Disabilities Act of 1990, public accommodations must meet certain federal requirements related to access and use by disabled persons. If the Property were not in compliance, the Partnership may be required to pay for improvements to effect compliance with the ADA. To comply with the ADA requirements, the Partnership could be required to remove access barriers at significant cost and non-compliance could result in the imposition of fines by the federal government or an award of damages to private litigants. State and federal laws in this area are constantly evolving, and could place a greater cost or burden in the future on the Partnership as the owners of the Property. While the Partnership believes the Property currently complies in all material respects with the ADA, there can be no assurance that ADA violations do not or will not exist at the Property.

Fair Housing Compliance

The Fair Housing Amendments Act of 1988 ("FHAA") requires apartment communities first occupied after March 13, 1990, to be accessible to the handicapped. Noncompliance with the FHAA could result in the imposition of fines or an award of damages to private litigants.

Effect of Market Conditions on Holding Periods

The determination of when the Property should be sold will be made by the General Partner in its sole discretion and consideration of relevant factors, including existing economic conditions and real estate and capital market conditions. While the General Partner expects that the Partnership will sell its properties for cash, market conditions may require the Partnership to accept a promissory note or other evidence or indebtedness in lieu of immediate total cash payment on the sale price of the Property. Depending on market conditions at the time when the Property is liquidated, the terms of repayment of any such debt could be disadvantageous to the Partnership.

Delays

Any delays encountered by the Partnership in the acquisition, renovation, enhancement, and disposition of the Property could adversely affect investor returns. The Partnership may not be able to obtain permits, complete the work, or obtain third party or governmental approvals necessary to realize desired returns on the Property.

Terrorism

The impact on economic conditions of terrorist attacks or the outbreak or escalation of armed conflict involving the United States may reduce the value of multifamily housing and land, and have an adverse impact on interest rates, the availability of financing, raw materials, oil, gas, electricity, water, energy, or other factors. These events could reduce the value of the Property.

Lack of Insurance

The Partnership may not be able to obtain adequate insurance with respect to the Property, or may not be able to obtain insurance on reasonable terms. Failure to obtain insurance or the excessive costs of insurance may expose the Partnership to additional risk of loss or additional expenses to which it would not otherwise be subject.

Unit Ownership Risk Considerations

Lack of Diversification

The Partnership expects that the Property will be the only significant asset of the Partnership. This lack of diversity in the type or number of properties and investments held by the Partnership may increase the risk of loss to the Partnership. For example, if the market in which the Property is located experiences an economic downturn or suffers from a catastrophic natural disaster, such as a hurricane, tornado, earthquake, flood, mudslide, or severe erosion or accretion, the value of the Property may decrease rapidly.

No Operating History

The Partnership and the General Partner are recently formed and have no operating history. Accordingly, an investor cannot make any evaluation of the merits of this investment based on past performance of these entities. While principals of the General Partner have prior experience in acquiring, operating, and selling multifamily projects, there is no assurance that such experience will benefit the Company in meeting its investment objectives.

Investors must rely upon the judgment of the General Partner with respect to the acquisition, refurbishing, operation, and refinancing of the Property, and must rely on the judgment of the General Partner in the disposition of all or any portion of the Property.

Lack of Experience or Knowledge with the Target Market

The Partnership and the General Partner may face risks associated with a lack of market knowledge or understanding of the local economy, forging new business relationships, and unfamiliarity with local government and permitting procedures in the [CITY], [STATE] regional market. The Partnership and the General Partner will work to mitigate such risks through diligence, research, and associations with experienced partners, there can be no guarantee that all or any of such risks will be eliminated.

Lack of Control Over the Partnership

A Limited Partner has no right to manage the business and affairs of the Partnership, including without limitation, to make any decision regarding any sale, exchange, or refinancing of the Property. The management, investment, financing, leasing, and divestiture policies of the Partnership and its policies with respect to certain other activities, including its distributions and operating policies, will be determined by the General Partner in its sole discretion. No assurance can be given that the General

Partner will be successful in implementing such policies or that the Partnership will achieve projected returns.

Furthermore, the Limited Partnership Agreement may be amended by the affirmative vote of the General Partner and the Limited Partners holding 67% of the Units. Accordingly, your rights as a Limited Partner may be subject to change.

Securities and Other Regulatory Matters

The Partnership will be subject to regulation, including regulation of the Offering under applicable securities laws. The Offering will not be registered under the Securities Act or any state securities laws in reliance upon an exemption from such registration. Any claim of non-compliance with applicable laws or regulations would cause the Partnership to incur costs to defend such claims and to incur fines or penalties in the event of actual non-compliance. The Partnership may be required to offer rescission rights to persons subscribing for Units in the event it was determined that the Offering violated applicable securities laws.

Best Efforts Offering

The Units are being offered on a "best effort" basis. The General Partner has discretion to accept subscriptions for Units in any amount it determines and intends to accept subscriptions as soon as possible to fund the acquisition of the Property. There can be no assurance that the Partnership will raise the full amount of the Offering.

Purchases of Units by Affiliates

Units purchased by the General Partner or its Affiliates will be counted in determining if the Offering amount is met. Investors should not expect that the sale of all Units offered indicates that such sales have been made to investors who have no financial or other interest in the Offering, or who are otherwise exercising independent investment discretion. The requirement for the sale of QQ Units to close the Offering is not designed as a protection to investors or to indicate that their investment decision is shared by other unaffiliated investors. Because purchases of Units by the General Partner or its Affiliates may be substantial, no individual investor should place reliance on the sale of the required amount of Units to close the Offering as an indication of the merits of this Offering.

Timing of Distributions

The General Partner will have considerable discretion in determining the amount and timing of distributions to be made by the Partnership to its Limited Partners. There is no assurance that the Partnership will generate cash flow sufficient to make distributions to Limited Partners at any particular time or in any particular amount.

No Market for Units

No market for the Units exists, and it is not anticipated that one will develop. The Units are not redeemable. Purchasers of the Units will be required to bear the economic risk of their investment for an indefinite period of time. The Units are not registered under the Securities Act or applicable state securities laws and may not be resold unless they are subsequently registered or an exemption from registration is available. Investors have no right to require, and the Partnership has no intention of effecting, such registration. Consequently, an investor may not be able to liquidate an investment in the Units, and a bank may be unwilling to accept the Units as collateral for a loan. The Units will not be readily marketable, and purchasers thereof may not be able to liquidate their investments in the event of an emergency.

Conflicts of Interest

Neither the General Partner nor its Affiliates will spend full time or even a major portion of their time in connection with the Partnership's operations. The General Partner may form and operate other entities employing investment strategies identical to the Partnership's strategy. The General Partner may charge certain market rate fees, including property management fees, as set forth in the LPA. As to any services provided by the General Partner or its Affiliates to the Partnership or the Property, neither the General Partner nor the Partnership can guarantee that these services will be performed in a manner that provides the Partnership with maximum benefits.

Limitations on Transfer, Pledge, Mortgage, or Encumbrance

No Limited Partner will be permitted to transfer, pledge, mortgage, or encumber any Units without first (i) obtaining the prior written consent of the General Partner; and (ii) executing all required documentation to make the transferee a substitute Limited Partner and preserve the status of the Partnership as a limited partnership. The General Partner will not consent to a transfer of any Units that would cause the Partnership to terminate for federal income tax purposes and unless the transfer is in compliance with applicable federal and state securities laws.

Reliance on the General Partner

The General Partner will exercise full control over all activities of the Partnership. The General Partner is a newly formed entity with limited experience and financial resources. The Limited Partners must rely solely on the General Partner's ability to manage the operations of the Partnership. Failure of the General Partner to fulfill its obligations to manage the Partnership could materially adversely affect the Partnership's operations and may cause the Partnership to be unable to successfully execute its investment strategy.

Furthermore, under the Limited Partnership Agreement, the General Partner may resign at any time upon thirty 30-day notice to the Limited Partners, and upon such resignation, a replacement General Partner will be appointed by a majority vote of the Limited Partners in accordance with the LPA. The Partnership cannot guarantee that the General Partner or its principals or Affiliates will continue to be involved in the management of the Partnership in perpetuity. A replacement General Partner may have less experience operating and managing multifamily residential real estate than the current General Partner.

Limited Financial Resources

The General Partner has limited financial resources, and its business is subject to significant risks and competition. The Partnership's profitability may be diminished if the General Partner incurs significant operating losses or becomes subject to significant liabilities that impede its operational efficiency.

Valuations and Appraisals

There is no requirement in the Limited Partnership Agreement for the General Partner to have a third party value or appraise any of the Partnership assets. Accordingly, the General Partner's determination of the value of the Partnership's assets may be a subjective analysis that provides no more than the General Partner's estimate of value. Valuations and appraisals may result in adjustments of the Partnership's gross and net asset values. Accordingly, there can be no assurance that the Partnership's gross or net asset values, as calculated based upon such valuations and appraisals, will be accurate on any given date, nor can there be any assurance that the sale of the Property would be at a price equivalent to the last estimated or appraised value of the Property.

Possible Loss of Limited Liability

Limited partners of limited partnerships, such as the Partnership, are generally not liable for debts of the company, except to the extent of personal guarantees of such debt. However, the law relating to limited partnerships is developing and there can be no assurance that the limited liability of limited partners of the Partnership will be respected under all circumstances.

Exoneration and Indemnification

In the LPA are set forth the circumstances under which the General Partner and its Affiliates, including their members, officers, directors, shareholders, and affiliates, are to be excused from liability to the Partnership and its investors for damages or losses that the Partnership or such investors may incur by virtue of any such person's performance of services for the Partnership. Neither the General Partner, its Affiliates, nor their members, officers, directors, shareholders, or affiliates, will generally be liable to the Partnership or the Unit holders for errors in judgment or other acts or omissions in connection with the business of the Partnership, provided such acts or omissions do not constitute fraud, a criminal act of moral turpitude, intentional misapplication of funds, deceit, or willful misconduct ("Wrongful Act"). As a result, the Partnership and its investors may have limited rights against these persons.

In the LPA, the General Partner and its Affiliates, including their members, officers, directors, shareholders and affiliates, are indemnified. The Partnership will indemnify the General Partner and its Affiliates for any claims made by a Limited Partner or third person related to the operations of the Partnership provided that the General Partner, its principals, or Affiliate actions or inactions do not constitute a Wrongful Act. To the extent that the indemnification provisions of the Limited Partnership Agreement are invoked, the assets of the Partnership would be reduced. See "Summary of the Limited Partnership Agreement - Indemnification and Exoneration" below.

Removal of General Partner

Investors will have the ability to remove the General Partner from such role only in the event the General Partner has committed a Wrongful Act. As a result, investors will have less control over the General Partner's investment strategies than they may have with other investments.

Lack of Separate Counsel

The Partnership has not been independently represented in connection with its organization or this Offering. The General Partner and the Partnership are represented by the same law firm with respect to this Offering. The General Partner and its Affiliates anticipate each will be represented by this law firm with respect to other offerings and other matters. No independent legal due diligence has been conducted by the Partnership on behalf of any investors with respect to this Offering. Investors are encouraged to engage independent legal counsel at their expense to advise them with respect to this Offering.

Arbitrary Unit Price

The offering price of the Units has been arbitrarily determined by the General Partner based primarily upon the expenses to be paid as a result of this Offering, the cost of organizing the Partnership, the amount of funds required to acquire the Property, and other financial needs. The offering price of the Units is not necessarily indicative of the value of the Partnership, the Units, or the Property. The Partnership cannot assure that any Unit, if transferable, could be sold for the offering price or for any amount.

Federal Income Tax Risks

General

An investment in the Partnership as a Limited Partner will subject the investor to the risk that the actual tax consequences resulting from such investment will be different from those anticipated by the General Partner. The following discussion points out those tax risks that the General Partner believes are the most significant. No assurance can be given that the risks described below are the only tax risks or that one or more of the risks will not be resolved adversely to the Partnership and the Limited Partners. If a tax risk is resolved unfavorably, an investment in the Partnership either will not be as profitable as anticipated (after considering the contemplated tax effects of such an investment) or could result in economic loss. No ruling or other advance determination will be sought from the Internal Revenue Service ("IRS") regarding the various tax issues described below.

The tax considerations of an investment in the Partnership that the General Partner believes are the most significant are discussed in the "Tax Aspects of the Offering" section below, and those considerations may involve additional tax risks not discussed in this section of the Memorandum. Each investor is urged to review that material and to discuss with his/her own tax counselors the application of the principles discussed in that section to his/her individual situation.

THE DISCUSSION OF CERTAIN TAX CONSEQUENCES IS ONLY FOR INFORMATIONAL PURPOSES AND PROVIDED IN CONNECTION WITH THE OFFERING OF UNITS AND CANNOT BE RELIED UPON TO AVOID PENALTIES THAT MAY BE PROPOSED BY THE IRS. THERE CAN BE NO ASSURANCE THAT THE INTENDED TAX CONSEQUENCES OF AN INVESTMENT IN THE COMPANY WILL BE ACHIEVED. PERSONS HOLDING UNITS SHOULD SEEK INDEPENDENT TAX ADVICE BASED ON THEIR PARTICULAR CIRCUMSTANCES.

IRS Audit

A ruling from the IRS has not been sought with respect to availability of certain tax benefits intended to be realized by Limited Partners and may be challenged upon audit by the IRS. See "Tax Aspects of the Offering" below. Any audit of the Partnership will be defended or settled by the General Partner as the Partnership's Tax Matters Partner ("Tax Matters Partner"). The Partnership will be responsible for costs incurred in such audit or related proceedings. Any adjustment resulting from an audit by the IRS could also result in adjustments to the tax returns of the Limited Partners and in the examination of other items in such return unrelated to the Partnership or an examination of prior years' tax returns. Moreover, Limited Partners could incur substantial legal and accounting costs in connection with any challenge by the IRS of the position taken by the Partnership on its tax returns regardless of the outcome of such a challenge.

Changes in Federal and State Tax Laws and Regulations and in Interpretations Thereof

Prospective investors should not unduly rely on the prospect that tax benefits provided by existing law will continue to be afforded. Prospective investors should be aware that changes in the administrative or judicial interpretation of applicable income tax laws could adversely affect the tax consequences of an investment in the Partnership. The tax benefits of an investment in the Partnership could be lost and/or substantial tax liabilities incurred by reason of changes in the tax law or its interpretation. Any legislative, administrative or judicial changes could be retroactive with respect to transactions entered into prior to the date of passage thereof.

Partnership Tax Status

The Internal Revenue Service has adopted regulations that will treat the Partnership as a partnership. Accordingly, the Partnership will be treated as a partnership for federal income tax purposes and will not be treated as an "association" taxable as a corporation. If the law were to change or if it were determined that the Partnership is taxable as a corporation rather than as a partnership, the changes in the tax consequence to a Limited Partners would be significant and adverse. See "Classification of the Partnership" below.

Allocations of Income and Expenses

Under the LPA, items of income and expense are allocated. The allocations are intended to reflect the economic arrangement of the Limited Partners, and should have the requisite "substantial economic effect" to be recognized by the IRS under current tax law. However, no assurance can be given that the specific allocations will not be challenged by the IRS or held to be invalid by a court. If the special allocations are not respected, the income and expenses of the Partnership allocated to Limited Partners will be determined in accordance with all of the Limited Partners' interests in the Partnership, taking into account all facts and circumstances.

Characterization of Apartment Properties

The General Partner believes that the Property should be characterized as a "trade or business" of the Partnership. However, because of the factual nature of such a determination, including the likelihood that events occurring after the acquisition of the Property by the Partnership will be deemed relevant, the General Partner is not able to determine whether the Property will be characterized as trade or business property, investment property, or property held primarily for sale in the ordinary course of business ("Dealer Property"). If the Property or a portion of the Property, is considered to be Dealer Property, any offering on the sale of the Property or such portion would be ordinary income (as opposed to capital gain) to the Limited Partners. Any sale of the Property made on a deferred-payment basis generally would result in a Limited Partner having to recognize his/her allocable share of the Offering realized upon the sale before the receipt of his/her share of the sale proceeds. Additionally, the costs incurred by the Partnership in carrying any portion of the Property characterized as Dealer Property would be treated as capital expenditures, which generally are not deductible, rather than trade or business expenses, which generally may be deducted. See "Tax Aspects of the Offering - Sale of the Property" herein.

Tax Liabilities in Excess of Cash Distributions

Each Limited Partner must include in his/her gross income the full amount of his/her share of Partnership income, if any, regardless of whether the Partnership has distributed cash to the Limited Partners. No assurance can be given that cash will be available for distribution or will be distributed at any specific time. Accordingly, there is a risk that the Limited Partners will incur tax liabilities resulting from an investment in the Partnership without receiving cash from the Partnership in amounts sufficient to pay for any part of liability. See "Tax Aspects of the Offering Cash Distributions" and "Installment Sales" below.

Factual Determinations by the General Partner

The determination of the correct amount of deductions and their availability and timing to the Partnership will depend on factual determinations that will be made by the General Partner relating to the nature of the fees paid by the Partnership and the nature of the investment in the Property. Although the General Partner will exercise its best judgment when the Partnership's information return is prepared, the IRS may assert that the General Partner's judgment of the facts is not correct, which could result in the disallowance or deferral of deductions in whole or part. Such adjustments could result in the assessment of additional tax liability to the Limited Partners.

ERISA and Tax Exempt Investors

The Employment Retirement Income Security Act of 1974 ("ERISA") subjects certain trustees and certain other parties in interest of ERISA plans to special standards. Tax exempt investors, including individual retirement accounts, are also subject to special rules that may affect their status and exemption from taxation. See "Tax Aspects of the Offering Unrelated Business Taxable Income" and "ERISA Aspects of the Offering" herein.

Unrelated Business Taxable Income

ERISA plans generally are exempt from federal income taxation, except to the extent they have "unrelated business taxable income" during any year. It is possible that the operation of the Property could generate unrelated business taxable income. Therefore, ERISA plans investing in Units could be subject to taxation on the income, if any, generated by the Partnership. See "Tax Aspects of the Offering Unrelated Business Taxable Income."

Potential Penalties

Under the Internal Revenue Code ("Code"), the IRS may impose a penalty on a taxpayer if he/she understates his/her income tax liability for any taxable year and the amount of the understatement exceeds the greater of 10% of the tax required to be shown on the return for that year or $5,000 (a "substantial understatement"). Different standards for imposition of the penalty are provided in the Code, depending on whether or not the substantial understatement of tax liability is attributable to a "tax shelter." Federal income tax deficiencies of a Limited Partner resulting from the reporting positions of the Partnership on its federal income tax information return may cause a Limited Partner to be liable for the penalty on "substantial understatement."

Additional Tax Issues Affecting the Company

The income tax effects of an investment in the Partnership on particular investors are unique. The Partnership will not undertake to advise the individual investor of all possible income tax consequences associated with an investment in the Partnership. However, the unique situation of a potential investor may require the investor to seek independent advice on the tax consequences of an investment in the Partnership.

EACH INVESTOR SHOULD CONSULT HIS OWN PERSONAL TAX ADVISOR REGARDING THE POTENTIAL INCOME TAX CONSEQUENCES OF AN INVESTMENT IN THE PARTNERSHIP.

Source and Application of Funds

Upon sale of all Units offered, the Partnership will have gross proceeds of $X. The funds received are expected to be used approximately as set forth below:

ESTIMATED USE OF PROCEEDS

SOURCE OF FUNDS :

    New Mortgage Loan   0

    Equity Offering (X Units)

      Total:

USES OF FUNDS:

    Purchase Price of Property

      Total:

CLOSING COSTS AND FEES:

    Appraisals, etc.

    Environmental

    Engineering

    Survey

    Title and Recording Fees

    Escrow Deposit and Real Estate Taxes

    Real Estate T ax Escrow

    Acquisition Fee to

    Due Diligence Fee

    Insurance

    Legal Fees

    Miscellaneous Closing Costs

    Repair Reserve Escrow

    Loan Fees

      Total:

RESERVES:

    Contingency Reserves

    Total:

TOTAL USES:

The amounts set forth above are only estimates of how the proceeds from the sale of Units will be used. The actual costs incurred for the items listed above may differ from these estimates. The General Partner reserves the right to use the proceeds as the General Partner deems necessary or advisable in connection with the purchase of the Property and the management and operation of the Partnership.

The Partnership will pay legal, accounting, and other expenses related to formation and offering and syndication expenses, which are estimated to be $25,000.

GENERAL PARTNER

GENERAL

The General Partner of the Partnership is ABC Investments, LLC. The General Partner was formed on [DATE].

The General Partner is managed and owned by …..

In 2000, Joe and Tom founded ABC Companies, which has developed or acquired approximately $500,000,000 in multi-family properties and manages over 10,000 units in the Western U.S. ABC Companies owns 10 businesses that provide services for multi-family properties and real estate investment.

BIOGRAPHICAL SUMMARIES

Joe

Tom

GENERAL PARTNER'S FINANCIAL INFORMATION

The General Partner was formed on or about [DATE]. The General Partner has represented that, after reimbursement of Partnership formation and offering expenses, it will have a minimal net worth, plus the value, if any, of its interest in the Partnership.

During the three years following this Offering, the General Partner anticipates no sources of revenue except: (i) the reimbursement of operating expenses for the Partnership; (ii) the General Partner's participation in the profits of the Partnership, which may not be forthcoming until future years; (iii) the reimbursement from the Partnership of some operating expenses; and (iv) fees payable by the Partnership.

COMPENSATION OF GENERAL PARTNER AND AFFILIATES

The General Partner and its Affiliates will receive compensation and fees as described below:

FEES ON ACQUISITION AND DISPOSITION

The General Partner will receive an Acquisition Fee of 2% of the purchase price of the Property when the purchase closes. Furthermore, the General Partner will receive a Disposition Fee from the Partnership equal to 1% of the sales price for the Property when the Property is sold.

DUE DILIGENCE FEE

The Partnership will pay ABC Management, LLC, an Affiliate of the General Partner, a Due Diligence Fee of $100 per Property unit ($XYZ) when the purchase of the Property closes for its due diligence services in evaluating the Property.

REFINANCING FEE

If the Property is refinanced after acquisition by the Partnership, the Partnership will pay the General Partner a Refinancing Fee equal to 1% of the amount of the loan as compensation for services rendered in refinancing the Property.

PROPERTY MANAGEMENT FEE

The Partnership will pay ABC MMMM, LLC, a Property Management Fee for managing the Property equal to 5% of the monthly gross revenues from the operations of the Property. In addition to the Property Management Fee, the Partnership shall reimburse the Property Manager for travel and related expenses (*e.g.*, air fare, lodging, meals, rental cars, etc.) associated with managing the Property.

OPERATING AND SALES PROCEEDS

As an incentive to increase the income and value of the Property, the General Partner will receive: (i) 33% of the Net Cash Flow after each Limited Partner has received distributions equal to his/her Preferred Return; and (ii) 33% of the Partnership's Major Capital Event Proceeds upon the sale or refinancing of the Property after each Limited Partner has received distributions equal to his/her unpaid Capital Contributions and any accrued but unpaid Preferred Return.

CONSTRUCTION MANAGEMENT FEE

Specialists, Inc., an Affiliate of Companies, will receive a Construction Management Fee equal to 5% of the cost of any capital improvements made to the Property for its services in overseeing and managing any capital improvements.

PRIOR EXPENSES

The Partnership will reimburse the General Partner for all actual out-of-pocket third-party expenses incurred in connection with the acquisition of the Property and formation of the Partnership, the offering of Units and the carrying out of the duties set forth in this Agreement and the management of the Property. The Partnership will pay all expenses of the Partnership, including, without limitation: (i) all costs of borrowed money, taxes, insurance and assessment with respect to the assets and operation of the Partnership; (ii) legal and accounting fees; and (iii) expenses for the acquisition, financing, operation, construction, and disposition of the assets of the Partnership.

DUTIES AND FIDUCIARY RESPONSIBILITIES OF GENERAL PARTNER

The General Partner will be responsible either directly or in a supervisory capacity for all material aspects of the Partnership's business. It will be directly responsible for every facet of the Partnership's business, including the decision to dispose of or encumber all or a portion of the Property. Under the Partnership's LPA, the General Partner is vested with broad powers over the business affairs and assets of the Partnership. Included among these powers is the authority to acquire, encumber, hold, refinance, and dispose of all or any portion of the Property.

Except for rights to approve certain major transactions, all decisions affecting the operation of the Partnership will be made by the General Partner. See "Summary of the Limited Partnership Agreement" below. LIMITED PARTNERS WILL HAVE NO RIGHT OR AUTHORITY TO PARTICIPATE TO ANY DEGREE IN THE MANAGEMENT OF OR TO BIND THE PARTNERSHIP.

The Limited Partnership Agreement and the Subscription Agreement require that any dispute arising out of an investment in the Partnership be submitted to mediation.

CONFLICTS OF INTEREST

The Partnership is subject to various conflicts of interest arising from its relationship with the General Partner. The conflicts include, but are not limited to, the following:

ACQUISITION OF UNITS

The General Partner or its Affiliates may acquire Units. If the General Partner or any Affiliates acquire Units, they will do so on the same terms and conditions as other Limited Partners. Units acquired by the General Partner or its Affiliates will count toward the number of Units required to be sold to close the Offering. See "Risk Factors Purchase of Units by Affiliates" above.

LACK OF SEPARATE REPRESENTATION

The Partnership, its Limited Partners and the General Partner are not represented by separate counsel. The attorneys and accountants who perform services for the Partnership may perform services for affiliates of the General Partner. It is anticipated that such dual representation will continue in the future. In the event that a dispute arises between the Partnership and the General Partner, or should there be a necessity to negotiate or prepare contracts and agreements between the Partnership and the General Partner other than those existing or contemplated on the effective date of this Memorandum, the General Partner may cause the Partnership to retain separate counsel for such matters.

NO LIMIT ON GENERAL PARTNER'S OTHER ACTIVITIES

The General Partner may engage for its own account, or for the account of others, including other limited liability companies, partnerships, or corporations, in other business ventures, including real estate or multi-family investments, and neither the Partnership nor any holder of Units shall be entitled to any interest therein. There may be conflicts of interest on the part of the General Partner between the Partnership and other real estate investments with which the General Partner is affiliated at such time as the Partnership attempts to sell properties as well as in other circumstances. The General Partner or its Affiliates may advise and receive commissions and fees from other persons or entities in connection with the acquisition and ownership of multi-family communities.

COMPETITION FOR MANAGEMENT SERVICES

The Partnership will not have independent management and must rely on the General Partner for the operation of the Partnership's business. The General Partner will devote only so much of its resources to the business of the Partnership as in its judgment is reasonably required. The General Partner anticipates that it will manage additional entities with operations similar to the Partnership's. The General Partner will have conflicts of interest in allocating management time, services, and functions between the Partnership and other present and future entities that it may organize or be affiliated with, as well as other business ventures in which it is or may become involved. The General Partner and its affiliates may engage for their own account, or for the accounts of others, in other business ventures and neither the Partnership nor any Member will be entitled to any interest therein.

COMPENSATION TO GENERAL PARTNER AND AFFILIATES

The compensation payable to the General Partner and its Affiliates described under "Compensation of General Partner and Affiliates" was not determined by arm's length negotiations. Under the Limited Partnership Agreement, the General Partner is permitted to obtain, from one or more of its Affiliates, certain services in connection with the Partnership's operations, and to cause the Partnership to pay for such services. The Limited Partnership Agreement requires that any payment by the Partnership to the General Partner or an Affiliate be consistent with the fair market value of such services.

TERMS OF THE OFFERING

The Partnership is offering QQ Units at a price of $100,000 per Unit. Until all QQ Units have been subscribed and paid for, all funds will be held in the Special Account. Upon subscription to and payment for QQ Units, the General Partner will accept the subscriptions on behalf of the Company, admit the persons purchasing Units as Limited Partners of the Partnership, and transfer proceeds from the Special Account to the Partnership. If QQ Units are not subscribed to and paid for on or before the Termination Date, all proceeds from the sale of the Units will be returned to subscribers. Unless terminated earlier by the Partnership, this Offering will terminate on the Termination Date.

The General Partner or its Affiliates may acquire Units to allow this Offering to close. See "Risk Factors Purchase of Units by Affiliates" above.

The General Partner reserves the right to reject any subscription in whole or in part. Each investor must meet the suitability standards discussed under the "Who Can Invest" section above. The General Partner and its Affiliates will be entitled to receive fees and compensation in connection with the operation of the Partnership. See "Compensation of General Partner and Affiliates" above.

SUBSCRIPTION AND PAYMENT FOR UNITS

A person desiring to subscribe for Units shall execute the Limited Partnership Agreement (Exhibit "B"), the Subscription Agreement (Exhibit "C") and the Purchaser Questionnaire (Exhibit "D"), forward these documents to the General Partner and tender to the General Partner the purchase price for the Units subscribed. A set of subscription documents will be supplied to the investor for signature.

This Offering is being made pursuant to the exemption from the registration requirements of the Securities Act provided by Section 4(a)(2) thereof for transactions by an issuer not involving any public offering and Rule 506(b) of Regulation D as promulgated under the Securities Act. In order to qualify this Offering as a private offering, restrictions must be placed on the type of persons to whom offers and sales may be made. Units will be offered and sold solely to "accredited investors" as defined in Regulation D. See "Who Can Invest" above.

The transferability of Units is severely restricted. They may be acquired for investment purposes only and not with a view toward resale in connection with any public distribution thereof. The Units will not be registered under the Securities Act or under the securities laws of any state and are being offered and sold in reliance upon the exemptions discussed above. The Units may be sold, transferred, assigned, or otherwise disposed of by a Limited Partner only if they are registered under the appropriate federal and state securities laws or, if, in the opinion of counsel, registration is not required under such securities laws. Limited Partners will not have the ability to withdraw their Capital Contributions or to receive the return of all or any portion of their Capital Contributions except upon the sale or refinancing of Partnership assets or the dissolution of the Partnership or as otherwise provided in the Partnership's Limited Partnership Agreement.

TAX ASPECTS OF THE OFFERING

GENERAL

This section describes some of the more important federal income tax consequences of participation in the Partnership. Other than a brief summary of some aspects of state tax law provided under the heading, "State and Local Taxes," no information regarding state and local tax laws is provided. Each prospective Limited Partner should consult his/her own tax adviser concerning his/her situation and the impact that his/her participation in the Partnership may have on his/her federal income tax liability, as well as which state and local income and other tax laws may apply to his/her participation and the impact those laws may have. While the Partnership will furnish the Limited Partners with such information regarding the Partnership as is required for income tax purposes, each Limited Partner will be responsible for preparing and filing his/her own tax returns.

The following summary of tax aspects (except as noted) generally assumes that the investor is an individual and is a citizen or resident of the United States. This summary is based on the Code, on existing Treasury Department regulations ("Regulations") and on administrative rulings and judicial decisions interpreting the Code. Significant uncertainty exists regarding certain tax aspects of limited liability companies investing in real estate. Such uncertainty is due, in part, to continuing changes in federal tax law. Only some of the changes in those acts have been interpreted by the issuance of regulations or by judicial decisions. No assurance can be provided that further legislation will not be enacted. Such legislation could change significantly the tax aspects of the Offering.

The discussion is limited to those areas of federal income tax law that are considered to be most important to investors owning interests in entities taxed as partnerships that invest in real property. Legislative or administrative changes and judicial decisions could modify or change completely statements and opinions expressed below about the federal income tax consequences of an investment in the Partnership. Judicial decisions nearly always accomplish a retroactive change in the law applicable to the issues presented and administrative decisions of the IRS frequently are retroactive in nature.

The interpretation of existing law and regulations described here may be challenged by the IRS during an audit of the Partnership's information return. Such a challenge may be based on judicial or administrative decisions issued after the date of this discussion but having retroactive effect, or on other factors. If successful, such a challenge generally would result in adjustment of a Limited Partner's individual return.

THE DISCUSSION BELOW CAN NOT BE RELIED UPON TO AVOID ANY PENALTIES THAT MAY BE PROPOSED BY THE IRS. THERE IS NO ASSURANCE THAT THE IRS MAY NOT SUCCESSFULLY CHALLENGE THE ANTICIPATED FEDERAL INCOME TAX TREATMENT OF SOME OR ALL ITEMS AS DISCUSSED HEREIN.

PROSPECTIVE LIMITED PARTNERS ARE URGED TO CONSULT THEIR OWN TAX ADVISER ABOUT THEIR INDIVIDUAL CIRCUMSTANCES AND THE FEDERAL, STATE, LOCAL AND OTHER TAX CONSEQUENCES ARISING OUT OF THEIR PARTICIPATION AS LIMITED PARTNERS IN THE PARTNERSHIP. IN EVALUATING THE INVESTMENT, A PROSPECTIVE LIMITED PARTNERS SHOULD TAKE INTO ACCOUNT THE COST OF OBTAINING SUCH ADVICE.

CLASSIFICATION OF THE PARTNERSHIP

It is intended that the Partnership be taxed as a partnership. A partnership generally incurs no federal income tax liability. Instead, each partner is required to take into account such partner's allocable share of the partnership's net income or loss and certain specially characterized items (*e.g.,* capital gains and losses) in computing his/her income tax liability. Distributions by a partnership to a partner generally are not taxable unless the distributions exceed the partner's adjusted basis in his/her partnership interest. The availability to Limited Partners of most of the tax treatment described in this summary requires that the Partnership be classified as a partnership for federal income tax purposes rather than as an association, which is taxed as a corporation under the federal income tax laws. The IRS has adopted regulations that provide that a partnership will be taxed as a partnership unless it elects to be taxed as a corporation. The Partnership does not intend to elect out of being taxed as a partnership and the discussion below assumes that the Partnership will be taxed as a partnership for federal income tax purposes.

Tax Consequences of Unit Ownership

GENERAL

No federal income tax will be paid by the Partnership as an entity. The Partnership will report on its federal information return its distributive share of the income, gain, losses, deductions, and credits of the Partnership, regardless of whether or not any actual distributions are made by the Partnership to the Partnership during the taxable year. In turn, each Limited Partner of the Partnership will be required to report on his/her income tax return his/her distributive share of items of income, gain, loss, deduction, or credit (and items of tax preference) of the Partnership, regardless of whether or not any actual Distribution is made to that Limited Partner during his/her taxable year. The characterization of an item of income of loss generally will be the same for the Limited Partners as it is for the Partnership.

The General Partner may retain reserves from income from the Property to allow the Partnership to improve the Property. Consequently, a Limited Partner's share of the taxable income of the Partnership may exceed the cash, if any, actually distributed to that Limited Partner. Conversely, except as set forth below, actual (or constructive) distributions of money from the Partnership will be taxable to the extent that such distributions exceed the adjusted basis of the Limited Partner's interest in the Partnership, regardless of whether or not the Partnership has current income.

A Limited Partner's distributive share of items of income, gain, loss, deduction, or credit will be determined in accordance with the allocations set forth in the LPA as long as such allocations are recognized for federal income tax purposes. See "Allocation of Income and Losses" below. Each Limited Partner will be entitled to claim as a deduction his/her distributive share of the Partnership's net losses, if any, to the extent of that Limited Partner's adjusted basis in his/her Units as of the end of such taxable year, although those losses are subject to various other limitations, such as the passive activity limitation, the investment interest limitation, the at-risk limitation and the floor on miscellaneous itemized deductions. See "Tax Basis of Units" below. To the extent that a Limited Partner's share of Partnership losses exceeds the basis of his/her Units, such excess losses cannot be utilized in that year by that Limited Partner for any purpose, but are allowed as a deduction (subject to the limitations described above) only when, and to the extent that Limited Partner's adjusted basis for his/her Units at the end of any year, exceeds zero (before reduction by the suspended loss).

Tax Basis of Units

Each Limited Partner's basis for his/her Units initially will be equal to the amount of his/her cash contributions to the Partnership. Subsequently, each Limited Partner must adjust his/her basis to reflect certain transactions of the Partnership. A Limited Partner's basis will be increased by (i) any additional capital actually paid to the Partnership by that Limited Partner; (ii) that Limited Partner's distributive share of the income of the Partnership; (iii) that Limited Partner's distributive share of any Partnership indebtedness for which no Limited Partner is personally liable (the "Non-Recourse Debt"), but such increase will be limited to the fair market value of the property securing such indebtedness; and (iv) that Limited Partner's distributive share of the Partnership's recourse debt to the extent that Limited Partner is in all events required to make additional Capital Contributions of fixed, specified amounts at a definite future date. A Limited Partner's basis is decreased, but not below zero, by (i) the amount of that Limited Partner's distributive share of items of Partnership loss and deduction, (ii) the amount of any money distributed or treated constructively as having been distributed to that Limited Partner and (iii) the adjusted basis of distributed property other than money. A reduction in the amount of a Limited Partner's share of Partnership debt will be treated as a constructive cash Distribution to the Limited Partner and will reduce the basis of that Limited Partner's Units.

Cash Distributions

Cash distributions by the Partnership to a Limited Partner will not result in taxable gain to the Limited Partner unless the distributions exceed the Limited Partner's adjusted basis for his/her Units, in which case the Limited Partner will recognize gain in the amount of such excess. Gain, if any, resulting from

Partnership cash distributions will be treated as a gain from the sale or exchange of a Unit. See "Sale of a Unit" below.

A reduction in a Limited Partner's share of the Partnership Non-Recourse Debt, if any, will be treated as a cash Distribution to that Limited Partner to the extent of such reduction. Investors should note that a reduction in each Limited Partner's share of non- recourse liabilities will be deemed to occur whenever the General Partner's share or Limited Partner's shares of Partnership profits are increased. If a constructive Distribution results from a shift in non-recourse indebtedness and, if that Distribution exceeds a Limited Partner's adjusted basis in the Units held by that Limited Partner at that time, that Limited Partner will recognize gain as described above. The Partnership will have no obligation to distribute any money from the Partnership to assist the Limited Partners in paying the tax on any such gain.

LIMITATIONS ON LOSSES FROM PASSIVE ACTIVITIES

In the Code, certain investment activities are characterized as producing either passive or portfolio income and loss. Deductions from passive activities, to the extent that they exceed the aggregated income from all such activities, generally are not allowed as a loss deduction against either the portfolio income or any other income of the taxpayer. Similarly, credits from passive activities generally are limited to the tax allocable to passive activities. Interest expense attributable to passive activities will not be subject to the limitation on investment interest expense deductions. See "Limitation on Interest Deductions" below.

Losses and credits disallowed by the passive activity rules are suspended and may be carried forward and treated as losses and credits from passive activities in each successive taxable year until offset by income from passive activities or allowed against other income as a result of a complete disposition of the taxpayer's interest in that activity. When a taxpayer's entire interest in an activity is disposed of in a taxable transaction (other than to a related party), any remaining suspended loss incurred in connection with that specific activity is allowed in full, first against income or gain from such activity during the year of disposition, second against net income or gain from all other passive activities and thereafter against income from all sources, including active income. The Regulations provide that such a disposition may occur either with respect to a disposition by an entity of a passive activity or when there is a complete disposition by a Limited Partner of his/her entire interest in an entity that holds the activity.

Passive activities are defined to include trade or business activities in which a taxpayer does not participate materially and rental activities. Because the Partnership will be engaged in the trade or business of renting and operating the Property, the General Partner anticipates that a Limited Partner's investment in the Partnership will be a passive activity. Accordingly, losses of the Partnership, which would otherwise be deductible by a Limited Partner, will be suspended until: (i) that Limited Partner either disposes of his/her interest in the Partnership or realizes passive activity income against which the suspended losses could be applied; or (ii) the Partnership terminates its activity, whichever occurs first. It should be noted that interest earned on reserved funds will be characterized as portfolio income to the Limited Partners.

APPLICATION OF AT-RISK LIMITATIONS

Generally, Section 465 of the Code limits losses that a taxpayer can claim in certain enumerated activities to the amount that the taxpayer has at risk with respect to such activities. Losses from an activity that are disallowed in any year because the at-risk limitations are carried over to succeeding years and can be used in those years to the extent that the taxpayer's at-risk amount with respect to that activity has increased. A taxpayer is considered at risk in an activity with respect to: (i) the net amount of money and the adjusted basis of property contributed by the taxpayer to the activity; (ii) any amount borrowed with respect to the activity if the taxpayer is personally liable for the repayment of that amount; and (iii) the taxpayer's share of any other amount borrowed with respect to the activity if the lender is an institutional lender and the loan is secured by real property used in the activity. A taxpayer's at-risk amount also is increased by profits earned in the activity and decreased by losses occurring in the activity.

LIMITATION ON INTEREST DEDUCTIONS

The deductibility of a taxpayer's investment interest expense generally is limited to the amount of that taxpayer's net investment income. Investment interest expense does not include any interest expense that is taken into account in determining the income or loss from a passive activity, but does include: (i) interest on indebtedness incurred or continued to purchase or carry property "held for investment;" (ii) a partnership's interest expense attributable to portfolio income under the passive loss rules; and (iii) the portion of interest expense incurred or continued to purchase or carry an interest in a passive activity to the extent attributable to portfolio income (within the meaning of the passive loss rules). Specifically, a Limited Partner would treat as investment interest his/her allocable portion of the Partnership's total interest expense attributable to the Partnership's gross portfolio income less deductible expenses directly connected with that portfolio income. Interest on debt incurred by a Limited Partner to purchase or carry Units also may be investment interest to the extent the Partnership does not engage in a passive activity. Under temporary Treasury Regulations, debt of a taxpayer generally is allocated among the taxpayer's activities by tracing the proceeds of each debt. A detailed discussion of the tracing rules contained in the temporary Treasury Regulations is beyond the scope of this discussion. Consequently, Limited Partners who intend to use borrowed funds to purchase their Units should consult their own tax advisors before borrowing such funds. Limited Partners should maintain careful records of any debt they incur to carry or acquire their Units. See "Limitations on Losses From Passive Activities" above.

Net investment income is equal to the sum of gross income from property held for investment, gain attributable to the disposition of property held for investment, and amounts treated as gross portfolio income pursuant to the passive loss rules, less deductible expenses (other than interest) directly connected with the production of investment income. Investment interest deductions that are disallowed may be carried forward and deducted in subsequent years to the extent of net investment income in such years.

If any portion of the Property is considered to be "held for investment" rather than used in a "trade or business" (see "Sale of the Property" below), the investment interest rules should be applicable to limit, to the extent of net investment income, the Limited Partners' ability to currently deduct both the interest paid by the Partnership to carry that portion of the Property and the interest, if any, paid by the Limited Partners to carry an allocable portion of their Units.

FLOOR ON MISCELLANEOUS ITEMIZED DEDUCTIONS

An individual may deduct certain "miscellaneous itemized deductions" only to the extent they cumulatively exceed 2% of his/her adjusted gross income. Miscellaneous itemized deductions include all itemized deductions other than those for interest, taxes, casualty losses, charitable donations, medical expenses, and certain other deductions. The legislative history of this new provision makes it clear that the floor applies with respect to indirect, non-business deductions through pass-through entities. The application of the new rules with respect to miscellaneous itemized deductions to the Partnership will depend on whether it is characterized as a passive activity. To the extent the activities of the Partnership do not constitute an active trade or business, each individual Limited Partner's share of any "miscellaneous itemized deductions," would be subject to the 2% floor. See "Sale of the Property" below.

APPENDIX

Unrelated Business Taxable Income

Organizations generally exempt from federal income taxation under Section 501(a) of the Code may, nevertheless, be taxable on their allocable share of income to the extent such income constitutes "unrelated business taxable income" ("UBTI"). For this purpose, unrelated business income ("UBI") means the gross income derived by a tax-exempt organization from an unrelated trade or business (including income derived through ownership by the tax-exempt entity of an interest in a pass through entity), less deductions directly connected with such gross income. There is an exclusion for UBTI for rents from real property subject to meeting the exemption for debt financed real property provided below.

Generally, a qualified pension, profit sharing, or stock bonus trust ("Qualified Plan") may acquire real property by using debt financing without subjecting itself to unrelated business income from the debt finance portion of the property. However, if the property is encumbered with indebtedness on which the time for payments or the amount of payment is dependent on future revenues, income or profits from the property, then such organization will be subject to unrelated business taxable income for debt-financed income. Further, if a property is seller financed and seller financing is on other than commercially reasonable terms or is dependent on revenue, income or profits, the property will be treated as debt-financed property. Accordingly, the General Partner does not intend to finance the Property where the financing is dependent as to the time of payment or the amount of payments or the revenues, income or profits of the property. Further, if the Property is acquired with seller financing, the General Partner intends that such financing be on commercially reasonable terms.

Indebtedness incurred on real property acquisitions by a partnership may be subject to unrelated business taxable income if the partnership has partners who are not Qualified Plans unless the partnership meets one of two tests: (i) each allocation to a partner or partnership is a "qualified allocation;" or (ii) the Partnership meets "disproportionate allocation" rules and each allocation to the Partnership has substantial economic effect. The Manager believes that the Partnership may fail to meet the qualified allocation test. Accordingly, the Partnership will strive to meet the disproportionate allocation test. A company meets the disproportionate allocation test if: (i) no distributive share of overall partnership income allocable to a tax exempt partner exceeds such partner's smallest distributive share of overall partnership loss for any taxable year; and (ii) each partnership allocation has substantial economic effect. Qualified Plans are cautioned that the requirements necessary to satisfy the above tests are highly technical and little authority provides guidance as to the proper interpretation of these requirements. It is possible that the provisions of any agreement governing the Partnership would be determined to violate the above requirements. If such a determination were made, qualified organizations investing in the Partnership could be required to recognize greater amounts of UBTI.

An annual specific deduction of $1,000 from UBI is allowable in computing UBTI. Therefore, if a tax-exempt Limited Partner were to be subject to tax on UBI from the Partnership only to the extent that such UBI, plus its UBI from other sources, exceeds $1,000 in any particular year. A tax-exempt organization, however, must file a tax return for each year in which it has $1,000 or more of gross income included in computing UBTI, even if no tax is due.

No assurance can be given that the IRS will concur with the conclusions regarding the tax consequences set forth above. No ruling has been or will be requested by the Partnership from the IRS as to such matters.

IN THIS MEMORANDUM, WE DO NOT ADDRESS ALL OF THE INCOME TAX AND ERISA CONSEQUENCES OF AN INVESTMENT IN THE PARTNERSHIP. PROSPECTIVE INVESTORS WHO ARE SUBJECT TO ERISA OR WHO ARE TAX-EXEMPT ARE URGED TO CONSULT WITH THEIR OWN LEGAL AND TAX COUNSEL WITH RESPECT TO ANY INVESTMENT IN THE PARTNERSHIP.

ALTERNATIVE MINIMUM TAX

Individual taxpayers are subject to an "alternative minimum tax" if such tax exceeds the individual's regular income tax. The alternative minimum tax is the excess of 24% of the amount by which the alternative minimum taxable income exceeds the exemption amount of taxpayer's regular federal income tax. Special rates exist for long- term capital gains.

Alternative minimum taxable income, generally, is the taxpayer's adjusted gross income increased by the amount of certain preference items, less certain itemized deductions. A credit is allowed against the regular tax for prior years' minimum tax liability attributable to deferral preferences. The itemized deductions allowable in calculating the alternative minimum tax are medical expenses in excess of 10% of adjusted gross income, casualty and theft losses, gambling losses to the extent of gambling gains, charitable contributions, certain estate taxes, and qualified housing interest and other investment interest to the extent of net investment income. Special rules apply if a taxpayer has net operating loss deductions.

The impact of the alternative minimum tax on a Limited Partner's overall federal income tax liability may vary, generally depending on a Limited Partner's other items of income, gain, loss, deduction, and credit, from no impact to a substantial increase in tax. Accordingly, each prospective investor should consult with his/her tax adviser regarding the impact of an investment in the Partnership on the calculation of his/her alternative minimum tax, as well as on his/her overall federal income tax liability.

ALLOCATION OF INCOME AND LOSSES

Under Section 704(b) of the Code, a Limited Partner's distributive share of income, gain, loss, deduction or credit (or any item thereof) will be determined in accordance with the Limited Partnership Agreement only if that allocation under the agreement has "substantial economic effect." In determining whether an allocation has substantial economic effect, the principal considerations are: (i) whether the allocation actually affects the eventual amount of money or other property allocable to a Limited Partner (*i.e.*, it has economic effect), without regard to tax consequences; and (ii) whether the effect described in (i) is substantial. If an allocation under a Limited Partnership Agreement does not have substantial effect, the profits and losses will be reallocated by the IRS among the Limited Partners in accordance with their interest in the Partnership determined by taking into consideration all facts and circumstances.

For a general description of how the income and losses of the Partnership are allocated, see "Summary of the Limited Partnership Agreement - Allocation of Income and Losses" below. In addition to that general description, two specific points should be noted. First, if a Limited Partner has, or is expected to have, a deficit distribution, some items of income and gain may be allocated specially to that Limited Partner to more quickly reduce the existing or expected distribution deficit. This is done to ensure that the allocations have substantial economic effect as required by the Code and as discussed below. Second, the Partnership's Limited Partnership Agreement does not require the Limited Partners with deficit distributions upon liquidation to restore those deficits to the Partnership. Since an allocation of losses attributable to the Partnership's recourse debt that reduces a Limited Partner's distribution (as specially adjusted pursuant to the "qualified income offset" provisions in the Limited Partnership Agreement) below zero would not have economic effect to the extent that the Limited Partner is not required to restore that deficit, the Limited Partnership Agreement requires gross income to be allocated to such Limited Partner to restore his/her distribution to zero. The LPA contains a curative allocation that reverses any required tax allocations as quickly as possible and attempts to put all Limited Partners into the same economic position as existed before the required tax allocations were made.

The allocations should have economic effect under the alternative test for economic effect set forth in the Regulations because: (i) distributions will be maintained by the Limited Partners in accordance with the standards as set forth in the Regulations; (ii) upon liquidation of the Partnership, distributions will be made to the Limited Partners in accordance with their positive Capital Account balances after any curative allocations of profits are made, and (iii) the LPA contains a "qualified income offset."

Although an allocation of losses attributable to non-recourse liabilities of a partnership cannot technically have economic effect because no Limited Partner bears the actual risk of economic loss, an allocation of such losses is deemed to have economic effect under the Regulations if four requirements are met: (i) the first two economic effect requirements listed above are satisfied throughout the full term of the Partnership; (ii) the allocation of non-recourse deductions among the Limited Partners is reasonably consistent with allocations of other significant items; (iii) a "minimum gain charge-back" (as defined in the Regulations) is provided for in the Limited Partnership Agreement; and (iv) all other material allocations and distribution adjustments under the Limited Partnership Agreement are recognized under the Regulations. Those requirements should be satisfied under the terms of the LPA.

In addition to having economic effect, an allocation must be substantial. An allocation is substantial if there is a reasonable possibility that the allocation will affect substantially the dollar amounts to be received by the Limited Partners, independent of tax consequences. Because liquidation proceeds are, in all cases, distributed in accordance with distributions, allocations under the LPA may significantly affect the dollar amounts to be received by the Limited Partners. Therefore, it appears that allocations in the Partnership's LPA are substantial; however, because whether an allocation is "substantial" involves a question of fact, counsel has rendered no opinion on this issue.

Tax Treatment of Partnership Operations

Taxable Year and Method of Accounting

Under the Code, the Partnership is required to report its operations on a calendar year basis and also will be required to use the accrual method of accounting. Under the accrual method of accounting, income is included for the taxable year when "all events" have occurred that fix the right to receive such income and the amount thereof can be determined with reasonable accuracy. Consequently, the Partnership will be required to recognize taxable income as it is earned, regardless of the fact that the Partnership may not have received the cash associated with such income. Thus, the Partnership (and the Limited Partners) may have taxable income for a period in an amount in excess of the cash actually received by the Partnership.

In general, deductions under the accrual method are allowed for the taxable year in which "all events" have occurred that establish the fact of the liability giving rise to such deduction if the amount thereof can be determined with reasonable accuracy. Thus, it is anticipated that interest and other expenses will be deductible or amortized by the Partnership as accrued, regardless of when paid. Certain liabilities are not considered to be incurred, however, during any taxable year any earlier than the time that "economic performance" with respect to such item occurs. As an example, economic performance for property or services to be provided to the Partnership by another person should occur when such person actually provides such property or services.

Depreciation

The Partnership will depreciate the improvements on the Property and some personal properties used in connection with operations on the basis recommended by the Partnership's accountant. Further, to the extent the Partnership purchases new equipment, such equipment may be expensed as provided in the Code. The limit on this ability to expense equipment will generally be applied at the Limited Partner level and not at the Partnership level.

ACTIVITIES NOT ENGAGED IN FOR PROFIT

Section 183 of the Code provides that no deductions are allowed for an individual for "activities not engaged in for a profit." If Section 183 were deemed to apply to the Property, a deduction is allowed for items such as interest and state and local property taxes because they may be deducted without regard to whether they are incurred in a trade or business or for the production of income. However, other deductions (such as depreciation) are allowed only to the extend they do not exceed gross income derived from the activity. Accordingly, the General Partner does not anticipate that Section 183 will limit deductions of the Partnership.

SALE OF THE PROPERTY

The treatment of any gain or loss on the sale, exchange or other disposition of the Property by the Partnership will be dependent upon all of the facts and circumstances existing at the time of disposition. Depending upon decisions of the General Partner with respect to the use and disposition of the Property, the Property will be classified as either: (i) a capital asset; (ii) property used in the trade or business of the Partnership; or (iii) Dealer Property. The federal income tax treatment of these categories is different.

The determination of whether all or any portion of the Property will be considered to be Dealer Property is a question that depends on the facts that exist at the time the Partnership's interest in the Property is terminated. No single fact is determinative. Factors often considered by the courts include: (i) the nature and purpose of the acquisition of the property and the duration of the ownership; (ii) the extent and nature of the taxpayer's efforts to sell the property; (iii) the number, extent, continuity and substantiality of the sales; (iv) the extent of subdividing, developing and advertising to increase sales; (v) the use of a business office for the sale of the property; (vi) the character and degree of supervision or control exercised by the taxpayer over any representative selling the property; and (vii) the time and effort the taxpayer devoted to the sales. Other factors considered are the reason for disposing of the property and the taxpayer's business history as well as factors that may be unique to the particular case being examined. No particular weighting of the factors may be discerned from the decisions, and several cases are in direct conflict with one another.

The current plan of the General Partner is to hold the Property solely for rental in trade or business and to obtain appreciation through a sale of the Property at the appropriate time. The General Partner believes that if it is successful in executing its plan, the Property should not be treated as Dealer Property. Rather, the Property should be treated as being used in the trade or business of the Partnership. Accordingly, the Partnership's distributive share of the gain or loss resulting from the sale of all or any portion of the Property should be capital gain and, consequently, each Limited Partner's distributive share of the Partnership's gain should be capital gain. If the Property is held for more than 12 months, the gain would be eligible for the treatment accorded to long-term capital gain and losses would be subject to the limitations applicable to long-term capital losses.

DEPRECIATION RECAPTURE

It is anticipated that gains realized from the sale or disposition of real estate held by the Partnership generally will be treated as capital gains (unless such disposition takes the form of a like kind exchange or other tax-free transaction, in which case all or a part of such realized gains would not be recognized). However, Limited Partners will be subject to tax at applicable ordinary income tax rates to the extent of depreciation recapture attributable to the disposition of certain personal and real property by the Partnership. In addition, corporate Limited Partners will be subject to tax at ordinary income rates on a portion of the depreciation recapture attributable to the disposition of real property by the Partnership. Any remaining gains will be subject to taxation at the applicable capital gain tax rates, including, with regard to a Limited Partner who is an individual, the 25% rate applicable to such Limited Partner's share of the "unrecaptured Section 1250 gain" (*i.e.*, previously claimed depreciation deductions with respect to depreciable real property that would not otherwise be recaptured as ordinary income pursuant to Code section 1250) of the Partnership and to the portion of REIT capital gain dividends attributable to unrecaptured Section 1250 gain. An exception to capital gains treatment exists for gains realized from the sale or other disposition of dealer property unless such property qualifies as "Section 1231 property." Generally, Code section 1231 provides that "Section 1231 property" includes real property and depreciable assets used in a trade or business that have been held for more than one year, but does not include inventory or other property held primarily for sale to customers in the ordinary course of a trade or business.

INSTALLMENT SALES

Upon a sale of the Property, the Partnership may take as part payment purchase money obligations in the form of a Promissory Note and Deed of Trust, a Promissory Note and Mortgage or an Agreement of Sale or other form of security instrument. In that instance, the Partnership would not have to report the entire amount of taxable gain on the disposition of the Property if the Partnership is eligible to report its gain under the installment sales rules. Under the Code, property held for use in a trade or business may be sold under the installment sales rules, subject to certain limitations. Under one of those limitations, if the aggregate face amount of all obligations held by a taxpayer that arise during any one taxable year from sales of property on the installment method is greater than $5,000,000, interest must be paid on the portion of the deferred tax liability attributable to the excess of the outstanding face amount of those obligations as of the close of that taxable year over $5,000,000. Because the Property will be depreciable property, any amount of gain realized from depreciation recapture would not be eligible for installment sale treatment.

UNIFORM CAPITALIZATION RULES

Under the Code, direct costs, and an allocable portion of most indirect costs, relating to Dealer Property must be capitalized. The indirect costs required to be capitalized include administrative expenses, taxes and certain interest costs, including imputed interest. As discussed in "Sale of the Property" section above, the determination of whether the Property held by the Partnership will be considered to be Dealer Property is a question that depends on the facts that exist at the time the interest in each portion of the property is terminated. In order to apply the uniform capitalization rules, however, it would seem that the determination of whether the Property is Dealer Property must be made at the time the direct and allocable indirect costs are incurred.

Since the Partnership's plans, which are subject to change, do not contemplate activities that would be likely to result in the Property being treated as Dealer Property, the General Partner does not believe the uniform capitalization rules should apply to the Partnership. Nevertheless, whether as a result of a departure by the General Partner from the plans or otherwise, if the Property is subsequently determined to be Dealer Property, a Limited Partner may be denied the privilege of currently deducting the administrative expenses, taxes and interest expenses relating thereto and may be required to file amended tax returns if he/she previously has done so.

FEES PAYABLE TO GENERAL PARTNER AND AFFILIATES

The General Partner and its Affiliates will receive various fees for services to be rendered in administering the business and affairs of the Partnership in connection with the purchase and sale of the Property. If questioned, the deduction for such fees would depend on a factual determination as to the nature of the services actually performed, an inquiry that cannot be predicted with certainty. As a consequence of the factual nature of the question, no opinion has been or will be received from counsel with respect to the deductibility of these payments. See "Organizational and Syndication Costs" below. Although the General Partner believes that the amount of the fees charged are customary and reasonable based on the services, no assurance can be given (and no opinion of Counsel has been received) that the IRS will not seek to treat the various fees as constituting an allocation of income or a distribution of the capital of the Partnership, rather than as a capitalizable or deductible expense of the Partnership.

ORGANIZATIONAL AND SYNDICATION COSTS

Expenses of organizing the Partnership and of promoting the sale of Units in the Partnership must be capitalized by the Partnership. The Partnership, however, may elect to deduct a portion of organizational expenses but not syndication expenses such as sales commissions, organizational fees, professional fees for preparing an offering memorandum and printing costs) and amortize the remaining organizational expenses over a period of 180 months. Specifically, up to $5,000 of certain organizational expenses incurred by the Partnership may be deducted in the current year; however, if organizational expenses of the Partnership exceed $50,000, then the deductible amount of $5,000 will be reduced dollar-for-dollar. The remaining organizational expenses after the current-year deduction may then be amortized over a period of 180 months. In light of the floor on miscellaneous itemized deductions, however, the General Partner may not make such an election for the Partnership. See "Floor on Miscellaneous Itemized Deductions" above.

Under Section 709(a) of the Code, expenses paid in connection with the syndication must be capitalized without the benefit of amortization. Regulations under Section 709(a) include within the definition of syndication expenses, legal fees of the issuer (the general Limited Partner) for securities law advice and for tax advice pertaining to the adequacy of tax disclosures in the offering memorandum and accounting fees for the preparation of representations to be included in the offering materials. Some of the expenses that will be incurred by the Partnership will be difficult to classify under the Regulations.

Transfers and Liquidation

SALE OF A UNIT

The sale of a Unit by a Limited Partner that has held that Unit for more than 12 months generally should result in long-term capital gain or loss, except that any gain attributable to a Limited Partner's share of the Partnership's substantially appreciated inventory or depreciation recapture will be taxed as ordinary income. The Partnership will have substantially appreciated inventory if: (a) it is determined to hold any portion of the Property primarily for sale to customers in the ordinary course of business; and (b) the fair market value of that portion of the Property is greater than: (i) 120% of the Partnership's basis in that portion of the Property; and (ii) 10% of the fair market value of all Partnership property other than money. See "Sale of the Property" above. The amount of gain realized on the sale of a Unit will be the sales price received by the Limited Partner, plus that Limited Partner's allocable share of Partnership Non-Recourse Debt relieved, less the adjusted basis of the Unit in the hands of the Limited Partner.

In the event of a sale or other transfer of a Unit by a Limited Partner, the distributive share of Partnership income, gain, loss, deduction, or credit for the entire year allocable to that Unit generally will be allocated between the transferor and the transferee, based upon the period of time during the taxable year that each owned such Unit and regardless of the timing or amounts or any distributions from the Partnership. Gain or loss from the sale of property by the Partnership, however, will be allocated to those persons that are Limited Partners on the date of sale.

APPENDIX

Limited Partners may not be able to sell their Units because it is not anticipated that a market will develop for Units, and the Partnership's Limited Partnership Agreement contains restrictions on their sale. See "Summary of the Limited Partnership Agreement" below.

GIFT OF A UNIT

Generally, no gain or loss is recognized for income tax purposes as a result of a gift of property. If a gift of a Unit is made at a time when a Limited Partner's allocable share of the Partnership's non-recourse indebtedness exceeds the adjusted basis of the Unit in the Limited Partner's hands, however, that Limited Partner may realize gain for income tax purposes to the extent of such excess. Such gain generally should be treated as capital gain, except to the extent it is attributable to any unrealized receivables or substantially appreciated inventory items of the Partnership, which generally will be treated as ordinary income. Gifts of Units also may be subject to a gift tax.

TERMINATION OF A PARTNERSHIP FOR FEDERAL INCOME TAX PURPOSES

If interests in the Partnership representing 50% or more of the total interests in the capital and profits of the Partnership are sold or exchanged within any consecutive 12-month period, the Partnership will be considered terminated for federal income tax purposes. A termination of a partnership for federal income tax purposes will cause that partnership's taxable year to end with respect to all partners of the partnership and could have potentially adverse federal income tax consequences, including a change in the adjusted basis of any property held by the partnership and a bunching of more than one year's taxable income from the partnership within a single taxable year of any member whose taxable year does not coincide with the partnership's calendar taxable year. Under the Partnership's LPA, no sale or exchange of any interest in the capital or profits of the Partnership may be made if, as a result of such sale or exchange, the Partnership would be terminated under federal income tax law. Although such a provision is common in limited partnership agreements, no case has ever been decided determining the validity of such clause for federal income tax purposes. Therefore, a risk exists that such a sale or exchange might take place and that such a sale or exchange would be deemed to terminate the Partnership.

LIQUIDATION OF THE PARTNERSHIP

Upon liquidation of the Partnership, any Gain or Loss recognized from a distribution to the Limited Partner generally will be considered as gain or loss from the sale or exchange of a capital asset, except to the extent of substantially appreciated inventory items. See "Sale of a Unit" above. Gain to a Limited Partner on a liquidating distribution will be recognized to the extent that any money received, together with any reduction in that Limited Partner's share of non-recourse partnership debt, exceeds that Limited Partner's adjusted basis in his/her interest. A Loss will not be recognized unless the Limited Partner receives no property in the distribution other than money, unrealized receivables or substantially appreciated inventory, and then only to the extent that the money and the basis to the Limited Partner of the unrealized receivables and substantially appreciated inventory are less than the adjusted basis of the partnership interest in the Limited Partner's hands.

SECTION 754 ELECTION

A partnership may make an election under Section 754 of the Code, which results in various items of partnership income, gain, loss, and deduction being treated differently for tax purposes than for accounting purposes. Under this election, the Code provides for adjustments to the basis of partnership property for measuring gain upon distributions of partnership property and transfers of any partnership interests. The general effect of such an election is that transferees of any partnership interests are treated, for purposes of computing depreciation and gain, as though they had acquired a direct interest in the partnership assets and the partnership is treated for such purposes, upon certain distributions to members, as though the partnership had acquired a new cost basis for such assets. Any such election, once made, cannot be revoked without the consent of the IRS.

In view of the inherent tax accounting complexities and the substantial expense that would be incurred in making such elections under Section 754 of the Code, the General Partner cannot at this time determine whether it will make such elections on behalf of the Partnership, although it is empowered to do so by the Partnership's Limited Partnership Agreement. Therefore, no benefits may be available to the Partnership by reason of such adjustments.

If no elections are made, the Limited Partners may have greater difficulty selling their Units than they would have if such elections were made, because any transferees will obtain no current tax benefits from their investment to the extent their investment cost exceeds their allocable share of the basis in the assets of the Partnership. A failure to make such elections also may adversely affect the beneficiary of a decedent Limited Partner for the same reason.

Administrative and Compliance Matters

Audit Risk

The IRS has adopted a policy of auditing, selectively, a large number of partnership information returns. The focus of such audits is on "tax shelters," including those investing in real estate. The term "tax shelter" has a variety of definitions, depending upon the context in which it is used. The Partnership's information return may be selected for audit. If the IRS audits the information return of the Partnership, it is more likely that the returns of the Limited Partners also will be audited. It is not expected that the Partnership would make cash distributions to assist the Limited Partners in paying a tax liability resulting from such an audit.

Resolution of Disputes Involving Partnership Items

Limited partnerships generally are treated as separate entities for purposes of federal tax audits, judicial review of administrative adjustments by the IRS and tax settlement proceedings. The tax treatment of partnership items of income, gain, loss, deduction, and credit are determined at the partnership level in a unified partnership proceeding rather than in separate proceedings with the members. The Code provides for one member to be designated as the "Tax Matters Partner" for these purposes. In the Partnership's LPA, the General Partner is appointed as the Tax Matters Partner of the Partnership.

The Tax Matters Partner is entitled to make certain elections on behalf of the Partnership and Limited Partners and can extend the statute of limitations for assessment of tax deficiencies against Limited Partners with respect to Partnership items. The Tax Matters Partner may bind to a settlement with the IRS any Limited Partners with less than a 1% profits interest in the Partnership unless the Limited Partners elect, by filing a statement with the IRS, not to give such authority to the Tax Matters Partner. The Tax Matters Partner may seek judicial review (to which all Limited Partners are bound) of a final partnership administrative adjustment and, if the Tax Matters Partner fails to seek judicial review, such review may be sought by any Limited Partners having in the aggregate at least a 5% profits interest. Only one action for judicial review will go forward, however, and Limited Partners with an interest in the outcome may participate.

The Limited Partners generally will be required to treat Partnership items on their personal federal income tax returns consistent with the treatment of the items on the Partnership information return. In general, this consistency requirement is waived if a Limited Partner files a statement with the IRS identifying the inconsistency. Failure to satisfy the consistency requirement, if not waived, will result in an adjustment to conform the treatment of the item by the Limited Partners with its treatment on the Partnership return. Even if the consistency requirement is waived, adjustments to a Limited Partners' tax liability with respect to Partnership items may result from an audit of the Partnership's or the Limited Partners' tax returns. Intentional or negligent disregard of the consistency requirement may subject a Limited Partner to substantial penalties.

POTENTIAL PENALTIES

A taxpayer is subject to an understatement penalty if the taxpayer's actual federal income tax liability is understated by the greater of $5,000 or 10% of the tax shown on the return. If the penalty applies, it is equal to 25% of the understatement. There are broad exceptions to this penalty provision, which applies different standards based on whether or not the item giving rise to the tax understatement resulted from a "tax shelter." The term "tax shelter" is defined to include a partnership if the principal purpose of such partnership is the avoidance or evasion of federal income tax. This definition is significantly different from the definition of "tax shelter" that applies in the context of the tax shelter registration requirements (which the General Partner does not believe are not applicable to this Partnership.) The determination of principal purpose is based upon objective evidence that the purpose of avoiding or evading federal income tax exceeds any other purpose. Although the principal purpose of a partnership is a question of fact, it is the belief of the General Partner that the principal purpose of the Partnership is to hold the Property and realize economic gain from the appreciation of the Property rather than the avoidance or evasion of federal income tax. Therefore, the Partnership should not be classified as a tax shelter for purposes of the understatement penalty.

Generally, if a tax shelter does not exist, the understatement penalty is reduced by an amount attributable to the tax treatment of an item if: (i) there is or was "substantial authority" for such treatment; or (ii) the relevant facts affecting the item's tax treatment are adequately disclosed in the tax return. The Code does not contain a definition of "substantial authority." The proposed regulations provide that the standard of "substantial authority" is less stringent than "more likely than not" and more stringent than a "reasonable basis" standard. The position must be "stronger than one that is arguable but fairly unlikely to prevail in court." The General Partner could take legal positions, in filing the Partnership's federal income tax information return, that authority for a particular legal position is substantial authority for purposes of the penalty and could be challenged by the IRS. No assurance can be given that the judgment of the General Partner in such matters would be found to be correct if tested in court.

If a tax shelter does exist, the understatement penalty will not be reduced upon adequate disclosure of the relevant facts on the tax return. Rather, an understatement with respect to a tax shelter will be reduced only if, in addition to being supported by substantial authority, the taxpayer reasonably believed that treatment of such items on his/her return was "more likely than not" the proper treatment.

There are several other penalties that could be applicable to the Partnership. For example, there is a penalty for failure to include correct information on an information return. Also, the failure to report on a tax return any amount reported on an information return is considered negligence in the absence of clear and convincing evidence to the contrary.

TAX SHELTER REGISTRATION

Under the Code and applicable Regulations, a "tax shelter" is defined as an investment in which the investor can reasonably infer from representations made in promotional material that the "tax shelter ratio" will be greater than two-to-one as of the close of any of the five taxable years after the investment is offered. The "tax shelter ratio" is determined by dividing the investor's share of aggregate deductions derived from the investment, determined without regard to income, by the amount of the investor's contribution. The Partnership does not believe it will be classified as a "tax shelter" under these rules and it does not intend to register as such with the IRS. However, if the Partnership is required to register and fails to do so, it could expose the Partnership to penalties. Registration as a "tax shelter" may also increase the likelihood of an audit of the Company's tax returns.

IMPOSITION OF MEDICARE TAX ON UNEARNED INCOME

Effective for tax years after December 31, 2012, under the Health Care and Education Reconciliation Act of 2010, a new tax is imposed on certain individuals equal to the lesser of 3.8% of the taxpayer's net investment income or the excess (if any) of the taxpayer's modified adjusted gross income over a threshold amount, which is $250,000 for taxpayers filing joint returns, $125,000 for married taxpayers filing separately, and $200,000 for all other taxpayers. For the purpose of this tax, net investment income includes gross income from interest, dividends, annuities, royalties and rents (other than from a trade or business), income from passive activities or from trading in financial instruments or commodities. Individual Unit holders may be subject to this additional tax on such Unit holder's allocations of income from the Partnership, as well as on a sale or other disposition of Units.

POSSIBLE CHANGES IN FEDERAL TAX LAWS

The Code is subject to change by Congress and interpretations of the Code may be modified or affected by judicial decisions, by the Treasury Department through changes in Regulations and by the IRS through its audit policy, announcements and published and private rulings. Such changes may be retroactive. Accordingly, the ultimate effect on a member's tax situation may be governed by laws, regulations, or interpretations of laws or regulations that have not yet been proposed, passed, or made, as the case may be. While significant changes historically have been given prospective application, no assurance can be given that any changes made in the tax law affecting an investment in the Partnership would be limited to prospective effect.

FOREIGN INVESTORS

This Memorandum does not attempt to discuss the effect of foreign taxes on an investment in the Partnership. Each non-U.S. resident investor should consult his or her own tax advisor. It should be noted, however, that federal law will require the Partnership to withhold income taxes on distributions to investors who are non-U.S. persons.

STATE AND LOCAL TAXES

The Property is located in [State], which does not impose an income tax on all income earned by non-residents from properties located within the state. However, [State] may impose a franchise tax or similar taxes on the Partnership. Prospective Limited Partners are urged to consult their own tax advisers concerning those matters.

ERISA ASPECTS OF THE OFFERING

INTRODUCTION

ERISA subjects trustees of Qualified Plans to special fiduciary standards with respect to the affairs of such Qualified Plans. The prohibited transaction rules under ERISA proscribe certain dealings between employee benefit plans and related persons. The purpose of the prohibited transaction rules is to curb all forms of fiduciary misconduct through prohibition of certain types of conduct in the first instance. A discussion of the general duties and restrictions imposed by ERISA, such as the duty to diversify the investments of Qualified Plans, is beyond the scope of this discussion, this material being limited to certain of the prohibited transaction rules under ERISA that most likely would bear upon the holding of Units by Qualified Plans.

BEFORE PURCHASING UNITS, TRUSTEES OF QUALIFIED PLANS SHOULD SEEK LEGAL COUNSEL HAVING EXPERTISE IN ERISA TO ASSURE THAT THE INVESTMENT BY THE QUALIFIED PLANS IN UNITS IS NOT, AND IS NOT LIKELY TO BECOME, A VIOLATION OF ANY RULES OR LAWS RELATING TO INVESTMENTS BY QUALIFIED PLANS. THE COSTS OF OBTAINING SUCH ADVICE SHOULD BE TAKEN INTO ACCOUNT IN EVALUATING ANY INVESTMENT.

PLAN ASSET RULES

The Department of Labor ("DOL") has finalized regulations ("DOL Regulations") pursuant to ERISA that treat the underlying assets held by certain entities in which exempt plans have beneficial ownership interests as plan assets, as opposed to treating the equity interest in the entity as a plan asset. DOL Regulations Section 2510.3-101(a)(2) sets forth the general rule that when a Qualified Plan invests in another entity, its assets include the investment, but do not, solely by reason of such investment, include any of the underlying assets of the entity. However, a special rule set forth therein provides that if a Qualified Plan acquires an equity interest in an entity that is neither a publicly-offered security nor a security issued by certain registered investment companies, its assets include both the equity interest and an individual interest in each of the underlying assets of the entity, unless: (i) the entity is an "operating company;" or (ii) the equity interests of certain "benefit plan investors" are not significant. The Units will be neither publicly offered nor issued by a prescribed investment company. Thus, one of the two exceptions must apply in order for the Property not to be treated under the DOL Regulations as a plan asset of a Qualified Plan holding Units.

An "operating company" is defined for these purposes as an entity primarily engaged in the production or sale of a product or service other than the investment of capital. A special category of "operating company" referred to as a "real estate operating company" is set forth for entities engaged in real estate activities. A "real estate operating company" is an entity at least 50% of the assets of which are devoted directly to the management or development of real estate. The examples to the Regulation the definition make it clear that the entity must devote substantial resources to its management or development activities to constitute a "real estate operating company," as opposed to merely holding real property for appreciation. Thus, in the examples to the DOL Regulations, a plan that invests in assets in equity positions in real property subject to long-term leases under which substantially all the management and maintenance activities with respect to the property are the responsibility of the lessee are not engaged in management or development of real estate and is not a real estate operating company. However, under another example to the DOL Regulation, if the same plan invests in equity interest in a shopping center in which individual stores are leased for relatively short periods and independent contractors are retained to manage and operate the properties and undertake the owner's obligations to maintain common areas and conduct maintenance activities with respect to the property, then the plan can be a real estate operating company. Under this example, so long as the Partnership engages in active management of the Property and does not enter into long-term leasing of the Property, the Partnership should be a real estate operating company. Accordingly, the General Partner should not be a fiduciary of plans investing in the Partnership under the plan asset rules.

Conflicts of Interest

GENERAL

Fiduciaries and other parties in interest are not to compromise their fiduciary duties or exploit their relationships with Qualified Plans to confer benefit upon themselves other than to receive reasonable compensation for services rendered. ERISA Sections 406(a)(1)(A)-(D) and 406(b)(1)-(3) and Code

Sections 4975(c)(1)(A)-(F) prohibit (i) direct or indirect sales or exchanges of property between Qualified Plans and parties in interest; (ii) the direct or indirect lending of money or extension of credit between Qualified Plans and parties in interest; (iii) the direct or indirect furnishing of goods, services, or facilities between Qualified Plans and parties in interests; (iv) direct or indirect transfers of plan assets to parties in interest; (v) fiduciaries from dealing with plan assets for their own account; (vi) fiduciaries from acting on the behalf of parties whose interests are adverse to the interests of the Qualified Plan; and (vii) the receipt by fiduciaries of consideration ("kickbacks") from any party dealing with the Qualified Plan with respect to plan assets.

Under Section 3(21)(A) of ERISA and Section 4975(e)(3)(A) of the Code, the term "fiduciary" is defined as including any person who exercises any authority or control respecting the management or disposition of the assets of a Qualified Plan. The General Partner will have full control over the affairs and assets of the Partnership. For the reason set forth above under the heading, "Plan Asset Rules," the Property should not be treated as a plan asset of Qualified Plan holding Units. Accordingly, the General Partner should not be deemed to be a Fiduciary of Qualified Plans holding Units for purposes of ERISA.

Even if the General Partner is not treated as a fiduciary, it nevertheless could be deemed to be a service provider and thereby a party in interest with respect to all Qualified Plans holding Units. A "party in interest" is defined at section 3(14)(B) of ERISA and Section 4975(e)(2)(B) of the Code as including any person "providing services to the plan."

If the General Partner does become a fiduciary for purposes of ERISA, it would be subject to a much stricter standard of loyalty to Qualified Plans holding Units than a mere party in interest. ERISA exacts undivided loyalty of fiduciaries to Qualified Plans. Pursuant to such duty, the General Partner would be required to refrain from dealing with the Partnership on its own behalf or on the behalf of those with interests adverse to those of Qualified Plans holding Units. In that regard, a conflict potential could exist by virtue of the General Partner's interest in the Partnership. Although the General Partner believes that its common law obligation to manage the Partnership in accordance with the best interests of the majority interest holders would prevent it from acting adversely to the interests of the Limited Partners, no assurances can be given that such common ownership would not be deemed to be a volatile conflict of interest per se.

If the General Partner engages in conduct that results in a violation of the prohibited transaction rules, the General Partner could be subject to prohibited transaction excise taxes under the Code, the General Partner would be liable for any losses incurred by the Qualified Plan occasioned by such conduct, and all aspects of the activity comprising the violation could be required to be reversed. Such violation should not, however, produce direct adverse consequences for Qualified Plans under the prohibited transaction rules.

Conflicts of interest that could result in violations of one or more of the prohibited transaction rules also could occur if Units are purchased by a Limited Partner upon the decision or recommendation of a fiduciary or any other party in interest with respect to that Qualified Plan in a position to affect the determination as to whether or not to purchase Units, if such party also bears any affiliation to the General Partner (other than through the ownership by the Limited Partner of Units purchased from the General Partner). The General Partner is not in a position to and makes no representations as to the existence or absence of such relationships.

POTENTIAL CONFLICTS IN OPERATION

If the General Partner is deemed to be a fiduciary or party in interest, the question arises as to whether the performance of the management duties and the receipt of the real estate commission by an Affiliate of the General Partner would violate the prohibited transaction rule against the direct or indirect furnishing of goods, services or facilities between Qualified Plans and parties of interest. Even assuming that the General Partner is a fiduciary, the General Partner believes that the rendition of those services should not violate the multiple services rule because it would not be exercising the powers that would make it a fiduciary to appoint affiliates to perform additional services. Rather, the General Partner believes that it and its Affiliates should be considered pre-appointed managers and the fees to be pre-established pursuant to the Offering documents, the appointment of and the payment of fees to the General Partner and its Affiliates are ratified by the named fiduciaries of the investing Qualified Plans through their decision to invest.

In addition, such services and fees should fall within the exceptions set forth at Section 408(c)(2) of ERISA and Section 4975(d)(10) of the Code, each of which exempt from the prohibited transaction rules the receipt of reasonable compensation for services rendered or for the reimbursement of expenses properly and actually incurred in the establishment or operation of Qualified Plans. Those exceptions also should prevent the payment to the General Partner of reimbursement of the expenses incurred by them in the organization and formation of the Partnership and the acquisition of the Property from being a violation of the prohibited transaction rule precluding the transfer of plan assets to a party in interest. However, no assurance can be given as to the applicability of those exceptions because they could be deemed to apply only to the payment for services and the reimbursement of expenses incurred in the administration of Qualified Plans as opposed to those incurred in connection with investments.

The status of the General Partner as a fiduciary of Qualified Plans that hold Units is discussed in detail under the section entitled "Plan Asset Rules" above. As to the status of the General Partner as a party in interest other than as a fiduciary, absent any pre-existing relationships between the investing Qualified Plans and the General Partner, the General Partner's status as a party in interest depends upon whether or not it is a "service provider" by virtue of the functions it perform as General Partner. Section 3(14)(B) of ERISA and Code Section 4975(e)(2)(B) each include within the definition of party in interest any person "providing services to the plan." There are no rulings determining whether the rendition of service of the nature of those to be performed by the General Partner make a person a service provider. However, ERISA is designed to be prophylactic in nature and the DOL has broadly construed the definition in its private rulings. Due to the lack of authority with respect to the issue, a definitive statement cannot be made as to whether the General Partner shall be a party in interest with respect to the Qualified Plans holding Units.

With respect to each of the potential conflicts of interest described above, the broad manner in which ERISA is drafted precludes the making of a definitive statement as to whether any such potential conflicts would be deemed to be violations of the prohibited transaction rules. If a violation of a prohibited transaction rule occurs, any person participating in such transaction could be subjected to prohibited transaction excise taxes under the Code. If a fiduciary participates in the violation, he/she can be held liable for any losses incurred by the Qualified Plan that are occasioned by the misconduct. For example, if a trustee of a Qualified Plan determines to invest in Units and knows or should know that the investment entails an inherent prohibited transaction, the trustee could be held personally accountable for all losses occasioned by the investment. Furthermore, all aspects of the activity comprising the violations could be required by the DOL to be reversed.

SUMMARY OF THE LIMITED PARTNERSHIP AGREEMENT

The rights and obligations of the General Partner and Limited Partners will be governed by the Partnership's LPA, which is set out in its entirety as Exhibit "B" this Memorandum". Prospective investors should study its provisions carefully before signing the Subscription Agreement, which is attached to this Memorandum as Exhibit "C." The following statement and other statements in this Memorandum concerning the Agreement are merely an outline and do not purport to be complete and in no way modify or amend the Agreement.

TERM

The Partnership was formed on [DATE]. If the Partnership has received completed subscriptions to and payments for QQ Units, the Partnership will admit such subscribers as Limited Partners at the time of the closing of the Offering.

The Partnership will be dissolved upon the:

1. Written consent of the General Partner and the Limited Partners holding at least 50% of all the Units;
2. Occurrence of an event specified under the laws of the State of Arizona as one effecting dissolution; or
3. Sale or other disposition of all or substantially all of the assets of the Partnership and the receipt in cash of all consideration therefor.

DISTRIBUTION UPON DISSOLUTION

Following the dissolution of the Partnership, any remaining assets will be liquidated by the General Partner and, after payment or making provision for payment of the liabilities of the Partnership and allocating all Income and Losses as provided in the Agreement, distributed among the Partners in accordance with the positive balance of the Partners' Capital Accounts. Thereafter, the Partnership will terminate, subject to any requirements necessary to effect the winding up and termination of the Partnership under applicable law.

NET CASH FLOW

The Net Cash Flow shall consist of all cash received by the Partnership from any source other than Major Capital Event Proceeds (as defined below) and, less the portion thereof used to pay (or establish reserves for) Partnership expenses and fees, including payments to the General Partner, principal and interest payments on Partnership debt, if any, capital improvements and contingencies, all as determined by the General Partner in its discretion. Distributions of Net Cash Flow shall be made in the following priority:

1. To the Limited Partners, pro rata, based on the number of Units owned by each Limited Partner, until each Limited Partner has received distributions equal to the Preferred Return on such amount of the Capital Contributions as is outstanding from time to time; and
2. Thereafter, 67% to the Limited Partners, *pro rata*, based on the number of Units owned by each Limited Partner, and 33% to the General Partner.

The Preferred Return will commence on the later of the date the Partnership closes on the purchase of the Property or the date each Limited Partner contributes capital to the Partnership.

MAJOR CAPITAL EVENT PROCEEDS

Major Capital Event Proceeds will consist of proceeds from the sale, exchange, transfer, condemnation, insurance claim, or refinance of the Property remaining after the payment of or the establishment of reserves for the payment of any indebtedness secured by the Property, costs of the refinancing or sale of the Property, and contingencies related to the sale of the Property. Distributions of Major Capital Event Proceeds shall be made in the following priority:

1. to the Limited Partners until the Limited Partners have received distributions equal to their Preferred Return not previously paid from Net Cash Flow;
2. next, to the Limited Partners until the Limited Partners have received distributions equal to their Capital Contributions; and
3. thereafter, 67% to the Limited Partners, *pro rata*, based on the number of Units owned by each Limited Partner, and 33% to the General Partner.

ALLOCATION OF INCOME AND LOSSES

Income will generally be allocated to the Limited Partner and General Partner to the extent of Losses previously allocated to the Limited Partner and General Partner, next to the Limited Partners in the amount of their Preferred Return, and thereafter 67% to the Limited Partners and 33% to the General Partner. Losses will generally be allocated to the Limited Partners and the General Partner to the extent of Income previously allocated to the Limited Partners or General Partner less any distributions associated with such Income, next to the Limited Partners to the extent their Capital Contributions exceed distributions associated with the Capital Contributions, next, to the Limited Partners and General Partner to the extent of the positive balances of their Capital Accounts, and thereafter, to the Limited Partners.

INTERESTS OF LIMITED PARTNERS

Limited Partners are required to make an initial cash contribution to the Partnership in the amount of $100,000 per Unit. No Limited Partner, in his/her capacity as such, will be personally liable for the obligations of the Partnership, but his/her capital in the Partnership is subject to normal risks of the Partnership business and the claims of its creditors. A Limited Partner may, however, be liable to the creditors of the Partnership for part or all of his/her *pro rata* share of the Capital Contributions that are returned to him/her by the Partnership if a creditor extends credit and has a claim that arose prior to the return of such capital.

RESTRICTIONS ON TRANSFERS

In the LPA, substantial restrictions are imposed on the transfer or assignment by a Limited Partner of a Unit in the Partnership. The General Partner must consent to any transfer. The General Partner will not approve any transfer that would cause the Partnership to terminate for federal income tax purposes or unless the transfer is in compliance with applicable securities laws.

MANAGEMENT

The General Partner will have exclusive discretion in the management and control of the business and affairs of the Partnership. In the LPA, Limited Partners grant the General Partner very broad authority in the exercise of the management and control of the Partnership. The General Partner will have full and complete power to do any and all things necessary or incident to the management and conduct of the Partnership's business subject to the Limited Partners' right to consent on limited matters set forth in the LPA.

RIGHTS OF THE LIMITED PARTNERS

The Limited Partners, as such, will not have the right to take part in the management or control of the business or affairs of the Partnership, to transact any business for the Partnership or to sign for or bind the Partnership.

Upon the requisite vote of the Limited Partners, the Limited Partners will have the right to: (i) amend the Agreement with the consent of the General Partner; (ii) dissolve the Partnership with the consent of the General Partner; and (iii) elect one or more new General Partners or continue the Partnership upon the occurrence of any event of withdrawal of the General Partner. Amendment of the LPA and certain other actions specified in the LPA requires the affirmative vote of the General Partner and the Limited Partners holding 67% of the Units, and the affirmative vote of the Limited Partners holding 50% of the Units is required to dissolve the Partnership or to appoint a new General Partner.

AMENDMENT OF THE PARTNERSHIP'S LPA

Subject to certain limitations, Limited Partners owning at least 67% of the Units may, with the consent of the General Partner, amend the LPA. Amendments to the LPA may be made by the General Partner without the vote of the Limited Partners so long as such amendments are of an inconsequential nature and do not adversely affect the Limited Partners in any material respect, are necessary or desirable to comply with any applicable law or governmental regulations, or are required or contemplated by the LPA.

BOOKS AND RECORDS

Under the LPA, the General Partner is required to furnish each Limited Partner with annual information necessary for tax purposes following the close of the Partnership's year and with quarterly reports. The General Partner is required to maintain at the principal office of the Partnership a copy of the Certificate of Limited Partnership and a copy of the LPA. The Limited Partners and their representatives also will be permitted limited access to records of the Partnership at reasonable times upon reasonable notice.

RESIGNATION AND REMOVAL OF THE GENERAL PARTNER

The General Partner may resign upon giving a 30-day notice to the Limited Partners. The General Partner may be removed upon occurrence of a Wrongful Act by the affirmative vote of Limited Partners holding a majority of the Units.

EXONERATION AND INDEMNIFICATION

Under the LPA, neither the General Partner or its Affiliates will be liable to the Partnership or any Limited Partner for any act or omission provided such act or omission did not constitute a Wrongful Act. The Partnership, its receiver or trustee shall, to the maximum extent provided by law, indemnify, defend, and hold harmless the General Partner and its Affiliates, including their members, officers, directors, shareholders, and affiliates, to the extent of the Partnership's assets, for, from, and against any liability, damage, cost, expense, loss, claim, or judgment incurred or arising out of or relating to any claim based upon acts performed or omitted to be performed by the General Partner in connection with the business of the Partnership, including, without limitation, attorneys' fees and costs incurred by the General Partner in settlement or defense of such claims. Notwithstanding the foregoing, the General Partner shall not be so indemnified, defended, or held harmless for claims based upon its acts or omissions that constitute a Wrongful Act. The Partnership is required to advance all amounts incurred by any or all of the General Partner and Affiliates, including their members, officers, directors, shareholders, and affiliates, in connection with any action or suit arising out of or in connection with Partnership affairs and, if judged to be liable of a Wrongful Act by the highest court to which an appeal is taken, the one or more such parties found to be liable shall reimburse the Partnership such amounts as required in the final judgment of liability.

MEDIATION

Under the Agreement and the Subscription Agreement, any dispute arising out of an investment in the Partnership must be submitted to mediation.

APPENDIX

The Agreement contains, and is required to contain, pursuant to the terms of the loan agreement for the indebtedness encumbering the Property, certain provisions relating to restrictions on the operations of activities of the Partnership. Specifically, without the approval of the lender, the Partnership may not, among other things, acquire or own any material assets other than the Property, merge into or consolidate with any other entity, or incur any debt except in the ordinary course of owning and operating the Property. See LPA Section 7.11.

GLOSSARY OF TERMS

As used in this Memorandum, the following terms will have the meanings described below:

"Acquisition Fee" means 2% of the purchase price of the Property to be paid to the General Partner or its Affiliates when the purchase of the Property is closed.

"Affiliate" of a particular Person means: (i) any other Person that, directly or indirectly, is in control of, is controlled by or is under common control with, such Person; (ii) any other Person who has the power to direct or cause the direction of, directly or indirectly, through ownership of voting rights, by contract, or through position or office of (A) such Person, (B) any subsidiary of such Person, or (C) any Person described in clause (i) above; or (iii) with respect to an individual, such member's family members.

"Agreement" means the Partnership's LPA substantially in the form attached as Exhibit "B" to this Memorandum, as originally executed and as amended from time to time.

"Capital Account" means an individual capital account that shall be maintained for each Partner in accordance with the requirements of Treasury Regulation §1.704-1(b)(2)(iv) or any successor regulatory or statutory provision.

"Capital Contribution(s)" means all sums contributed by Limited Partners to the capital of the Partnership in connection with the purchase of Units pursuant to the LPA.

"Code" means the Internal Revenue Code of 1986, as amended.

"Construction Management Fee" means 5% of the cost of the capital improvements made to the Property to be paid to Specialists, Inc., an Affiliate of Companies, for its services in overseeing and managing capital improvements.

"Disposition Fee" means 1% of the sale price to be paid to the General Partner or its Affiliates if and when the Property is sold.

"Due Diligence Fee" means the fee of $XYZ per unit (or $15,000) to be paid to Management, LLC, an Affiliate of the General Partner when the purchase of the Property closes for its due diligence services in evaluating the Property.

"General Partner" means ABC Investments, LLC, a Colorado limited liability company, or an entity controlled by the principals of the General Partner.

"Income" and "Losses" means for each year or other period, an amount equal to the Partnership's taxable income or loss for that year or period, determined in accordance with Code Section 703(a) (for this purpose, all items of income except gains from the sale of assets, gains, losses or deductions required to be stated separately pursuant to Code Section 703(a)(1) shall be included in taxable income or loss), with certain adjustments as required by Code Section 704 and the Regulation thereunder:

"IRS" means the Internal Revenue Service.

"Limited Partner" means any person that executes the Limited Partnership Agreement either personally or by a duly constituted attorney-in-fact as a Limited Partner, and any other person admitted to the Partnership as an additional or substituted Limited Partner and that has not made a transfer of such person's entire partnership interest. The term "Limited Partner" includes the General Partner in its capacity as a Limited Partner to the extent the General Partner acquires Units.

"Major Capital Event Proceeds" means proceeds from the sale, exchange, transfer, condemnation, insurance claim, or refinance of the Property remaining after the payment of or the establishment of reserves for the payment of any indebtedness secured by the Property, costs of the refinancing or sale of the Property, and contingencies related to the sale of the Property.

"Memorandum" means this Private Offering Memorandum effective as of [DATE], as supplemented or amended.

"Net Cash Flow" means the Partnership's net cash flow from ordinary operations, which consists of all cash received by the Partnership (other than Major Capital Event Proceeds), less any portion used to pay or establish reserves for Partnership expenses, fees, taxes, principal, and interest on Partnership debt, capital improvements, and contingencies.

"Offering" means the offering of Units of limited partnership interests made pursuant to this Memorandum.

"Partnership" means ABC Apartments, LP, a Colorado limited partnership.

"Person" means an individual, firm, partnership, corporation, estate, trust, pension plan, or other entity.

"Preferred Return" means the distributions to the Limited Partners of a X% per annum, cumulative, but not compounded, return on the unreturned portions of the Limited Partners' Capital Contributions as are outstanding from time to time. Each Limited Partner's Preferred Return shall commence on the later of the date the Partnership closes on the purchase of the Property or the date each Limited Partner contributes capital to the Partnership.

"Property" means the XYZ-unit, multifamily apartment complex on approximately ZZZZ acres located at 1234 Main Street, [CITY], [STATE], and known as the ABC Building, as further described in this Offering memorandum.

"Property Management Fee" means 5% of the monthly gross revenue of the Property to be paid to ZZZ, LLC, a property management company owned by Companies.

"Property Manager" means ZZZZZZZ, LLC, a property management company owned by Companies.

"Purchaser Questionnaire" means the purchaser questionnaire attached as Exhibit "D" to this Memorandum.

"Qualified Plans" means any qualified pension, profit sharing and stock bonus plans, or Keogh plan as described in Section 401 of the Code.

"Refinance Fee" means a fee equal to 1% of the amount of the loan for any refinance of the Property payable to the General Partner upon completion of any refinance of the Property.

"Regulations" means the Treasury Department regulations.

"Securities Act" means the Securities Act of 1933, as amended.

"Special Account" means the non-interest bearing account established in the Partnership's name in which the Partnership will deposit investors' Capital Contributions until subscription for all Units has been received and accepted.

"Subscription Agreement" means the Subscription Agreement substantially in the form of Exhibit "C" attached to this Memorandum pursuant to which a prospective Limited Partner subscribes for Units.

"Termination Date" means the Offering will terminate on the first to occur of the date the Partnership terminates the Offering or [DATE], provided that the date of termination may be extended by the General Partner with notice to all persons previously subscribing for Units.

"Unit" means a Limited Partner's interest in the Partnership requiring a total Capital Contribution of $100,000 for each Unit issued.

"Wrongful Act" means the non-appealable determination that the General Partner or a controlling principal of the General Partner committed in connection with its actions as the General Partner fraud, a criminal act of moral turpitude, intentional misapplication of funds, deceit, or willful misconduct.

ADDITIONAL INFORMATION

Potential investors may receive answers to questions relating to the Partnership's LPA, the Property, and the conditions of the Offering of the Units and obtain any other information available to the General Partner without unreasonable expense or burden at the offices of the General Partner. Unaudited financial statements of the General Partner may be reviewed at the offices of the General Partner.

THIS MEMORANDUM, THE BUSINESS PLAN AND ANY OTHER INFORMATION PROVIDED IN CONNECTION WITH THE SALE OF UNITS INCLUDES CERTAIN PROJECTIONS AND OTHER FORWARD-LOOKING INFORMATION WITH RESPECT TO THE PARTNERSHIP'S FUTURE PERFORMANCE. SUCH STATEMENTS ARE SUBJECT TO A NUMBER OF ESTIMATES AND ASSUMPTIONS WHICH ARE SUBJECT TO SIGNIFICANT BUSINESS, ECONOMIC, REGULATORY AND COMPETITIVE UNCERTAINTIES AND CONTINGENCIES. THE PARTNERSHIP'S ACTUAL RESULTS AND FUTURE DEVELOPMENT COULD DIFFER MATERIALLY FROM THE RESULTS EXPRESSED IN, OR IMPLIED BY, SUCH STATEMENTS. FACTORS THAT COULD CAUSE OR CONTRIBUTE TO SUCH DIFFERENCES INCLUDE, BUT ARE NOT LIMITED TO, THOSE DISCUSSED UNDER THE CAPTION "RISK FACTORS" AND ELSEWHERE IN THE MEMORANDUM. NO REPRESENTATIONS OR WARRANTIES ARE MADE AS TO THE ACCURACY OF SUCH FORWARD-LOOKING INFORMATION.

LEGAL COUNSEL

PQRS, Denver, Colorado, has advised the Partnership with respect to the Offering. Amos Smith, Denver, Colorado, has advised the Partnership with respect to its formation and the acquisition of the Property.

LIST OF EXHIBITS

Exhibit A	Certificate of Limited Partnership
Exhibit B	Limited Partnership Agreement
Exhibit C	Subscription Agreement
Exhibit D	Purchaser Questionnaire
Exhibit E	Business Plan

SAMPLE: LIMITED PARTNERSHIP AGREEMENT

LIMITED PARTNERSHIP AGREEMENT
OF
ABC APARTMENTS, LP

THIS LIMITED PARTNERSHIP AGREEMENT ("Agreement") is entered into effective as of the Xth day of YYY, 20XX ("Effective Date"), by and among ABC Investments, LLC, a Colorado limited liability company, as the general partner ("General Partner") and those individuals, trusts, corporations or other persons executing this Agreement as additional and/or substitute limited partners (hereinafter singularly referred to as a "Limited Partner" and collectively as "Limited Partners").

BACKGROUND INFORMATION

The General Partner and the Initial Limited Partner formed a limited partnership ("Partnership") for the single purpose of acquiring, owning, operating, selling and otherwise dealing with that certain multi-family apartment community more commonly known as "ABC Building" located 1234 Main Street, [CITY], [STATE]. Upon the closing of the sale of Units as described in the Memorandum, the Initial Limited Partner shall withdraw and all persons purchasing Units will be admitted as Limited Partners.

This Agreement sets forth the understanding between and among the parties with respect to the formation, capitalization, management and operation of the Partnership and the distribution of the profits, proceeds and/or losses that are incurred or received from the operation of the Partnership business.

AGREEMENT

The General and the Limited Partner do hereby form the Partnership pursuant to the Revised Uniform Limited Partnership Act, as enacted in the State of Colorado, C.R.S.§ _____, *et seq.*, as amended ("Act") and for their mutual convenience and protection, and in consideration of the mutual covenants and benefits herein contained, do hereby agree as follows:

ARTICLE I
NAME

The name of the Partnership shall be ABC APARTMENTS, LP.

ARTICLE II
PURPOSES OF THE PARTNERSHIP

2.01   General Purposes. The purpose of the Partnership is to acquire, own, operate, manage and/or sell that certain multi-family apartment community more commonly known as the "ABC Building" located at 1234 Main Street, [CITY], [STATE] ("Property") and to engage in any further business permitted under the Act and to have the power to take whatever action the General Partner deems necessary or appropriate in the furtherance of the Partnership's business. The Partnership, as Borrower, shall comply with the single asset requirements described in Section 4.02(d) of the Loan Agreement, until such time as the Indebtedness is paid in full.

2.02   Authority of the Partnership. The Partnership is authorized to engage in all business permitted by the Act. If the Partnership qualifies to do business in a foreign jurisdiction, then it may transact all business permitted in that jurisdiction. There is no jurisdictional restriction upon property or activity of the Partnership.

2.03   Limited Liability Partnership Status. In accordance with the provisions of C.R.S. § _____, *et seq.*, the parties hereby agree to elect to be a limited liability partnership and to file a statement of qualification with the office of the Colorado Secretary of State in the form required to properly elect such status.

ARTICLE III
DEFINITIONS

The following terms used in this Agreement shall (unless otherwise expressly provided herein or unless the context otherwise requires) have the following respective meanings. In the event of a conflict in the meaning of the terms defined herein and in the Deed of Trust, being one of the Loan Documents referenced herein, the definition in the Deed of Trust shall apply.

3.01   "Affiliate" of a particular Person means: (i) any other Person that, directly or indirectly, is in control of, is controlled by or is under common control with, such Person; (ii) any other Person who has the power to direct or cause the direction of, directly or indirectly, through ownership of voting rights, by contract, or through position or office, of (A) such Person, (B) any subsidiary of such Person, or (C) any Person described in clause (i) above; or (iii) with respect to an individual, such member's family members.

3.02   "Agreement" means this Limited Partnership Agreement, as amended from time to time.

3.03   "Assignee" mean a person who is assigned Units but who is not a substitute Limited Partner.

3.04   "Capital Account" means the account established and maintained for the General Partner and each Limited Partner, which shall be:

(i)   increased by (A) the aggregate amount of Capital Contributions made by the General Partner or Limited Partner, (B) such General Partner's or Limited Partner's share of Income or any item thereof, (C) the fair market value of Capital Contributions of property net of liabilities secured by such property that the Partnership is considered to assume or take subject to under IRC Section 752, and (D) the amount of any other upward adjustment to the General Partner's or Limited Partner's Capital Account required under Treasury Regulation Section 1.704-1(b); and

(ii)   decreased by (A) cash distributions to the General Partner or Limited Partner from the Partnership (other than in repayment of any loan or advance to the Partnership), (B) such General Partner's or Limited Partner's share of Losses or any item thereof, (C) the fair market value of property distributed to the General Partner or Limited Partner by the Partnership net of liabilities secured by such property that the General Partner or Limited Partner is considered to assume or take subject to under IRC Section 752, and (D) the amount of any other downward adjustment to the General Partner's or Limited Partner's Capital Account required under Treasury Regulation Section 1.704-1(b).

For purposes of computing the balance in a Capital Account, no credit shall be given for any Capital Contribution that the General Partner or Limited Partner is obligated to make until such contribution is actually made. Unless otherwise specified with respect to the transfer, any transferee of Units that is admitted as a Limited Partner shall succeed to the transferring Limited Partner's Capital Account in proportion to the Units transferred. Notwithstanding any other provision in this Agreement to the contrary, the Capital Accounts of the General Partner and Limited Partners shall be maintained in accordance with Treasury Regulation Section 1.704-1(b) and any successor thereto.

3.05 **"Capital Contribution"** means the total amount of money or other property contributed or agreed to be contributed to the Partnership by each Partner pursuant to the terms of this Agreement. The term shall not include loans or advances made to the Partnership by the General Partner or any Limited Partner. Any reference to a Capital Contribution of a Partner shall include the Capital Contribution made by a predecessor holder of the Units of such Partner.

3.06 **"Certificate"** means the certificate of limited partnership, as amended from time to time, which is required under the laws of the State of Colorado or such other state to be signed and acknowledged by the Partners of the Partnership and filed with the appropriate public office.

3.07 **"Code"** or **"IRC"** refers to the Internal Revenue Code of 1986, as amended from time to time.

3.08 **"Deed of Trust"** means the Multifamily Deed of Trust, Assignment of Leases and Rents, Security Agreement and Fixture Filing securing the Indebtedness.

3.09 **"General Partner"** means ABC Investments, LLC, a Colorado limited liability company, or to any other person or entity that succeeds it in such capacity.

3.10 **"Income"** and **"Losses"** shall be determined as of December 31 or any other year end of each fiscal year of the Partnership, and Income shall mean the items of income, gain, and credit, and Losses shall mean the items of expense, cost, amortization, and losses of the Partnership for federal income tax purposes as determined by the General Partner on the advice of the accountant who prepares the Partnership's federal income tax returns. "Income" shall include any item of income exempt from federal income taxation and "Losses" shall include any item of expenditures, charges, and losses described in IRC Section705(a)(2)(B) or treated as such under Treasury Regulation Section 1.704-1(b).

3.11 **"Indebtedness"** means the principal of, interest at the fixed rate set forth in the Note on, and all other amounts due at any time under, the Note, or any other Loan Document (including prepayment premiums, late charges, default interest, and advances) to protect the security of the Loan, as provided in the Deed of Trust.

3.12 **"Initial Limited Partner"** means an Affiliate of the General Partner who was the initial limited partner of the Partnership and who has withdrawn upon the closing of the sale of Units as described in the Memorandum and admission of the purchasers of such Units as Limited Partners.

3.13 **"Invested Capital"** means with respect to any Partner, as of a date of reference, the total amount of such Partner's Capital Contributions under **Article VI**, reduced (but not below zero) by the aggregate amount of any prior return of Capital Contributions to such Partner pursuant to **Section 8.02(B) (2)**.

3.14 **"Limited Partners"** means the Initial Limited Partner and to any other persons who are admitted to the Partnership as additional and/or substitute Limited Partners.

3.15 **"Loan Agreement"** means the Multifamily Loan and Security Agreement (Non-Recourse) evidencing the Indebtedness

3.16 **"Loan Documents"** means the Loan Agreement, Note, Deed of Trust and all other documents evidencing the Indebtedness.

3.17 **"Major Capital Event"** means: (i) the sale, exchange, or other transfer of the Property; (ii) the recovery of damage awards, condemnation awards, and insurance proceeds (other than business or rental interruption proceeds) related to the Property; or (iii) the refinance of the Property.

3.18 **"Major Capital Event Proceeds"** means the net cash proceeds received by the Partnership resulting from a Major Capital Event available after paying all ordinary and necessary operating and capital expenses and current amortization of any debt of the Partnership, and after establishing reserves to meet current or reasonably expected obligations of the Partnership and other purposes and uses of the Partnership to the extent the General Partner, in its sole and absolute discretion, determines that such reserves are necessary or advisable; provided, however, that Major Capital Event proceeds shall not include any cash if the distribution of such cash to the Limited Partners would be restricted or prohibited by any note, mortgage, deed of trust, or other agreement to which the Partnership is a party or by which the Partnership is bound.

3.19 **"Memorandum"** means the Partnership's Private Offering Memorandum dated [DATE] describing the offering of Units and terms of holding Units under this Agreement.

3.20 **"Minimum Gain"** has the meaning set forth in Treasury Regulation Section 1.704-2(d).

3.21 **"Mortgaged Property"** as the term applies to **Section 7.18**, Mortgaged Property shall have the meaning as set forth in the Deed of Trust.

3.22 **"Nonrecourse Debt"** has the meaning set forth in Section 1.704-2(b)(4) of the Treasury Regulations.

3.23 **"Nonrecourse Debt Minimum Gain"** means an amount with respect to each Nonrecourse Debt equal to the Minimum Gain that would result if such Nonrecourse Debt were treated as a nonrecourse liability, determined in accordance with Section 1.704-2(i)(3) of the Regulations.

3.24 **"Nonrecourse Deductions"** has the meaning set forth in Treasury Regulation Section 1.704-2(b).

3.25 **"Net Cash Flow"** means the excess of "Partnership Cash Receipts" over "Partnership Disbursements."

3.26 **"Note"** means the Multifamily Note as defined in the Deed of Trust, including all schedules, riders and addenda; as such Multifamily Note may be amended from time to time.

3.27 **"Partners"** means collectively the General Partner and to the Limited Partners, and reference to a "Partner" shall be to any one of the Partners.

3.28 **"Partnership"** means the limited partnership created under this Agreement.

3.29 **"Partnership Cash Receipts"** means, without limitation, all revenue received by the Partnership from whatever source, but excluding Major Capital Event proceeds.

3.30 **"Partnership Disbursements"** means:

A. operating expenses of the Partnership, including without limitation, wages, salaries, utilities, costs of repairs and maintenance, costs of inventory and supplies, rents, advertising, taxes, insurance premiums and all other expenses related to the operation of the Partnership business or incurred in connection with the production of Partnership income;

B. cost of acquisition of any real or personal property or any interest therein used by the Partnership;

C. the cost of improvements made to Partnership property;

D. the payment of amounts of principal and interest due on Partnership loans (including loans to the Partnership by any Partner) during the forthcoming one year period;

E. such reserve for future expenses as the General Partner reasonably deems necessary for current and future operations of the Partnership and current and future investment opportunities, all in keeping with the Partnership purposes set forth in **Section 2.01** hereof; and

F. such additional reserve in an amount not to exceed X percent (X%) of the Net Cash Flow of the Partnership each year determined without regard to this **Subsection**, as the General Partner may determine is necessary for the future expansion of Partnership business or investments. Such reserves may be built up for a period not to exceed five years and, thereafter, if such reserve is not expended or committed for expansion of Partnership business or properties, the reserve held pursuant to this **Subsection** shall be distributed to the Partners in the same percentages as Net Cash Flow is then being distributed. The reserve accumulated pursuant to this **Subsection** shall not be allowed to exceed $500,000.

3.31 **"Percentage Interest"** means, with respect to each Limited Partner and General Partner, the percentage set forth opposite that Limited Partner's or General Partner's name and Units on **Exhibit A**, as amended from time to time. All Percentage Interests of the Limited Partners are indivisible from the Units to which they relate. If a Limited Partner's Units are transferred pursuant to this Agreement, the person who acquires those Units shall succeed to the Percentage Interest to the extent the Percentage Interest relates to the transferred Units.

3.32 **"Person"** means any natural person, sole proprietorship, corporation, general partnership, limited partnership, limited liability company, limited liability limited partnership, joint venture, association, joint stock company, bank, trust, estate, unincorporated organization, any federal, state, county or municipal government (or any agency or political subdivision thereof), endowment fund or any other form of entity.

3.33 **"Preferred Return"** means the payment of a cumulative, non-compounded return on a Partner's Invested Capital equal to X Percent (X%) per annum, which shall commence upon the later of the acquisition of the Property or the issuance of Units as provided under **Section 6.02**.

3.34 **"Property Manager"** shall mean LMNO, LLC, a Colorado limited liability company.

3.35 **"Treasury Regulations"** means the Regulations issued by the Internal Revenue Service under the Code.

3.36 **"Units"** is described in **Section 6.01** hereof.

3.37 **"Wrongful Act"** means the determination by a nonappealable court or arbitration order, judgment, decree, or decision that the General Partner or a controlling principal of the General Partner committed in connection with its actions as the General Partner of the Partnership, fraud, a criminal act of moral turpitude, intentional misapplication of funds, deceit, or willful misconduct.

ARTICLE IV
TERM OF THE PARTNERSHIP

The Partnership shall commence as of the Effective Date, and shall continue until terminated by the provisions of this Agreement or as provided by law.

ARTICLE V
PARTNERSHIP BUSINESS; OFFICE; AGENT

The office of the Partnership shall be located at 1111 Elm Street, [CITY], [STATE], or at such other place or places as the General Partner may hereafter determine from time to time. The agent for service of process on the Partnership shall be Agent, 5678 North Drive, [CITY], [STATE].

ARTICLE VI
CAPITAL AND CONTRIBUTIONS

6.01   Partnership Capital. The capital of the Partnership shall consist of QQ interests, denominated in "Units."

6.02   Capital Contribution; Allocation of Units.

   A.   **By General Partner.** The General Partner shall contribute the assets and properties listed on **Exhibit A** at the agreed net value set forth on **Exhibit A**.

   B.   **Allocation of Units and Percentage Interests.** One (1) Unit shall be issued for each $100,000 Capital Contribution made by a Limited Partner. The General Partner and the Limited Partners shall be allocated the Percentage Interests as more particularly listed on **Exhibit A**.

   C.   **General Partner's Right to Admit Limited Partners and Revise Percentage Interests.** The General Partner will have the power and authority to admit Limited Partners to the Partnership and issue Units and Percentage Interests for those Capital Contributions until [DATE] ("Termination Date"). General Partner shall have the authority, from time to time, and upon written notice to the Limited Partners, to extend the expiration of the Termination Date, at the reasonable discretion of the General Partner, in order to sell all Units. General Partner shall have the unilateral right from time to time, until the Termination Date to revise **Exhibit A** to reflect the addition of new Limited Partners, their respective Capital Contributions, and the number of Units issued to and Percentage Interests allocated to each Limited Partner admitted.

6.03   Withdrawals. A Partner shall not be entitled to withdraw any part of his or her or its Capital Contribution or to receive any distributions from the Partnership except as provided in the Agreement and regardless of the nature of a Partner's contribution, no partner may demand or be entitled to receive a distribution from the Partnership in any form other than cash. A Limited Partner may withdraw from the Partnership in accordance with the provisions of Section _____ of the Act. Each Partner shall look only to the property of the Partnership for return of its Capital Contributions. If the Partnership's property remaining after satisfaction of its obligations is insufficient to return the Capital Contributions of any Partner, that Partner shall have no recourse against the Partnership or any Partner except in the case of gross negligence, bad faith or fraud. Except as otherwise provided in this Agreement, neither a Partner's capital account nor its Capital Contribution shall earn interest.

6.04   Additional Capital Contributions. No additional Capital Contributions of the Partners shall be required.

6.05   Terms of Loans. Any Partner loans to the Partnership shall bear interest at two points above the General Partner's cost of funds, shall be unsecured, and shall be repaid in full out of available funds of the Partnership before any distribution may be made to any Partners. If more than one Partner has made a loan, then, in that event, repayments shall be made in the order said loans were advanced (*i.e.*, the oldest loan balance shall be paid first) according to the ratio of principle amounts advanced by said Partner.

6.06   No Third Party Beneficiary. No creditor or other third party having dealings with the Partnership shall have the right to enforce the right or obligation of any Partner to make Capital Contributions or to pursue any other right or remedy hereunder or at law or in equity, it being understood and agreed that the provisions of this Agreement shall be solely for the benefit of, and may be enforced solely by, the parties hereto and their respective successors and assigns. None of the rights or obligations of the Partners set forth in this Agreement to make Capital Contributions to the Partnership shall be deemed an asset of the Partnership for any purpose by any creditor or other third party, nor may such rights or obligations be sold, transferred or assigned by the Partnership or pledged or encumbered by the Partnership to secure any debt or other obligation of the Partnership or of any of the Partners.

ARTICLE VII
RIGHTS, POWERS AND LIMITATIONS
OF THE GENERAL PARTNER

7.01   Authority of General Partner. The General Partner shall have exclusive authority to manage the operation and affairs of the Partnership and to make all decisions regarding the business of the Partnership. It is understood and agreed that the General Partner shall have all the rights and powers of a general partner as provided in the Act and, except as may otherwise be provided by law, any action taken by the General Partner shall constitute the act of and serve to bind the Partnership. In dealing with the General Partner, acting on behalf of the Partnership, no person shall be required to inquire into its authority to bind the Partnership. Persons dealing with the Partnership are entitled to rely exclusively on the power and authority of the General Partner as set forth in this Agreement.

7.02   Specific Powers. The General Partner is hereby granted the right, power and authority to do, on behalf of the Partnership, all things that it in its sole judgment deems necessary, proper or desirable to carry out the aforementioned duties and responsibilities; including, by way of illustration only and not by way of limitation, the right, power and authority:

A.   to take all actions with respect to the Property, including all actions related to the acquisition, operations, management, maintenance, financing, sale, exchange, or other disposition of the Property;

B.   to borrow money on behalf of the Partnership and, in connection with such borrowing, to pledge, hypothecate, encumber and grant security interests in the Partnership's property (including the Property) to secure repayment thereof, including but not limited to, any acquisition loan, modifications of Partnership financing, any financing or assumption documentation for existing financing for the purpose of acquiring the Partnership and any subsequent financing or refinancing thereof in connection with the Property, all upon such terms and conditions as General Partner, in its sole discretion, shall determine reasonable under the circumstances;

C.   to manage the Partnership's cash assets (including short-term investments thereof);

D.   to execute on behalf of the Partnership all instruments and documents that the General Partner reasonably believes are necessary to accomplish the purposes of the Partnership;

E.   to select, engage, and supervise, on behalf of the Partnership, all employees, agents, architects, engineers, attorneys, accountants, managers, consultants or other persons, including the General Partner or its Affiliates, as the General Partner, in its reasonable discretion, deems appropriate in connection with the conduct, operation and management of the Partnership's business and for the performance of its legal and accounting requirements, all on such terms and for such compensation as the General Partner, in its reasonable discretion, deems proper, provided that any compensation that is not specifically designated by this Agreement to be paid to the General Partner or an Affiliate shall be consistent with the fair market value of such services;

F.   to file on behalf of the Partnership any tax returns or execute any other agreements or documents in connection with tax matters affecting the Partnership that the General Partner deems necessary, and make any elections permitted under the IRC or other applicable tax law that the General Partner, in its sole discretion, deem appropriate; and

G.   to do and perform all other acts as may be necessary or appropriate to accomplish the purposes of the Partnership.

7.03   Quarterly Report. The General Partner shall provide all Partners, on a quarterly basis, with a report identifying the current condition of all Property leases and the current budget for the Property.

7.04   Consent of the Partners. In addition to those actions for which this Agreement specifically requires the vote of the Partners, the Partnership shall not take any of the following actions without first obtaining the affirmative vote of Limited Partners holding sixty seven percent (67%) of the Units outstanding:

A.   approve a plan of merger or consolidation of the Partnership with or into one or more business entities;

B.   engage in any business other than owning, operating, and selling the Partnership's assets;

C.   increase the compensation of any General Partner or any affiliates of the General Partner or its principals;

D.   assign, transfer or pledge any debts due the Partnership for amounts in excess of $250,000 or release any debts due in amounts in excess of $250,000, except in payment in full;

E.   compromise any claim due the Partnership for amounts in excess of $250,000 or submit to mediation, arbitration or any other jurisdiction any dispute or controversy involving the Partnership for amounts in excess of $250,000; or

F.   confess a judgment for amounts in excess of $250,000 against the Partnership or its assets.

7.05   Reports. On or before April 1st of each calendar year, the General Partner shall provide all Partners, with complete financial statements of the Partnership for the preceding fiscal year.

7.06   Non-Exclusivity. The General Partner shall devote as much time as is reasonably required to carry out the Partnership's business, but shall not necessarily be required to work on Partnership matters on a full-time basis.

7.07   Resignation. A General Partner may resign as a General Partner at any time by giving at least thirty (30) days written notice to all the Partners.

7.08   Removal of General Partner. The General Partner may be removed by the affirmative vote of Limited Partners holding a majority of the Units upon the occurrence of a Wrongful Act.

7.09   Replacement of General Partner. If a General Partner resigns or is removed, a new General Partner shall be appointed by the affirmative vote of Limited Partners holding a majority of the Units outstanding.

7.10   Fiduciary Duty. The Partner agrees that each Partner shall be accountable to the Partner and the Partnership, and shall have the same duties of care and loyalty that Colorado law imposes on general partners in a partnership.

7.11   Non-Exclusivity. The Partners hereby acknowledge and agree that each Partner may engage in any other business or investment activity. No Partner shall, solely by virtue of this Agreement or its relationship to the Partnership or the Partners, be liable or accountable to the Partnership or any Partner for failure to disclose or make available to the Partnership any business opportunity of which it becomes aware or be obligated to allow the Partnership or any Partner to share or participate in any such other investments.

7.12   Separateness/Operations Matters. In the event that the activities described below are inconsistent with **Section 7.18**, or to the extent that the activities conflict with **Section 7.18**, the meanings in **Section 7.18** shall apply until such time as the Indebtedness referenced herein is paid in full. The Partnership has not and shall not:

A. acquire or own any material assets other than: (i) the Property; and (ii) such incidental personal property as may be necessary for the operation of the Partnership;

B. merge into or consolidate with any person or entity or dissolve, terminate or liquidate in whole or in part, transfer or otherwise dispose of all or substantially all of its assets or change its legal structure, without in each case obtaining the consent of the Property acquisition loan lender;

C. fail to preserve its existence as an entity duly organized, validly existing and in good standing under the laws of the State of Colorado, or without the prior written consent of lenders, amend, modify, terminate or fail to comply with the provisions of this Agreement, as same may be further amended or supplemented, if such amendment, modification, termination or failure to comply would adversely affect the ability of the Partnership to perform its obligations under the applicable loan documents;

D. own any subsidiary or make any investment in, any person or entity without the consent of lenders;

E. commingle its assets with the assets of any of its affiliates, principals or of any other person or entity;

F. incur any debt, secured or unsecured, direct or contingent (including guaranteeing any obligation), except in the ordinary course of its business of owning and operating the Property, provided that such debt is paid when due;

G. become insolvent or fail to pay its debts and liabilities from its assets as the same shall become due;

H. fail to maintain its records, books of account and bank accounts separate and apart from those of the Partners, principals and affiliates of the Partnership, the affiliates of a Partner, and any other person or entity;

I. except as otherwise expressly permitted herein, enter into any contract or agreement with any Partner or affiliate of the Partnership, any guarantor or indemnitor, or any affiliate thereof, except upon terms and conditions that are intrinsically fair and substantially similar to those that would be available on an arms-length basis with third parties other than any Partner or affiliate of the Partnership, any guarantor or indemnitor, or any affiliate thereof;

J. seek the dissolution or winding up in whole, or in part, of the Partnership;

K. maintain its assets in such a manner that it will be costly or difficult to segregate, ascertain or identify its individual assets from those of any, Partner or affiliate of the Partnership, or any other person;

L. hold itself out to be responsible for the debts of another person or entity;

M. make any loans or advances to any third party, including any Partner, or affiliate of the Partnership;

N. fail to file its own tax returns;

O. agree to, enter into or consummate any transaction that would render the Partnership unable to furnish a certification that: (i) the Partnership is not an "employee benefit plan" as defined in Section 3(3) of ERISA, which is subject to Title I of ERISA, or a "governmental plan" within the meaning of Section 3(32) of ERISA; (ii) mortgagor is not subject to state statutes regulating investments and fiduciary obligations with respect to governmental plans; and (iii) one or more of the following circumstances is true: (a) equity interests in the Partnership are publicly offered securities, within the meaning of 29 C.F.R. Section 2510.3-101(b)(2), (b) less than 25% of each outstanding class of equity interests in the Partnership are held by "benefit plan investors" within the meaning of 29 C.F.R. Section 2510.3-101(f)(2), or (c) the Partnership qualifies as an "operating company" or a "real estate operating company" within the meaning of 29 C.F.R. Section 2510.3-101(c) or (e) or an investment company registered under The Investment Company Act of 1940;

P. fail either to hold itself out to the public as a legal entity separate and distinct from any other entity or person or to conduct its business solely in its own name in order not: (i) to mislead others as to the identity with which such other party is transacting business, or (ii) to suggest that any mortgagor is responsible for the debts of any third party (including any Partner, or affiliate of the Partnership);

Q. fail to maintain adequate capital for the normal obligations reasonably foreseeable in a business of its size and character and in light of its contemplated business operations; or

R. file or consent to the filing of any petition, either voluntary or involuntary, to take advantage of any applicable insolvency, bankruptcy, liquidation or reorganization statute, or make an assignment for the benefit of creditors.

7.13   Auditor. If the Partners determine by a majority vote of the Partners that it is necessary for an independent third party to audit and review the Partnership's financial books and records, then the Partners shall select the accounting firm designated by the General Partner.

7.14   Fees and Compensation to General Partner. Each Partner acknowledges and consents to the following fees to be paid to General Partner and/or its Affiliates:

A. Acquisition fee totaling Two Percent (2%) of the acquisition price of the Property will be paid to ABC Advisors, an Affiliate of the General Partner. In consideration for this fee, ABC Advisers, LLC will do the following: negotiate any letters of intent; deposit its own non-refundable at-risk funds into escrow; apply for the loan to the Partnership; use ABC Advisers, LLC's and its principals' financial strength to qualify for financing; coordinate and manage the closing process; coordinate all legal work; organize and oversee the close of escrow; and, manage all investor equity.

B. The operation of the residential apartment complex situated on the Property may be managed by an independent property management firm or an affiliate of General Partner, which will also generate reports and remit operating returns for Partners, for a fee equal to an amount not greater than Five Percent (5%) of the monthly gross income from the Property.

C. A disposition fee equal to One Percent (1%) of the sale price for the Property shall be paid to General Partner at the closing of any future sale thereof as reasonable compensation for its negotiation of any letter of intent and purchase agreement to sell the Property, and conducting and coordinating due diligence in connection therewith.

D. A refinancing fee equal to One Percent (1%) of the amount of any refinanced loan on the Property shall be paid to General Partner at the closing of any refinancing as reasonable compensation for its negotiation of loan terms, delivering carve-out guarantees, and coordinating all due diligence in connection therewith.

E. A due diligence fee equal to $X ($Y per Property unit) for service in evaluating the property payable at the closing of the purchase of the Property.

F. A construction management fee equal to Five Percent (5%) of the cost of any capital improvement made to the Property for service related to overseeing and managing the capital improvements.

7.15   Limitation of Liability. The General Partner shall not be liable, responsible or accountable in damages or otherwise to the Partnership or any Limited Partner for any action taken or failure to act by it on behalf of the Partnership within the scope of the authority conferred on the General Partner by this Agreement or by law unless such action or omission was performed or omitted fraudulently or in bad faith or constituted wanton or willful misconduct to gross negligence. The Partnership shall indemnify and hold harmless the General Partner and its agents and employees from and against any loss, expense, damage or injury suffered or sustained by it by reason of or in furtherance of the interest of the Partnership, including but not limited to any judgment, award, settlement, reasonable attorney's fees and other costs or expenses incurred in connection with the defense of any action or threatened action, proceeding or claim, provided that the acts, omissions, or alleged acts or omissions upon which such action or threatened action, proceedings or claims are based were in good faith and were not performed or omitted fraudulently or in bad faith or as a result of wanton and willful misconduct or gross negligence by such party.

7.16   Limitations of Limited Partners. The Limited Partners shall, in their capacities as such, in no event: (i) be permitted to take part in the control of the business or affairs of the Partnership; (ii) have any voice in the management or affairs of the Partnership; or (iii) have the authority or power to act as agent for or on behalf of the Partnership or any other Partner or to do any act that would be binding on the Partnership or any other Partner or to incur any expenditures with respect to the Partnership or its assets.

7.17   Liability of Limited Partner. Notwithstanding anything in the Agreement to the contrary, the liability of each of the Limited Partners for the losses of the Partnership shall in no event exceed the aggregate amount of their Capital Contributions and/or the amount of capital credited to him or her pursuant to **Section 6.03** and, in no circumstances, shall the Limited Partners be required to make additional contributions to the capital of the Partnership for the purpose of restoring a negative balance in a capital account, or for any other purpose whatsoever.

7.18   Mortgage Loan Requirements. Notwithstanding anything herein to the contrary, the purpose of the Partnership shall be solely to engage in owning, operating, and managing the Property; and further, the Partnership shall hold no material assets other than the Property, have no material debt other than a loan ("Loan") with Wells Fargo, in the approximate amount of $7,000,000.

7.19   Indemnification and Exoneration. Neither the General Partner nor its Affiliates, including their partners, members officers, directors, shareholders and affiliates, will be liable to the Partnership or any Limited Partner for any act or omission provided such act or omission did not constitute a Wrongful Act. The Partnership, its receiver or trustee shall, to the maximum extent provided by law, indemnify, defend and hold harmless the General Partner and its Affiliates, including their partners, members officers, directors, shareholders and affiliates, to the extent of the Partnership's assets, for, from and against any liability, damage, cost, expense, loss, claim or judgment incurred or arising out of or relating to any claim based upon acts performed or omitted to be performed by the General Partner in connection with the business of the Partnership, including, without limitation, attorneys' fees and costs incurred by the General Partner in settlement or defense of such claims. Notwithstanding the foregoing, the General Partner shall not be so indemnified, defended or held harmless for claims based upon a Wrongful Act. The Partnership shall pay in advance of any determination all amounts incurred by any or all of the General Partner and its Affiliates, including their partners, members, officers, directors, shareholders, or other affiliates, in connection with any action or suit arising out of or in connection with Partnership affairs and, if judged to be liable for a Wrongful Act by the highest court to which an appeal is taken, the one or more such parties found to be liable for a Wrongful Act shall reimburse the Partnership for amounts advanced as determined in the final judgment of liability.

APPENDIX

ARTICLE VIII
INCOME, LOSSES; CASH FLOW
DISTRIBUTIONS; CAPITAL TRANSACTIONS

8.01　**Income and Losses**. Subject to **Section 8.04,**

A.　Income and items thereof shall be allocated:
1.　first, to the Limited Partners in the amount of cumulative Losses allocated to the Limited Partners under **Section 8.01(B)(5)**;
2.　next, to the Limited Partners and the General Partner in the amount of cumulative Losses allocated to the Limited Partners and the General Partner under **Section 8.01(B) (4)**;
3.　next, to the Limited Partners in the amount of cumulative Losses allocated to the Limited Partners under **Section 8.01(B)(3)**;
4.　next, to the Limited Partners in the amount of the cumulative accrued Preferred Return; and
5.　thereafter, to the Limited Partners and the General Partner in accordance with the Percentage Interests.

B.　Losses and items thereof shall be allocated:
1.　first, to the Limited Partners and the General Partner in the cumulative amount of Income allocated to the Limited Partners and the Manger under **Section 8.01(A)(5)**, less cumulative distributions made to the Limited Partners and the General Partner under **Sections 8.02(A)(2) and 8.02(B)(3)**;
2.　next, to the Limited Partners in the cumulative amount of Income allocated to the Limited Partners under **Section 8.01(A)(4)**, less cumulative distributions made to the Limited Partners under **Sections 8.02(A)(1) and 8.02(B)(1)**;
3.　Next, to the Limited Partners in the cumulative amount Capital Contributions made by the Limited Partners, less cumulative distributions made to the Limited Partners under **Section 8.02(B)(2)**;
4.　next, to the Limited Partners and the General Partner in the cumulative amount of the positive balances of the Capital Accounts, if any, of the Limited Partners and General Partner, in proportion to such positive balances; and
5.　thereafter, to the Limited Partners.

C.　Income allocated under **Sections 8.01(A)(1), (2), and (3)** shall, to the extent possible, be of the same type and character of Losses allocated under **Sections 8.01(B)(4) and (5), and 8.01(A)(3)**, respectively, and Losses allocated under **Sections 8.01(B)(1) and (2)** shall, to the extent possible, be of the same type and character of Income allocated under **Sections 8.01(A)(4) and (5)**, respectively.

D.　The provisions of this **Section 8.01**, together with **Section 8.04**, are intended: (i) to produce Capital Account balances that will permit the liquidation distributions made in accordance with **Section 12.02(C)** below to be made in a manner identical to the distributions to be made in accordance with **Section 8.02**; and (ii) comply with the requirements to cause indebtedness incurred by the Partnership to not be treated as acquisition indebtedness under IRC Section 514(c)(9). To the extent that any allocations of Income or Losses are required to be modified to give effect to such intent, the provisions of **Section 8.01** shall be modified to the least extent necessary to cause such intent to be given full effect and to cause such allocations to have substantial economic effect under IRC Section 704(b) and to comply with IRC Section 514(c)(9).

8.02   **Distributions.**

A.   Distributions of Net Cash Flow shall be made as follows:
   1.   first, to the Limited Partners, in the cumulative amount of the Preferred Return due to the Limited Partners; and
   2.   thereafter, to the Limited Partners and General Partner in accordance with their Percentage Interests.

B.   Except upon dissolution and winding up of the Partnership, distributions of Major Capital Event Proceeds shall be made as follows:
   1.   first, to the Limited Partners, in the cumulative amount of the Preferred Return due to the Limited Partners;
   2.   next, to the Limited Partners in the amount of the unreturned Invested Capital of the Limited Partners; and
   3.   thereafter, to the Limited Partners and General Partner in accordance with their Percentage Interests.

8.03   **Allocations and Distributions among Limited Partners.** Allocations of Income and Losses and distributions of Net Cash Flow and Major Capital Event Proceeds shall be allocated and distributed among the Limited Partners pro rata in accordance with the Units held by the Limited Partners.

8.04   **Compliance with Allocation Requirements of the Code.**

A.   Allocations of book and tax items with respect to property contributed by any Partner or distributions or revaluations of Partnership property shall be made solely for federal income tax purposes as required by IRC Section 704(c) and the applicable Treasury Regulations thereunder including Treasury Regulation Section 1.704-1(b)(2)(iv).

B.   Except as otherwise provided in Section 1.704-2(f), if there is a net decrease in Minimum Gain during any fiscal year of the Partnership, and if a Limited Partner would otherwise have a deficit in its Capital Account at the end of such year, the Limited Partner shall be specially allocated items of Income for such year (and, if necessary, subsequent years) in an amount and manner sufficient to eliminate such deficit as quickly as possible. The items to be so allocated shall be determined in accordance with Treasury Regulation Section 1.704-2. This **Section 8.04(B)** is intended to comply with the minimum gain chargeback requirement of Treasury Regulation Section 1.704-2(f) and shall be interpreted consistently therewith.

C.   Except as otherwise provided in Treasury Regulation Section 1.704-2(i)(4), if there is a net decrease in Nonrecourse Debt Minimum Gain attributable to a Nonrecourse Debt during any taxable year, each Limited Partner who has a share of the Nonrecourse Debt Minimum Gain attributable to such Nonrecourse Debt, determined in accordance with Treasury Regulation Section 1.704-2(i)(5), shall be specially allocated items of Partnership income and gain for such taxable year (and, if necessary, subsequent taxable years) in an amount equal to such Limited Partner's share of the net decrease in Nonrecourse Debt Minimum Gain attributable to such Nonrecourse Debt, determined in accordance with Treasury Regulation Section 1.704-2(i)(4). Allocations pursuant to the previous sentence shall be made in proportion to the respective amounts required to be allocated to each Limited Partner under this **Section 8.04(C)**. The items to be so allocated shall be determined in accordance with Treasury Regulation Sections 1.704-2(i)(4) and 1.704-2(j)(2). This **Section 8.04(C)** is intended to comply with the minimum gain chargeback requirement in Section 1.704-2(i)(4) of the Treasury Regulations and shall be interpreted consistently therewith.

D. In the event a Limited Partner unexpectedly receives any adjustments, allocations, or distributions described in Treasury Regulations Sections 1.704-1(b)(2)(ii)(d)(4), 1.704-1(b)(2)(ii)(d)(5), or 1.704-1(b)(2)(ii)(d)(6), items of Income shall be specially allocated to such Limited Partner in an amount and manner sufficient to eliminate, to the extent required by the Treasury Regulations, the deficit of such Limited Partner's Capital Account as quickly as possible, provided that an allocation pursuant to this **Section 8.04(D)** shall be made only if and to the extent that the Limited Partner would have a deficit in its Capital Account after all other allocations provided for in this Agreement have been tentatively made.

E. Except as provided in the following sentence, Nonrecourse Deductions shall be allocated to the Limited Partners as items of Income or Losses as provided in **Section 8.01**. Nonrecourse Deductions for which any Limited Partner bears the economic risk of loss as provided in Treasury Regulation Section 1.704-2(i) shall be allocated to such Limited Partner as provided in such Treasury Regulation.

F. Any allocations of items of Income or Losses pursuant to **Section 8.04(A) (B), (C), or (D)** shall be in the order as provided in the Treasury Regulations promulgated under IRC Section 704(b) and shall be taken into account in computing subsequent allocations of Income or Losses pursuant to **Section 8.01** so that the net amounts of the allocations under this **Section 8.04** shall, to the maximum extent possible, be equal to the net amounts that would have been allocated pursuant to **Section 8.01** if there had been no allocations pursuant to **Section 8.04(A), (B), (C), or (D)**.

G. Notwithstanding anything to the contrary in this Agreement, no Limited Partner shall be allocated any item of Losses under this Agreement if such allocation would not have economic effect or otherwise be recognized under the Treasury Regulations promulgated under IRC Section 704(b) or any successor thereto. Any such item of Losses shall instead be allocated solely to other Partners in a manner having economic effect or otherwise being allowed under IRC Section 704(b). Income otherwise allocable to the Partners under this Agreement from any source, except for allocations required under **Section 8.04(A), (B), (C), or (D)**, shall first be allocated to the Partners receiving such allocations of Losses to the extent and in the proportion that Losses from that source have been reallocated to the such Partners pursuant to this **Section 8.04(G)**.

8.05 **Withholding Obligations.**

A. The Partnership shall comply with all applicable federal, state, local, or foreign withholding tax obligations, as the same may change from time to time under applicable law. In all cases, the Partnership shall withhold from distributions payable to a Limited Partner and pay over such amounts to the appropriate taxing agency the amount as required under applicable law as determined by the General Partner in its sole discretion.

B. To the extent the Partnership fails to comply with any withholding obligation under this **Section 8.05** as a result of a Limited Partner's false certification or failure to affirmatively notify the General Partner of such Limited Partner's status, all taxes, penalties, and interest (and all related attorneys' fees and costs) shall be borne by and paid by such Limited Partner.

C. Except as otherwise provided in this **Section 8.05**, any amount withheld by the Partnership with respect to a Limited Partner shall be treated for purposes of this Agreement as an amount actually distributed to such Limited Partner pursuant to **Section 8.02**. An amount shall be considered withheld by the Partnership if and at the time such amount is remitted to a governmental agency without regard to whether such remittance occurs at the same time as the distribution or allocation to which it relates; provided, however, that an amount withheld from a specific distribution or designated by the General Partner as withheld with respect to a specific allocation shall be treated as distributed at the time such distribution or allocation occurs.

    D.   In the event that the General Partner determines in its reasonable discretion that the Partnership lacks sufficient cash available to pay withholding taxes with respect to any Limited Partner, the General Partner may require that an amount equal to such taxes with respect to a Limited Partner be paid promptly to the Partnership, by such Limited Partner.

    E.   Taxes withheld by third parties from payments to the Partnership shall be treated as if withheld by the Partnership for purposes of this **Section 8.05**. In the event that the Partnership receives a refund of taxes previously withheld by a third party from one or more payments to the Partnership, the economic benefit of such refund shall be apportioned to each Limited Partner to which such refund is directly attributable in a manner reasonably determined by the General Partner to offset the prior operation of this **Section 8.05** with respect to such withheld taxes.

8.06   **Withholding Distributions for Business Needs.** Notwithstanding anything to the contrary in **Section 8.02**, if the General Partner so elects, distributions of Net Cash Flow may be withheld if General Partner in the exercise of its reasonable business judgment, and with due deference to its duty of the care and loyalty to the Partnership and the Partners, determines that all or any portion of such funds are reasonably necessary to accomplish the business purposes of the Partnership as set forth in **Section 2.01**.

ARTICLE IX
STATUS OF LIMITED PARTNERS

9.01   **Limited Liability.** A Limited Partner shall not be bound by or be personally liable for, the expenses, liabilities or obligations of the Partnership except to the extent of his, her or its total contributions to Partnership capital.

9.02   **No Voice in Management.** A Limited Partner shall take no part in, or interfere in any manner with, the conduct or control of the business affairs of the Partnership, and shall have no right or authority to act for or the bind the Partnership or to incur expenditures with respect to the Partnership or its properties.

9.03   **Fully Paid and Nonassessable.** Each Unit owned by Limited Partner shall be fully paid and nonassessable.

9.04   **Partitions.** No Limited Partner shall have the right to bring an action for partition against the Partnership. Except as otherwise specifically set forth in this Agreement, no Partner shall have priority over any other Partner, either as to the return of Capital Contribution or distributions or allocations of profit, losses, deductions, credits or allowances.

9.05   **Meetings of Partners.** Meetings of the Partners may be called by the General Partner and shall be called by the General Partner at the request of Limited Partners holding at least twenty-five percent (25%) of all Units held by Limited Partners. Notice of such meeting shall be given by the General Partner within ten (10) days after receipt of such request. Such request shall state the purpose of the proposed meeting and the matters proposed to be acted upon thereat. Such meeting shall be held at the principal office of the Partnership or at such other place, inside or outside the State of Colorado, as may be designated by the General Partner. Each Partner shall be entitled to one vote times his, her or its Units. Partners shall vote as one class on all matters on which the Partners are entitled to vote. A notice of any such meeting shall be given personally or by mail, not less than five days or more than 60 days before the date of the meeting, to each Limited Partner at his, her or its record address or at such address that may have furnished in writing to the General Partner. Such notice shall be in writing, shall state the place, date and hour of the meeting and shall indicate that it is being issued at or by the direction of the Partner or Partners calling the meeting. If a meeting is adjourned to another time or place, and if any announcement of the adjournment of time or place is made at the meeting, it shall not be necessary to give notice of the adjourned meeting. The presence in person or by proxy of an agent of the General Partner and Limited Partners holding at least fifty percent (50%) of the number of Units then held by the Limited Partners shall constitute a quorum at all meetings of the Limited Partners; provided, however, that if there be no such quorum, the agent of the General Partner and the holders of a majority in interest of such Limited Partners so present or so represented may be adjourn the meeting from time to time without further notice until a quorum shall have been obtained. No notice of the time, place, or purpose of any meeting of Limited Partners need be given to any Limited Partner who attends in person or is represented by proxy (except when the Limited Partner attends a meeting for the express purpose of objecting at the beginning of the meeting to the transaction of any business on the grounds that the meeting is not lawfully called or convened), or to any Limited Partner entitled to such notice who, in writing, executed and filed with the records of the meeting either before or after the time thereof, waives such notice. A Partner or his, her or its proxy may attend a meeting by telephonic means. Every proxy shall be revocable at the pleasure of the Limited Partner executing it. At each meeting of Limited Partners, the General Partner and the Limited Partners present or represented by proxy shall adopt such rules for the conduct of such meeting as they shall deem appropriate.

9.06 Waiver of Notice. When any notice is required to be given to any Partner, a waiver thereof in writing signed by the person entitled to such notice, whether before, at, or after the time stated herein, shall be equivalent to the giving of such notice.

9.07 Proxies. At all meetings of Partners, a Partner may vote in person or by proxy executed in writing by the Partner or by a duly authorized attorney-in-fact. Such proxy shall be filed with one or more other Partners before or at the time of the meeting. No proxy shall be valid after 11 months from the date of its execution, unless otherwise provided in the proxy.

9.08 Action by Partners without a Meeting. Any action required or permitted to be taken at a meeting of Partners may be taken without a meeting if the actions evidenced by one or more written consents describing the action taken, signed by the Partners owning the requisite Units necessary to adopt and approve the action as provided herein, and delivered to one or more other Partners for inclusion in the minutes or for filing with the Partnership records. The record date for determining Partners entitled to take action without a meeting shall be the date the first Partner signs a written consent.

9.09 Confidentiality. The Partners acknowledge that from time to time they may receive information from or regarding the Partnership in the nature of trade secrets or that otherwise is confidential, the release of which may be damaging to the Partnership or persons with which it does business. Each Partner shall hold in strict confidence any information he, she, or it receives regarding the Partnership that is identified as being confidential (and if that information is provided in writing, that is so marked) and may not disclose it to any person other than another Partner except for disclosures: (i) compelled by law (but the Partner must notify the General Partner promptly of any request for that information, before disclosing it, if practicable); (ii) to advisers or representatives of the Partners, but only if the recipients have agreed to be bound by the provisions of this **Section**; or (iii) of information that Partner also has received from a source independent of the Partnership that the Partner reasonably believes obtained that information without breach of any obligation of confidentiality. The Partners acknowledge that breach of the provisions of this **Section** may cause irreparable injury to the Partnership for which monetary damages are inadequate, difficult to compute, or both. Accordingly, the Partners agree that the provisions of this **Section** may be enforced by specific performance, injunction or other appropriate equitable relief.

ARTICLE X
WITHDRAWAL, DEATH, BANKRUPTCY, RECEIVERSHIP OR INCOMPETENCY OF GENERAL PARTNER; ASSIGNMENT OF UNITS

10.01   Voluntary Withdrawal of General Partner. The General Partner may withdraw as the general partner and may transfer all of its Units only if the proposed transferee agrees to become a general partner and be bound by all the duties and responsibilities imposed herein and Limited Partners holding at least fifty percent (50%) of the number of Units then held by the Limited Partners vote, at a meeting duly called for that purpose, or by an action without a meeting pursuant to **Article IX**, in favor of such transferee becoming the sole General Partner or consent, in writing, to such transferee becoming the sole General Partner.

10.02   Dissolution, etc. of the General Partner. In the event of the death, bankruptcy or incapacity, dissolution or cessation to exist of any General Partner, the Partnership shall not be dissolved. Within 120 days thereafter, the remaining Limited Partners shall elect a new General Partner of the Partnership. Such withdrawing General Partner or its personal representative, trustee or successor in interest, as the case may be, shall become a Limited Partner in the Partnership, its Units shall be transferable only in accordance with the provisions of **Article XI** and its Units shall thereinafter be held by it as a Limited Partner except that any amounts assessed against the withdrawing General Partner prior to the transfer shall be paid, in full, upon such transfer or such withdrawing General Partner or its personal representative, trustee or successor in interest, as the case may be, shall continue as a personal obligor on such obligation.

ARTICLE XI
RESTRICTIONS ON TRANSFER

11.01   Sale or Transfer of Units.

A.   **Prohibition on Transfers.** No Partner shall transfer all or any part of its Units or other interest in the Partnership without strictly complying with the provisions of this **Article XI**. Any purported transfer in violation of this **Article XI** shall not be recognized, be valid, or be given effect by the Partnership.

B.   **Consent to Transfers.** A Partner may transfer its Units solely with the prior written consent of the General Partner, which may be withheld in the sole and absolute discretion of the General Partner. The General Partner intends to not permit any transfer that would require the Partnership to terminate for federal income tax purposes or that is not in compliance with applicable federal and state securities law. The General Partner may require any Partner desiring to transfer a Unit to obtain an opinion of counsel satisfactory to the General Partner to the effect that the transfer will not cause a termination of the Partnership for federal income tax purposes or violate applicable federal or state securities laws.

C.   **Permitted Transfers.** Notwithstanding anything to the contrary contained herein, any transfer by a Partner to another Partner, to a trust, corporation, partnership or limited liability company for the benefit of that Partner, or to any of that Partner's lineal descendants, or to a trust for the benefit of such lineal descendants (in every case, the non-transferring Partners shall be notified of such transfer), shall not be deemed to be a transfer of a Partner's Units in the Partnership that requires prior written consent or gives rise to a right of first refusal.

The Partners acknowledge that the prohibitions on transfers contained in this Agreement are reasonable and necessary restrictions and may be enforced by specific performance. Any attempted transfer in violation of this Agreement shall be void *ab initio* and of no force or effect, and the purported transferee shall not have any rights in the Units or the Partnership. Notwithstanding anything to the contrary set forth herein, a Partner may acquire the Units of another Partner, so long as said acquisition of such Units is not a default under any loan agreement with a lender to the Partnership and approved by a majority of Partners.

11.02 Form of Assignment; Agreement to be Bound. Before any assignment of any Units shall be effective, the assignor or transferor and the Assignee or transferee as the case may be, shall both execute as assignment in the form and substance satisfactory to counsel of the Partnership that, among other matters, contains, an acknowledgment that the Assignee or transferee assumes the responsibilities and agrees to the terms of this Partnership Agreement, including, but not limited to, the restrictions on transfer contained in this **Article**.

11.03 Substitution of Assignee. No Assignee or transferee, as the case may be, may become a substituted Limited Partner until the following requirements are complied with:

A. **Execution of Assignment.** An assignment in form and substance satisfactory to the General Partner shall be executed and delivered to the Partnership that, among other matters, contains an acknowledgment that the Assignee or transferee, as the case may be, assumes the responsibilities and agrees to the terms of this Agreement. Such instrument or transfer shall set forth the intention of the assignor or transferor, as the case may be, that the Assignee or transferee, as the case may be, become a substitute Limited Partner in his, her or its place and stead;

B. **Investment Letter.** The Assignee or transferee, as the case may be, shall deliver to the General Partner an investment letter, in form acceptable to the General Partner, stating that such assignee or transferee, as the case may be, is acquiring the Units for investment purposes only and not for the purpose of reselling or otherwise distributing such Units to the public;

C. **Other Instruments.** The assignor and Assignee or transferor and transferee, as the case may be, shall execute and acknowledge such other instruments as the General Partner or its legal counsel shall deem necessary or desirable to effect the substitution of the transferee or Assignee, as the case may be, for the transferor or assignor, as the case may be, including the written acceptance and adoption by the Assignee or transferee, as the case may be, of the provisions of this Agreement and his, her or its written execution, acknowledgement and delivery to the General Partner of a power of attorney, the form and content of which are more fully described in **Article XV**;

D. **Consent to Assignment.** The Assignee or transferee, as the case may be, shall be accepted as a substitute Limited Partner by the General Partner; and

E. **Transfer Fee and Costs.** The payment or reimbursement of the Partnership for all costs incurred by the Partnership in connection with the transfer (including, without limitation, all legal fees incurred by the Partnership) on or before the tenth (10th) day after the receipt by the transferee, or Assignee of the Partnership's invoice for the amount due. If payment is not made by the date due, the transferee shall pay interest on the unpaid amount from the date due until paid at a rate per annum equal to the then prime rate charged by [BANK], [CITY], [STATE] or any successor in interest, plus four percent (4%) per annum.

11.04 Effective Date of Assignment or Substitution. The effective date of an assignment shall be the later of the date set forth in the instrument or assignment or the satisfaction of the requirements of this **Article** and the effective date of a substitution shall be the later of the date of the assignment is effective or the date that the requirements of this **Article** are complied with; provided, however, that the record date for cash distributions determined by the General Partner shall govern whether the payment of cash distributions shall be made to the transferor/assignor or the transferee/Assignee.

11.05 Treatment of Assignee as Substituted Limited Partner. The General Partner may elect to treat an Assignee who has not become a substitute Limited Partner as a substitute Limited Partner in the place of the assignor should the General Partner, in the exercise of its reasonable discretion, deem such action to be in the best interests of the Partnership, even though the provisions of **Section 11.03** have not been fully complied with.

11.06 Effect of Substitution. A transferee or Assignee, as the case may be, who becomes a substitute Limited Partner has, to the extent assigned, the rights and powers and is subject to the restrictions and liabilities of a Limited Partner under this Partnership Agreement and the Act. Unless otherwise provided by this Partnership Agreement, a transferee or Assignee, as the case may be, who becomes a substitute Limited Partner also is liable for the obligations of the transferor or assignor, as the case may be, to make contributions but is not obligated for liabilities unknown to the transferee or Assignee, as the case may at the time he, she or it became a Limited Partner and that could not be ascertained from this Agreement. Regardless of whether a transferee or assignor, as the case may be, of Units becomes a substitute Limited Partner, the transferor or assignor, as the case may be, is not released from his, her or its liability to the Partnership hereunder.

11.07 Status of Transferor or Assignor. Until a transferee or Assignee, as the case may be, becomes a substitute Limited Partner, the transferor or assignor Limited Partner continues to be a Limited Partner and to have the power to exercise any rights or powers of a Limited Partner, except to the extent those rights or powers are assigned.

11.08 Indirect Transfers and Assignments.

A.   A Limited Partner that is not a natural person may not cause or permit any Units, direct or indirect, in itself to be disposed of such that, after the disposition: (i) the Partnership would be considered to have terminated within the meaning of IRC Section 708; or (ii) without the consent of the General Partner, that Limited Partner shall cease to be controlled by substantially the same persons who control it as of the date of its admission to the Partnership.

B.   Notwithstanding anything in this Agreement to the contrary (including but not limited to the restrictions on transfers in **Section 11.01**, a Limited Partner that is not a natural person may transfer or distribute its Units in the Partnership to the respective Limited Partners or partners of such Limited Partner; provided that: (i) such Limited Partner obtains the prior written approval of the General Partner, which approval shall be at the General Partner's sole and absolute discretion; and (ii) the transferee(s) of such Limited Partner's Units comply with the requirements of this **Article XI** in order to be admitted as a substitute Limited Partner of the Partnership.

11.09 Concerning Securities Matters. Each Partner hereby represents and warrants to the Partnership and the other Partners that:

A.   Subject to the requirements of any law, it is acquiring the Units solely for the Partner's own account as a principal and not with a view to resale or distribution.

B.   In connection with the acquisition of its Units, and to the extent that Units in the Partnership are determined to be securities under federal or state securities laws: (i) the Partner has been fully informed as to the circumstances under which it is required to take and hold such interest pursuant to the requirements of the Securities Act of 1933, as amended ("1933 Act"), the rules and regulations thereunder, and the applicable state securities or "blue sky" law or laws; (ii) it knows that none of the Units have been registered under the 1933 Act and may not be transferred, assigned or otherwise disposed of unless such interest is subsequently registered under the 1933 Act or an exemption from such registration is available; and (iii) the Partner understands that: (A) the Partnership is under no obligation to register such Interests under the 1933 Act or to comply with any applicable exemption under the 1933 Act and any applicable exemption or exemptions under the applicable state securities or "blue sky" law or laws with respect to such Interest; and (B) the Partnership will not be required to supply any Partner with any information necessary to enable the Partner to make a casual sale of such Units pursuant to Rule 144 under the 1933 Act (assuming such Rule is applicable and is otherwise available with respect to such interest).

C. Each Partner understands that this Agreement contains restrictions on the transfer of all of the Units and that, in addition to such restrictions, the Partners covenants and agrees that such Units shall not be transferred or otherwise disposed of unless such transfer or other disposition is exempt from registration under the 1933 Act and the applicable state securities or "blue sky" law.

D. Each Partner hereby represents that it is an "accredited investor" under Rule 501(c), Regulation D of the 1933 Act.

ARTICLE XII
TERMINATION, DISSOLUTION AND LIQUIDATION

12.01 Events of Dissolution. The Partnership shall be terminated and dissolved and its assets liquidated and distributed on the happening of any of the following events:

A. **Written Consent.** Upon the written consent of the General Partner and Limited Partners holding at least fifty percent (50%) of all Units held by Limited Partners.

B. **State Law.** Upon the occurrence of an event specified under the laws of the State of Colorado as one affecting dissolution (except as otherwise provided in this Agreement).

C. **Sale of All Assets.** Upon the sale of all or substantially all of assets of the Partnership at any one time to one purchaser in one transaction and the receipt of all proceeds of such sale in cash unless all the Partners unanimously consent or agree to continue the Partnership.

12.02 Liquidation Distributions. Upon the termination of the Partnership, the Partnership shall engage in no further business other than that necessary to wind up the business and affairs of the Partnership and liquidate the assets of the Partnership, although the General Partner, in the sole discretion of the General Partner, may distribute assets in kind or in cash, or a combination thereof. The General Partner shall manage the liquidation and winding up of the Partnership. Unless otherwise determined by the General Partner, the Partnership shall implement and complete any and all activities that the Partnership has commenced. Except as otherwise provided, the proceeds from the liquidation and winding up of the Partnership shall be distributed in the following order:

A. **Expenses of Liquidation.** First, to pay the expenses of the liquidation;

B. **Outside Creditors.** To creditors of the Partnership in order of priority as provided by law;

C. **Balance.** The balance, if any, shall be distributed to the Limited Partners and the General Partner in accordance with the positive balance of their respective Capital Accounts.

12.03 Deficits. Each Limited Partner shall look solely to the assets of the Partnership for the return of his, her or its interest in the Partnership and if the Partnership property remaining after the payment or discharge of the debts and liabilities of the Partnership is insufficient to return the investment of each Partner, such Partner shall have no recourse against any other Partner, his, her or its employees or agents for indemnification, contribution or reimbursement.

ARTICLE XIII
BOOKS, RECORDS AND REPORTS

The Partnership's books and records and this Agreement and all amendments hereto shall be maintained at the principal office of the Partnership, or at such other place as the General Partner may determine. Such books and records shall be kept on a cash or accrual basis as determined by the General Partner on advice of the Partnership's counsel and/or accountant in accordance with sound income tax accounting principles applied on a consistent basis. On or before April 1 of each year the General Partner shall send information showing the amount of the taxable income or loss that each Partner should include in his, her or its federal and state income tax return for the prior tax year. Upon 30-day written notice, a Limited Partner may inspect the books and records of the Partnership, in person or by agent or attorney, during normal business hours, and to make copies of such records. Any Limited Partner desiring to inspect the books and records of the Company shall furnish an affidavit under oath that such inspection relates solely to the Limited Partner's interest in the Partnership. No Limited Partner shall be entitled to inspect or have access to any books or records of the Partnership that contain confidential information of the Partnership, and such confidential information shall specifically include a list of the Limited Partners, the Limited Partners' contact information, and the number of Units held by any Limited Partner.

ARTICLE XIV
ACCOUNTING YEAR

The accounting year of the Partnership shall be the calendar year or such other fiscal year as the General Partner may properly select.

ARTICLE XV
POWER OF ATTORNEY

15.01 General Purpose. Each Limited Partner does hereby constitute and appoint [Mr. X] and/or [Mr. Y] as his, her, or its true and lawful agents and attorney-in-fact, in his, her or its name, place and stead, to make execute, acknowledge, swear to, and file:

A. **Certificate of Partnership.** Any certificate or other instrument that may be required to be filed by the Partnership under the laws of any state or of the United States.
B. **Amendments.** Any and all amendments, modifications, or cancellations of such certificates or instruments, including any amendment to the Limited Partnership Certificate required to admit any substitute or additional Limited Partner or General Partner in accordance with the provisions of this Agreement.
C. **Registration.** Any application for the registration of the Limited Partnership or of the offering of Partnership Units in accordance with the securities law of the United States or of any state.
D. **Other.** Any other instrument that may be required to be filed by the Partnership by any governmental agency, or that the General Partner deems advisable to file.

15.02 Power; Procedures. The power of attorney to be concurrently granted by each Partner to [Mr. X] and/or [Mr. Y]:

A. **Irrevocable.** Shall represent a special power of attorney, be irrevocable, and survive the death of the Partner.

B. **Signatures.** May be exercised by [Mr. X] and/or [Mr. Y] for each Partner by a facsimile signature of an agent or employee of [Mr. X] and/or [Mr. Y] or by listing all of the Partners executing any instrument with a single signature by such attorney-in-fact.

C. **Survival.** Shall survive the delivery of an assignment by a Limited Partner of the whole or any portion of his, her or its Units; except that where the Assignee thereof has been approved by the General Partner for admission to the Partnership as a substituted Limited Partner, the power of attorney shall survive the delivery of such assignment for the sole purpose of enabling [Mr. X] and/or [Mr. Y] to execute, acknowledge and file any instrument necessary to effect such substitution.

ARTICLE XVI
AMENDMENTS TO
CERTIFICATE OF LIMITED PARTNERSHIP

The Certificate of Limited Partnership may be amended by the General Partner without consent of the Limited partners whenever the Act requires such Certificate to be amended due to a change in this Agreement, the Partnership or the Partners.

ARTICLE XVII
RESTRICTIONS ON AMENDMENT
OF LIMITED PARTNERSHIP AGREEMENT

This Agreement may be amended upon the written consent or affirmative vote of the General Partner and Limited Partners holding at least sixty seven percent (67%) of the then outstanding Units then held by Limited Partners. No amendment, however, shall without the affirmative consent of all Partners:

- enlarge the obligations of any Partner under this Agreement;
- enlarge the responsibilities of the General Partner to the Limited Partners; or
- amend this **Article**, or **Articles VI, XI or XII.**

ARTICLE XVIII
INTEREST OF SPOUSES

18.01 Management. Insofar as the Partnership and the Partners are concerned, the Units in the Partnership of each Partner is in the sole name of a Partner and shall be deemed to be his or her property, and the Partner shall have sole management and control over such Units, including the right to vote or sell such Units. This **Section** is not intended to and shall not affect the existence or extension of any community property or other interest that a spouse may have in such Units.

18.02 Death of Spouse. In the event that the spouse of a Partner shall predecease the Partner and the spouse has a community property or other interest in the Units in the Partnership standing in the sole name of the Partner, the Partner shall continue to own all of the Units standing in his or her name. The spouse shall duly implement this provision by providing in his or her will for the devise of his or her Units in the Partnership or the Partner. In the event that the community property or other interest of the spouse in such Units does not pass entirely to the Partner by intestate succession or through the spouse's will, then the Partner and the Partner's spouse shall be deemed to own such Units not as community property and not as tenants-in-common, but as joint tenants with the right of survivorship.

18.03 Dissolution of Marriage. In the event a Partner's spouse is determined to own a community property or other interest in the Units in the Partnership standing in the sole name of a Partner, and their marriage is dissolved otherwise than by death, all of such interest shall pass to the Partner upon such dissolution. The Partner and spouse shall duly effectuate this provision in a property settlement agreement or other like instrument.

18.04 Subsequent Marriage of Partner. Any Partner who marries subsequent to the execution of this Agreement shall cause such new spouse to consent to this Agreement and specifically to the provisions of this **Article**, and the failure to do so shall constitute a material breach of this Agreement by such Partner.

ARTICLE XIX
GENERAL PROVISIONS

19.01 Notices. All notices under this Agreement shall be in writing and shall be given to the Partner entitled thereto by personal service or by mail to the address set forth in this Agreement for such Partner or at such other address as may be specified in writing.

19.02 Titles and Captions. Article, Section and **Subsection** titles or captions contained in this Agreement are inserted only as a matter of convenience and for reference and in no way define, limit, extend or proscribe the scope of this Agreement or the intent of any provisions hereof.

19.03 Gender and Number. Whenever the singular number is used in this Agreement and when required by the context, the same shall include the plural, and the masculine gender shall include the feminine and neuter genders, and the word "person" shall include any corporation, firm, partnership, trust, entity, or other form of association.

19.04 Execution in Counterparts. This Agreement may be executed in several counterparts and all so executed shall constitute one agreement, binding on all of the parties hereto, notwithstanding that all parties are not signatory to the original or the same counterpart.

19.05 Binding Effect. The terms and provisions of this Agreement shall be binding upon and inure to the benefit of the successors and assigns of the respective Partners.

19.06 Entire Agreement; Amendment. This Agreement shall constitute the entire and whole agreement among the parties hereto and may not be modified or amended except in accordance with **Article XV**.

19.07 Mediation. In the event that there is an unresolved dispute not provided for in any other **Section** of this Agreement, either party may make written demand for mediation to the other party and to a special mediator. The parties shall appoint one person to hear and determine the disputed matter. If the parties are unable to agree upon a single mediator within 30 days after the matter has been submitted to mediation, then each party shall designate a mediator and if the number of mediators chosen is less than three the two persons so chosen shall select a third impartial mediator whose decision shall be final and conclusive upon the parties. The cost of such mediation shall be borne by the Partnership and such cost shall be taken into account by the mediator.

Within five days after receipt of such a demand, the responding party may forward to the mediator and the initiating party a written response setting forth any other issues and concerns that they believe are relevant to the issues presented for mediation. Unless otherwise agreed, once a demand for mediation has been filed, there shall be no *ex parte* communications with the mediator.

The mediator shall promptly determine if all parties are in possession of adequate information necessary to evaluate the issues and concerns set forth in the demand notice and/or the response thereto (collectively, "Claims"). In the event he deems that they are not, he shall utilize his best efforts to obtain the information in a prompt manner. The mediator shall immediately prepare an agenda consisting of the various issues and concerns comprising the Claims, and shall deliver the agenda to both parties within 15 days after the demand for mediation was received. The mediator shall then schedule a conference among the parties, to occur within 30 days after the demand for mediation was received. The conference will be attended by the persons most familiar with the issues set forth in the Claims, and by a representative of each party, who is authorized to act on behalf of such party as to reaching an agreement on the Claims. The mediator shall lead negotiations between the parties in an impartial manner, and shall endeavor to develop a consensus and agreement as to all of the issues and concerns. Agreements as to any issues, if reached, shall be acknowledged by the parties upon preparation of a written summary by the mediator. The proceedings and all documents prepared exclusively for use in these proceedings shall be deemed to be matters pertaining to settlement negotiations, and not subsequently admissible at any further proceeding, except for the summaries of agreements prepared by the mediator and acknowledged by the parties. Upon a determination by the mediator that further negotiations are unlikely to achieve further meaningful results, he shall declare the mediation procedure terminated, and any matter not resolved may be referred to litigation.

19.08 Legal Representation. This Agreement was prepared by the [Law Firm], solely in its capacity as counsel for General Partner and not of the benefit of the Partnership, or any of its Limited Partners. The Partners also acknowledged that they have personally read this Agreement and are fully aware of its contents and legal effect. The Partners further acknowledge that each Partner has been advised to consult an attorney of their own choosing before executing this Agreement and have had this Agreement reviewed by a qualified attorney for their and all liability for the draftsmanship of this Agreement. The Partners further acknowledge that the [Law Firm] is not giving any tax, business or securities advice in connection with the preparation of this Agreement or any other documents for the Partnership.

[Signature Pages Follow]

IN WITNESS WHEREOF, the parties hereto have executed the Agreement on the day and year first above written.

GENERAL PARTNER:

ABC INVESTMENTS, LLC,
a Colorado limited liability company

By: General Partner

By: _____

                Mr. X

By: General Partner

By: _____

                Mr. Y

INITIAL LIMITED PARTNER

_____

                Mr. Z

EXHIBIT "A"

**LIST OF PARTNERS, CAPITAL CONTRIBUTIONS,
UNITS AND PERCENTAGE INTEREST OF EACH PARTNER**

SAMPLE: SUBSCRIPTION AGREEMENT

ABC APARTMENTS, LP
Subscription Documents

DIRECTIONS FOR THE COMPLETION OF THE SUBSCRIPTION DOCUMENTS

Prospective investors must complete all of the Subscription Documents contained in this package in the manner described below. For purposes of these Subscription Documents, the "Investor" is the person for whose account the Interests are being purchased. Another person with investment authority may execute the Subscription Documents on behalf of the Investor, but should indicate the capacity in which it is doing so and the name of the Investor.

1. Subscription Agreement:
   a. Fill in amount of the investment.
   b. Date, print the name of the investor and sign (and print name, capacity and title, if applicable).
   c. Complete the appropriate acknowledgment form and have the form notarized.
2. Investor Questionnaire:
   a. In Section A, each Investor should fill in the Investor's name, address, tax identification or social security number and telephone and telecopier numbers and respond to the questions in items 7, 8 and 9.
   b. Each Investor should check the box or boxes in Section B that are next to the categories under which the Investor qualifies as an accredited investor.
   c. Each entity should respond to the questions in Section C.
   d. Each Investor should respond to the questions in Section D.
   e. Each Investor should check the box or boxes in Section E that are next to the categories under which the Investor qualifies as a qualified purchaser.
   f. Date, print the name of the Investor and sign (and print name, capacity and title, if applicable).
3. W-9 Tax Form:
   Fill in and sign and date the attached Form W-9 in accordance with the instructions to the Form.
4. Delivery of Subscription Documents:
   Two completed and signed copies of the Subscription Agreement and the Investor Questionnaire, together with any required evidence of authorization, should be delivered to the Partnership at the following address:

   > ABC Investments, LLC
   > 1111 Elm Street
   > [CITY], [STATE]
   > [phone]
   > [email]
   > Attention: Mr. X

In addition, please send copies of: (i) the completed and executed signature page of the Subscription Documents; and (ii) the completed Investor Questionnaire.

Inquiries regarding subscription procedures should be directed to ABC Investments, LLC, 1111 Elm Street, [City], [State], Attention: Mr. X, telephone number: (ZXZ) 111-1111. If the

Investor's subscription is accepted by the General Partner, a fully executed set of the Subscription Documents will be returned to the Investor.

5. Payment of Subscription:

    Payment of the cash (or in kind at the General Partner's discretion) amount of the Investor's subscription should be made on the closing date of the Investor's subscription by wire transfer to the Partnership's account specified in Section 7 of the Subscription Agreement on in the case of an in kind payment accepted by the Partnership in its sole discretion, by such means as agreed to between the Investor and the Partnership.

ABC APARTMENTS, LP

SUBSCRIPTION AGREEMENT—SAMPLE

ABC Apartments, LP
c/o ABC Investments, LLC
1111 Elm Street
[CITY], [STATE]

Gentlemen:

1. Subscription. The undersigned ("Investor") subscribes for and agrees to purchase the amount of Limited Partnership interests ("Interests") in ABC Apartments, LP, a Colorado limited partnership ("Partnership"), set forth on the signature page below. The Investor acknowledges that this subscription: (i) is irrevocable; (ii) is conditioned upon acceptance by or on behalf of ABC Investments, LLC, as the general partner of the Partnership ("General Partner") on behalf of the Partnership and may be accepted or rejected in whole or in part by the General Partner in its sole discretion; and (iii) will expire if not accepted by the General Partner on or prior to two months from the date hereof. The Investor agrees to be bound by all the terms and provisions of the LPA of the Partnership (as amended from time to time, the "LPA") in the form previously provided to the Investor. Capitalized terms not defined herein are used as defined in the LPA.

2. Representations and Warranties. To induce the Partnership to accept this subscription, the Investor represents, warrants, understands, acknowledges and agrees as follows:

    (a) The Investor has been furnished the Private Placement Memorandum (as amended or supplemented from time to time, "PPM") dated ZZZ XX, 20YZ, relating to the Partnership and the LPA (which, together with this Subscription Agreement, constitute the "Partnership Documents"). The Investor has carefully read the Partnership Documents and any other documentary information, if any, requested of the General Partner by the Investor. The Investor has such knowledge and experience in financial and business matters as to be capable of evaluating the merits and risks of an investment in the Interests, is able to bear the risks of an investment in the Interests and understands the risks of, and other considerations relating to, a purchase of an Interest, including the matters set forth under the caption "RISK FACTORS" and "CONFLICTS OF INTEREST" in the PPM.

    (b) The Investor:

        (i)   will not transfer or deliver any interest in the Interests except in accordance with the restrictions set forth in the LPA and the PPM; and

        (ii) is acquiring the Interests to be acquired hereunder for the Investor's own account for investment purposes only and not with a view to resale or distribution.

(c) The Interests have not been registered under the Securities Act of 1933, as amended ("Securities Act"), the securities laws of any state or the securities laws of any other jurisdiction, nor is such registration contemplated. Subject to the limited withdrawal rights set forth in the LPA, the Interests must be held indefinitely unless they are subsequently registered under the Securities Act and these laws or an exemption from registration under the Securities Act and these laws covering the sale of Interests is available. Even if such an exemption is available, the assignability and transferability of the Interests will be governed by the LPA, under which are imposed substantial restrictions on transfer. Legends stating that the Interests have not been registered under the Securities Act and these laws and setting out or referring to the restrictions on the transferability and resale of the Interests will be placed on all documents, if any, evidencing the Interests. The Investor's overall commitment to the Partnership and other investments that are not readily marketable is not disproportionate to the Investor's net worth and the Investor has no need for immediate liquidity in the Investor's investment in Interests.

(d) To the full satisfaction of the Investor, the Investor has been furnished with any materials the Investor has requested relating to the Partnership, the offering of Interests or any statement made in the PPM, and the Investor has been afforded the opportunity to ask questions of representatives of the Partnership concerning the terms and conditions of the offering and to obtain any additional information necessary to verify the accuracy of any representations or information set forth in the PPM.

(e) Other than as set forth in the PPM and other Partnership Documents, the Investor is not relying upon any other information, representation or warranty by the Partnership, the General Partner or any agent of them in determining to invest in the Partnership. The Investor has consulted to the extent deemed appropriate by the Investor with the Investor's own advisers as to the financial, tax, legal and related matters concerning an investment in Interests and on that basis believes that an investment in the Interests is suitable and appropriate for the Investor. Any placement agent used in connection with the offer and sale of the Interests did not prepare the PPM or any other Partnership Document.

(f) (i) If the Investor is not a natural person, the Investor has the power and authority to enter into this Subscription Agreement, the LPA and each other document required to be executed and delivered by or on behalf of the Investor in connection with this subscription for Interests, and to perform its obligations thereunder and consummate the transactions contemplated thereby, and the person signing this Subscription Agreement on behalf of the Investor has been duly authorized to execute and deliver this Subscription Agreement, the LPA and each other document required to be executed and delivered by the Investor in connection with this subscription for Interests.

(ii) If the Investor is an individual, the Investor has all requisite legal capacity to acquire and hold the Interests and to execute, deliver and comply with the terms of each of the documents required to be executed and delivered by the Investor in connection with this subscription for Interests. Such execution, delivery and compliance by the Investor does not represent a breach of, or constitute a default under, any instruments governing the Investor, any applicable law, regulation or order to which the Investor is subject, or any agreement to which the Investor is a party or by which the Investor is bound. This Subscription Agreement has been duly executed by the Investor and constitutes, and the LPA, when the Investor is admitted as a Member, will constitute, a valid and legally binding agreement of the Investor.

(g) If the Investor is, or is acting on behalf of, an employee benefit plan within the meaning of Section 3(3) of the Employee Retirement Income Security Act of 1974, as amended

("ERISA"), or an entity that is deemed to hold the assets of any such employee benefit plan pursuant to 29 C.F.R. § 2510.3-101, which plan or entity is subject to Title I of ERISA or Section 4975 of the Internal Revenue Code of 1986, as amended (the "Code") (collectively, a "Plan"):

(i) the decision to invest in the Partnership was made by a fiduciary (within the meaning of Section 3(21) of ERISA and the regulations thereunder) ("Fiduciary") of the Plan that is unrelated to the General Partner or any of its employees, representatives or affiliates .and that is duly authorized to make such an investment decision on behalf of the Plan (the "Plan Fiduciary");

(ii) the Plan Fiduciary has taken into consideration its fiduciary duties under ERISA, including the diversification requirements of Section 404(a)(1)(c) of ERISA, in authorizing; the Plan's investment in the Partnership, and has concluded that such investment is prudent;

(iii) the Plan's subscription to invest in the Partnership and the purchase of Interests contemplated thereby is in accordance with the terms of the Plan's governing instruments and complies with all applicable requirements of ERISA and the Code; and

(iv) neither the General Partner nor any of its employees, representatives or affiliates will be a fiduciary with respect to the Plan as a result of the Plan's investment in the Partnership, and the Plan Fiduciary has not relied on, and is not relying on, the investment advice of any such person with respect to the Plan's investment in the Partnership.

(h) The Partnership may require a mandatory redemption of all or part of the Interests held by the Investor at any time, including to assure that the Partnership will not be deemed to hold "plan assets" within the meaning of ERISA, provided that any mandatory redemption made for the purpose of effecting an overall reduction in the capital of the Partnership shall only be made *pro rata* among all of the Partners.

(i) The Investor was offered the Interests in the State listed in the Investor's permanent address set forth in the Investor Questionnaire attached hereto or previously provided to the, General Partner and intends that the securities law of that State govern the Investor's subscription.

3. Tax Information. Under penalties of perjury, the investor has provided:

(a) (i) the Investor's name, taxpayer identification or social security number and address provided in the Investor Questionnaire is correct; and

(ii) the Investor will complete and return with this Subscription Agreement IRS Form W-9, Payer's Request for Taxpayer Identification Number and Certification; and

(b) (i) the Investor is not a non-resident alien individual, foreign corporation, foreign partnership, foreign trust or foreign estate (as defined in the Code); and

(ii) the Investor will notify the Partnership within 60 days of a change to foreign status. The Investor shall properly execute and provide to the Partnership in a timely manner any tax documentation that may be reasonably required by the General Partner.

4. Further Advice and Assurances. All information that the Investor has provided to the Partnership, including the information in the attached Investor Questionnaire, is correct and complete as of the date hereof, and the Investor shall notify the General Partner immediately if any representation, warranty or information contained in this Subscription Agreement, including in the attached Investor Questionnaire, becomes untrue at any time. The Investor shall provide such information and execute and deliver such documents as the Partnership may reasonably request from time to time to verify the accuracy of the Investor's representations

and warranties herein or to comply with any law or regulation to which the Partnership may be subject.

5. Power of Attorney. By executing this Subscription Agreement, the Investor appoints the General Partner and each of its managers and officers, with full power of substitution, as the Investor's true and lawful representative and attorney-in-fact, in the Investor's name, place and stead to make, execute, sign, acknowledge, swear to and file the LPA, any amendments to the LPA or any other agreement or instrument that the General Partner deems appropriate to admit the Investor as a Partner. This power of attorney is coupled with an interest, is irrevocable and shall survive, and shall not be affected by, the subsequent death, disability, incapacity, incompetency, termination, bankruptcy, insolvency or dissolution of the Investor.

6. Indemnity. The information provided herein will be relied upon by the Partnership for the purpose of determining the eligibility of the Investor to purchase Interests. The Investor shall provide, if requested, any additional information that may reasonably be required to determine the eligibility of the Investor to purchase Interests in the Partnership. To the maximum extent permitted by law, the Investor shall indemnify and hold harmless the Partnership and each Member thereof from and against any loss, damage, or liability due to or arising out of a breach of any representation, warranty or agreement of the Investor contained in this Subscription Agreement or in any other document provided by the Investor to the Partnership or the General Partner in connection with the Investor's investment in Interests. Notwithstanding any provision of this Subscription Agreement, the Investor does not waive any rights granted to it under applicable securities laws.

7. Payment of Subscription.

    (a) The Investor shall pay the amount of the Investor's subscription hereunder by wire transfer to the account set forth below, on the closing date of the Investor's subscription, or make an in kind payment to the Partnership acceptable to the Partnership in its sole discretion. If the Investor's subscription is rejected in whole or in part, the amount rejected shall be promptly returned by wire transfer to an account designated by the Investor.

    (b) Wire transfer payments shall be made to the following account:

    >   Routing 111111111
    >   Account #999999999
    >   XYZ Bank
    >   100 East Street
    >   [City], [State]

8. Miscellaneous. This Subscription Agreement is not assignable by the Investor without the consent of the. General Partner. The representations and warranties made by the. Investor in this Subscription Agreement shall survive the closing of the transactions contemplated hereby and any investigation made by the Partnership or the General Partner. The attached Investor Questionnaire is an integral part of this Subscription Agreement and shall be deemed incorporated by reference herein. This Subscription Agreement may be executed in one or more counterparts, all of which together shall constitute one instrument, and shall be governed by and construed in accordance with the laws of the State of Colorado, without regard to principles of conflicts of law thereof.

IN WITNESS WHEREOF, the undersigned has executed this Subscription Agreement on the date set forth below.

Date: _____

Amount of Subscription:

$ _____

If a placement agent has been used in connection with the offer and sale of the Interests, the name of the placement agent is indicated below (any placement fee will be paid by General Partner):

_____
(name of placement agent)

PARTNERSHIP, CORPORATION, TRUST, CUSTODIAL ACCOUNT, OTHER ENTITY:

_____
(Print Name of Entity)

By:

_____
(Signature)

_____
(Print Name and Title)

INDIVIDUAL INVESTOR:

_____
(Signature)

_____
(Print Name and Title)

The General Partner hereby accepts the above application for subscription for Interests on behalf of the Partnership.

ABC INVESTMENTS, LLC
By: _____
        Name: Mr. X
                Managing Member

Date: _____

PARTNERSHIP ACKNOWLEDGMENT

STATE OF _____)

                                   : ss.:

COUNTY OF _____)

On the day of _____, _____, before me personally came_____, to me known to be the individual described in and who executed the foregoing instrument, and acknowledged that he (she) executed the same as a general partner of the foregoing partnership.

                           _____

                           Notary Public

                           Address: _____

                                        _____

[seal]

My commission expires:

_____

CORPORATE ACKNOWLEDGMENT

STATE OF _____)
                                    : ss.:

COUNTY OF _____)

On the _____ day of _____, 20_____ before me personally came_____, to me known, who, being by me duly sworn, did dispose and say that he (she) is the of _____, the corporation described in and that executed the foregoing instrument; that he (she) executed said instrument on behalf of said corporation by authority of its board of directors or pursuant to its by-laws and that the same is the free act and deed by said corporation.

_____

Notary Public

Address: _____

            _____

[seal]

My commission expires:

_____

TRUST ACKNOWLEDGMENT

STATE OF _____)

: ss.:

COUNTY OF _____)

On the _____ day of _____, 20_____ before me personally appeared _____, to me known, who duly acknowledged to me that he (she) (they) (it) is (are) the trustee(s) of _____, trust described in the foregoing instrument, that the foregoing instrument was signed on behalf of said trust and that the same is the free act and deed of said trust.

_____

Notary Public

Address: _____

_____

[seal]

My commission expires:

_____

REAL ESTATE SECURITIES

INDIVIDUAL ACKNOWLEDGMENT

STATE OF _____)

                                   : ss.:

COUNTY OF _____)

On the _____ day of _____, 20_____ before me, the undersigned, a Notary Public of said State, duly commissioned and sworn, personally appeared _____, to me known to be the person (or persons) whose name is (or whose names are) subscribed to on the foregoing instrument, and acknowledged that he (or she or they) executed the same.

IN WITNESS WHEREOF, I have hereunto set my hand and affixed my official seal the day and year in this certificate first above written.

_____
Notary Public

Address: _____

_____

[seal]

My commission expires:

_____

LIMITED LIABILITY COMPANY ACKNOWLEDGMENT

STATE OF _____)

: ss.:

COUNTY OF _____)

On the _____ day of _____, 20____ before me personally came_____ , to me known to be the individual described in and who executed the foregoing instrument, and acknowledged that he (she) executed the same as a managing member of the foregoing limited liability company.

IN WITNESS WHEREOF, I have hereunto set my hand and affixed my official seal the day and year in this certificate first above written:

_____

Notary Public

Address: _____

_____

[seal]

My commission expires:

_____

SAMPLE: INVESTOR QUESTIONNAIRE

The Investor represents, warrants, understands, acknowledges and agrees as follows:

A. GENERAL INFORMATION

1. Print Full Name of Investor: _____

2. Address and Contact Person
   for Notices: _____

   Attention: _____

3. Telephone Number: _____

4. Tele copier Number: _____

5. Permanent Address:
   (if different from above) _____

6. U.S. Taxpayer
   Identification or Social
   Security Number: _____

7. If the Investor would like to receive information in connection with the Partnership by e-mail, please specify the e-mail address of the Investor: _____

8. Would the Investor like to access information regarding the Partnership via the Internet when available?

   ☐ Yes   ☐ No

   If the above question was answered "yes", the General Partner will contact the Investor with instructions.

B. ACCREDITED INVESTOR STATUS

The Investor is an "accredited investor" within the meaning of Rule 501 of Regulation D under the Securities Act of 1933, as amended ("Securities Act"), and has checked the box or boxes below that are next to the categories under which the Investor qualifies as an accredited investor:

1. FOR ENTITIES

   a. ☐ An entity, including a grantor trust, in which all of the equity owners are accredited investors (for this purpose, a beneficiary of a trust is not an equity owner, but the grantor of a grantor trust may be an equity owner).

   b. ☐ A bank as defined in Securities Act Section 3(a)(2) or any savings and loan association or other, institution as defined in Securities Act Section 3(a)(5)(A), whether acting in its individual or fiduciary capacity.

c. ☐ An insurance company as defined in Securities Act Section 2(13).

d. ☐ A broker-dealer registered pursuant to Section 15 of the Securities Exchange Act of 1934, as amended.

e. ☐ An investment company registered under the Investment Company Act of 1940, as amended ("IC Act").

f. ☐ A business development company as defined in IC Act Section 2(a)(48).

g. ☐ A small business investment company licensed by the Small Business Administration under Section 301(c) or (d) of the Small Business. Investment Act of 1958, as amended.

h. ☐ A private business development company as defined in Section 202(a)(22) of the Investment Advisers Act of 1940, as amended ("IA Act").

i. ☐ An organization described in Section 501(c)(3) of the Internal Revenue Code, a corporation, Massachusetts or similar business trust, or partnership, in each case not formed for the specific purpose of acquiring Interests, with total assets in excess of $5 million.

j. ☐ A trust with total assets in excess of $5 million not formed for the specific purpose of acquiring Interests, whose purchase is directed by a person with such knowledge and experience in financial and business matters as to be capable of evaluating the merits and risks of an investment in the Interests.

k. ☐ An employee benefit plan within the meaning of ERISA if the decision to invest in the Interests is made by a plan fiduciary, as defined in Section 3(21) of ERISA, which is either a bank, savings and loan association, insurance company, or registered investment adviser, or if the employee benefit plan has total assets in excess of $5 million or, if a self-directed plan, with investment decisions made solely by persons that are accredited investors.

l. ☐ A plan established and maintained by a state, its political subdivisions, or any agency or instrumentality of a state or its political subdivisions, for the benefit of its employees, if the plan has total assets in excess of $5 million.

2. FOR INDIVIDUALS:

a. ☐ A natural person with individual net worth (or joint net worth with spouse) in excess of $1 million: For purposes of this item, "net worth" means the excess of total assets at fair market value, including home, home furnishings and automobiles (and including property owned by a spouse), over total liabilities.

b. ☐ A natural person with individual income (without including any income of the Investor's spouse) in excess of $200,000, or joint income with spouse of $300,000, in each of the two most recent years and who reasonably expects to reach the same income level in the current year.

C. Supplemental Data for Entities

If the Investor is an entity, furnish the following: supplemental data (natural persons may skip this Section of the Investor Questionnaire):

1. Legal form of entity (corporation, partnership, trust, etc.): _____

    Jurisdiction of organization: _____

2. Was the Investor organized for the specific purpose of acquiring Interests?

    ☐ Yes   ☐ No

    If the answer to the above question is "Yes," please contact the General Partner for additional information that will be required.

3. Are shareholders, partners or other holders of equity or beneficial interests in the Investor able to decide individually whether to participate, or the extent of their participation, in the Investor's investment in the Partnership (*i.e.*, can equity holders in the Investor determine whether their capital will form part of the capital invested by the Investor in the Partnership)?

    ☐ Yes   ☐ No

    If the answer to the above question is "Yes," please contact the General Partner for additional information that will be required.

4. Please indicate whether or not the Investor is, or is acting on behalf of:

    (i)   an employee benefit plan within the meaning of Section 3(3) of ERISA, whether or not such plan is subject to ERISA; or

    (ii) an entity that is deemed to hold the assets of any such employee benefit plan pursuant to 29 C.F.R. § 2510.3-101.

    For example, a plan that is maintained by a foreign corporation, governmental entity or church, a Keogh plan covering no common-law employees and an individual retirement account are employee benefit plans within the meaning of Section 3(3) of ERISA but generally are not subject to ERISA (collectively "Non-ERISA Plans"). In general, a foreign or U.S. entity that is not an operating company and that is not publicly traded or registered as an investment company under the Investment Partnership Act of 1940, as amended, and in which 25% or more of the value of any class of equity interests is held by employee pension or welfare plans (including an entity that is deemed to hold the assets of any such plan), would be deemed to hold the assets of one or more employee benefit plans pursuant to 29 C.F.R. § 2510.3-101. However, if only Non-ERISA Plans were invested in such an entity, the entity generally would not be subject to ERISA. For purposes of determining whether this 25% threshold has been met or exceeded, the value of any equity interests held by a person (other than such a plan or entity) who has discretionary authority or control with respect to the assets of the entity, or any person who provides investment advice for a fee (direct or indirect) with respect to such assets, or any affiliate of such a person, is disregarded.

    ☐ Yes   ☐ No

If the Investor is, or is acting on behalf of, such an employee benefit plan, or is an entity deemed to hold the assets of any such plan or plans, please indicate whether or not the Investor is subject to ERISA.

☐ Yes　　　　　　☐ No

Please indicate whether or not the Investor is a U.S. pension trust or governmental plan qualified under section 401(a) of the Code or a U.S. tax-exempt organization qualified under section 501(c)(3) of the Code.

☐ Yes　　　　　　☐ No

5.　Does the amount of the Investor's subscription for Interests in the Partnership exceed 40% of the total assets (on a consolidated basis with its subsidiaries) of the Investor?

☐ Yes　　　　　　☐ No

If the question above was answered "Yes," please contact the General Partner for additional information that will be required.

6.　(a)　(i)　Is the Investor a private investment company that is not registered under the IC Act, in reliance on IC Act Section 3(c)(1) or 3(c)(7)?

☐ Yes　　　　☐ No

(ii)　Was the Investor formed prior to April 30, 1996?

☐ Yes　　　　☐ No

(b)　If questions 6(a)(i) and (ii) were both answered "Yes," please indicate whether or not the Investor has obtained the consent of its direct and indirect beneficial owners to be treated as a "Qualified Purchaser" as provided in Section 2(a)(5 1)(C) of the Investment Partnership Act and the rules and regulations thereunder:

☐ Yes　　　☐ No

If the question above was answered "No," please contact the General Partner for additional information that will be required.

7.　If the Investor has a taxable year that ends other than on December 3l, please indicate such taxable year end: _____.

8.　(a)　Is the Investor a grantor trust, a partnership or an S-Corporation for U.S. federal income tax purposes?

☐ Yes　　　☐ No

(b)   If the question above was answered "Yes," please indicate whether or not

    (i)   more than 50% of the value of the ownership interest of any beneficial owner in the Investor is (or may at any time during the term of the Partnership be) attributable to the Investor's (direct or indirect) interest in it; or

       ☐ Yes   ☐ No

    (ii)   is a principal purpose of the Investor's participation in the Partnership to permit the Partnership to satisfy the 100 partner limitation contained in U.S. Treasury Regulation Section 1.7704-1(h)(3)?

       ☐ Yes   ☐ No

    If either question above was answered "Yes," please contact the General Partner for additional information that will be required.

D. RELATED PARTIES

Will any other person or persons have a beneficial interest in the Interests to be acquired hereunder (other than as a shareholder, partner or other beneficial owner of equity interests in the Investor)?

    ☐ Yes   ☐ No

If the question above was answered "Yes," please contact the General Partner for additional information that will be required.

E. QUALIFIED PURCHASER:

The Investor is a "qualified purchaser" within the meaning of IC Act Section 2(a)(51) ("Qualified Purchaser") and has checked the box or boxes below that are next to the categories under which the Investor qualifies as a Qualified Purchaser:

1.   ☐   A natural person (including any person who holds a joint, community property, or other similar shared ownership interest in an issuer that is excepted under IC Act Section 3(c)(7) with that person's qualified purchaser spouse) who owns not less than $5 million in "investments."

2.   ☐   A company that owns not less than $5,000,000 in "investments" and is owned directly or indirectly by or for two or more natural persons who are related as siblings or spouse (including former spouses), or direct lineal descendants by birth or adoption, spouses of such persons, the estates of such persons, or foundations, charitable organizations or trusts established by or for the benefit of such persons ("Family Partnership").

3.   ☐   A trust that is not covered by (2) above as to which the trustee or other person authorized to make decisions with respect to the trust, and each settlor or other person who has contributed assets to the trust, is a person described in clause (1), (2) or (4) of this Section E.

4. ☐ A person (which may be a natural person or a corporation, partnership, limited liability company, trust or other entity) acting for its own account or the accounts of other Qualified Purchasers, who in the aggregate owns and invests on a discretionary basis not less than $25,000,000 in "investments."

The foregoing information will be relied upon by the Partnership for the purpose of determining the eligibility of the Investor to purchase Interests in the Partnership. The Investor shall provide, if requested, any additional information that may be reasonably required to substantiate the Investor's status as an accredited investor, a qualified eligible participant or qualified investor or to otherwise determine the eligibility of the Investor to purchase Interests in the Partnership to the maximum extent permitted by law. The Investor shall indemnify and hold harmless the Partnership and each Partner thereof from and against any loss, damage or liability due to or arising out of a breach of any representation, warranty or agreement of the Investor contained herein.

SIGNATURE PAGE FOLLOWS

Date: _____

Signatures:

PARTNERSHIP, CORPORATION, TRUST, CUSTODIAL ACCOUNT OR OTHER ENTITY:

_____
(Name of Entity)

By: _____
(Signature)

_____
(Print Name and Title)

INDIVIDUAL:

_____
(Signature)

_____
(Print Name)

REAL ESTATE SECURITIES

SAMPLE: "BAD ACTOR" QUESTIONNAIRE

Name of Person Completing Questionnaire:

_____
(Please print or type)

_____
("*Company*")

EXECUTIVE MANAGEMENT QUESTIONNAIRE

The purpose of this questionnaire is to obtain information as necessary for due diligence and disclosure requirements in connection with a private placement of securities to be issued by [issuer] ("Company") or an entity affiliated with the Company. The person completing this questionnaire will be a member of the executive management of the Company or of an entity serving as manager of the Company ("Management").

Information requested in the questionnaire is as of the date you complete the questionnaire, unless otherwise indicated. We assume that Company's fiscal year end is December 31 unless you advise otherwise. Please read each question in its entirety before completing any portion of the question. If additional space is required to complete an answer, please attach additional pages. You may respond do a question by including any relevant information (such as your bio) and so indicating on the question.

If a matter comes to your attention that is not specifically covered by these questions, whether you feel the issue may or may not be material, please raise the issue so that it may be discussed and resolved. If there is any question in your mind as to whether a matter is material, relevant, important or should for any reason be discussed or disclosed, you should disclose the matter to counsel.

PLEASE ANSWER EVERY QUESTION COMPLETELY AND FILL IN ALL BLANKS. IF A PARTICULAR QUESTION OR BLANK IS NOT APPLICABLE, INSERT "N/A."

SECTION I: DEFINITIONS

In answering the questions that follow, the following definitions apply:

a. An *"affiliate"* of a person is any corporation, partnership, association, or other business or professional entity that, directly or indirectly, through one or more intermediaries, controls or is controlled by, or is under common control with the person. See definition of *"parent"* and *"subsidiary."* below.

b. An *"associate"* of yours means any of the following:
    (1) a corporation or entity (other than the Company),
         (a) of which you are a manager, partner or executive officer; or
         (b) in which you beneficially own, directly or indirectly, ten percent (10%) or more of any class or equity securities.
    (2) any trust or estate,
         (a) in which you have a substantial beneficial interest; or
         (b) as to which you are a trustee or serve in a similar fiduciary capacity; and
    (3) your spouse, parents, children, siblings, mothers- and fathers-in-law, sons- and daughters-in-law, and brothers- and sisters-in-law.

c. A *"beneficial owner"* of a security includes any of the following:

    (1) a person who, directly or indirectly, through any contract, arrangement, understanding, relationship, or otherwise has or shares:

        (a) voting power that includes the power to vote, or to direct the voting of, such security; and/or

        (b) investment power that includes the power to dispose, or direct the disposition of, such security;

    (Please note that either voting power or investment power, or both, is sufficient for you to be considered the beneficial owner of shares);

    (2) a person who, directly or indirectly, creates or uses a trust, proxy, power of attorney, pooling arrangement, or any other contract, arrangement, or device with the purpose or effect of divesting such person of beneficial ownership of a security or preventing the vesting of such beneficial ownership as part of a plan or scheme to evade the reporting requirements of the federal securities acts; or

    (3) a person who has the right to acquire beneficial ownership of a security within sixty (60) days, including but not limited to any right to acquire: (i) through the exercise of any option, warrant, or right; (ii) through the conversion of a security; (iii) pursuant to the power to revoke a trust, discretionary account, or similar arrangement; or (iv) pursuant to the automatic termination of a trust, discretionary account, or similar arrangement; provided however, that any person who acquires a security or power specified in (i), (ii) or (iii), above, with the purpose or effect of changing or influencing the control of the issuer, or in connection with or as a participant in any transaction having such purpose or effect, immediately upon such acquisition is deemed to be the beneficial owner of the securities that may be acquired through the exercise or conversion of such security or power.

d. *"Equitable ownership,"* for purposes of this questionnaire, means ownership of any *"equity security"*.

e. An *"equity security"* any stock or similar security, certificate of interest. or participation in any profit- sharing agreement, preorganization certificate, or subscription, transferable share, voting trust certificate, or certificate of deposit for an equity security, limited partnership interest, interest in a joint venture, or certificate of interest in a business trust; or any security convertible, with or without consideration, into such security or carrying any warrant or right to subscribe to or purchase such a security; or any such warrant or right; or any put, call, straddle, or other option or privilege of buying such a security from or selling such a security to another without being bound to do so.

f. *"Executive officer"* means any manager, partner, director, president, secretary, treasurer, or vice president in charge of a principal business unit, division of function (such as sales, administration, or finance or similar office), and any person who performs a policy-making function or any other person who performs similar policy-making functions for the entity.

g. *"Family relationship"* means any relationship by blood, marriage or adoption, not more remote than first cousin.

h. *"Group"* means two or more persons acting as a partnership, limited partnership, syndicate, or other group for the purpose of acquiring, holding, or disposing of securities of an issuer.

i. A *"parent"* is any corporation, partnership, association, or other entity that directly, or indirectly through one or more intermediaries, controls the subject entity.

j. *"Plan"* includes but is not limited to the following: any plan, contract, authorization, or arrangement, whether or not set forth in any formal documents, pursuant to which the following may be received: cash, stock, restricted stock, phantom stock, stock options, stock appreciation rights, warrants, convertible securities, performance units and performance shares. A plan may be applicable to one person. For purposes of this document *"Plan"* does not include any group life, health, hospitalization, medical reimbursement or relocation program that does not discriminate in scope, terms or operation in favor of executive management and that are generally available to all employees.

    k.   A *"subsidiary"* is any corporation, partnership, association or other entity that is, directly or indirectly, through one or more intermediaries, controlled by the subject entity.

SECTION 2. GENERAL INFORMATION

A.   Name: _____

b.   Date of Birth: _____

c.   Residence: _____

d.   Citizenship: _____

e.   Education: _____

SECTION 3. COMPANY

A.   List all positions you currently hold with the Company and/or the Company's manager and all positions and offices previously held with the Company and/or the Company's manager and any of their affiliates; indicate the term for which you have been elected or appointed to each current office or position and the time periods during which you served in any prior offices or positions.

POSITION OR OFFICE	PERIOD HELD	TERM OF OFFICE

b.   Describe any arrangement or understanding between you and any other person or entity pursuant to which you were or are to be selected as Management.

c.   State the nature of any family relationship between you and any other member of Management.

SECTION 4. PRIOR EXPERIENCE

A.   Give a brief account of your professional, business and employment experience during at least the past 10 years, including your principal occupations and employment and the name and principal business of any organization in which such occupations and employment were conducted. Please indicate whether such organization is an affiliate of the Company. Give a brief explanation of the nature of the responsibilities undertaken by you in your prior positions, including the size of the operation supervised.

POSITION HELD	NAME OF ORGANIZATION	AFFILIATE NAME	PERIOD (MONTH AND YEAR)

<u>PRINCIPAL BUSINESS AND</u>
<u>SIZE OFORGANIZATION</u>

<u>NATURE OF YOUR RESPONSIBILITIES</u>

b. Indicate any other entities for which you serve as a director, manager or executive officer, or in which you are the beneficial owner of 5% or more of the equity.

			PERCENT OF
NAME OF COMPANY	POSITION HELD	PERIOD OF SERVICE	OWNERSHIP

SECTION 5. SECURITIES TRANSACTIONS

A. Are you now, or have you ever been engaged in the business of buying or selling securities, part or full-time, as a broker, dealer or salesman?

Yes _____   No _____

If your answer is *"yes,"* please provide the following information:

DATES OF EMPLOYMENT	NAME OF BROKERAGE FIRM	POSITION HELD	STATE(S) IN WHICH YOUR FIRM CONDUCTS BUSINESS

b. Are you now acting, or have you ever acted as a member of executive management of any entity in which you participated in selling securities issued by such entity?

Yes _____   No _____

If your answer is *"yes,"* please provide the following information:

PARTNERSHIP NAME	STATE(S) IN WHICH SECURITIES WERE SOLD	DATES DURING WHICH SECURITIES WERE SOLD

c. (1) Have you ever had, or have you ever been affiliated with any entity that has had, a license or registration as a dealer, broker, investment adviser or salesman with respect to securities denied, suspended or revoked?

(2) Have you or any entity with which you were affiliated ever been suspended or expelled from membership in any securities exchange, association of securities dealers or investment advisers or counsel?

Yes _____   No _____

If you answered *"yes"* to the foregoing question, please explain the circumstances in detail on a separate sheet of paper, including a statement, if applicable, regarding the subsequent suspension, reversal or other subsequent action taken by the court or administrative tribunal.

d. (1) Do you or any member of your family have any direct or indirect affiliation or association as an officer, director, general partner, employee or agent with any firm regulated by the Financial Industry Regulatory Authority ("FINRA")?

Yes _____   No _____

(2) Are you or any member of your family a senior officer of a bank, savings and loan institution, insurance company, registered investment company, registered investment

advisory firm or any similar institutional-type investor that has influence over the buying or selling of securities by any such entity?

Yes _____ No _____

If you answered *"yes"* to (1) or (2) above, please provide the following information for each applicable person:

NAME	NAME OF INSTITUTION	TYPE OF INSTITUTION	POSITION

SECTION 6. LITIGATION

A. Have you been, or are you, or any entity that you control or have controlled, or with which you are affiliated or were affiliated, a party (as a plaintiff or a defendant) to any presently pending civil litigation involving a claim of $10,000 or more?

Yes _____ No _____

If your answer is *"yes,"* please provide the following information:

Court:_____

Date:_____

Case No.:_____

Allegations:_____

Events Surrounding:_____

Opposing Party(ies):_____

b. Are there any judgments outstanding against you?

Yes _____ No _____

If your answer is *"yes,"* please provide the following information:

AMOUNT	NATURE OF JUDGMENT	COURT (TYPE AND ADDRESS)

c.   Have you ever been indemnified by any company for any reason as a result of being a director, manager, executive officer, employee or agent of such company?

   Yes _____   No _____

If you answered *"yes,"* please provide the following information:

NAME OF INDEMNIFYING PARTY	REASON FOR INDEMNIFICATION	MANNER OF INDEMNIFICATION

d.   Please indicate whether, at any time:
   (1)   has a petition under the federal bankruptcy laws or any state insolvency law ever been filed by or against you, or has a receiver, fiscal agent or similar officer ever been appointed by a court over your business or property, or any partnership in which you were a general partner at or within two (2) years before the time of such filing, or any corporation or business association of which you were an executive officer at or within two (2) years before the time of such filing?

      Yes _____   No _____

   (2)   have you ever been convicted in a criminal proceeding, or do you have pending against you, or have been named as a subject of a pending criminal proceeding (excluding traffic violations and other minor offenses)?

      Yes _____   No _____

   (3)   have you ever been the subject of any order, judgment or decree of any court of competent jurisdiction permanently or temporarily enjoining you from, or otherwise limiting, the following activities:
      (A)   engaging in any activity in connection with the purchase or sale of any security or in connection with any violation of federal or state securities laws or federal commodities laws?

         Yes _____   No _____

      (B)   engaging in any type of business practice?

         Yes _____   No _____

      (C)   acting as an investment adviser, underwriter, broker, dealer, municipal securities dealer, government securities broker or dealer or as a futures commission merchant, introducing broker, commodity trading advisor, commodity pool operator, floor broker. leverage transaction merchant, any person regulated by the Commodity Futures Trading Commission, any person required to be registered under the Commodity Exchange Act, or an associated person of any of the foregoing or as an affiliated person, director, or employee of any investment company, bank, savings and loan association, or insurance company, or engaging in or continuing any conduct or practice in connection with such activity?

Yes _____   No _____

(4)   have you ever been the subject of any order, judgment or decree of any federal or state authority barring, suspending or otherwise limiting your right to engage in any activity described in subparagraph (3) above, or to be associated with persons engaged in any such activity?

Yes _____   No _____

(5)   have you ever been found by a court of competent jurisdiction in a civil action or by the Securities and Exchange Commission or a state securities regulatory authority to have violated any federal or state securities law?

Yes _____   No _____

(6)   have you ever been found by a court of competent jurisdiction in a civil action or by the Commodity Futures Trading Commission to have violated any federal commodities law? and

Yes _____   No _____

(7)   have you ever been associated with any person who has been the subject of any order, judgment or decree, not subsequently reversed, suspended or vacated, outlined in subparts (3), (4), (5) or (6) above?

Yes _____   No _____

If you answered "*yes*" to any of the foregoing questions, please explain the circumstances in detail on a separate sheet of paper, including a statement, if applicable, regarding the subsequent suspension, reversal or other subsequent action taken by the court or administrative tribunal.

SECTION 7. TRANSACTIONS WITH THE COMPANY AND COMPENSATION

PRELIMINARY NOTES:

- A person or entity may be considered to have a direct material interest in a transaction to which the Company or any of its affiliates is a party if that person or entity stands to receive any compensation or thing of value from the Company or any of their affiliates as a result of the transaction.
- A person or an entity may be considered to have an indirect material interest in a transaction to which the Company or any of its affiliates if a firm, corporation, partnership, or other entity in which such person or entity is or has been an officer, director, partner (including a limited partner), manager, member, equity owner or employee, or in which such person or entity owns

or has owned an equity interest, stands to receive any compensation or thing of value from the Company or any of its affiliates as a result of the transaction.
- If it is not practicable to state the approximate amount of the interest held in a certain transaction, state the total approximate amount involved in the transaction and so indicate with an asterisk (*).

a. To the best of your knowledge, will any of the following people have a direct or indirect material interest in any presently proposed transaction that would include, without limitation, the provision of services, the lease of assets or the sale of equipment, supplies or other assets to which the Company or any of its affiliates is a party?
   (1) you? or
   (2) your spouse?

   Yes _____   No _____

   If your answer is "yes," please provide the following information:

NAME OF INTERESTED PERSON	RELATIONSHIP OF INTERESTED PERSON TO COMPANY	NATURE OF TRANSACTION	NATURE OF INTEREST IN TRANSACTION	AMOUNT OF INTEREST IN TRANSACTION

b. If in answering part (a) above, you disclosed a transaction involving the purchase or sale of assets by or to the Company or its affiliates, otherwise than in the ordinary course of business, please provide the following information with respect to each such transaction: (i) the identity of the purchaser; (ii) the identity of the seller; (iii) the nature of the assets; (iv) the cost of the assets to the purchaser; and (v) if the seller acquired the assets within two (2) years prior to the subject transaction, the cost of the assets to the seller. Also indicate the principle followed in determining the purchase or sale price and the name of the person making the determination.

c. Describe any other form of compensation not listed above paid or to be paid by the Company, directly or indirectly, to you, your spouse, your parents, children, siblings, mothers- or fathers-in-law. sons- or daughters-in- law, or brothers- or sisters-in-law.

d. Other than transactions and compensation specified in any agreement between you and the Company described in the Company's disclosure documents and as set forth above, please confirm, to the best of your knowledge, that you are unaware of any transactions or contemplated transactions between the Company or any of its affiliates.

   _____   Confirmed

   _____   I am aware of the following transactions:

SECTION 8. RELATIONSHIP WITH ACCOUNTANTS

Have you or any of your associates at any time been interested in or affiliated or otherwise connected with, or had any significant relationship with, the independent certified public accountants for the Company?

   Yes _____   No _____   Not Applicable _____

If, at any time prior to the closing of the offering contemplated by the Company, any of the information set forth in my responses to this Questionnaire changes due to the passage of time, or any development occurs that requires a modification in my answer, or such information has for any other reason become incorrect, I will forthwith furnish to counsel any necessary or appropriate correcting information. Otherwise, the Company and its counsel are to understand that the above information continues to be, to the best of the undersigned's knowledge, complete and correct.

I have reviewed, or will review, the disclosure document related to the Company's offering. I am unaware of any statement set forth therein that is inaccurate or of any statement omitted therefrom that would be necessary to cause all statements set forth therein to not be misleading in the context in which such statements were made. If I become aware of any such statement or omission, I will advise counsel.

Dated: _____, 201__.

_____
(Signature)

_____
(Type or Print Name)

Made in the USA
Coppell, TX
28 May 2020

26597930R00214